10/12/09

3
|13
3

ANTI-SEMITISM

A History and Psychoanalysis of Contemporary Hatred

A V N E R   F A L K

PRAEGER

Westport, Connecticut
London

Library of Congress Cataloging-in-Publication Data

Falk, Avner.
   Anti-semitism : a history and psychoanalysis of contemporary hatred / Avner Falk.
      p. cm.
   Includes bibliographical references and index.
   ISBN 978–0–313–35384–0 (alk. paper)
1. Antisemitism—Psychological aspects. 2. Antisemitism. 3. Antisemitism—Germany—
History—20th century. 4. Judaism and psychoanalysis. I. Title.
DS145.F353 2008
305.892'4—dc22   2007052856

British Library Cataloguing in Publication Data is available.

Library of Congress Catalog Card Number: 2007052856
ISBN: 978–0–313–35384–0

First published in 2008

Praeger Publishers, 88 Post Road West, Westport, CT 06881
An imprint of Greenwood Publishing Group, Inc.
www.praeger.com

Printed in the United States of America

The paper used in this book complies with the
Permanent Paper Standard issued by the National
Information Standards Organization (Z39.48–1984).

10 9 8 7 6 5 4 3 2 1

Contents

Jew-hatred, Judeophobia, and Anti-Judaism

During the second Lebanon war in the summer of 2006, I received a jolting "instant message" on my computer from an obscure Englishman whom I had never heard of before: "Love the Nazis KILL THE JEWS DEAD." What could have prompted a complete stranger in the United Kingdom of Great Britain and Northern Ireland to send such a hate-filled message to an Israeli Jew whom he had never met? What could make an unknown Englishman hate the Jews so much that a war between Israel—the tiny Jewish state in the Middle East with its Arab minority—and a fundamentalist Shiite Muslim Lebanese Arab group called *Hezbollah* (Party of Allah) could make him want to "kill the Jews dead"?

The sender of this hate message was a certain John Anderson of Southampton. Searching the Internet for this gentleman yielded no result. The obscurity of the sender may be a key to our psychological riddle. A person with a healthy self-esteem who has done anything worthwhile does not need to hate whole nations or religious groups. Four centuries earlier, a better-known and more enlightened Englishman lived in Southampton. He was Henry Wriothesley, Third Earl of Southampton (1573–1624), and for many years he was the patron of the English playwright William Shakespeare (1564–1616), whom the founder of psycho-analysis, Sigmund Freud (1856–1939), greatly admired. In the last decade of the sixteenth century, Shakespeare wrote *The Merchant of Venice,* a drama in which a greedy and cruel Jewish merchant named Shylock wants to carry out his contract with his Christian debtor and cut a pound of flesh from his debtor's body for nonpayment of his debt, but is foiled by the wise and beautiful Portia, the debtor's beloved, who defies Shylock to cut his pound of flesh without shedding one drop of blood from his borrower's body. In this "anti-Jewish" play, however, Shakespeare put one of his most eloquent and best-known speeches into the Jewish "villain's" mouth:

> Hath not a Jew eyes? Hath not a Jew hands, organs
> dimensions, senses, affections, passions; fed with
> the same food, hurt with the same weapons, subject
> to the same diseases, heal'd by the same means
> warm'd and cool'd by the same winter and summer
> as a Christian is? If you prick us, do we not bleed?
> If you tickle us, do we not laugh? If you poison us,
> do we not die? And if you wrong us, shall we not revenge?
>   (Shakespeare, *The Merchant of Venice*, Act III, Scene 1)

Like most of Shakespeare's characters, from Richard III to Hamlet to Macbeth, Shylock has a complex and multifaceted personality. He is greedy and vengeful, but he is also honest and courageous. His daughter's elopement with a Christian friend of Shylock's borrower and her stealing of his money enrages Shylock and leads him to insist on his pound of flesh from his debtor.

There have been many different readings of *The Merchant of Venice*. Some scholars have called it anti-Semitic, others sympathetic to the Jews, still others saw Shylock as the most morally upright of the play's characters. Some read his famous speech as a proud and courageous defense of Jewish identity in the face of Christian anti-Semitism, while others saw it as cloying (Clark 1894; Carlton 1934; Sinsheimer 1947; Lelyveld 1961; Shatzmiller 1990; Bloom 1991; Gross 1992). The German-born Argentinian Jewish psychiatrist Eduardo Krapf (1901–1963), a victim of Nazi persecution who fled Adolf Hitler's Germany and became the first president of the *Sociedad interamericana de psychología* and the head of the Mental Health Division in the World Health Organization (he died in Geneva, Switzerland), saw the play as an expression of Shakespeare's anti-Semitism (Krapf 1951, 1955). In fact, anti-Jewish feeling was common in Shakespeare's England, and Shakespeare's own feelings about the Jews were quite complex and ambivalent (Shapiro 1997).

England had expelled its Jews in 1290, but after the expulsion of the Jews from Iberia in the late fifteenth century, some Marranos and New Christians, "converted" Jews who outwardly professed Christianity but secretly practiced their Judaism, had settled again in England, and there were a few hundred Jews in Shakespeare's sixteenth-century England (Katz 1994; Shapiro 1997; Holden 1999, p. 142). Because the Jews were barred from most professions, while Christians could not commit usury, most Jews in Shakespeare's England (as in other Christian countries) were forced to lend their money at usurious interest rates because of the very high risk of never being repaid by their borrowers. This situation fueled Christian Jew-hatred. The American Jewish scholar James Shapiro believed that there was a crisis of cultural identity in Elizabethan England and that the Elizabethans imagined the Jews to be utterly different from themselves in religion, race, nationality, even sexuality. There were strange cases of English Christians masquerading as Jews and bizarre proposals to settle foreign Jews in Ireland. (Shapiro 1997).

Shakespeare's feelings about the Jews were shaped by a sequence of emotional events in his thirties. In 1589–1590, his friend Christopher Marlowe (1564–1593) had written *The Jew of Malta,* a virulently anti-Jewish play which was staged in 1592. The play's protagonist is an immensely wealthy Jewish merchant named Barabas, a namesake of the New Testament murderer who was imprisoned along with Jesus Christ but was released by Pontius Pilate when the Jews clamored for the latter's crucifixion. Barabas freely engages in intrigue, manipulation, blackmail, betrayal, lying, cheating, murder, and every other conceivable evil. He ends up boiling to death in a giant cauldron he had prepared for the Turks. Marlowe may have been among the spies of Sir Francis Walsingham (1530–1590), the spymaster of Queen Elizabeth I (1533–1603). In 1593, the 29-year-old Marlowe was accidentally killed or murdered in a brawl 10 days after being arrested for spying and heresy and released by the Queen's Privy Council on condition "that he give his daily attendance on their Lordships, until he shall be licensed to the contrary."

Marlowe's death was a traumatic loss to Shakespeare. The following year, he suffered another terrible shock. Robert Devereux, the Second Earl of Essex (1566–1601), a favorite of Queen Elizabeth who had married Walsingham's daughter, falsely accused Rodrigo Lopez (1525–1594), Walsingham's former follower and Queen Elizabeth's Portuguese-born Marrano physician, of trying to poison the Queen. The 69-year-old Lopez was tried, found guilty, sentenced to die, castrated, hanged, cut down while alive, disemboweled, and quartered "in front of a baying ground that may have included an inquisitive (if appalled) Shakespeare" (Holden 1999, p. 143).

Shakespeare wrote *The Merchant of Venice* shortly after Lopez's execution, and the play has a reference to a Wolf, the English translation of the name Lopez, as one of the play's Christian characters harangues its Jewish protagonist in the fourth act. (Shakespeare, *The Merchant of Venice,* Act IV, Scene 1; Holden 1999, p. 143):

O, be thou damn'd, inexecrable dog!
And for thy life let justice be accused.
Thou almost makest me waver in my faith
To hold opinion with Pythagoras,
That souls of animals infuse themselves
Into the trunks of men: thy currish spirit
Govern'd a Wolf, who, hang'd for human slaughter,
Even from the gallows did his fell soul fleet,
And, whilst thou lay'st in thy unhallow'd dam,

Infused itself in thee; for thy desires
Are wolvish, bloody, starved and ravenous.

In fact, Shakespeare's psychological portrayal of the Jew Shylock was much more subtle than Marlowe's portrayal of the Jew Barabas. As Shakespeare's biographer Anthony Holden put it, Marlowe's *Jew of Malta* "merely reflected stereotypical Elizabethan altitudes to Jews" while Shakespeare's *Merchant of Venice* "painted a more profound portrait of racism and religious prejudices reeking of contemporary resonance for every subsequent era, not least our own" (Holden 1999, p. 145).

In 1986, the 53-year-old American Jewish writer Philip Roth won the National Book Critics Circle Award for his novel *The Counterlife* (Roth 1986), in which, as in his other "Zuckerman novels," Roth's lifelong preoccupation with Judaism, anti-Semitism, and Israel was prominent. Twenty years later, the American Jewish scholar Alana Newhouse discussed *The Counterlife* and cited a section of the novel in which the writer and his Israeli Jewish journalist friend each disparages his own people and idealizes the other:

> Less a linear tale than five riffs revolving around the same set of characters, the book acts as a kind of narrative kaleidoscope on Jewish identity—with each slight shift of perspective, a whole new picture emerges (think "Sliding Doors," but smarter). The structure is designed to put the author's famed alter ego, Nathan Zuckerman, face to face with characters who challenge his identity as a Jew—vis-à-vis signature Roth topics (sex, family, psychoanalysis, sex, assimilation, sex) as well as broader ones: the Holocaust, antisemitism and, most evocatively here, Israel. Nathan's good, moderate, American values are challenged—from his resistance to religious ritual and distaste for the political right ("We do not wish to crush the Arab," [an Israeli] settler leader explains, "we simply will not allow him to crush us"), to his subtle romanticization of Israeli life. "Whenever I meet you American-Jewish intellectuals," says his friend Shuki, a wearied Israeli journalist, "with your non-Jewish wives and your good Jewish brains, well-bred, smooth, soft-spoken men, educated men who know how to order in a good restaurant, and to appreciate a good wine, and to listen courteously to another point of view, I think exactly that: We are the excitable, ghettoized, jittery little Jews of the Diaspora, and you are the Jews with all the confidence and cultivation that comes of feeling at home where you are." The book is not exclusively about Israel, but it was these sections that moved me. (Newhouse 2006)

Roth's preoccupation with anti-Semitism and with Israel is not unique to American Jews or even to American Jewish writers. Our entire world today seems preoccupied with the little Jewish state and its wars with its Arab neighbors. Anti-Semitism, anti-Zionism (often, though not always, a cover for anti-Semitism), and anti-Israeli diatribes have become a global phenomenon. The U.S. Department of State thought that "global anti-Semitism in recent years has had four main sources: 1. Traditional anti-Jewish prejudice that has pervaded Europe and some countries in other parts of the world for centuries. This includes ultra-nationalists and others who assert that the Jewish community controls governments, the media, international business, and the financial world. 2. Strong anti-Israel sentiment that crosses the line between objective criticism of Israeli policies and anti-Semitism. 3. Anti-Jewish sentiment expressed by some in Europe's growing Muslim population, based on longstanding antipathy toward both Israel and Jews, as well as Muslim opposition to developments in Israel and the occupied territories, and more recently in Iraq. 4. Criticism of both the United States and globalization that spills over to Israel, and to Jews in general who are identified with both" (U.S. Department of State, 2005). Anti-Semitism has been with us for millennia. Let us see what it is and what its psychological causes may be.

WHAT IS ANTI-SEMITISM?

While most of us know intuitively what anti-Semitism is about—Jew-hatred, Judeophobia, and anti-Judaism—scholars disagree on a definition of anti-Semitism. Though the general definition of anti-Semitism is hostility or prejudice towards Jews, a number of authorities have developed more formal definitions. The American Jewish scholar Helen Fein defined anti-Semitism as "a persisting latent structure of hostile beliefs towards Jews as a collective manifested in individuals as attitudes, and in culture as myth, ideology, folklore and imagery, and in actions—social or legal discrimination, political mobilization against the Jews, and collective or state violence—which results in and/or is designed to distance, displace, or destroy Jews as Jews" (Fein 1987, p. 3). Fein distinguished three "schools" in the historical explanation of anti-Semitism: that which stresses Christian persecution, that which stresses "the interaction of Jews with others, and the neo-Marxist school (ibid.).

The German scholar Dietz Bering expanded Fein's definition by describing the structure of anti-Semitic beliefs. To anti-Semites, he wrote, "Jews are not only partially but totally bad by nature, that is, their bad traits are incorrigible. Because of this bad nature: (1) Jews have to be seen not as individuals but as a collective. (2) Jews remain essentially alien in the surrounding societies. (3) Jews bring disaster on their 'host societies' or on the whole world, they are doing it secretly, therefore the antisemites feel obliged to unmask the conspiratorial, bad Jewish character" (Bering 1992). It is noteworthy that Bering did not mention the anti-Semites' wish to eliminate the Jews altogether. This was done by Daniel Goldhagen a few years later (Goldhagen 1996).

Several scholars thought that anti-Semitism was not monolithic. The Canadian-born American scholar Gavin I. Langmuir distinguished "irrational" anti-Semitism from "rational" anti-Judaism (Langmuir 1990). The South African

Jewish scholar Milton Shain pointed out the "gradations in the nature and substance of hostility toward the Jews" and defined anti-Semitism as "unprovoked and irrational hostility towards Jews" (Shain 1997, pp. 2, 5). The methodological problem, of course, is how to distinguish what is rational from what is not.

The twenty-first century saw efforts by international and governmental bodies, mainly in the "West," to formally define anti-Semitism. In early 2005, the U.S. Department of State submitted its *Report on Global Anti-Semitism* to the U.S. Senate's Committee on Foreign Relations and to the U.S. House of Representatives' Committee on International Relations. In this report, the State Department defined anti-Semitism as "hatred toward Jews—individually and as a group—that can be attributed to the Jewish religion and/or ethnicity." It immediately added that "an important issue is the distinction between legitimate criticism of policies and practices of the State of Israel, and commentary that assumes an anti-Semitic character. The demonization of Israel, or vilification of Israeli leaders, sometimes through comparisons with Nazi leaders, and through the use of Nazi symbols to caricature them, indicates an anti-Semitic bias rather than a valid criticism of policy concerning a controversial issue."

The European Monitoring Center on Racism and Xenophobia (EUMC) came up with a more detailed definition: "Antisemitism is a certain perception of Jews, which may be expressed as hatred toward Jews. Rhetorical and physical manifestations of antisemitism are directed toward Jewish or non-Jewish individuals and/or their property, toward Jewish community institutions and religious facilities. In addition, such manifestations could also target the state of Israel, conceived as a Jewish collectivity. Antisemitism frequently charges Jews with conspiring to harm humanity, and it is often used to blame Jews for 'why things go wrong.'" The EUMC then listed "contemporary examples of antisemitism in public life, the media, schools, the workplace, and in the religious sphere." These included making mendacious, dehumanizing, demonizing, or stereotypical allegations about Jews; accusing Jews as a people of being responsible for real or imagined wrongdoing committed by a single Jewish person or group; denying the Holocaust; and accusing Jewish citizens of being more loyal to Israel, or to the alleged priorities of Jews worldwide, than to the interests of their own nations. The EUMC also discussed ways in which attacking Israel could be anti-Semitic, depending on the context. In 2007, the EUMC became the EU's Agency for Fundamental Rights.

One of the best scholars of antisemitism has been Gavin I. Langmuir (1921–2005), a non-Jewish professor at Stanford University. Being non-Jewish may have given Langmuir a more objective stance on the subject. Gary Dickson, a British historian at the University of Edinburgh who was a Stanford undergraduate and a student of Langmuir's in the 1960s, has described his mentor as a pioneering scholar in the field of medieval anti-Semitism. Although some scholars were researching the subject in Europe, Dickson said, Langmuir was virtually an isolated figure in the United States. A half-century later, the field of anti-Semitism is of broad interest to medievalists, as well as to students of prejudice, multiculturalism, and the Holocaust. Langmuir's work on the formation and nature of anti-Semitism earned him an international reputation.

At the relatively advanced age of 69, Langmuir published an impressive two-volume collection of his studies on anti-Semitism (Langmuir 1990). The collection made Langmuir's innovative work on the subject available to scholars in medieval and Jewish history and in religious studies. In the first volume, *Toward a Definition of Antisemitism,* the underlying question is: what is anti-Semitism, where and when did it emerge, and why? After two chapters that highlighted the failure of historians to depict Jews and attitudes toward them fairly and objectively, the other chapters were historical studies of crucial developments in the legal status of Jews and in beliefs about them during the Middle Ages. The two concluding chapters provided an overview of the subject. In the first, Langmuir summarized the historical developments, indicating concretely when and where anti-Semitism as he defines it emerged. In the second, he criticized recent theories about anti-Semitism, prejudice, and racism and developed his own general theory about the nature and dynamics of anti-Semitism.

In his second volume, *History, Religion, and Antisemitism,* Langmuir confronted the problems that arise when historians have to describe and explain religious phenomena, as any historian of anti-Semitism must. How, and to what extent, can the historian be objective? Is it possible to discuss Christian attitudes toward Jews, for example, without adopting the historical explanations of those whose thoughts and actions one is discussing? What, exactly, does the historian mean by "religion" or "religious"? Langmuir's original, stimulating, and interdisciplinary approach integrated anthropology, sociology, and psychology, and recent empirical research on the functioning of the mind and the nature of thought. His key distinction between *religiosity,* a property of individuals, and *religion,* a social phenomenon, allowed him to place unusual emphasis on the role of Christian religious doubts and tensions and on the irrationality they can produce. *Defining anti-Semitism as irrational beliefs about Jews,* he distinguished Christian *anti-Judaism* from Christian *anti-Semitism,* argued that *anti-Semitism emerged in the twelfth and thirteenth centuries* because of rising Christian doubts about their own religion, and sketched how the revolutionary changes in religion and mentality in the modern period brought new faiths, new kinds of religious doubt, and a deadlier expression of anti-Semitism. Although he developed it in dealing with the difficult question of anti-Semitism, Langmuir's approach to religious history is important for scholars in all areas.

The late-medieval Christians did indeed suffer from many doubts and fears. Fearful of the Devil, whom they also called Satan and Lucifer, these Christians imagined the Jews as his children. They also imagined the Antichrist as the offspring of the sexual union of the Devil with a Jewish whore (Trachtenberg 1943;

Poliakov 1965, p. 144; Russell 1984; Bonfil 1988; Gilman 1991; Shain 1997, pp. 34–35; Wistrich 1999). This was a classical case of unconscious projection, the Devil and the Antichrist being concrete representations of the evil or bad feelings within the Christian mind itself. One of the best-known Christian thinkers on anti-Semitism, John Maria Oesterreicher, considered anti-Semitism to be an equivalent of racism and anti-Christianism (Oesterreicher 1940, 1993).

DIFFERENT TYPES OF ANTI-SEMITISM

Many historians have treated anti-Semitism as a single phenomenon with a continuous history. Thus, the French Jewish historian Léon Poliakov (1910–1997) wrote a monumental, multivolume "history of antisemitism" (Poliakov 1955–1977, 1965–1985). Nine years after Langmuir's groundbreaking studies, however, the British scholar Ritchie Robertson pointed out that there were many different kinds of anti-Semitism and raised some poignant questions about the monolithic nature and anachronistic historiography of anti-Semitism.

> Is anti-Semitism a single phenomenon? Can a term coined in the 1870s be applied retrospectively to the hostility to Jews found in the Roman Empire, in Europe in the High Middle Ages, and in Europe since the Enlightenment, without imposing a spurious unity upon diverse phenomena?...one may be tempted to propose a discrimination of anti-Semitisms that would dissolve the unity of the concept. Under the impact of the Holocaust, however, and feeling that such an immense catastrophe must have correspondingly tenacious historical roots, attempts have been made to write a continuous history of anti-Semitism from the ancient world till the twentieth century. Some writers have insisted on particular continuities. Holocaust theologians try to trace modern anti-Semitism back to the Church Fathers' denunciations of "Old Israel" and its obdurate rejection of the Christian message. Others trace it back to the anti-Jewish superstitions—the charges of worshipping the Devil and carrying out ritual murders of Christian children—that arose in the Middle Ages. This, however, is broad-brush history, and on closer examination the continuities tend to dissolve. (Robertson 1999, pp. 151–152, citing Trachtenberg 1943, Poliakov 1961–1975, Ruether 1974, Thoma 1980, Zimmermann 1986, Gilman & Katz 1991, and Wistrich 1991)

Several other scholars have distinguished different types of anti-Semitism—religious, political, murderous, "benign," "eliminatory," racial, economic, Nazi and so on—treating them as if they were separate, different, and distinct from one another. (Friedman 1987). The interesting thing about these distinctions is that they leave out "psychological anti-Semitism," which is common to all the other types. As we have seen, during the late European Middle Ages, people firmly believed in the existence of "the Devil" as author of all evil in our world: everything bad people did was an act or wish of the Devil, and people were not to blame ("the Devil made me do it"). Just as the ancient fantasy of the gods and goddesses was an unconscious externalization of internal images of the father and mother of one's early life, and just as man created his gods in his own image, so the fantasy of the Devil was an unconscious projection of one's unacceptable bad feelings. To medieval Christians, the Devil was as real as God, and they were sure that the Jews were the Devil's children by the Evil Sow, an unconscious externalization of an internalized "bad mother" image (Trachtenberg 1943; Shachar 1974; Russell 1981, 1984; Falk 1996, pp. 368–369).

Even in the "enlightened" eighteenth century, the great French philosopher Voltaire (François-Marie Arouet, 1694–1778) wound up hating the Jews. In 1750, while staying with the Francophile king Friedrich II of Prussia (Frederick the Great, 1712–1786), Voltaire got himself into financial and legal trouble. Voltaire's self-destructive gambling propensity had led him to supply a Berlin Jewish jeweler named Abraham Hirsch or Hirschl with money and send him to the Saxon capital of Dresden to buy depreciated banknotes at a large discount. Hirsch seems to have attended to his own business and neglected Voltaire's. He was recalled to Berlin, and Voltaire abandoned his speculation, but Hirsch was not easily shaken off. Voltaire could not yield, while Hirsch was just as persistent and apparently also unscrupulous. After several months of litigation, Voltaire won his suit against Hirsch, but at the cost of his own humiliation and of disgust-ing King Friedrich, who could not tolerate a Christian's lawsuit with a lowly Jew.

In fact, Voltaire had made Friedrich very upset. The outcome of Voltaire's legal battle with the Jew Abraham Hirsch was that a furious King Friedrich II expelled Voltaire from his court of *Sans Souci* at Potsdam and even had him arrested on his way to France. A hurt and humiliated Voltaire wrote venomously of the Jews, "They are, all of them, born with raging fanaticism in their hearts, just as the Bretons and the Germans are born with blond hair. I would not be in the least bit surprised if these people would not some day become deadly to the human race" (Potok 1978, pp. 365–366, quoting Voltaire 1764). Voltaire bitterly denounced the Jews for "their stubbornness, their new superstitions, and their hallowed usury." Addressing some French Jewish leaders, he wrote, "You have surpassed all nations in impertinent fables, in bad conduct, and in barbarism. You deserve to be punished, for this is your destiny" (Potok 1978, p. 366, quoting Voltaire 1764; Blümner 1863; Graetz 1868; Lazard 1884; Calais 1996; Scharfstein 1996–1997; Bayme 1997). Did Voltaire unconsciously project his own unpleasant and difficult character on the Jews?

Friedrich II did not like the Jews much more than Voltaire did. In his time, only *Schutzjuden* (protected Jews) and *Hofjuden* (Court Jews) could live in the Prussian capital of Berlin; most Prussian Jews had to live in the provinces. The anti-Jewish Prussian-Jewry law of 1730 had attempted to restrict rabbinic activity to ceremonial and ritual functions, depriving the rabbis of legal jurisdic-tion in Jewish civil and economic affairs. The Jewish rabbinical court (*beth din*), a pillar of Jewish communal autonomy for centuries, was to be stripped of its judicial competence and fated to disappear. However, this *General-Privilegium and Reglement* (Friedrich loved the French language over and above his native German) was not effective in putting a definitive halt to the Jewish law courts, for Friedrich II reiterated this demand more explicitly in another *Reglement* of 1750. That regulation made plain that, except for patently religious disputes, Jews were to rely on a regular court of justice (*ordentliches Justiz-Forum*). The Jewish courts were permitted to survive only as arbitration courts (*per modum arbitrii*) to which Jews could repair *if they so desired*. If they were not satisfied with the decision of the Jewish arbitrators, however, they could seek binding justice in the Prussian civil courts. For centuries, the possibility and occasional actuality of Jewish defection to civil jurisdiction had threatened the autonomy of the Jewish communities. Now the Prussian state had institutionalized the threat. Although *parnassim* (community leaders) from many communities fought to temper the finality of the regulation, they were unsuccessful. The Prussian state was adamant in its campaign against traditional autonomy. (Kochan 1990, pp. 52–53; Mittleman 2001, pp. 3–4).

In 1750, Friedrich II enacted a new oppressive anti-Jewish law entitled *Neue revidierte General-Privilegium und Reglement vor die Judenschaft in Preussen und der Mark Brandenburg* (New Revised General Privilege and Regulation for the Jewry in Prussia and the Margraviate of Brandenburg), which required all Prussian *Schutzjuden* either to abstain from marriage or leave Berlin. However, this act was not promulgated until 1756. The Berlin Jewish community, then consisting of 333 families numbering some 1,945 souls, had the number of its *Schutzjuden* fixed at 150, and only an eldest son could inherit his father's rights. All other Prussian Jews were declared to be "extraordinary," which meant that they were not allowed to transmit their privilege of residence to their children. Throughout the kingdom, this law was enforced with rigor. In Silesia and West Prussia, no Jews could live in the open country (*plattes Land*). Jewish servants were not allowed to marry, and Jewish beggars and peddlers were inhibited. All this was child's play, of course, compared with what the Germans did to the Jews of Europe two centuries later.

Eugenics, Racism, and Genocide

Raphael Lemkin (1900–1959) was a Polish-born Jewish lawyer who fought the German occupiers of Poland in 1939–1940, fled to neutral Sweden in 1940 and to the United States in 1941, and coined the term *genocide* (the killing of a people) in 1943. From 1948, Lemkin taught law at Yale University and campaigned for The Convention on the Prevention and Punishment of the Crime of Genocide, which was adopted by the United Nations General Assembly in December 1948 and took effect in January 1951. It defines and outlaws genocide. The total number of UN members that have ratified the convention is 137. The United States ratified the convention only in 1988, and with the all-important proviso that it was immune from prosecution for genocide without its consent. This proviso was also made by Bahrain, Bangladesh, India, Malaysia, the Philippines, Singapore, Vietnam, Yemen, and Yugoslavia.

In dry, legal language, the UN convention defines genocide as "any of the following acts committed with intent to destroy, in whole or in part, a national, ethnical, racial or religious group, as such: (a) Killing members of the group; (b) Causing serious bodily or mental harm to members of the group; (c) Deliberately inflicting on the group conditions of life calculated to bring about its physical destruction in whole or in part; (d) Imposing measures intended to prevent births within the group; (e) Forcibly transferring children of the group to another group." The convention was passed in order to outlaw actions similar to the Holocaust by Nazi Germany during World War II. Because the adoption of the convention by the United Nations General Assembly required the support of the Soviet Union and the Communist bloc, it excluded actions undertaken by those nations. As a result, the convention excludes from the definition of genocide the killing of members of a social class, the killing of members of a political or ideological group, and cultural killings.

Human genocide is nothing new. According to the Hebrew Bible, the ancient Israelites believed that their god Yahweh had commanded them to exterminate the Amalekites (Exodus 17:8–16; Numbers 24:20; Deuteronomy 25:17–19; Judges 3:13, 6:3, 6:33, 7:12; 1 Sam. 15:2–3, 28:16–18; I Chronicles 4:42–43). Genocide has been a regular and widespread event in the history of civilization. The phrase "never again," which is often used in relation to genocide, has been proven wrong in Rwanda, Bosnia, Darfur, and many other places in recent times (Charny 1999). Despite the UN convention, determining which historical events constitute genocide and which are merely criminal or inhuman behavior is not a clear-cut matter. In nearly every case in which accusations of genocide have been made, partisans of various sides have fiercely disputed the interpretation and details of the event, promoting wildly different versions of the facts. An accusation of genocide is certainly not taken lightly and will almost always be controversial. "Revisionist" attempts to deny or challenge genocides are, in some countries, illegal.

The tragic age-old human phenomenon of anti-Semitism, a euphemism for the hatred and fear of Jews, which in the twentieth century led to the worst genocide in human history, has enjoyed an incredible resurgence in the twenty-first century. It is widespread not only in its birthplace of Europe but also in the entire Arab and Muslim world, fueled by the Arab-Israeli conflict (Falk 2004). The mass-communication media, including the Internet, abound with anti-Semitic, anti-Israel, and anti-Zionist literature. Once again, as in the infamous *Protocols of the Sages of Zion* (Nilus 1905, 1920; Segel 1934; Bernstein 1935; Cohn 1967; Bach 1973; Taguieff 1992; Conan 1999; Bishop 1999; Eisner 2005), the anti-Semites are trying to prove their fantasies that the Jews control the world.

During the terrible Second World War (1939–1945), the Germans, led by their deeply disturbed *Führer* Adolf Hitler (1889–1945) and his murderous Nazi party, with the help of their non-German collaborators, mass-murdered six million European Jews. This genocide is known as the *Shoah* or Holocaust. The British writer Eric Arthur Blair (1903–1950), better known as George Orwell, was one of the most clear-sighted men of the twentieth century (Hitchens 2002). By the end of the war Orwell understood the illogical and fantastic nature of anti-Semitic feelings: "Anti-Semitism is an irrational thing. The Jews are accused of specific offences which the person speaking feels strongly about, but it is obvious that these accusations merely rationalise some deep-rooted prejudice. To attempt to counter them with facts and statistics is useless, and may sometimes be worse than useless. People can remain antisemitic, or at least anti-Jewish, while being fully aware that their outlook is indefensible. If you dislike somebody, you dislike him and there is an end of it: your feelings are not made any better by a recital of his virtues" (Orwell 1945).

While some scholars have distinguished "anti-Judaism" from "Judeophobia" and "anti-Semitism," the latter has become the standard modern term for fear and hatred of Jews. After the Second World War, the non-Jewish French philoso-pher Jean-Paul Sartre (1905–1980), who in his thirties had been a prisoner of war in Germany, thought that anti-Semitism did not require the presence of Jews, as it derived from purely projective fantasies. The anti-Semite feared him-self, his consciousness, his liberty, everything *but* the Jew (Sartre 1948, p. 53). Sartre defined anti-Semitism as "attributing all or part of one's own misfortunes, and those of one's country, to the presence of Jewish elements in the community, and proposing to remedying this state of affairs by depriving the Jews of certain of their rights; by keeping them out of certain economic or social activities, by expelling them from the country, by exterminating them, etc." Sartre's "attribu-tion" is the unconscious defensive processes of *projection* and *externalization* by which we attribute to others feelings and traits that we cannot bear about ourselves.

While the activist left-wing Jean-Paul Sartre fought the right-wing French anti-Semites in his writings, his attitude toward the Jews was ambivalent, as is that of many other non-Jews. Sartre had some close Jewish friends, such as Claude Lanzmann and Jean Daniel. His last personal secretary, Benny Lévy (1945–2003), a.k.a. Pierre Victor, claimed that at the end of his life, the dying, secular, and left-wing Sartre embraced orthodox Judaism (Sartre & Lévy 1980, 1996). This secretary, however, was an unreliable Egyptian-born French Jewish "scholar" who had renamed himself "Pierre Victor" and who had been manipu-lating Sartre for years. A year before Sartre's death, the Palestinian-American scholar Edward W. Said (1935–2003) came to Paris to take part in a seminar on "peace in the Middle East" organized by Sartre's journal, *Les Temps modernes*. Said met Sartre, accompanied by Benny Lévy, and, 20 years later, published this unflattering memoir of the latter:

> When the great man finally appeared, well past the appointed time, I was shocked at how old and frail he seemed. I recall rather needlessly and idiotically introduc-ing [Michel] Foucault to him, and I also recall that Sartre was constantly surrounded, supported, prompted by a small retinue of people on whom he was totally dependent. They, in turn, had made him the main business of their lives. One was his adopted daughter [Arlette Elkaïm, Sartre's Algerian Jewish mistress] who, I later learned, was his literary executor...Another was Pierre Victor, a for-mer Maoist and co-publisher with Sartre of the now defunct *Gauche prolétarienne*, who had become a deeply religious and, I supposed, Orthodox Jew; it stunned me to find out later from one of the journal's assistants that he was an Egyptian Jew called Benny Lévy, the brother of Adel Ref'at (né Lévy), one of the so-called Mahmoud Hussein pair (the other being a Muslim Egyptian [Bahgat Elnadi]: the two men worked at UNESCO and as "Mahmoud Hussein" wrote *La Lutte des* [sic] *classes en Egypte* [Hussein 1969], a well-known study published by Maspero). There seemed to be nothing Egyptian about Victor: he came across as a Left Bank intellectual, part-thinker, part-hustler. (Said 2000)

The "Mahmoud Hussein pair" were Adel Rifaat (the former Eddy Lévy) and Bahgat Elnadi, who used that pseudonym. The title of their book was *La Lutte de classes en Egypte* (The Class Struggle in Egypt), but Said's slight grammatical error in French is more than made up for by the insight he gave us into the character of Benny Lévy, whose biography may help us understand the complex psychological aspects of Judaism and anti-Semitism.

Born in Egypt in 1945, the little boy Benjamin (Benny) Lévy grew up in an Egyptian Jewish family. His elder brother Edouard (Eddy) had been born in 1938. Most of the Egyptian Jews spoke French as well as Arabic. In 1956, the 11-year-old Benny's parents took him to France as part of the mass exodus of Egyptian Jews following the Suez War, in which the British and French had fought on Israel's side against Egypt. The war had forced most Egyptian Jews, including the Lévys, to flee Egypt, which had begun to persecute and expel its Jews. But Benny's 18-year-old brother Eddy found another solution. He stayed in Egypt, converted to Islam, and took the Arabic name of "Adel Rifaat."

It is hard to exaggerate the emotional conflict provoked by the elder brother's actions in the boy Benny. As he saw it, his revered idol had abandoned him, let him down, and betrayed him. At the same time, however, Benny's chief rival for his parents' love was left behind, while his parents had taken Benny with them. Before his death in 2003, Lévy said that Sartre was an "elder brother" to him, "the only great one" (Finkielkraut & Lévy 2003). In Benny's unconscious mind, Sartre had clearly replaced his elder brother.

Adel Rifaat remained in Egypt and wrote for the French-language newspaper *Courrier de l'UNESCO* with his friend Bahgat Elnadi. Together those "twins of Islam" later published several books under the *nom de plume* of "Mahmoud Hussein" (Hussein 1969, 1973; Hussein et al. 1974; Friedländer & Hussein 1975; cf. Galinier 2005). Meanwhile, in France, the young Benny Lévy became a brilliant student. In 1963, he came to Paris at the age of 18 to attend the *École Normale Supérieure,* studying under key intellectual figures such as Louis Althusser and Jacques Derrida. Under their influence, he was drawn to the far-left French Radical movement, aligning himself with the Maoists and taking the *nom de guerre* of "Pierre Victor." The two Egyptian Jewish brothers Eddy and Benny Lévy were no longer to be found under their original names. Such name changes indicate profound disturbances of identity and the self (Falk 1975–1976).

In 1966 the 28-year-old Adel Rifaat got himself exiled from Egypt and went to France to join his family. His friend Bahgat Elnadi also came to France. The two sibling rivals Adel Rifaat and Pierre Victor became rivals in intellectual achievement. When French students tried to bring down the government of Charles de Gaulle in 1968, the 23-year-old Pierre Victor played a key role in the uprising. His elder brother Adel Rifaat was less violent. Together with Bahgat Elnadi, he published French-language books under the *nom de plume* of Mahmoud Hussein (1969, 1973, 2005).

Pierre Victor helped found *La Gauche prolétarienne,* a radical and violent Maoist group that was dissolved by a special French law in 1970. "Pierre Victor" met Jean-Paul Sartre in this group and became his disciple. Four years later, he became Sartre's personal secretary. Adel Rifaat and Bahgat Elnadi had many heated arguments with Adel's younger brother. Finally, in 1972, after many "white nights" of passionate argument, the "twins of Islam" succeeded in getting Adel's younger Maoist brother to renounce terrorism and violence. After his death in 2003, they described him as a rigid perfectionist: "Everything that Benny Lévy undertook was inscribed in an absolute quest...A few years ago, Benny Lévy had planned a writing project: to confront our crossed paths, a dialogue between brothers. But it was too early" (Galinier 2005, my translation from the French).

Pierre Victor, a.k.a. Benny Lévy, remained Sartre's personal secretary until Sartre's death in 1980. The two published books together (Victor et al. 1974, Lévy & Sartre 1984, Sartre & Lévy 1996). Pierre Victor also manipulated Sartre into getting President Valéry Giscard d'Estaing to bestow French citizenship upon Benny Lévy. After becoming French, however, Pierre Victor underwent a great religious and political conversion, changing from Maoist to ultra-orthodox Jew. While working with his "elder brother" Sartre, he began to discover orthodox Judaism through his research into Jewish mysticism, which he conducted with his mentor. Their work together greatly upset the circle of intellectuals around Sartre, especially after Sartre began introducing Jewish religious ideas like redemption and messianism into his philosophy. Simone-Lucie-Ernestine-Marie-Bertrand de Beauvoir (1908–1986), who was Sartre's lifelong companion, and her friends angrily accused Lévy of brainwashing Sartre and faking his writings. Shortly before his death, however, Sartre publicly declared that he had willingly and consciously abandoned some of his earlier ideas in favor of his later ones.

Pierre Victor had begun studying in a Jewish *yeshivah,* or rabbinical school, in Strasbourg and practicing orthodox Judaism. He wore the black garb of the medieval Polish nobility that ultra-orthodox Jews take for uniquely Jewish clothing. He went back to his original name of Benny Lévy. In March 1980, a month before Jean-Paul Sartre's death, the French intellectual weekly *Le Nouvel Observateur* published a series of interviews that Sartre had purportedly given to Benny Lévy, the last ever given by the blind, debilitated, and dying Sartre. In those interviews, Sartre reportedly told Lévy that he had abandoned his lifelong leftist convictions, rejected his intimate friends, including Simone de Beauvoir, in favor of his mistress and adopted daughter Arlette Elkaïm, and cast aside his fervent beliefs in the primacy of individual consciousness, the inevitability of violence, and Maoist Marxism, in favor of Lévy's messianic Judaism (Sartre & Lévy 1980, 1996).

Many *Nouvel Observateur* readers were outraged by the publication of Sartre's purported interviews with Lévy and denounced them as distorted, inauthentic, tendentious, even faked. Simone de Beauvoir was beside herself with fury. When the dying Sartre publicly confirmed the authenticity of the interviews, Lévy's critics claimed that he had exploited Sartre's fear of his impending death and manipulated him into abandoning his leftist convictions and adopting Lévy's messianic Judaism, and also into rejecting his lifelong companion Simone de Beauvoir in favor of his adopted daughter and former mistress Arlette Elkaïm. Sartre's followers and Lévy's detractors argued that his interviewer Benny Lévy, the former extreme-left-wing, now ultra-right-wing activist, had twisted the words of the dying Sartre to his own ends. Simone de Beauvoir died six years later of alcohol and drug abuse. Sartre had given other interviews to the French luminaries Dominique Desanti, Jean-Bertrand Pontalis, Claude Lanzmann, André Glucksmann, Olivier Todd, Serge July, and Jean Daniel, all of which can be found on the French *Bibliothèque nationale* Web site, whereas the Benny Lévy interviews are conspicuously missing from it.

Benny Lévy's elder brother Adel Rifaat obtained French citizenship in 1983, three years after Sartre's death. In the 1990s Benny Lévy immigrated to Israel, set up a "doctoral school" under the auspices of the university of Paris VII (which closed within a short time due to the hostility of his Israeli colleagues and his own character), then founded an *Institut d'études lévinassiennes* to teach the work of the Lithuanian-French Jewish philosopher Emmanuel Lévinas (1906–1995), and manipulated the French Jewish intellectuals Bernard-Henri Lévy (born Bernard Lévy in 1948) and Alain Finkielkraut (born 1949) into joining him in his public "intellectual" shows in France and in Israel. Before his own death in 2003, Benny Lévy said that Jean-Paul Sartre had been "more an elder brother than a father to him" (Finkielkraut & Lévy 2003).

As we have seen, Benny Lévy's elder brother Adel Rifaat had been a key figure in his emotional life. After Benny Lévy's death, Adel Rifaat, who may have suffered from "survivor guilt" (Krystal & Niederland 1968), published a book with Bahgat Elnadi under the *nom de plume* of Mahmoud Hussein in which he argued for a free and democratic Arab world and praised the "dialogue" between Jews and Arabs (like his brother and himself). Rifaat and Elnadi assembled the Arabic writings of the first two centuries of Islam and presented the prophet Muhammad as "an exceptional man, but also one who doubts, who errs, who wavers, who is afraid" (Galinier 2005, quoting Hussein 2005; my translation from the French).

ANTI-SEMITISM, EUGENICS, AND RACISM

Anti-Semitism is closely related to racism, which developed out of eugenics, originally an ancient philosophy advocating the improvement of human hereditary traits through social intervention. Selective breeding of human beings had been suggested by Plato, but modern eugenics was first created in the mid-nineteenth century by Sir Francis Galton (1822–1911), using (or misusing) the evolutionary theory of his older cousin, Charles Darwin (1809–1882)—who had used the word "race" in a sense similar to "species" rather than in Galton's sense (Darwin 1859; Galton 1869, 1909; Haller 1963; Mehler 1983, 1988, 1989, 1997; Kevles 1985; Allen 1986; Adams 1990; Kühl 1994; Kenny 2002).

The official goals of eugenics had been benign—to create more intelligent people, save social resources, lessen human suffering, and reduce health problems. The official means of achieving these goals have included birth control, selective breeding, and genetic engineering—but not mass murder or genocide. The new science of eugenics was initially supported by prominent and respected thinkers, including Alexander Graham Bell and W. E. B. Du Bois, and in the late nineteenth and early twentieth century, it was a respected academic discipline at many universities. Its scientific reputation, however, was destroyed in the 1930s, after the Swiss-German "genetic psychiatrist" Ernst Rüdin (1874–1952) began incorporating eugenics rhetoric into the murderous racist policies of Nazi Germany. The Nazi abuse of eugenics culminated in coercive state-sponsored discrimination, human-rights violations, mass murder, extermination, and genocide.

In 1913 the Eugenics Research Association was founded in the United States. While eugenics did not start out as racism, there has been a slippery slope from one to the other. One example was the notorious American eugenicist Wickliffe Preston Draper (1891–1972), who began his career as a wealthy benefactor of the scientific study of heredity and human differences, notably those related to race and intelligence, and ended it as a fanatical Nazi racist and anti-Semite (Kenny 2002, Tucker 2002). Draper at first supported charitable causes and scientific endeavors, including history (mainly military), archaeology, conservation, and population problems. Among the organizations he supported was the Eugenics Research Association and the American Eugenics Society, founded in 1926.

Draper gradually became a virulent racist. In 1935, with Adolf Hitler as Germany's *Führer,* Draper traveled to Berlin to attend the racist International Congress for the Scientific Investigation of Population Problems, presided over by Wilhelm Frick (1877–1946), Hitler's interior minister, who was later condemned and sentenced to death at the Nuremberg Trials and hanged for his crimes against humanity. At the Berlin conference, Draper's fellow delegate was Dr. Clarence Gordon Campbell (1868–1956), the first president of the Eugenics Research Association, and a Nazi sympathizer. Campbell delivered a fiery racist oration: "The Leader of the German Nation, Adolf Hitler, ably supported by Dr. Frick and guided by Germany's anthropologists and social philosophers, has been able to construct a comprehensive racial policy of population development and improvement. This policy promises to be epochal in racial history!"

Chiding good folk who think of marriage as something sentimental and religious, with its sexual details omitted from consideration until after the wedding ceremony, Dr. Campbell reported: "A decided tendency is now to be observed in enlightened minds no longer to place implicit faith in rhetorical principles which have no foundation in fact, and to explore the realities of nature." Campbell concluded his speech: "The difference between the Jew and the Aryan is as unsurmountable [*sic*] as that between black and white...Germany has set a pattern which other nations must follow." He toasted "that great leader, Adolf Hitler!" Ironically, one of the prosecutors at the Nuremberg trials of former Nazi leaders, including Frick, was another Clarence Campbell—Clarence Sutherland Campbell (1905–1984), the Canadian-born president of the American-dominated National Hockey League.

Hitler's bizarre ideas about the ethnic origin of the Germans in the ancient "Aryans" who came from northern Europe and invaded India from Persia were pure fantasy (Poliakov 1974, Goodrick-Clarke 1998). The ancient "Aryan" culture had preceded both the Vedic Indian and Avestan Persian ones, and "Aryan" unity had probably begun around 2,500 BCE. Draper and Campbell, however, fervently believed in this fantasy.

In 1937, Draper founded the Pioneer Fund, a racist foundation intended to give scholarships to descendants of colonial-era white American families and to support research into "race betterment" through "scientific" eugenics. The Pioneer Fund was headed by the American eugenicist Harry Hamilton Laughlin (1880–1943), who had directed the U.S. Eugenics Record Office from its inception in 1910 to its closing in 1939. The racist Laughlin was among the most active individuals influencing American eugenics policy. He had lobbied hard for restrictive U.S. immigration laws and for national programs of the compulsory sterilization of the mentally ill and mentally retarded.

Draper paid to reprint and publicize the racist book *White America* (1923) by the American white supremacist leader Earnest Sevier Cox (1880–1966), and a personal copy was delivered to *Reichminister* Frick in Berlin. The Pioneer Fund scholarships were never given. The first project of the Fund was to distribute in the United States two documentary films from Nazi Germany depicting its claimed success with eugenics. Though years before the Holocaust and its eventual public disclosure, Germany's eugenic policies were still very controversial for their far-reaching scope and coercive public policies.

Having served as a soldier in both world wars, Draper returned to active philanthropy after the Second World War in 1945, and his Pioneer Fund supported the work of several racist "researchers," including William Shockley, Arthur Jensen, J. Philippe Rushton, and Roger Pearson. Though he never personally served as the Pioneer Fund's president, Draper remained on the Fund's board until his death and left his entire estate to the Fund, having never married. Was his inability to form a lasting, intimate relationship connected to his racism? Subsequent Pioneer Fund boards have continued Draper's support for "eugenics researchers" studying race and intelligence. Draper also donated considerable funds to racist right-wing political organizations and candidates. In addition to the Pioneer Fund, Draper also gave money directly to support the racist causes that he favored. In 1963, at the peak of the Civil Rights Movement, Draper secretly sent $215,000 to the Mississippi State Sovereignty Commission in order to support racial segregation. The gifts came to light only in the 1990s, when the commission's records were made public.

Throughout his life, Draper maintained a low profile, as did the Pioneer Fund. When he died from prostate cancer, he left $1.4 million to the Pioneer Fund. Since his death in 1972, Draper and the Pioneer Fund have been criticized for funding "race and intelligence research," which is a euphemism for "scientific" racism (Kenny 2002, Tucker 2002). Draper has become even more controversial since the publication of *The Bell Curve* (Herrnstein & Murray 1994), which purported to prove that white people's intelligence was superior to black people's intelligence, because the Pioneer Fund supported the controversial research in the book (Fraser 1995; Jacoby & Glauberman 1995; Baum 2004). So much for the slippery slope from eugenics to racism, of which Draper and Hitler were examples. After the Holocaust, most of the world associated eugenics with Nazi racism, including its enforced "racial hygiene," mass murder and genocide, while several regional and national governments maintained eugenics programs until the 1970s. Contemporary scholars consider eugenics a pseudoscience with a dangerous potential for "objectifying" human character traits, a precursor of modern racism (Winfield 2006).

Sartre's definition of anti-Semitism may be applied to racism, which in turn may be defined as the delusional view of the human species as divided into "races" arranged by hierarchical order so that some races (such as the white or "Aryan" races) are superior to others (such as the black or Jewish races), the "lower races" must submit to the "higher races," and the "subhuman" lower races are the cause of all of humanity's ills. While having roots in the ancient world, the pernicious, modern variety of racism, which has led to many genocides, began in the nineteenth and twentieth centuries, when "scientific" anthropological theories dividing humankind into "superior" and "inferior" races were propagated by racist "scholars" such as the French nobleman Joseph-Arthur de Gobineau (1816–1882) and the English "philosopher" Houston Stewart Chamberlain (1855–1927), who lived in Germany and wrote in German (Gobineau 1855–1857, 1915; Chamberlain 1899, 1911). According to these "scholars," the white-skinned "Aryan" races were vastly superior to the "subhuman" dark-skinned "Semitic" and "Hamitic" races from Africa and Asia.

Ironically, the word "Aryan" comes from a Persian-Indian word meaning "noble," the *Hakenkreuz,* or swastika, the emblem of the German Nazis (the common name for Hitler's *Nationalsozialistische deutsche Arbeiterpartei* or *NSDAP,* the National-Socialist German Workers Party), is an inverted old Hindu religious symbol, while the "Star of David," the "Jewish" symbol that the Nazis forced the Jews of Europe to wear, is in fact an old non-Jewish astrological symbol.

The shape of that star is the hexagram, a symbol from other religions that predates its use by the Jews. Its prevalent usage before and outside Judaism was the occult. The hexagram is a *mandala* symbol found on Indian temples built thousands of years ago. It symbolizes the *nara-narayana* or perfect meditative state of balance achieved between Man and God, and, if maintained, results in *moksha*, or *nirvana*, the release from the bounds of the earthly world and its material trappings. The Star of David can be found all over Asia and Africa. The Star of David is known as the "King's Star" in astrological circles and was an important astrological symbol in Persian Zoroastrianism. Like beauty, therefore, in the last analysis, the meaning of symbols is in the eye of the beholder.

One of the most prolific scholars of anti-Semitism and the Holocaust was the German-born American Jewish historian George L. Mosse (Gerhard Lachmann-Mosse, 1918–1999). He was born into one of Berlin's wealthiest Jewish families. The Mosse family owned a large chain of newspapers including several of the most prestigious papers in Germany, most notably the *Berliner Tageblatt*. Mosse was educated at the exclusive German boys' school *Schloß Salem* (Salem Castle) near the *Bodensee* (Lake Constance), which was run by former German army officers, and where, as a frail youth, he had difficulty with the demanding physical education regime imposed on the pupils. Most of Mosse's teachers were supporters of the German National People's Party and anti-Semites. Mosse's experience there left him with a lifelong sense of being an outsider.

In 1933, the Mosses fled Germany to Britain. During his time in Britain, Mosse was educated at the Bootham School. It was there that he discovered that he was a homosexual (Mosse 2000). In 1936, the Mosses moved to the United States and "George Mosse" went to college. Despite his upper-class background, he was a self-proclaimed "Marxist of the heart." In 1941, he graduated from Haverford College and, in 1946, from Harvard University with a PhD in history. He taught at the University of Iowa from 1944 to 1955 and at the University of Wisconsin from 1955 to 1988. On his sabbaticals, the pro-Zionist Mosse often taught at the Hebrew University of Jerusalem.

After the Second World War, the Mosse family attempted to recover their lost German property, and in the 1950s, they obtained the restitution of Mosse family properties located in the western sector of Berlin. Since most of their real estate was located in the Soviet-occupied zone (later the German Democratic Republic), however, their efforts were only partially successful. After the unification of Germany, in 1990, George Mosse successfully petitioned the German government to reclaim his family property that had been expropriated by the Nazis and the Communists. At his death in 1999, George Mosse was a wealthy man. He left the bulk of his estate to fund history scholarships at the University of Wisconsin and at the Hebrew University of Jerusalem.

Mosse began his academic career as an expert on family life in Tudor and Stuart England, but later studied Nazi Germany, fascism, anti-Semitism, and

Jewish history (Mosse 1964, 1970, 1978, 1987). The homosexual Mosse also studied the history of sexuality (Mosse 1985). Interested in the psychology of political leadership, he studied how symbols were created and used by leaders to win and keep their followers. Another major interest for Mosse was the brutalization of politics, especially in the Nazi era. He correctly saw fascism and Nazism not as rational ideologies but as the expression of irrational feelings. Yet another area of interest for Mosse was the intellectual origin of Nazism.

Like many of his colleagues, George Mosse studied the notorious history of racism, including its "scientific" varieties. (Hirschfeld 1938; Katz 1976; Mosse 1970, 1978; Chase 1979; Billig 1979, 1981; Mehler 1983; Brown 1985; Barkan 1992; Ferraroti 1994; Shipman 1994; Kühl 1994; Tucker 1994, 2002; Loewenberg 1995b; Dunbar 1995; Tarnero 1995; Richards 1997; Winston 1998, 2004; Wistrich 1999; Moss 2001, 2003; Fredrickson 2002; Clarke 2003; Levine & Patak 2004). In most cases, racism has involved anti-Semitism.

"SCIENTIFIC" ANTI-SEMITISM

As we have seen, even though the term "anti-Semitism" is used universally for the fear and hatred of the Jews, it is a misleading euphemism. The German word *antisemitisch* was first used in 1860 by the Austrian Jewish scholar Moritz Steinschneider (1816–1907) in the phrase *antisemitische Vorurteile* (anti-Semitic prejudices). Steinschneider used this phrase to characterize the French philosopher Ernest Renan's false ideas about how "Semitic races" were inferior to "Aryan races" (Renan 1855). A linguist, historian, and writer, Renan had toyed with the "new idea" of race, regarding it as the cornerstone of human civilization. He saw himself, in the European tradition, mainly as a man of science. Renan's belief in science gave his theorizing an air of unshakable scientific truth. Although the distinction between superior Aryans and inferior Semites was not always to his liking, he felt duty-bound to speak the truth, in the spirit of value-free science, *avant la lettre*. Renan's training for the priesthood added a strong moral note to his devotion to the "gospel" of science. Ironically, this Catholic priest almost succeeded in rejecting traditional Christianity in favor of his imagined Indo-European ancestry of European civilization (Almog 1988).

"Scientific" theories of race, civilization, and progress had become popular in Europe in the second half of the nineteenth century. The nationalistic Prussian historian Heinrich Gotthard von Treitschke (1834–1896) did much to promote "scientific" racism. (Treitschke 1880). In Treitschke's writings, the term "Semitic" was almost synonymous with "Jewish," in contrast to its usage by Renan, who used it to denote a whole range of peoples: the Akkadians (Assyrians and Babylonians), Chaldeans, Eblaites, Aramaeans, Syriacs, Ugarites, Canaanites, Amorites (Amurru or Martu), Ammonites, Edomites, Eberites (Hebrews), Jews, Moabites, Phoenicians, Sabaeans (of Yemen, Eritrea and Ethiopia), Semitic Ethiopians, Arabs, Nabataeans, and "Saracens."

The "scientific" term *Antisemitismus* was coined in 1879, eight years after the unification of Germany by the Prussian chancellor Otto von Bismarck, by an unemployed, angry and self-hating German gutter journalist and political agitator named Wilhelm Marr (1819–1904), who had serious emotional trouble with his unloved wife, with his Jewish father-in-law (who had converted to Christianity)—and with himself. Via unconscious projection, Marr blamed the loss of his job and his other personal failures and troubles on the Jews. Like many other Germans (and German speakers in neighboring countries), Marr supported Bismarck's *Kulturkampf* (cultural struggle) against the Catholic Church, which lasted through the 1870s and 1880s, until Bismarck resigned in 1890 (Zimmermann 1986).

Bismarck himself had his own emotional problems, though he was able to cope with them at a much higher psychological level than Marr (Hughes 1977; Hughes 1983, pp. 45–76). After the Congress of Berlin in 1878, which divided the Balkans among Great Britain, Russia, and Austria, with Bismarck overseeing the process, Marr took the anti-Jewish and racist philosophies of the German scholars Johann Gottfried von Herder (1744–1803) and the aforementioned Heinrich von Treitschke an insidious step further by giving Jew-hatred intellectual and ideological respectability and, unconsciously, denying its evil power and insidious racism, which eventually led to the greatest tragedy in human history, the Holocaust, which not only saw the mass murder of six million Jews but also left hundreds of thousands of massively traumatized survivors (Herder 1784; Treitschke 1880; Marr 1879, 1880a, 1880b; Hilberg 1961, Améry 1966, 1980; Krystal 1968).

Some scholars have studied the so-called "new anti-Semitism" that began after the Second World War and the Holocaust (Forster & Epstein 1974; Chesler 2003; Iganski & Kosmin 2003; Taguieff 2004; Frindte et al. 2005; Joffe 2005; Nirenstein 2005). Whether or not this "new" anti-Semitism is essentially different from the "old" variety remains an open question. Be that as it may, in view of its highly irrational fantasies, which we shall examine below, and its tragic and murderous actions, of which we shall study some key examples, it is impossible to understand anti-Semitism without understanding its unconscious aspects, the defensive unconscious psychological processes operating on the individual and collective levels. It is on these unconscious aspects, as opposed to numerous other studies of anti-Semitism that examine its conscious aspects, that this book focuses (Falk 2006).

XENOPHOBIA, NATIONALISM, AND ANTI-SEMITISM

The history of Judeophobia among the ancient Greek and Romans (Stern 1980) makes it clear that to truly understand anti-Semitism we need to analyze the psychological roots of ethnocentrism, racism, and xenophobia—all of them age-old, universal human phenomena. Xenophobia, the fear and hatred of foreigners, has existed since ancient times and has persisted into modern German society. The German psychoanalyst Werner Bohleber found psychological similarities and links between xenophobia, nationalism, and anti-Semitism (Bohleber 1992, 1997). He thought that social crises, high unemployment, scarce housing, or the absence of better future-life prospects do not suffice to explain the aggressive nationalism and the new xenophobia in Germany.

Bohleber thought that while xenophobia and anti-Semitism have been extensively studied by German psychoanalysts, the fantasy of the German "nation" as a living organism still defied a clear psychoanalytic understanding. Through a psychoanalytic case vignette, the author showed that assuming nationalist ideologies, which, in Germany, perceived the nation as a living organism, could prevent the breaking out of an individual neurosis and act as an "oblique healing" in Freud's sense. Bohleber thought that the fantasy of the "nation" opens up a psychological space for the patient, which fulfills the unconscious wish for the pre-ambivalent fusion with an object (the early mother) in which there is nothing separate, different, strange, heterogenous, foreign, or autonomous. In other words, the "nation" unconsciously replaces the early mother. In fact, this is hardly a new idea. There is a large body of psychoanalytic literature on the unconscious meaning of the nation as the mother and as an extension of the self (cf. Mack 1983; Kristeva 1993; Falk 2004, pp. 87–102).

The "strangeness" of the ancient Jews, their being different in some ways—though similar in other ways—to the ancient Greeks and Romans, made it possible for the latter to unconsciously *externalize and project* upon the Jews their own undesirable or unacceptable qualities or the painful feelings they had about themselves. Those aspects of the ethnic (or religious) "group self" that were *split off* and barred from awareness were externalized and projected upon the Jews. The Jews were unconsciously *dehumanized* and demonized—their humanity was *denied,* and they were thought of as animals or subhuman beings—making it emotionally easier for the Greeks and Romans to hate them and kill them. *Dehumanization* and *demonization* of "the enemy" are well-known defensive psychological processes that involve an unconscious *denial* of the enemy's humanity and occur under great stress and emotional regression, denial being an early infantile defensive process. (Volkan 1997, pp. 112–115). We shall also see that our "adult" feelings that other human groups are "strange" or "foreign" echo our early infantile feelings about our mother's body and our refusal to give up the fusion with her.

The ancient Romans probably exaggerated when they put the number of Jews whom they had killed during their "Jewish War" of 66–70 CE at one million, but it is still true that during the tragic Bar-Kochba revolt against the Romans of 132–135 CE, hundreds of thousands of Jews were massacred by the Roman troops. It was the worst military catastrophe in Jewish history. No Jews were left in Judaea, and none were permitted within sight of Aelia Capitolina, the new Roman city built upon the ruins of Jerusalem. Jews now lived only in the Galilee and in the *diaspora*, the Greek name for the Jewish "dispersion" outside Palestine—the Graeco-Roman name for "the land of Israel"—"among the nations." The term *diaspora* has survived in the Zionist view of the world: all Jews living outside Israel are said to live in the "diaspora" and in "exile." Both terms are anachronistic and unrealistic, however: most U.S. Jews, for example, do not think of themselves as either "dispersed" or "exiled," nor even as part of "the Jewish people." To them, Judaism is their religion only. They are Jewish Americans rather than American Jews (Ouzan 2008). Therefore, in Israel, a "post-Zionist" view of Jewish and Israeli history has developed, especially among the "new Israeli historians" such as Benny Morris, Ilan Pappé and Avi Shlaim, who are much maligned by their Zionist colleagues. The last two now live in the UK.

At the same time as the "pagans" hated the Jews, there were also Greeks and Romans, both pagan and Christian, who converted to Judaism or observed Jewish traditions. This Judaizing movement, which began in the time of Saint Paul in the first century, was so strong that by the fourth century, the Greek church father Johannes Chrysostomos (347–407), whose last name means "golden-mouthed," felt compelled to denounce it in a special "discourse" (Chrysostom 1979, Stern 1980). The Judaizing movement indicates the great *ambivalence* that the ancient Greeks and Romans—and their Christian successors—felt for the Jews. This ambivalence was noted by modern psychoanalysts as part of overt anti-Semitism (Stern 1980; Stein 1987; Blumenberg 1997).

Nevertheless, the overt Greek and Roman hatred of the Jews had its subtle effect on the Jewish collective self-image. A child who is repeatedly attacked or berated by an angry, disturbed, paranoid parent, upbraided, yelled at and told that it is "bad" cannot remain emotionally healthy. Unconsciously, the child will internalize these attitudes, develop a bad self-image, hate itself and feel that it really is bad. The child will also act "badly" to confirm to its bad self-image. In a human society, a minority group consistently derided, segregated, discriminated against, persecuted or hated by the majority is in the same predicament. It cannot retain a healthy self. Its members internalize the majority's feelings about them and develop a bad "group self." They will act "badly" to confirm this self, creating a tragic vicious circle. This "identification with the aggressor" is what happened to the Jews as a group. While, on the one hand, feeling superior and elected by God, on the other hand, they gradually became emotionally ill, fearful of non-Jews, unhappy with themselves, and feeling inferior, suspicious, and insecure. This was the origin of the strange phenomenon of Jewish self-hatred, which the American Jewish scholar Sander Gilman has analyzed (Gilman 1986). We shall return to this tragic and fascinating subject below.

Some Aspects of the History of Anti-Semitism

The complete history of anti-Semitism, including anti-Judaism, Judeophobia, and Jew-hatred, would fill many lengthy tomes (cf. Long 1953; Factor 1956; Poliakov 1961–1975; Morais 1976; Weiberg 1986). Despite Langmuir's interesting distinctions, and his idea that anti-Semitism as we know it arose in the Middle Ages, Judeophobia has existed for millennia, while the term "anti-Semitism" only came into being in the late nineteenth century. However, not only among non-Jews, or "Gentiles," but also among Jews and Jewish scholars, the term "anti-Semitism" has almost universally replaced "anti-Judaism," Jew-hatred" and "Judeophobia" (Schäfer 1997; Smith 1997; Fischer 1998; Perednik 2001; Taguieff 2002). The Austrian-born (and concentration-camp survivor) American Jewish psychoanalyst Ernest Rappaport (1903–1974) purposely used the term "anti-Judaism" in the title of his fascinating book on the subject (Rappaport 1975). "Anti-Judaism," "Judeophobia," and "Jew-hatred" better describe the tragic, psychopathological and irrational phenomenon that we are studying here than "anti-Semitism," a "scientific" and ideological euphemism coined in the nineteenth century by the emotionally disturbed, Jew-hating gutter journalist Wilhelm Marr (1819–1904). Let us now examine the history of Jew-hatred through the ages.

HUMAN CHILD SACRIFICE AND ANTI-SEMITISM

Sigmund Freud considered the father-son conflict and the internal "oedipus complex" as basic to the psychological understanding of the human family, the human condition, and human civilization. He speculated that since ancient times non-Jews unconsciously identified "the Jew" with the loved-and-hated father (Bergmann 1988, p. 17). They also unconsciously projected their own patricidal and filicidal wishes on the Jews. One of the most dangerous and tragic fantasies of medieval European Christians was the "ritual-murder libel" or "blood libel" against the Jews: the Christians seriously and fervently believed that the Jews killed Christian children in order to use their blood for the baking of their unleavened Passover bread. When a Christian child was found dead, the Jews were accused of having murdered him and were often violently attacked and massacred. Several psychoanalytic scholars have shown that, because every father has filicidal wishes, which he unconsciously represses or denies, this terrible murderous fantasy resulted from the Christian accuser's unconscious *projection* of his own infanticidal wishes and guilt feelings (Hsia 1988; Heinsohn 1988; Dundes 1991; Chasseguet-Smirgel 2004).

Ancient child sacrifice, in which the firstborn son was sacrificed to the imagined sun god or fire god to appease them and make them benevolent towards us, resulted from the unconscious projection of the father's filicidal wishes upon the gods—who themselves were projections of internalized parental images in early life or an anthropomorphizing of natural forces. Child sacrifice had a profound impact on the development of Judaism and Christianity (Bergmann 1992, Falk 1996). It also helps us understand Jew-hatred as an unconscious projection of the father's inner conflict about his son—his fear of his son replacing him and his wish to kill him struggling with his love of his son and his wish to keep him. This painful inner conflict, which found its outward expression in the sacrifice of one's firstborn son to the gods, in the Genesis myth of the *Akedah*—Abraham's binding of his son Isaac in order to sacrifice him to Yahweh—and in the Jewish (and Muslim) practice of circumcision may have given rise to both Judaism and Christianity (Falk 1996).

The perceptive American Jewish psychoanthropologist Howard F. Stein thought that this ancient Laios-Oedipus or Abraham-Isaac father-son conflict underlay both Jewish "anti-Gentilism" and Christian anti-Judaism:

> Each accretion of ritual following ritual, new defense replacing old defense—from human sacrifice of the firstborn male to animal sacrifice, to the abolition of animal sacrifice and the institution of personal pietism, to the self-sacrifice of Jesus on the Cross—was less a theological advance than symptomatic of the fact that the conflict underlying the *Akedah* had never been sufficiently countercathected by myth or ritual...in the psychodynamic sense Judaism *never* abolished the *original* sacrifice. The nature of the sacrifice transformed the sacrificial dyad...into the relationship between God and the entire people of Israel. Jews, in sadomasochistic identification with both father...and son, became the Jewish Paschal lamb who, as scapegoat, takes away the sins of the world. Christianity continued the *displacement* and dissociation of the sacrifice; Judaism became the religion of a people who *remain the sacrifice itself*. (Stein 1987, pp. 155–156)

Stein thought that by identifying with the aggressor, accepting their assigned role as victims, making martyrdom holy, and adopting a superior anti-Gentile attitude, the Jews unwittingly contributed to this paradoxical vicious circle of survival through persecution, all the way up to the Nazi holocaust of our own times (Stein 1977, 1978, 1987, 1994). Far from blaming the Jews for their own predicament, Stein was trying to outline the *vicious circle* that arose out of their initial persecution and their hatred by the non-Jews.

Stein's studies, however, are part of the "interactionist" model of anti-Semitism, which seeks to explain anti-Semitism as the outcome of a subtle "interaction" between Jews and non-Jews. This was the view of the British scholar Colin Holmes, who saw modern British anti-Semitism as a common reaction to unemployment, housing shortages and economic hardships which were linked to the involvement of Jews in some British financial scandals (Holmes 1979). The American Jewish historian Albert Lindemann thought that anti-Semitism was partly due to "the experience of real people in the real world" (Lindemann 1991, p. 9), namely as the non-Jewish reaction to the high visibility and upward mobility of Jews in modern Europe and America. The non-Jews "felt threatened by the rise of the Jews, and some had good reason to feel threatened, for Jews were indeed encroaching on areas that previously had been exclusively Gentile, and Jews were helping make life, as those Gentiles had traditionally experienced it, difficult or impossible" (Lindemann 1991, p. 12).

The British literary scholar Bryan Cheyette challenged the "interactionist" model of antisemitism (Cheyette 1989). He showed that long before the Marconi Scandal in Great Britain (1911–1914), which alleged financial abuses by prominent British Jews, one of its instigators, the British writer Joseph Hilaire Pierre René Belloc (1870–1953), had written anti-Semitic fiction (Belloc 1904, 1908, 1910). The Marconi Scandal began in 1911 with allegations by Hilaire Belloc in his new scandal sheet, *Eye-Witness,* that highly placed members of the Liberal government of Britain, under Prime Minister Herbert Henry Asquith (1852–1928), had profited from the improper use of inside information about the government's intentions with respect to the Marconi Company Ltd., which had been founded in 1897 by Guglielmo Marconi as the Wireless Telegraph & Signal Company (also known as as the Wireless Telegraph Trading Signal Company).

The allegations centered on insider trading in Marconi company shares by the British Jewish Solicitor-General and Attorney-General Rufus Daniel Isaacs (1860–1935) and by his law firm of Rufus Isaacs and Associates. The allegations cited the fact that Isaacs's brother Godfrey was the president of Marconi's subsidiary, the American Marconi Company. Some British periodicals ran an anti-Semitic publicity campaign, which was rather rare in British public life at that time. Most active was *The New Witness,* edited by the anti-Semitic British journalist Cecil Edward Chesterton (1879–1918), who had converted to Catholicism and bought *Eye-Witness,* the scandal sheet founded in 1911 by Belloc.

Chesterton and Belloc accused Solicitor-General and Attorney-General Rufus Daniel Isaacs, Postmaster General Herbert Louis Samuel (1870–1963), and Chancellor of the Exchequer David Lloyd George (1863–1945) of insider trading, bribery, and corruption. Their allegations were investigated by a British parliamentary commission, which found only that Rufus Isaacs and David Lloyd George had indeed purchased shares in Marconi's American subsidiary. However, Chesterton's persistent attacks on prominent Jewish figures during the Marconi Scandal and his public defense of his position in terms of a "Jewish problem" left him with a permanent reputation as an anti-Semite.

Godfrey Isaacs brought suit against Cecil Chesterton for libel. Chesterton lost the case and was fined £100. Despite a long history of British anti-Semitism, the anti-Semitic venom in this scandal was remarkable (Donaldson 1962; Lunn 1978; Cheyette 1989, 1993). Cheyette pointed out that Belloc and Chesterton were anti-Semites long before *they* instigated the Marconi Scandal. "Interactionism, by concentrating on the particular 'conflict situation,' fails to take account of the fact that representations of Jews saturated all aspects of British society long before they were institutionalized by particular 'antisemitic' groups or individuals" (Cheyette 1989, p. 139; Cheyette 1993, 1996, 2007).

Like Cheyette, the outstanding American Jewish scholar Sander Gilman studied the psychological aspects of anti-Semitism, including the bizarre antisemitic fantasies about Jewish bodies (Gilman 1991). He found that since ancient times, the non-Jewish mind has entertained all manner of incredibly deformed, exaggerated, ridiculous, malignant, absurd, and grotesque fantasies about the Jewish body. As Gilman's South African Jewish friend and colleague Milton Shain put it, "the point at issue is that [anti-Semitic] preconceptions about Jews precede attitudes and actions" (Shain 1997, p. 74).

The American Jewish psychoanalyst Jacob Arlow cited the German writer Heinrich Heine's treatment of the ritual-child-murder theme in his fragmentary novel *Der Rabbi von Bacherach* (Heine 1840; Arlow 1992, 1994). Heine was a Jew who converted to Christianity. Arlow identified the hatred for and rage at the "foreign" as a key aspect of anti-Semitism, and linked them with infantile sibling rivalry. I have pointed out that "the tragic irony of this ritual-murder libel was that the Passover ritual of the Jews had originated in their attempt to avoid child sacrifice in the first place" (Falk 1996, p. 369). Oedipal guilt was also projected, and the Jews were also accused of deicide (Reed 1992). By their very existence, the Jews, who had abandoned and condemned human sacrifice, became the unwitting accusers of the Christians who have sacrificed their Christ Jesus to their God the Father, and, by "a perverse move of the spirit," the Jews became the target of the sacrificers' unconscious projections of guilt feelings (Chasseguet-Smirgel 2004, p. 60).

Another prevalent fantasy about the Jews among medieval Christians was that of the "host-desecration libel." In the Roman Catholic and other Christian churches, the host or Eucharist is a wafer symbolizing the body of Jesus Christ, and the wine symbolizes his blood. The Eucharist was called *hostia mirifica* in medieval Church Latin because the Christians believed that it could work miracles, healing the sick and saving the sinners. The Christians imagined that the Jews repeatedly desecrated their *hostia mirifica* just as they had killed their Messiah. The thirteenth century was especially tragic in that respect. In 1215, the Fourth Lateran Council formally established the Christian doctrine of *transubstantiation,* by which the host actually becomes the body of Christ and the wine his blood. Twenty years later, Jews were massacred in various parts of Germany for having "desecrated the sacred host." When the Mongols raided Europe in 1241–1242, the Jews were falsely accused of aiding them, and were massacred. In 1243, near the newly founded Berlin, the Jews were formally accused in court of having defiled, tortured, stabbed, trampled upon, and desecrated the host, which was "the body of Jesus Christ," and of having used the blood that flowed from it to bake their bread. The irrationality of this fantasy is clear from the fact that the Jews, isolated in their own religious and social world, did not know about the host or the belief in transubstantiation and had no interest in them. The murderous fantasy came from the projection of the Christians' unconscious wishes to kill their own sons, symbolized by Jesus Christ (Falk 1996, pp. 480–481).

ANTI-SEMITISM IN ANTIQUITY

While not monolithic or uniform, the history of Jew-hatred goes back to ancient times. In ancient Greece and Rome, from Alexander the Great (353–323 BCE) to Justinian the Great (483–565), the Jews were often discriminated against, despised, and persecuted (Feldman 1993). One of the chief proponents of Jew-hatred was the third-century Graeco-Roman Sophist philosopher Flavius Philostratus the Athenian (170–245), who came from a Lemnos Island literary family, studied at Athens, and lived through the reigns of several Roman emperors. In 193 CE, the new Roman emperor Lucius Septimius Severus Pertinax (146–211), better known as Severus, replaced his traditional Prætorian Guard with his own Danubian legions and assumed the role of an absolute despot over the Roman Empire. Severus was a patron of Sophism, a rhetorical philosophical school and forerunner of pragmatism.

After 202 CE, Philostratus was patronized by Severus's second wife, the Roman empress Julia Domna (c. 170–217), who wielded great power but whose end was tragic. Empress Julia Domna gathered about her in Rome a group of scholars and other intellectuals whose activities are best known through the writings of Philostratus. Political assassination was commonplace in ancient Rome. When Emperor Severus died in 211, his two sons by Julia Domna, Marcus Aurelius Severus Antoninus Augustus (188–217), better known as Caracalla, and Publius Septimius Geta (189–212), became joint emperors. Their

murderous fraternal rivalry led to Geta's assassination by "the mad" Caracalla—
in their mother's arms—in 212. Julia Domna was deeply traumatized. Caracalla
became Rome's sole emperor, but in 217, he too was assassinated by one of
his own officers while leading his army in Parthia, allegedly at the instigation of
his successor, Caesar Marcus Opellius Severus Macrinus Augustus (164–218).
The grieving Julia Domna died soon thereafter. She had either starved herself
to death out of suicidal depression or killed herself on the orders of the new
emperor, Macrinus.

After Julia Domna's death, Flavius Philostratus moved to Tyre (now in
Lebanon). Macrinus concluded an unsatisfactory peace treaty with Parthia,
losing the support of his troops to Caracalla's cousin's son, Varius Avitus
Bassianus (204–222), also known as Elagabalus. Macrinus fled Parthia toward
Italy, but was overtaken by the vengeful Elagabalus, who defeated Macrinus near
Antioch, captured him, and murdered him. Elagabalus became emperor as
Cæsar Marcus Aurelius Antoninus Augustus, but he too was in turn killed by
the mutinous Prætorian guards in 222. Philostratus wrote his most important
philosophical works—the *Life of Apollonius of Tyana,* the *Gymnastikos,* and the
Lives of the Sophists—around 217–218 CE, after the assassination of Caracalla
and the tragic death of his mother Julia Domna. Philostratus really hated the
Jews. They were so very *different* from the Greeks and Romans, he complained,
declaring that the Jews "are separated from ourselves by a greater gulf than
divides us from Susa or Bactra or the most distant Indies" (Philostratus 2005,
5:33; Stern 1980). In those days, Susa was the remote capital of Elam (now in
Iran), and Bactra was in the faraway kingdom of Bactria (now in Afghanistan).

The xenophobic Philostratus was not alone in his fear and hatred of the Jews.
His contemporary historian Cassius Dio Cocceianus (150–235), also known
as Dion Cassius, thought that the Jews were "distinguished from the rest of
mankind in practically every detail of life." The modern historian Michael Grant
considered Philostratus's statements one indication of how "the incomprehension of the Jewish religion shown by even the most intelligent Greeks remained
almost as complete as it had ever been" (Grant 1978, p. 270, quoting Dion
Cassius; Stern 1980)

Were the Jews, who had been Hellenized after the conquests of Alexander
the Great, really that different from the Greeks and Romans "in every respect"
(Stern 1980)? Whence came this deep incomprehension of the Jews by the most
intelligent Greeks and Romans? Was it really something about the Jews that provoked such deep fear, hostility, and hatred—or was it something unconscious
within the Jew-haters themselves? The German classical historian Emil Schürer
(1844–1910) thought that the Jews were "properly and essentially...*strangers
in the pagan world.* The restoration of the Jewish commonwealth in the
Holy Land was, and continued even to be, a subject of religious hope, which
they held by with unconquerable tenacity" (Schürer 1961, p. 308, italics added).

This statement, however, leaves the irrational fantasies of Jew-haters unexplained.

The xenophobic ancient Greeks called those who could not speak their language *barbaroi* (barbarians) because their incomprehensible speech sounded to them like "bar, bar." Dion Cassius thought that the Jews were "strangers" among the polytheistic Greeks and Romans by virtue of their "extreme reverence for one particular god" and that they were also different from the Greeks and Romans in everything else—their habits, clothes, dietary laws, circumcision rites, Sabbath observance, and other "strange" features of their religion. The fourth-century Roman historian Ammianus Marcellinus, author of the 31-volume *Rerum gestarum libri* (Books of Events), wrote that the Roman emperor and philosopher Caesar Marcus Aurelius Antoninus Augustus (121–180) had disliked the Jews, whom he found strange, unpleasant, disgusting, smelly and rebellious (Grant 1978, p. 265, quoting Dion Cassius; Stern 1980). Yet the same Marcus Aurelius and his son Lucius Aelius Aurelius Commodus (161–192) had also passed pro-Jewish laws admitting Jews as guardians over non-Jews, as well as to other offices. This indicates the Greek and Roman *ambivalence* about the Jews, which may be one of the psychological keys to the understanding of anti-Semitism (Stein 1987, 1994; Blumenberg 1997).

During the second and third centuries of the Christian Era, most of the Jews of the Roman Empire in the east were Hellenized and spoke Greek. Aramaic and Hebrew were second tongues to them. The Jews came from all walks of life and generally accepted Roman rule no less than the Greeks. Their tragic revolt against Rome in Judea in 66–70, forced upon the Jews by their own fanatical zealots, had earned them the hatred of even intellectual Romans. The Roman historian Publius Gaius Cornelius Tacitus (55–117), author of 30 *Histories* and *Annals,* wrote extensively about the Jews in Chapters 1–13 of his *Fifth History.* Tacitus propounded the anti-Jewish myths and fantasies that were common in his time. He attributed to the Jews low birth, despicable origins, national arrogance, hatred of non-Jews, selfishness and, once again, "strangeness." The Roman satirical poet Decimus Junius Juvenalis (55–127), better known as Juvenal, also hatefully derided the Jews (Stern 1980).

If an "arrogant" anti-Gentile attitude is part of traditional Jewish religion (Jeremiah 10:25; Micah 5:14), this in itself cannot explain the virulence of Graeco-Roman Jew-hatred. Were the ancient Jews really as unpleasant and loathsome as Tacitus and Juvenal made them out to be? Was Roman Jew-hatred based on the qualities of the Jews alone? Was there more to Roman Judeophobia than met the eye? Was it in the eye of the beholder? The irrational hatred of the Jews by the larger ethnic groups around them could not have resulted only from their being "strange," "different," or "smelly," or from their worship of one god only. In fact, even their monotheism was not pure and unadulterated. As their ancestors in Canaan during the First Temple period had worshiped the Canaanite goddess Asherah (and Baal) alongside Yahweh, the Jews of the Græco-Roman world worshiped Helios (and Jupiter) along with Yahweh, well into the Byzantine period, as we know from sixth-century Byzantine Jewish synagogue mosaics in Israel and all over the Middle East. Greeks, Romans and Jews lived side by side in the cities of the Eastern Roman empire, such as Alexandria, Cæsarea, and Antioch (Stern 1980). The tensions between the groups, which often erupted into violence, pillage, and massacres of the Jews, resulted from the collective unconscious processes of *externalization* and *projection* and the unconscious need for enemies (Volkan 1988).

CHRISTIANITY AND ANTI-SEMITISM

European Christian anti-Semitism has a long history. Over the 20 centuries of the Christian era, as Europe became increasingly Christian, it also became increasingly anti-Jewish. The Jews were blamed for killing Jesus Christ—the crime of deicide—and European Christian painting and sculpture depicted the "passion of the Christ" as a sequence of sadistic torments by the "evil Jews" that ended in His death on the Cross. The Romans, who had actually tried and sentenced Jesus to death (if, in fact, he ever existed) were depicted as incited by the Jews. The Jews of Europe were repeatedly persecuted, charged with horrible crimes, and murdered (Parkes 1936, 1938a, 1938b; Hay 1950; Loewenstein 1951; Berdyayev 1952; Glock & Stark 1966; Ruether 1974, 1987, 1991; Klein 1978; Thoma 1980; Falwell 1981; Krigier 1985; Aho 1990; Langmuir 1990; Athans 1991a, 1991b; Siker 1991; Perry & Schweitzer 1994; Abulafia 1995, 2002; Nicholls 1993; Freudmann 1994; Olster 1994; Taylor 1995; Bergen 1996; Simon 1996; Zanicky 1997; Grunberger & Dessuant 1997; Salamon 1999; Konig et al. 2000).

The great musical composers of Europe were no less anti-Semitic than other Christians of their time. One of the greatest European composers, Johann Sebastian Bach (1685–1750), wrote dramatic oratorios called "passions" describing the "passion" of Jesus Christ according to the gospels of the evangelists Matthew and John (and also, though less known, Luke and Mark), which are infused with violent anti-Jewish feeling. Bach's sublime *Matthäus-Passion* (St. Matthew Passion) has the Jews screaming for the crucifixion of Jesus Christ, and his *Johannes-Passion* (St. John Passion) portrays the Jews as bloodthirsty and merciless (Marissen 1998). Yet, the Israeli-American Jewish psychoanalyst Ruth Stein had this to say about the *St. Matthew Passion* in her study of suicidal murder:

> I have always been deeply impressed by the intimate, loving discourse a believer holds with God while praying and supplicating. Particularly poignant to me was the theme of a son praying to his God-father. One can palpably hear the sweet plaintive murmur of the Psalmist, "My God, so numerous became those who hunt me, so many are those who stand over me, who say to my soul, you have no

redemption in God, and You, my God, giveth back to me my breath and saveth me with Thy love." And one is not only riveted by the music, but also by the lyrics of Jesus Christ's love songs to God in Bach's *Matthäuspassion, "Dein Mund hat mich gelabet mit Milch und höchster Kost"* (Your mouth has pleasurably fed me with milk and the highest nourishment). Both the Psalms and St. Matthew are profound works of great beauty and inspiration, where joy and pain intertwine. (Stein 2002, p. 398)

Bach, however, was not the only German anti-Semitic composer. One of Hitler's greatest inspirations was the anti-Semitic German opera composer Richard Wagner (1813–1883), whose fantasies about the "evil Jews" were as wild and irrational as his operas based on the ancient Germanic myths, which are rife with the psychopathological themes of incest, parricide, matricide, fratricide, infanticide, and suicide (Katz 1986, Weiner 1995).

Bach's "passions" are not the only dramatic or musical works that have inspired German anti-Semitism. The dramatic passion of Jesus Christ has been enacted since 1634 as a theatrical play on a regular basis by the people of the Bavarian town of Oberammergau, and the Jews have consistently been portrayed in this drama as evil, bloodthirsty, murderous, and diabolical. It is they, not the Romans, who try, condemn, sentence to death, and execute Jesus in the Oberammergau passion play. At the beginning of the twentieth century, an American rabbi who saw the Oberammergau passion play found it "unhistoric in fact, false in interpretation, and cruel in inference" (Krauskopf 1901, p. 19).

Incredibly, the Oberammergauers themselves believe that their passion play is a drama of reconciliation and peace (Friedman 1984, p. 80). The current German-born pope, Benedict XVI, the former Joseph Cardinal Ratzinger (born 1927), has supported this belief. To this day, though slightly attenuated, the Oberammergau passion play draws many anti-Semites and stirs powerful racist and anti-Jewish feelings. In 2004, the anti-Semitic and alcoholic Australian-American actor-director Mel Gibson made *The Passion of the Christ,* an "Aramaic-speaking life of Jesus," without any serious historical foundation, in which the Jews were dehumanized and depicted as bloodthirsty demons (Landres & Berenbaum 2004, Bartchy 2005). During the second Lebanon war in 2006, Gibson was arrested in California for drunken driving and, in his rage, blamed the Jews for all the world's ills. The idea of anti-Semitism as a symptom of emotional illness received yet another confirmation.

Unfortunately, many intelligent scholars see our complex world in black and white. Like infants, they split their world into all-good and all-bad parts. The feminist American Christian theologian Rosemary Radford Ruether blamed the Holocaust on Christianity's centuries-old anti-Jewish theology (Ruether 1974, 1987, 1991). Ruether's colleague Walter Burghardt thought the moralizing Ruether saw things in black and white: "I regret the unrelieved darkness, a failure to balance the picture with [the] grays and whites of Christian-Jewish relations"

(Burghardt 1977, p. 83). The American Jewish historian Yosef Hayim Yerushalmi also criticized Ruether (Yerushalmi 1977). The seemingly pro-Jewish Ruether later adopted the Palestinian Arab propaganda against Israel, blaming Israel for its "wicked" policies in the Palestinian Arab territories (Ruether & Ruether 1989). As a scholar, Ruether "explored" the historical roots of Zionism, the efforts to establish a Jewish state, the development of the Israeli-Palestinian conflict, and the Christian responses to all three, but as an activist fighter for "Palestinian human rights," she edited two virulently anti-Israeli volumes (Ruether & Ellis 1990, Ateek et al. 1992).

MEDIEVAL ANTI-JUDAISM

From ancient times, anti-Semitism has persisted through our present day. European Christianity, and more specifically the Roman Catholic Church and later the Protestant churches, played a major role, portraying the Jews as deicides, the murderers of Jesus Christ, the children of the Devil and of the Evil Sow (Shachar 1974; Carroll 2001; see below). The fantasies of the Christians about the Jews and what they did had little to do with reality. During the Middle Ages, Jews were segregated, persecuted, driven away from their homes, and massacred. They were accused of poisoning the water wells, of murdering Christian children and using their blood in their Passover bread, of desecrating the Scared Host, of blaspheming and cursing Jesus Christ in their scriptures, and of a host of other imaginary crimes.

Anti-Semitism has always increased dramatically in times of economic, political, or social trouble, when the large group's identity and very existence are threatened. During the European plague, or Black Death, of the fourteenth century, the number of deaths was enormous, reaching in various parts of Europe two-thirds or three-fourths of the population in the first pestilence. It has been calculated that one-fourth of the population of Europe, or 25 million persons, died from the plague during the great epidemic. The terrified Christians believed that the Jews had poisoned their wells, and that this was why they were dying by the millions. Massacres of Jews occurred all over Europe in the midst of the plague. The real cause of the plague was a bacillus transmitted to humans by rat fleas, but the European Christians were convinced that it was poisoned water. At that time, water, which came from unhygienic wells, was a persistent health hazard, but it only became a public obsession in Europe when it seemed plausible to accuse the Jews of poisoning the wells. Howard Stein thought that in such cases, the collapse of reliable, safety-giving boundaries and the rise of unbearable anxiety cause the very existence of the Jews to provide "the foundation upon which and against which the new defensive identity can be built" (Stein 1994, p. 45).

To understand the projective roots of the Christian persecution of the Jews, it is illuminating to examine the late Middle Ages. The fantasies of medieval

Christians about the Jews revealed their innermost emotional preoccupations. Medieval Christians viewed the Jew as the Devil incarnate—or as his children (Trachtenberg 1943). The Devil was usually pictured with goat's legs and beard, a frightful, long, sword-like penis—and with a woman's breasts—attended by Jews. In the Christian unconscious mind, this was a "contaminated" externalization of the internalized Bad Father and "Phallic" Mother in the child's fantasy. Medieval German Christians really believed that the Jews rode a *Judensau* (Sow of the Jews), that they drank her milk and ate her excrement, that Jewish women gave birth to piglets, and that Jews murdered Christian children to use their blood for their Passover ritual (Shachar 1974).

The *Judensau* was an unconscious projection of the Bad Mother image that every child carries within himself from early on in his or her life. Those Christian fantasies about the Jews were unconscious *projections* of their own infantile, unacceptable wishes. The strict upbringing of medieval children, especially in matters of toilet training, produced painful feelings in them. The infant wanted to suck his mother's milk and eat her excrement, to carve her up in pieces, and to devour her. He feared both his parents even as he loved them. Most medieval Christians were peasants who lived with pigs and sows all their lives. It was natural for them to unconsciously displace their frightening feelings about their mothers and fathers to the Sow (bad mother) and to the Devil (bad father), which were unconscious externalizations of their internalized early parents. The profound Christian fear and hatred of the Jews derived from the unconscious *projection* upon the minority of "evil" feelings and wishes within the Christian mind itself.

The old English word "parricide" is a euphemistic defense against the horror of *patricide*. The Christians' unbearable feelings and wishes included deicide (an unconscious form of parricide), fratricide, infanticide, blood thirst, incest, and matricide. The Christians were unconsciously telling themselves, " *We* do not wish to kill our children nor our fathers! It is *the Jews* who are the filicides and parricides." The medieval Christians, who believed that they drank their Savior's blood through the transubstantiation of the sacrament of the wine, thought the Jews *actually* drank the blood of Christian children. The "bloodthirsty" Jews were accused of having killed Jesus Christ, the son-god of the Christians, and of murdering Christian children and of drinking their blood, or using it for their Passover ritual. The irony of this Christian ritual-murder libel against the Jews was that the Passover ritual of the Jews had originated in their attempt to avoid child sacrifice in the first place.

Historically, in early medieval Christian Europe, from the fifth to the early seventh century, the Jews spread all over eastern, southern, and western Europe. They settled and became minorities in the new kingdoms that replaced the old Roman Empire. These included the newly established Frankish empires of central and western Europe, the Visigothic kingdom of Spain, and the Byzantine Empire of eastern Europe and the Mediterranean basin. In all of these Christian lands, the hatred and the persecution of the Jews kept surging during early medieval times, especially during times of crisis. Laws were enacted progressively barring the Jews from many occupations. Other laws forced them to convert to Christianity and to attend all Christian feasts. Still others imposed sentences of 100 lashes, shaving of the beard, confiscation of the property, and banishment on Jews found guilty of offending the Church. Many Jews were put to death as well, often for fabricated offenses.

The European Christians forced the Jews to engage in loathsome occupations that they themselves would not exercise—usury, slave trading or prostitution. In 826, when Bishop Agobard of Lugdunum (died 840 and later canonized) railed against "Jewish insolence" in his letter to King Louis the Pious (Agobard 1981, *Opusculum XI,* pp. 191–195) and condemned the Jewish slave trade, he failed to mention that the Jews had been officially commissioned by the Burgundian and Frankish kings, including the king's own father, Emperor Charlemagne, to buy and sell slaves for them. Neither did he say that most of those slaves were pagan Slavs who had been taken prisoner by German Christians, sold to Jews, and resold to Muslims. In fact, the Latin word for Slave and for Slav, *sclavus,* was one and the same. In the ninth century, the slave trade was legal, socially and psychologically acceptable, and deemed economically necessary (Grayzel 1969, p. 312). No one thought it was wrong, because people had little empathy for the feelings of others, especially slaves. The sanctimonious Agobard was enraged about the Jews' refusal to surrender to the church without charge those slaves who converted to Christianity while passing through the Christian lands. It seems that during the Middle Ages, the Jews were fully integrated into their surrounding society (Grayzel 1969, pp. 312–313).

Modern Judeophobia

MARTIN LUTHER, THE GERMAN REFORMATION, AND THE JEWS

The Dutch-born American historian Heiko Augustinus Oberman (1930–2001) believed that European anti-Semitism had escalated in the late Middle Ages and early modern era (Oberman 1984, 1989b). In the fourteenth and fifteenth centuries, the Jews were persecuted and massacred, especially in times of trouble like the Plague or Black Death of 1348–1349. In the sixteenth century came the German Christian reformer Martin Luther (1483–1546), who began his religious career as a Roman Catholic Augustinian monk, only to become history's greatest rebel against the Roman Catholic Church. In 1517, Luther threw off the "yoke" of the "corrupt" Pope Leo X (Giovanni de' Medici, 1475–1521) and started the German Protestant Reformation in Wittenberg, southwest of Berlin (Erikson 1958, Oberman 1982, 1989a). Pope Leo X, who reigned from 1513 to 1521, was one of the most extravagant of the Renaissance popes. He made Rome a center of European culture and raised the papacy to significant political power in Europe. He also depleted the papal treasury, and, by his response to the developing Reformation, he contributed to the dissolution of the Western Christian church. Leo X excommunicated Luther in 1521.

Martin Luther's act of defiance against the Holy Father led to terrible religious wars. In 1523, Luther penned a statement, which for his time was pro-Jewish, entitled *Daß Jesus Christus ein geborner Jude sei* (That Jesus Christ was a born Jew). It said that the "sinful" Jews could be saved by converting them to Christianity. Luther advocated converting the Jews by stages: first convincing them that Jesus was the Messiah, then that he was God. "It is my request and advice that they shall be treated properly and be instructed in Scripture, so that quite a few will join [Christianity]. But now, when we are using violence against then and are telling lies about them, accusing them that they need the blood of Christians in order not to stink and further foolish things so that they might be regarded as dogs—what good can we do with them? Furthermore, how can they be made better, if they are forbidden to do work and to do business among us and to maintain other human connections, as they are driven into usury?" (Luther 1523, reprinted in Luther 1955–1976).

Martin Luther's irascible, violent, and tyrannical father, Hans Luder, the unconscious target of Martin's rebellion against the pope, died in 1530. Martin's mother, Margarethe Luder, died in 1531. A grieving Martin now felt face to face with death. In early 1543, after his efforts to convert the Jews had failed, the 59-year-old Luther was filled with righteous rage. Fifty-nine years in those days was old age—death was approaching. He did not know it, of course, but in fact, he was to die three years later. Luther wrote a venomous anti-Jewish tract entitled *Über die Juden und ihre Lügen* (On the Jews and their Lies), accusing the Jews of all manner of vile behavior, evil deeds and devilish plots:

> Therefore know, my dear Christian, that next to the Devil you have no more bitter, more poisonous, more vehement an enemy than a real Jew...What now shall we Christians do with this unregenerate, damned people? To suffer them in our midst means laying ourselves open to indoctrination by their lies, curses, and blasphemies. It seems we can neither extinguish the inextinguishable wrath of God against them nor convert them. We must indeed with prayer and with the fear of God before our eyes exercise a sharp compassion towards them and seek to save at least some of them from the flames of hell. Avenge ourselves we dare not. (Luther 1543, reprinted in Luther 1955–1976).

An enraged Luther advocated that the Christians set fire to the Jewish synagogues and schools, break and destroy their houses, take away from them all their prayer books and Talmuds, prohibit their rabbis from teaching under pain of death, revoke their protection on the roads, prohibit their usury, force them to earn their living through hard labor, and finally, be expelled from all German lands. The idea of usury itself had old psychological roots. (Nelson and Starr 1944; Nelson 1949). The German Reformation also revived the ritual-murder libel against the Jews, as well as the belief in the Devil, witches, and magic (Hsia 1988). In the twentieth century, Hitler's German Nazis made extensive use of Luther's diatribe against the Jews as part of their racist and murderous anti-Jewish propaganda.

Despite Luther's anti-Judaism (or because of it), the German American psychoanalyst Erik H. Erikson (1902–1994), the son of a Danish Jewish mother and a father who had abandoned him at birth and whom he never knew, greatly admired Luther, with whom he deeply identified: consciously or not, Erikson, who coined the terms "ego identity" and "identity crisis," considered himself a reformer in the "church" of psychoanalysis (Erikson 1958; Friedman 1999, pp. 268–286). Erikson, who as a child had an adoptive Jewish stepfather named Homburger, later changed his last name from Homburger to Erikson, reducing his stepfather's last name to his middle initial—and became a practicing Christian. While Erikson felt that Luther had "facilitated the victory of the Renaissance spirit over Medieval construction" (Friedman 1999, p. 272), his colleague, the Austrian-born American Jewish psychoanalyst Ernest Rappaport (1903–1974), had these incisive comments about Luther—and Erikson:

> This is Martin Luther, the anti-Jew. Luther presents many similarities to Adolf Hitler in his biography as well as in his violent anti-Judaism. This has been recognized especially by Erikson, but makes it to a bizarre paradox if one reads that Erikson also compares Sigmund Freud with Luther and thus with Hitler, which puts psychoanalysis undeservedly into extremely bad company regardless if we call this ego psychology or what else. Luther's megalomania started in infancy and by his obstinate will power, his insistence to triumph over the impossible and a series of lucky circumstances was materialized in his position as a new pope. Of course, throughout his life he found willing sponsors who pushed him out of his frequent standstills and dead-end positions. "He taught that authority must be respected and obeyed except when it must be absolutely disobeyed for prohibiting the Gospel of Luther." Like most anti-Jews he was a disaster to his country. He perverted Humanism into his Reformation which delayed the unification of Germany for four hundred years and also split Germany permanently into two halves, the Protestant East and the Catholic West. The Reformation induced the Counter Reformation which led to the Thirty-Years War from 1618 to 1648 in which the population of Germany was reduced from 20 million to 2 million people. There was, of course, one thing that Germany definitely had no need for, that was a second church and a second pope. (Rappaport 1975, pp. 142–143)

Rappaport's book on anti-Judaism remains a classic in its field, very different from most conventional studies of anti-Semitism, and even from other psychoanalytic studies in its original thinking and in its well-considered application of psychoanalysis to history.

Like the medieval *Judensau* theme, among the most potent political weapons, as well as the most powerful expressions of unconscious fantasy, are the racist caricature and the political cartoon. The German Jewish cultural historian Eduard Fuchs (1870–1940) found that in modern times, anti-Jewish cartoons and caricatures replaced the woodcuts and sculptures of the Middle Ages (Fuchs 1921). The Jews were viciously caricatured as bloodthirsty, money-hungry, sexually depraved, or power-mad. The same themes were repeated in an Iranian Holocaust-cartoon exhibition in 2006 (Gerstenfeld 2007).

During Nazi rule in Germany (1933–1945), Alfred Rosenberg (1893–1946), who had joined the Nazi Party in 1919, became Hitler's racist theorist. Rosenberg had written "scholarly" books on the Jews and their history in various European countries (Rosenberg 1919, 1921), which became increasingly racist and filled with hate as he accused the Jews of a conspiracy with the Freemasons to take over the world (Rosenberg 1941). Interestingly enough, Rosenberg's last name was typically Jewish. He may well have feared being Jewish and, like Hitler and other anti-Semites, unconsciously projected his own unbearable wishes and qualities upon the Jews (Waite 1977, Rosenbaum 1998).

While Rosenberg edited the racist newspaper *Der völkischer Beobachter,* his colleague Julius Streicher (1885–1946) edited *Der Stürmer,* the most viciously anti-Jewish newspaper ever published, where the Jews were portrayed as demons and rats devouring the flesh of Mother Germany, as bloodthirsty animals sucking its blood, or as lecherous old men seducing its daughters. Reading it began the psychological process that prepared the Germans and the Austrians for the fanatical annihilation of the Jews (Nova 1986, Molau 1993). In the 1990s, the Jewish Theological Seminary of America had an exhibition of "a century of British caricature" showing the viciousness of anti-Jewish caricatures. Since the beginning of the Arab-Jewish conflict, and especially after the creation of the state of Israel in 1948, Arab and Muslim anti-Jewish caricatures have replaced and imitated the German Nazis ones (Stav 1999).

MODERN AND CONTEMPORARY ANTI-SEMITISM

As we have seen, as long as the Jews were a minority among a larger non-Jewish majority, in times of social, economic, political, cultural, or military crisis, the fear and hatred of the Jews among the surrounding majority population increased dramatically. One classic example was the German *Kulturkampf* of 1871–1887, the time that gave rise to modern "anti-Semitism." In 1870–1871, the Prussian "iron chancellor" Otto von Bismarck defeated France in a terrible war that led to the annexation of Alsace and Lorraine to a new unified Germany under Prussia's leadership, with its capital at the Prussian capital of Berlin. The new German empire became known as the Second *Reich* with King Wilhelm I of Prussia (1797–1888) as its *Kaiser* (emperor) and Bismarck himself as its *Kanzler* (chancellor).

In 1871, a bitter power struggle broke out between Bismarck's government and the Roman Catholic Church, as the staunchly Lutheran and tyrannical Bismarck sought to subject the Catholic church to German state controls. In 1873, the liberal Prussian politician Rudolf Virchow (1821–1902) gave it the name of *Kulturkampf.* The conflict began in July 1871, when Bismarck, supported by the German liberals, abolished the Roman Catholic bureau in the Ministry of Culture (which governed ecclesiastical affairs) and in November forbade priests from voicing political opinions from the pulpit. In March 1872, all German religious schools became subject to state inspection; in June, all religious teachers were excluded from state schools, and the Jesuit order was dissolved in Germany; and in December, diplomatic relations with the Vatican were severed. In 1873 the May Laws, promulgated by the minister of culture, Paul Ludwig Adalbert Falk (1827–1900), placed strict state controls over religious training and even over ecclesiastical appointments within the church. A German periodical named *Der Kulturkämpfer* fought for Bismarck's ideas (Weiland 2004).

The climax of the *Kulturkampf* came in 1875, when civil marriage was made obligatory throughout Germany. Dioceses that failed to comply with state regulations were cut off from state aid, and noncompliant clergy were exiled. The German Roman Catholics, however, strongly resisted Bismarck's measures and opposed him effectively in the German parliament, where they doubled their representation in the 1874 elections. Bismarck, a pragmatist, decided to retreat. He conceded that many of the measures were excessive and served only to strengthen the resistance of the Centre Party, whose support he needed for his new thrust against the Social Democrats. The advent of a new pope, Leo XIII, in 1878 eased a compromise. By 1887, when Leo XIII declared the conflict over, most of the German anti-Catholic legislation had been repealed or reduced in severity. The struggle had the consequence of assuring state control over education and public records, but it also alienated many Roman Catholics from German national life.

During the bitter *Kulturkampf*, Judeophobia and Jew-hatred became widespread in Central Europe. The fantastic age-old libel of ritual murder, accusing the Jews of killing Christian children and using their blood to bake their unleavened Passover bread, resurfaced. The German Catholic journal *Germania* blamed the Jews for the sufferings of the German people. In the 1870s, an angry 42-year-old anti-Jewish German journalist named Otto Glagau bitterly attacked the Jews for manipulating the Berlin stock exchange, which had collapsed in 1873 and ruined Glagau financially. Later, writing in *Der Kulturkämpfer,* Glagau spread fantastic stories of Christians being raped and murdered by Jews (Glagau 1876, 1877; Weiland 2004)

In 1878, the 43-year-old German Imperial Court preacher Adolph Stöcker founded the German Christian Social Workers Party, a precursor of Hitler's Nazis, which adopted a blatantly anti-Jewish platform and renewed the medieval ritual-murder libel. Glagau and Stöcker paved the way for modern anti-Semitism. Viewing the Jews as a "race" rather than an ethnic or religious group, they "invented" the new Judeophobia and Jew-hatred, which was *racist* rather than religious, claiming a pseudoscientific validity for its projective racist fantasies (Falk 1996, p. 637; Weiland 2004). The euphemism *Antisemitismus* for Jew-hatred, Judeophobia, and anti-Semitism was coined by the converted German Jewish "gutter journalist" Wilhelm Marr, who ascribed Germany's woes to its defeat in an imaginary struggle with Judaism (Marr 1879, 1880b). The new word was quickly adopted by the German press and public and gained currency in Austria and all over Central Europe. Several respectable German leaders exacerbated traditional "anti-Semitism" by pointing to the Jews as a principal cause of the upheavals.

In 1879, German anti-Semitism burst out into the open after the German Imperial Court Preacher Stöcker delivered an anti-Jewish address. The German historian Heinrich Gotthard von Treitschke wrote a long essay in which he claimed that the fundamental differences between German Jews and Christians—all in favor of the latter—could not be reconciled, and that the Jews had "usurped too large a place in our life" (Treitschke 1880) Treitschke assailed the Jews for their refusal to assimilate into German culture and for their "arrogance."

> What we have to demand of our Israelite fellow citizens is simple: they should become Germans. They should feel themselves, modestly and properly, Germans-and this without prejudicing their faith and their ancient, holy memories, which we all hold in reverence. For we do not want to see millennia of Germanic morality followed by an era of German-Jewish hybrid culture. It would be sinful to forget that a great many Jews, baptized and unbaptized, were German men in the best sense...But it is equally undeniable that numerous and mighty circles among our Jews simply lack the goodwill to become thoroughly German. It is painful to speak of these things...
>
> Nevertheless, I believe that many of my Jewish friends will concede, though with deep regret, that I am right when I assert that in recent times a dangerous spirit of arrogance has arisen in Jewish circles. The influence of Jewry on our national life, which created much good in earlier times, nowadays shows itself in many ways harmful...
>
> Our Jewish fellow citizens must resolve to be German—without qualification, as so many of them have already done, to our benefit and their own. The task can never be wholly completed. A cleft has always existed between Occidental and Semitic essences...There will always be Jews who are nothing more than German-speaking Orientals. A specific Jewish civilization will also always flourish, as befits a historically cosmopolitan power. But the conflict will lessen when the Jews, who speak so much of tolerance, really become tolerant and show respect for the faith, customs, and feelings of the German people, who have atoned for the old injustice and bestowed upon them the rights of man and citizen. That this respect is wholly missing in a section of our commercial and literary Jewry is the ultimate basis for the passionate embitterment of today.
>
> It is not a pretty picture-this storming and wrangling, this bubbling and boiling of half-baked ideas in the new Germany. But we are now the most passionate of peoples, even though we often berate ourselves as phlegmatic. New ideas have never established themselves among us without convulsive twitches. May God grant that we emerge from the rashness and ill humor of these restless years with a stricter conception of the state and its duties, a more powerful national feeling. (Treitschke 1880, in rough English translation)

Soon, readers of Treitschke's racist essay and other anti-Semitic tracts were advocating legal measures against Germany's Jewish population. By the mid-1890s, several laws had been proposed in the German *Reichstag* to limit Jewish education, participation in the professions, and other rights of German citizens. Although none of these measures had been enacted, racial prejudice against Judaism in Germany was growing.

In 1881, a time of murderous massacres against the Jews in Russia, an emotionally disturbed former Berlin University professor named Carl Eugen Dühring (1833–1921), who had been fired from his post for his irascible, violent behavior, blamed the Jews for his misfortune, and published a book of hate literature against them (Dühring 1881) The book became popular and went through several expanded editions. The Israeli Jewish historian Samuel Ettinger ascribed the new anti-Semitism to social, political, philosophical, and economic roots: "The power of the Jewish stereotype resulted from the fact that it combined the remnants of the mediaeval image of the 'evil Jew,' the images created under the impact of new ideological currents, and the fear aroused in the European town-dweller by the integration of the Jews into society and their steady advancement" (Ben-Sasson 1976, p. 874). The deeper causes of the fear and hatred of the Jews, however, remained unconscious. Once more, unbearable inner feelings of self-hatred were unconsciously projected upon the scapegoated Jews.

In the nineteenth century in Eastern Europe, especially Russia, fear and hatred of the Jews had been as deep-rooted as in Central Europe, although not as intellectualized. In 1881, following the assassination of Tsar Aleksandr II, bloody pogroms broke out against the Jews all over the Russian Empire. Thousands were massacred, women were raped, and children were murdered. The survivors were deeply traumatized. A mass wave of Russian Jewish emigration, mainly to the United States, began, ending when the Great War broke out in 1914, after about 2.5 million Jews had emigrated to America. Only a handful of Jews went to God-forsaken Ottoman Palestine. In Romania, an army scandal forced the aging anti-Jewish prime minister Ion Brătianu to resign in 1888; he was succeeded by other anti-Semitic leaders. In 1892, a year after Brătianu died, Dimitrie Alexandru Sturdza became the leader of the Romanian Liberal Party. In 1895 Sturdza became prime minister, serving, with some interruptions, until 1909. These were times of economic and political upheaval.

By the late nineteenth century, anti-Semitism had become respectable all over Europe. In 1895 the Romanian Antisemitic Society was created. Its bylaws called for its members to use every means to get the Jews to leave Romania. Many high Romanian officials joined it. In 1899–1900, there were bad harvests in Romania, and famine hit the land. As with the Bubonic Plague in 1348–1349, the Jews were blamed for it. A pogrom at the Moldavian town of Iaşi caused a wave of Jewish refugees to flee Romania for Vienna and London. Some managed to immigrate to Austria, England, and America. Many were turned back and forced to return "home" to Romania, where they faced further persecution.

In 1894, the infamous Dreyfus Affair broke out in France when a French spy in the German embassy in Paris discovered a handwritten *bordereau* (schedule or list), received by Major Max von Schwartzkoppen, the German military attaché in Paris, which listed secret French military documents. The French army, at this time the stronghold of monarchists and Catholics, and permeated by anti-Semitism, attempted to find the traitor. Suspicion fell on Captain Alfred Dreyfus, a wealthy Alsatian Jew, while the frenzied French press raised accusations of Jewish treason. Dreyfus was tried *in camera* by a French court-martial, found guilty, and sentenced to degradation and deportation for life. He was sent to Devil's Island, off the coast of French Guiana, for solitary confinement. Dreyfus protested his innocence, but public opinion generally applauded the conviction, and French public interest in the case lapsed.

The matter flared up again in 1896 and divided the Frenchmen into two irreconcilable factions, the *Dreyfusards* and *anti-Dreyfusards.* Colonel Georges Picquart, chief of the French military intelligence section, discovered evidence indicating that Major Ferdinand Walsin Esterhazy, who was deep in debt, was the real author of the *bordereau.* Picquart, however, was silenced by his superiors. In 1897 Alfred Dreyfus's brother, Mathieu, made the same discovery and increased pressure to reopen the case. Esterhazy was tried in early 1898 by a court-martial and acquitted in a matter of minutes.

Émile Zola, a leading *Dreyfusard,* promptly published an open letter entitled *J'accuse* to the president of the French republic, Félix Faure, in Georges Clemenceau's newspaper *l'Aurore,* accusing the judges of having obeyed illegal orders from the war office in their acquittal of Esterhazy. Zola was tried for libel and sentenced to jail, but he escaped to England. By this time the case had become a major political issue and *cause célèbre* in France and was fully exploited by royalist, militarist, and nationalist elements on the one hand and by republican, socialist, and anticlerical elements on the other.

The violent partisanship over the Dreyfus Affair dominated French life for a decade. Among the *anti-Dreyfusards* were the anti-Semites Édouard Drumont, Paul Déroulède, and Maurice Barrès. The *Dreyfusards,* who steadily gained strength, came to include Georges Clemenceau, in whose paper Zola's letter appeared, Jean Jaurès, René Waldeck-Rousseau, Anatole France, Charles Péguy, and Joseph Reinach. They were, politically, less concerned with the poor Dreyfus himself, who remained in solitary confinement on Devil's Island, than with discrediting the rightist French government.

Later in 1898, it was discovered that much of the evidence against Dreyfus had been fabricated or forged by a Colonel Joseph Henry of the French army intelligence. In August, Colonel Henry was arrested and committed suicide and Major Esterhazy fled to England. At this point, a revision of Dreyfus's sentence had become imperative. The case was referred to an appeals court in

September, and after Waldeck-Rousseau became premier in 1899, the court of appeals ordered a new court-martial.

There was worldwide indignation when the new military court, unable to admit error, found Dreyfus guilty again, though with extenuating circumstances and sentenced him to 10 years in prison. Nonetheless, a pardon was issued by President Émile Loubet, and in 1906 the supreme court of appeals exonerated Dreyfus completely. Captain Alfred Dreyfus was reinstated and promoted to major, and decorated with the Legion of Honor. In 1930, his innocence was reaffirmed by the publication of Schwartzkoppen's papers. The immediate result of the Dreyfus Affair was to unite and bring to power the French political left. Widespread anti-militarism and anti-clericalism also ensued; army influence declined, and in 1905, church and state were formally separated in France.

Modern and Contemporary Anti-Semitism

THE BEGINNING OF THE TWENTIETH CENTURY

The famous opening sentence of *A Tale of Two Cities,* a historical novel about the French Revolution by the great English writer Charles Dickens (1812–1870), reads as follows:

> It was the best of times, it was the worst of times, it was the age of wisdom, it was the age of foolishness, it was the epoch of belief, it was the epoch of incredulity, it was the season of Light, it was the season of Darkness, it was the spring of hope, it was the winter of despair, we had everything before us, we had nothing before us, we were all going direct to Heaven, we were all going direct the other way—in short, the period was so far like the present period, that some of its noisiest authorities insisted on its being received, for good or for evil, in the superlative degree of comparison only. (Dickens 1859, p. 1)

The same, and even more so, can be said of the twentieth century. In 1900, most people expected the new century to be more enlightened, compassionate, and humane than its predecessors. It was the age of the socialist, communist, and Zionist revolutions, the era of anticolonialism and anti-imperialism, the century that saw the oppressed peoples in the "Third World" of Asia, Africa, and Latin America gain their freedom and independence. Yet communism proved an oppressive and bloody tyranny, Zionism has not succeeded in resolving Israel's conflicts with its Arab neighbors, some of the new Third World regimes are more corrupt and more ruthless to their citizens than their colonial predecessors, and the twentieth century saw some of the worst horrors in human history, including two world wars, the Holocaust, and the atomic bombing of the Japanese cities of Hiroshima and Nagasaki.

Indeed, the horrible anti-Jewish pogroms of 1903 in the Russian city of Kishinyov (now the Moldovan capital of Chişinău), in which several dozen Jews were massacred and many more Jewish women were raped and murdered, pale beside the deaths of millions and the horrors of the Great War of 1914–1918, including the genocide of the Armenians by the Ottomans in 1915, the mass destruction of the Second World War in 1939–1945, including the German Nazi extermination of six million European Jews, known as the Holocaust, and the atomic bombing of the Japanese cities of Hiroshima and Nagasaki by the Americans at the end of the war, all of them unprecedented tragedies. These human catastrophes were followed by the interminable Arab-Israeli wars (Falk 2004), the African and Asian genocides in the 1970s, 1980s, and 1990s, and the "ethnic cleansing" in Somalia and in the former Yugoslavia in the 1990s. Only at the end of the twentieth century, after the fall of communism in Eastern Europe in 1989–1991, did a semblance of peace begin to appear in our turbulent world —along with terrorism, fundamentalism, "islamism," "jihadism," and other dangerous fanatical movements (Falwell et al. 1981; Ammerman 1989; Cohen 1990; Strozier 1994; Sidahmed & Ehteshami 1996).

The Tsarist government used anti-Jewish pogroms as counterrevolutionary measures. The Kishinyov riots of 1903 were a particularly poignant example of the horrors that result from anti-Semitism. During the nineteenth century, the Moldavian city of Kishinyov was part of the Imperial Russian province of Bessarabia. Kishinyov had a mixed Russian, Moldavian, Ukrainian, Romanian, and Jewish population and was part of the Jewish Pale of Settlement in southern and western Russia, to which the Russian Jews had been confined since 1791. Jew-hatred was endemic in Moldova. During the late nineteenth and early twentieth centuries, an emotionally unbalanced, Russianized Moldavian anti-Semite named Pavolaki or Pavel Krushevan (1860–1909) edited a government-subsidized newspaper entitled *Novoya Vremya* (New Times). In 1897, Krushevan began publishing anti-Jewish articles in his paper, inflaming Christian feelings against the Jews.

In early 1903, the dead body of a Christian boy was found in a small town in the Ukrainian province of Kherson, across the river from Moldavia. The boy had been killed by his own disturbed family, yet Krushevan told the Moldavian Christians that the Jews had killed him for ritual purposes. Krushevan, together with Bessarabia's Vice-Governor Ustrugov and a high-ranking police officer from St. Petersburg named Levendahl, secretly plotted an anti-Jewish pogrom. They printed posters falsely declaring that Tsar Nikolai II (1868–1918) had issued an imperial decree sanctioning a bloody retribution upon the Jews during the coming Easter holiday, which in Christian minds recalled the killing of Jesus Christ by the Jews. Anti-Jewish feeling ran high.

On Easter Sunday 1903, the murderous Christian rage against the Jews—based on totally false fantasies of what they had done—exploded in a bloody pogrom. On Easter Sunday and Monday, April 19–20, some 50 Jewish men, women, and children were murdered, several hundred wounded, and most Jewish shops and homes were burned. The atrocities committed by the emotionally disturbed rioters were unprecedented. Men were tortured to death, eyes were gouged, nails driven into people's skulls, babies hurled from high windows onto the pavement, bodies mutilated, women raped, their breasts slashed. The unconscious rage that many people harbor against their early mothers was displaced to the hapless Jewesses. Several hundred Jews were severely wounded. Homes and shops were looted, synagogues desecrated. At first, the Russian police did nothing to stop the massacre. Only on Monday evening did Interior Minister Plehve in St. Petersburg order the police to halt the riots. The Russian Hebrew poet Hayim Nahman Bialik (1873–1934) published a fiery lament on the massacre entitled *In the City of Slaughter.*

Under conditions of social and political unrest, Russian anti-Semitism flourished, the pogroms against Jews multiplied, and many Russian Jews left the country. From 1881 to 1914, some two and a half million Russian Jews emigrated to the United States (a figure comparable to the one million Russian immigrants to Israel from the 1970s to the 1990s, most of whom came for economic reasons, and many were not Jews). From 1903 to 1905 alone, some 125,000 Jews fled Russia for America. The Russo-Japanese war of 1904–1905 contributed to Russian anti-Semitism. Even though many Jews served in the Imperial Russian army—some with distinction—the virulently racist and anti-Semitic Russian press accused the Jews of aiding and abetting the Japanese enemy, to whom they were said to be "racially related," notwithstanding budding Japanese anti-Semitism (Kowner 1997b, 1999, 2001, 2006; Goodman & Miyazawa 1995). From 1905 to 1914, only a handful of Russian Jews went to Palestine. The anti-Jewish riots in Russia continued.

On Sunday, January 22, 1905, came the Russian "Bloody Sunday," also known as the "Winter Palace Revolution." A large crowd of Russian workers, led by the fiery young priest Father Georgi Apollonovich Gapon (1870–1906), marched in front of Tsar Nikolai II's Winter Palace in St. Petersburg, protesting his harsh government. Tragically, Russian army pickets fired into the crowd. Hundreds of people were killed and injured. Gapon had organized the Assembly of Russian Factory and Plant Workers of St. Petersburg, which was patronized by the Russian police and by the Russian secret police, *Okhranka.* Father Gapon was saved by his followers. He anathematized the emperor and called upon the workers to rise against the regime, but then escaped abroad, where he had ties with the Russian Socialist-Revolutionary Party. In October 1905, the tsar issued a manifesto that addressed the unrest in Russia and pledged to grant civil liberties to the people, including personal immunity, freedom of religion, freedom of speech, freedom of assembly, freedom of association, a broad participation in the *Duma,* the introduction of universal suffrage, and a decree that no law should come into force without the consent of the *Duma.* Thereupon Gapon returned to Russia and resumed his ties with *Okhranka.*

The two leaders of the Russian Socialist-Revolutionary Party, the Jewish-born Yevno Fishelevich Azef (1869–1918) and the non-Jewish Boris Viktorovich Savinkov (1879–1925), suspected Gapon of being an *agent provocateur.* They wanted him dead. Gapon's double agency had been exposed by the young Russian Jewish socialist engineer Pinkhas Rutenberg (1879–1942), a member of the Russian Socialist-Revolutionary Party who had followed Gapon in the Winter Palace Revolution and fled abroad with him. Gapon and Rutenberg had been welcomed in Europe by the prominent Russian emigrants Georgy Plekhanov, Vladimir Lenin and Pyotr Kropotkin, and by the French socialist leaders Jean Jaurès and Georges Clemenceau. By the end of 1905, however, Rutenberg had returned to Russia, and this time it was Gapon who followed Rutenberg. Gapon soon revealed to Rutenberg his contacts with the *Okhranka* and tried to recruit him as well, arguing that double loyalty helped the workers' cause. Rutenberg reported this "treacherous provocation" to his leaders, Azef and Savinkov. Azef demanded that Gapon be put to death.

On March 26, 1906, Gapon arrived to meet Rutenberg in a rented Finnish cottage outside St. Petersburg. A month later, he was found there hanged. Rutenberg later asserted that Gapon had been condemned to death by a Socialist-Revolutionary Party comrades' court. By another version of this tragic story, three Socialist-Revolutionary Party combatants overheard Gapon's and Rutenberg's conversation from an adjoining room. After Gapon had repeated his treacherous collaboration proposal, Rutenberg called the comrades into the room and left. When he returned, Gapon was dead by hanging. Azef and Savinkov, however, refused to take responsibility for Gapon's execution, claiming that it had been undertaken by Rutenberg on his own and that the cause was personal. Ironically, Azef himself was a double agent. He was exposed by the Russian revolutionary Vladimir Lvovich Burtsev (1862–1942) in late 1908 or early 1909. A Socialist-Revolutionary Court of Honor held in Paris to try Azef let him go home after he promised to provide convincing proof of his innocence the following day, but the guilty Azef fled to Germany. His wife, Liuba Mankin, who had been unaware of his double-dealing, divorced him and immigrated to the United States. Rutenberg immigrated to Palestine and founded its electrical power system.

The violent unrest in Russia continued. Poland, which in earlier times had been a haven for central and western European Jews, and which was now part of Russia, had become deeply anti-Semitic in the nineteenth century (Porter 2000). In October 1905, there was a nationwide railroad strike in Russia and the first Council of Workers' Deputies was formed in St. Petersburg. Foreign Minister Sergei Yulievich Witte persuaded Tsar Nikolai II to grant his people limited rights, and the tsar grudgingly issued the famed *October Manifesto.* Witte was made prime minister. Paranoid, extremist, and fanatical Russian right-wing groups such as the Black Hundreds agitated against the Jews. Bloody anti-Jewish riots broke out all over the Jewish Pale of Settlement. Within 12 days in October 1905, no less than 810 Jews were murdered in riots all over western and southern Russia, including the Ukraine, Belarus, the Crimea, Poland, and Lithuania. In Odessa alone, some 300 Jews were massacred over a four-day period. The murderous pogroms intensified the wave of Russian Jewish emigration to America, which had begun in 1881. Some 40,000 mostly Russian Jews emigrated to Palestine from 1905 to 1914, but the very harsh living conditions there caused a great turnover among them. Many of the new Palestinian Jews left for America or returned to Russia.

The Great War of 1914–1918, later known as the First World War or World War I, and the Russian Revolution which took place at that time, killed many millions of people in Europe and destroyed its old political and social order (Winter 1995, 2006). Many Jews in Eastern Europe were uprooted and displaced when their habitats changed hands. The Austrian Galician Jews became Polish, or migrated to a much-diminished Austria, mainly to Vienna. Russian anti-Semitism grew as the First World War broke out. On June 28, 1914 the 51-year-old Austrian archduke Franz Ferdinand was assassinated by a young Serbian nationalist student named Gavrilo Princip at Sarajevo, Bosnia, then an Austrian territory. In August Austria declared war on Serbia, and the Great War broke out. Russia allied itself with her Slavic "sister" Serbia, Germany with her Germanic "sister" Austria. The Russian authorities suspected the Jews of the Pale of Settlement that they had created in the Russian west and south of sympathizing, if not collaborating, with the German and Austrian enemies. They began expelling Jews from Galicia (now in Poland and the Ukraine) and from Bukovina (now in Romania and the Ukraine). Jewish hostages were taken to ensure the allegiance of the Russian Jewish community. All this was but a little prelude to the Holocaust of 1941–1945, committed by the Germans. This terrible tragedy is denied by "revisionist" historians, and we shall analyze this detail in another chapter.

A COLLECTIVE PSYCHOSIS?

One of the hallmarks of medieval anti-Judaism had been the "blood-libel myth" in which Christians imagined and accused Jews of murdering Christian children and using their blood for their religious rites, such as baking their Passover bread (Hsia 1988, 1992). The legend was traced back to the murder of William of Norwich in 1144, one of the first reported cases of ritualized murder attributed to Jews, through nineteenth-century Egyptian reports, Spanish examples, Catholic periodicals, modern English instances, and twentieth-century American cases. The essays deal not only with historical cases and surveys of blood libel in different locales, but also with literary renditions of the legend, including the ballad "Sir Hugh, or, the Jew's Daughter" and Chaucer's "The Prioress's Tale." In 1475, the Jews of the Tyrolean town of Trent were accused of having killed a two-year-old boy named Simonino (Little Simon) for this purpose. The infamous blood-libel legend was partly responsible for the expulsion of Jews from Spain in 1492, the basis of persecutions and actual courtroom trials throughout Europe, and exploited in Nazi propaganda (Dundes 1991).

In 1911, during the internal Russian struggle between the Tsarist and Socialist forces, occurred the infamous Beilis Affair, which may be called a "government blood libel" and which raises the question of whether it was a "collective psychosis." In February 1911, the liberal and socialist factions in the Third Russian *Duma* introduced a proposal to abolish the Jewish Pale of Settlement, where the Jews had been restricted to live since 1791, and to let them live anywhere in the Russian empire. The anti-Semitic right-wing and monarchist organizations such as the Union of the Russian People and the Congress of the United Nobility embarked on a campaign to harshen anti-Jewish policies instead of lessening them. For this anti-Jewish campaign, both organizations received secret state subsidies from the Tsarist government that had lost practically all support in the *Duma*.

In March 1911, the dead body of a young Russian Christian boy, Andrei Yushchinsky, was found in the Ukrainian capital of Kiev, then part of Russia. The Tsarist authorities seized the opportunity to revive the age-old ritual blood-libel accusation against the Jews. An innocent young Jewish inhabitant of Kiev, Menahem Mendel Beilis (1874–1934), the superintendent of a brick kiln, was arrested and charged with the murder, although by that time the authorities already knew who the true perpetrators were.

For more than two years, Beilis remained in prison while most of the Russian people believed that he was guilty. The Tsarist secret police, the *Okhranka,* tried to build a case against him by falsifying papers and pressurizing "witnesses" to perjure themselves. Then the Beilis case turned around and backfired on its perpetrators. The lamplighter, on whose testimony the indictment of Beilis rested, confessed that he had been confused by the secret police. In October 1913, the jury unanimously acquitted Beilis. His case drew international attention to the plight of the Jews in Russia and united the conservative Russian "Octobrists" with the radical Bolsheviks in their opposition to the Tsarist government.

After his release by the Russian police, Menahem Mendel Beilis and his family fled Russia for Palestine, then a poor province of the Ottoman Empire. In 1920, they left Palestine for the United States, where Beilis died in 1934. The Tsarist government of Russia would not accept its defeat. On the eve of the Bolshevik Revolution, Gheorghi Zamyslovsky, a Russian *Duma* member and one of the prosecutors in the Beilis case, repeated the false accusation against Beilis in an inflammatory book (Zamyslovsky 1917). Zamyslovsky had been paid the equivalent of several million U.S. dollars today by Tsar Nikolai himself to write the book and "expose the Hasidic occult, and its participation in the ritual murder of Yushchinsky." The book was published with the secret funds of the Interior Ministry that had been approved by the Tsar. Zamyslovsky himself was executed after the Bolshevik Revolution. Anti-Semites, of course, claimed that it was all a Jewish plot (Samuel 1966, Lindemann 1991). The Beilis trial was followed closely worldwide, and the anti-Semitic policies of the Russian empire were severely criticized by the international community.

The Beilis case has been compared with the Dreyfus Affair in France and with the Leo Frank case in the United States. In the latter, the American Jew Leo Frank (1884–1915), the manager of a pencil factory in Atlanta, Georgia, was falsely accused of raping and murdering a 12-year-old girl named Mary Phagan. The case is widely regarded as a miscarriage of justice. The trial was sensationalized by the American press, which promoted fantastic stories of orgies and rape at the factory. The anti-Semitic and racist Georgia politician and publisher Thomas Edward Watson (1856–1922) used the Frank case to build support for the renewal of the Ku Klux Klan, which had been destroyed by the U.S. government in the early 1870s. Shortly after Leo Frank's conviction, new evidence emerged that cast doubt on his guilt. The governor of Georgia commuted his death sentence to life imprisonment, but Frank was kidnaped from his prison by a mob of citizens calling itself "the Knights of Mary Phagan" and lynched. The lynch mob included the son of a senator, a former governor, lawyers, and a prosecutor. Crowds descended on the site of the lynching, removing pieces of the tree and rope as souvenirs, and for decades afterwards, shops in Atlanta sold pieces of rope to commemorate it (Lindemann 1991).

Was the Beilis Affair a "collective psychosis," in that a whole people seemingly believed in a patent delusion? Not necessarily. Most experts on large-group psychology, such as the Cypriot-Turkish-born American psychoanalyst Vamık Volkan, do not use the term "collective psychosis" (Volkan 1997, 2004). The "delusion," moreover, may have been a deception of the people by its own government. German Nazism has been called a "collective psychosis" by the German psychoanalyst Getrud Hardtmann (Hardtmann 1992, 1995, 2001). Nonetheless, most psychoanalysts prefer to reserve the term "psychosis" to describe individual conditions rather than collective ones.

JEWISH SELF-HATRED

The psychological phenomenon of self-hatred, both on the individual and on the collective level, is a puzzling one (Gilman 1986). Why should anyone hate himself or herself? Is it not natural for every person to love himself or herself? Or for large groups to glorify themselves? Is it not natural to do what is best for oneself? Unfortunately, an infant or child who is unwanted, unloved, rejected, attacked, punished, abused, rebuked, scolded, or made to feel that it is bad, tends to develop a bad sense of itself and to hate itself. This self-hatred then becomes part of oneself and may lead to sadism and masochism, self-destructive acts, even suicide. On the collective level, a minority group in a given society that is repeatedly told that it is bad, that is rejected and persecuted, may also develop a collective group self that is bad and negative.

Individual and collective Jewish self-hatred has occurred ever since the ancient Jews were besieged by the Assyrians, Babylonians, and Romans, defeated, massacred, exiled from their land, dispersed and persecuted. Right-wing American and Israeli Jews denounce left-wing Jews—including the prominent American Jewish journalist Thomas Friedman, the publishers and editors of the *New York Times,* and all Jewish liberals and leftists who disparage or condemn Israel—as anti-Semitic. Some of these Jews, they say, like Noam Chomsky, actively work to undermine Israel, and may qualify as anti-Semites. Many non-Jews, as well as Jews, do not understand Jewish self-hatred. Right-wing Jews and Israelis believe that Jewish self-hatred also occurs in the leadership of the successive Israeli governments and of a large portion of Israeli academic and media leftists.

Writing in 1941, when Hitler's German Nazis began their "final solution of the Jewish problem," the German-American Jewish social psychologist Kurt Lewin (1890–1947), who had fled Germany for the United States, thought that there was a tendency for some members of underprivileged groups in general, and Jews in particular, to display a degree of hatred towards their own group. He proposed that in any group, there are forces drawing people into the group, and forces drawing them away. Given a situation in which the need for status is an important determinant of behavior, the "member of an underprivileged group is more hampered by his group belongingness" (Lewin 1948, p. 192). As a result, some members of the underprivileged group desire to leave the group, but since the majority prevents them from leaving, they are left on the periphery of the group. According to Lewin, the desire to leave the group is exacerbated by a tendency among members of minority groups to accept the values of the majority, and therefore to see "things Jewish with the eyes of the unfriendly majority" (ibid., p. 198). Lewin believed that Jewish self-hatred was "both a group phenomenon and an individual phenomenon...the self-hatred of a Jew may be directed against the Jews, against his own family, or against himself. It may be directed against Jewish institutions, Jewish mannerisms, Jewish language, or Jewish ideals...the most dangerous forms, are a kind of indirect undercover self-hatred...In most cases, expressions of hatred of the Jew against his fellow Jew or against himself as a Jew is more subtle."

While a minority group that is chronically denigrated, persecuted, and humiliated by the majority tends to have serious problems with its self-image, other reactions to "inferiorization" are possible. The variety of Jewish reactions to anti-Semitic persecution have included fear, arrogance, rage, hatred (of the persecutors), nationalism, and violent resistance, as well as self-hatred (Loewenstein 1951; Schorsch 1972; Tal 1975; Adam 1978; Mack 1983; Roskies 1984; Marcus and Rosenberg 1989; Stein 1993; Abulafia 1995, 2002; Finlay 2004; Levin 2005). The American Jewish scholar Sander Gilman, without question one of the best scholars of both psychoanalysis and anti-Semitism, studied the history and psychology of Jewish self-hatred (Gilman 1986). The American cultural-history scholar Allan Janik, who teaches at the Austrian university of Vienna, disputed Gilman's "Jewish Self-Hatred Hypothesis" (Janik 1987).

While Gilman's analysis was scholarly, the American Jewish journalist Janice Booker wrote a popular book arguing that anti-Semitism was not confined to non-Jews; that Jews, too, could be anti-Semitic; and that when they were, what surfaced was a latent insecurity that arose from humiliation and oppression by non-Jews (Booker 1991). Booker accused American Jewish celebrities of expressing Jewish self-hatred: Joan Rivers exuded Jewish self-contempt, Phil Donahue reinforced anti-Jewish stereotypes, and Woody Allen exploited roles that fed negative images of Jewish men. She condemned Hannah Arendt's "obtuseness" in the face of Nazi evil, I. F. Stone's hatred of Israel, Lillian Hellman's negative images of Jews, and feminists who single out Judaism for its reputed inherent sexism. Jewish self-hatred is still being debated by scholars.

ZIONISM AND ANTI-SEMITISM

Most scholars agree that anti-Semitism gave rise to modern Zionism. Despite its Marxist Jewish detractors (Rubin 1987), Zionism, which became a political movement in 1897, was indeed a historical Jewish response to anti-Semitism. At least since 1860, the French-based *Alliance Israélite Universelle* had been fighting anti-Semitism, Jew-hatred, and Judeophobia, which in 1879 became known as "anti-Semitism." The German-Jewish philosopher Moses Hess (1812–1875) anticipated political Zionism many years before it came into being (Hess 1862, 1918). Hess was far in advance of his time, and not until well after his death did the originality of his ideas receive recognition. In 1891, following the pogroms in Russia, the German Jews set up a Central Committee for Russian Jewry in Berlin. In 1897, a 37-year-old Austrian Hungarian Jewish journalist named Theodor Herzl (1860–1904) convened the first Zionist Congress in Basel, Switzerland (Falk 1993). European Jewish politics split into Zionists, non-Zionists, and anti-Zionists. The notorious Dreyfus Affair (1894–1906), in which a French Jewish military officer was falsely accused of betraying French military secrets to "the enemy," split the French population into the pro-Jewish *Dreyfusards* and the anti-Semitic *anti-Dreyfusards,* who cried "Death to the Jews" (Johnson 1966; Marrus 1980; Wilson 1982; Lindemann 1991; Cahm 1994, 1996; Burns 1998).

At the outset of the twentieth century, organized European Jewry took steps to defend itself and to help Jews who had been victims of anti-Semitic persecution. In 1901, the German Jews created the *Hilfsverein der deutschen Juden* (German Jews' Aid Society) to help Jewish immigrants in both America and Palestine. It was led by Paul Nathan, James Simon, Ephraim Cohen, and Bernard Kahn, who in 1906 convened an international meeting of Jewish leaders in Brussels. In the United States, the formerly anti-Zionist American Jewish Committee (now a pro-Zionist organization) was created in 1906. In 1909, the Hebrew Immigrant Aid Society (HIAS) was formed in the United States, and in 1912, Paul Nathan succeeded in creating the international *Union des Associations Israélites.*

The name *Zion*—originally the name of one of the hills of Jerusalem—had attracted Jews throughout the ages. It had a dreamlike quality: "When Yahweh restored the fortunes of Zion, we were like dreamers" (Psalms 126:1). Longings for "Zion" had been part of the Jewish liturgy since the destruction of the First Temple in 586 BCE (Psalms 137:1), yet political Zionism came only 25 centuries later. The idea seemed sound: get the persecuted Jews out of their unhealthy "diaspora" and "exile" in anti-Semitic Christian Europe and back into their ancient homeland, where they can live a normal, healthy, national Jewish life. In actual practice, things were very different. Zionism led to the creation of modern Israel, which is beset by no less serious existential problems than were the Jews of nineteenth-century Europe (Falk 2004).

In every public matter, powerful unconscious private and personal emotions underlie political actions. Most of Theodor Herzl's Zionist writings are highly idealized views of Palestine as a great good mother (Falk 1993). His letters and diaries contain some scathing comments about Jews, bordering on anti-Semitism. When Herzl visited Palestine in 1898—to see Emperor Wilhelm II of Germany, who had come to visit the Ottoman sultan—he became ill, was disgusted with the filth of Jerusalem, and left for Vienna as fast as he could. Before Herzl converted himself to the Zionist idea in 1895, he had a young man's fantasies of solving the Jewish Question by duelling with prominent Austrian anti-Semites and leading the Jews into mass conversion to Catholicism. *Herzl's quest for the Jewish State was a desperate unconscious attempt to resolve his lifelong personal conflict of fusion vs. separation from his engulfing mother.* Christian Europe unconsciously stood for his Bad Mother, and Palestine for his idealized Good Mother. The Jewish people was unconsciously himself.

Herzl, the founder of political Zionism, imagined Palestine as an orderly, beautiful, cultured, lush, green land like Austria or Switzerland, with German as the language of the land and with a Central European way of life. When Herzl visited Jerusalem in 1898 to see Wilhelm II, he was so appalled by the sight and smell of Jerusalem that he wanted to tear down the entire city and replace it with a new one like Vienna. From the psychoanalytic viewpoint, such *psychogeograph-ical fantasies* betray the infantile *denial* and *idealization* that propelled them: as the baby and child idealizes its mother and denies her painful qualities, so Theo-dor Herzl did with Palestine. Earlier, Herzl had had fantasies of solving the Jew-ish Question in Austria by fighting duels with leading anti-Semitic leaders like Lueger and Schönerer or by leading the Jews into mass conversion to Christian-ity in Vienna's Saint Stephen's Cathedral. Now, like an infant that wants to repair its bad mother, he wanted to replace "bad mother Jerusalem" with "good mother Vienna." The popular notion that Herzl became a Zionist due to the anti-Semitic Dreyfus Affair in France, where he was a correspondent for Vienna's *Neue Freie Presse,* is another myth. Herzl's psychology was very complex and he had been in a deep depression due to his self-perceived failure as a dramatist before hitting on "the Zionist solution to anti-Semitism." (Stewart 1974; Elon 1975; Pawel 1989; Falk 1993).

In the twentieth century, Hitler's persecution of the Jews and Herzl's politi-cal Zionism sparked several waves of Jewish immigration, mainly from Europe to Palestine, which finally led to the creation of the "Jewish and democratic" state of Israel in 1948, after half a century of bloody conflict with the Palestin-ian Arabs. The terms "Jewish" and "democratic" are in conflict, however, for Israel has a large Arab minority (about 20 percent of its population) that does not have the same rights as the Israeli Jews. The Israeli "scroll of independ-ence" of 1948 promised equal rights to all its residents, but Arabs do not have the right of automatic citizenship under the Israeli Law of Return that Jews have.

Israel itself has been in conflict with the Palestinian Arabs, with its neighbor-ing Arab countries, and with the entire Arab and Muslim world ever since its creation, and that conflict has yet to be resolved, because of profound psycho-logical obstacles on both sides (Falk 2004). Many anti-Semites, however, have used "imperialist and colonialist Zionism" as an "explanation" or pretext for their anti-Semitism. In the former Soviet Union, especially after the paranoid Stalin succeeded Lenin as leader in 1924, nationalist movements were feared and persecuted, including Zionism, which was treated as anti-Soviet Jewish nationalism (Rappaport 1975, pp. 258–281). Soviet anti-Zionism borrowed slogans and fantasies from traditional Russian anti-Semitism, including the infa-mous "Protocols of the Elders of Zion" (Kostyrchenko 1995). A group of American Marxists and communists—mostly Jews—has published a "scholarly" collection of articles to "prove" that Zionism was the chief cause of anti-Semitism, rather than the reverse (Rubin 1987). Psychological "scholarship" can be mobilized in the service of anti-Semitism, while people who hate Jews are often those who also hate psychoanalysis (Billig 1979, Dvořak 1987). Currently, Russian anti-Semitism is growing more vociferous, violent, and public (Fenyvesi 2006).

FIGHTING ANTI-SEMITISM: ZIONISTS AND ANTI-ZIONISTS

The Russian-Jewish leader Vladimir Zhabotinsky (1880–1940), who later in Palestine hebraized his first name to Ze'ev, had many contradictory traits in his character. As a young man in 1906, he helped convene the anti-Zionist Helsingfors Conference (Helsingfors is the Swedish and German name for the Finnish capital of Helsinki), which called upon the Jews of Europe to engage in *Gegenwartsarbeit* (present work), and to join in the liberation struggle of the ethnic minorities in Russia. It called upon Russia to ensure the rights of these groups, and to grant the Jews full equality of rights. The Zionist leaders opposed these resolutions because they did not call upon the Jews to settle in Palestine. "Why should Jabotinsky have bothered to insist on full equality for the Jews [in Russia]," the Jewish Zionist historian Walter Laqueur wondered, "if he was convinced, with Pinkser and Herzl, that antisemitism was endemic in Europe and that east European Jewry was doomed?" (Laqueur 1972, p. 340).

After immigrating to Palestine, Zhabotinsky had fantasies of Jewish heroics. In the spring of 1920, the Palestinian Arabs, incited by Islamic leaders, rioted against the Jews. Many Jews were killed and injured. Zhabotinsky helped organize the new illegal Jewish defense force known as the *Haganah*. He and his colleagues were arrested by the British, court-martialed, and sentenced to 15 years at hard labor. A great outcry arose in the Palestinian Jewish community as well as among world Jewry. After a few months of intensive lobbying in London, Zhabotinsky was pardoned and released. In 1921, he was elected to the National Council of Palestinian Jewry, which the "Hebrews of the Land of Israel"—as the Palestinian Jews called themselves and imagined themselves to be—who then numbered less than 100,000—called *Assephath HaNivharim* (The Assembly of the Elected). From 1920 to 1928, this body had little or no authority, bowing to the Zionist Executive (Laqueur 1972, p. 447). Zhabotinsky was elected to the Political Department of the Zionist Executive and to the Executive board itself. He constantly disagreed with Chairman Chaim Weizmann (1874–1952) over the latter's pro-British policy. Weizmann was a cautious Zionist politician and came into conflict with extremists both left and right.

Political Zionism had been pursuing the creation of a Jewish homeland in Palestine, which later became the Jewish state of Israel—although it still had a sizable Arab minority. From the Zionist viewpoint, the Russian and Ukrainian riots were a disaster, but also a blessing in disguise. Zionism fought anti-Semitism, but the riots served its purpose by making the Jews wish to leave for Palestine (although many more chose to leave for the United States). In 1921, Zhabotinsky, who had been in Palestine during its takeover by the British, met in Prague, on his way to the 12th World Zionist Congress in Carlsbad, with Maxim Slavinsky, the ambassador of the Ukrainian government in exile led by Symon Vassilyevich Petlyura (1879–1926), proposing the creation of a Jewish police force within the Ukrainian state to protect Ukrainian Jews against pogroms. Zhabotinsky's meeting with the representative of Petlyura, who had murdered thousands of Jews, provoked an outcry in the Jewish and Zionist world (Laqueur 1972, p. 344).

In 1923, Zhabotinsky resigned from the Zionist Executive in protest against Weizmann's conciliatory policies, and, in 1925, he created Zionist Revisionism, a right-wing offshoot of Zionism that after 1948 spawned *Herut, Gahal,* and *Likkud,* the Israeli Jewish right-wing nationalist parties (Shavit 1988). One should note here that the word "revisionist" is an emotionally loaded one in the context of anti-Semitism, as it is now also used to disguise the anti-Semitic denial of the Holocaust. But in 1925, the word was used in a very different context—a nationalist-Jewish revolt against mainstream socialist and religious Zionism. In 1926, Petlyura was assassinated in Paris by a young Ukranian Jewish watchmaker named Schalom Schwarzbart, whose family had been massacred by Petlyura's men, and who was acquitted by a French jury in 1927.

While Zhabotinsky fought both the British and his Zionist rivals, the dead hero Joseph Trumpeldor, who had lost an arm in the Russo-Japanese War (1904–1905) and later migrated to Palestine, where he was killed in Jewish-Arab battle at the Galilean stronghold of Tel-Hai, became the hero of both left-wing and right-wing Zionists. In 1923, Zhabotinsky's ultranationalist Zionists set up a youth movement in Riga, Latvia, which they called *Bethar,* a Hebrew acronym for *Brith Joseph Trumpeldor.* Actually, Bethar had also been the name of an ancient Jewish stronghold during the disastrous Bar Kochba revolt against the Romans of 132–135 and is now again the name of a settlement outside Jerusalem. Bar Kochba, who had brought the worst military disaster upon the Jews in all their history—half a million Jews were massacred by Roman troops—was glorified by the Zionists as a hero.

The Jewish "Legion of Labor," founded in 1920 at a memorial meeting for Joseph Trumpeldor, and which built many roads, bridges, and houses in various parts of Palestine, broke up in 1923 and again in 1926 after fierce internal power struggles between its communist and socialist factions. The communist faction returned to the Soviet Union, set up a commune, and were ultimately destroyed in Stalin's paranoid "purges," a euphemism for mass murder. The socialist faction remained in Palestine, working on road and building construction projects. Trumpeldor remains in the Israeli Heroes' Hall of Fame. Every Israeli Jewish schoolchild learns to sing "In the Galilee, at Tel Hai, a hero fell." Every year, on the 11th day of Adar in the Hebrew calendar, a great pilgrimage is made to his monument in the shape of a roaring lion at Tel Hai.

In 1925, Zhabotinsky seceded from the Zionist Organization and created the Revisionist Zionist Alliance, known by its Hebrew acronym of *Hatsohar.* Henceforth, the Revisionists were the chief opposition to the Labor Zionists in Palestinian Jewish and world Zionist politics. At the 17th World Zionist Congress in Basel in 1931, Zhabotinsky's Revisionists moved to define Zionism's ultimate aims as the political possession of the whole of "Eretz Israel"—the Zionist name for Ottoman Palestine—in line with a pamphlet written in 1908 by the Dutch Zionist leader Jacobus Kann (Kann 1910) This motion was voted down by the assembly, at which the enraged Revisionist Zionists tore up their delegate cards and stormed out of the hall. In 1935, they seceded completely from the World Zionist Organization and set up the rival New Zionist Organization.

ARAB AND MUSLIM ANTI-SEMITISM

The prophet Muhammad fought the Arabian Jews, and the Kor'an has anti-Jewish verses. One Jewess is supposed to have tried to poison the Prophet to death. The Arabs and Muslims have had an ambivalent relationship with Jews. While some Muslims saved Jews from German Nazi persecution during World War II (Satloff 2006), others collaborated with the perpetrators of the Holocaust. The case of *Haj* Mohammad Amin al-Husayni (1895–1974), the Grand Mufti of Jerusalem who befriended Adolf Hitler and closely collaborated with Nazi Germany, is notorious. From 1941, the Grand Mufti established close contacts with Bosnian and Albanian Muslim leaders and spent the remainder of the war helping the formation of Muslim *Waffen SS* units in the Balkans and the formation of training centers for Muslim imams and mullahs who would accompany the Muslim *SS* and *Wehrmacht* units. Until the end of the World War II in 1945, al-Husayni worked for Nazi Germany as a propagandist for the Arabs and a recruiter of Muslim volunteers for the German armed forces.

Modern Islamic culture contains a strong element of anti-Semitism, which is quite widespread in the Muslim world. In some Arab countries, such as Syria and Egypt, television series portray the Jews as bloodthirsty child murderers, citing the *Protocol of the Elders of Zion,* which is printed in Arabic, as truthful works about reality rather than the sick fantasies that they really are (Heggy 1991, Mannes 2002, Radai 2007). The Muslim Council of Britain, as well as the Muslim Brotherhood in the United Kingdom of Great Britain and Northern Ireland, deny the Holocaust and actively seek to undermine the Jews and Israel, insisting that the Palestinian Arabs are the victims of "genocide" by Israel and that the Israelis are the new "Nazis." It is as if the Muslims and the Jews are living in two different worlds. Under British Muslim influence, during the first decade of the twenty-first century, two British university-teacher unions adopted resolutions boycotting their Israeli colleagues.

Two Jewish psychoanalysts, one British, the other American-Israeli, have pointed out the powerful role of unconscious *splitting, denial,* and *projection* in the fundamentalist Islamic outbursts against the Jews and Israel: "Whether unconsciously determined or not, in order to gain or maintain political power, the belief systems of the *jihadists* seem to exemplify these mechanisms. Thus, on one hand, they widely disseminate the *Protocols of the Elders of Zion* (a Russian anti-Semitic fabrication of 1905 'proving' that the Jews conspire to rule the world), in order to 'prove' a Jewish conspiracy to take-over the world. And, on the other hand, Sheik Mudaires [a fiery imam in Gaza], among others, publicly asserts: '(Moslems) have ruled the world before, and, by Allah, the day will come when we will rule...America, Britain, and the entire world.' In considering these words, one must not underestimate the power of projective processes" (Berke & Schneider 2006).

Among the psychoanalytic writers on Islamic anti-Semitism is the feminist American Jewish scholars Phyllis Chesler (Chesler 2003). Unfortunately, she carries her views of woman-abuse in Arab and Muslim society to extreme lengths, and reduces the complex causes of Muslim anti-Semitism to simplistic explanations. One of the basic problems in academic discourse is how to keep one's personal and political feelings from affecting one's scholarship. Chesler began her career as a political leftist, but she turned to the political right in response to what she came to see as the anti-Israeli and anti-Semitic viewpoints increasingly prevalent on the far left of political discourse in the United States, in Europe, and all over the academic world. As an American, a Jew, a woman, and a feminist, she has many sources of bias to overcome. She often confuses "Muslim" with "Islamic fundamentalist," thus aggravating the black-and-white "us and them" mentality, as if the entire Muslim world were of one piece. Black-and-white thinking is dangerous and unrealistic (Mack 2002, p. 174), and, as we have seen, the unconscious roots of Islamic antisemitism are far more complex that Chesler has tried to portray them (Falk 2004, pp. 159–173).

Holocaust denial is not restricted to Germany, Europe or the United States. It is also widespread in the Arab and Muslim world. Its center is in Iran, a non-Arab country whose government seems to hate Israel and seek its destruction more than any Arab country. Here is a report by the German scholar Matthias Küntzel on the Iranian exhibits at the Frankfurt Book Fair of 2005:

> Last week at the Frankfurt Book Fair, I happened to find myself in the International Publishers section and was simply astonished. At the stand of the Iranian publishers, in plain view, was the text that influenced Hitler's Holocaust fantasies like no other: "The Protocols of the Learned Elders of Zion," published in English by the Islamic Propagation Organization of the Islamic Republic of Iran. The first page of the tract makes clear that Israel is the target of this new edition. It shows a snake made of triangles, enclosing an area labeled "Greater Israel" that includes large areas of Egypt, Syria, Lebanon, Jordan, Iraq, parts of Turkey and northern Saudi Arabia. Each triangle, according to the annotation, symbolizes the "Freemason's Eye," supposedly a "symbol of Jewry." (Küntzel 2005)

Dr. Küntzel was shocked by what he saw, which was both virulently anti-Semitic and a violation of German law. But this was not all:

A few steps farther on, the second most important classic of modern anti-Semitism was on display: Henry Ford's "The International Jew," in a 200-page abbreviated version, published by the Iranian "Department of Translation and Publication, Islamic Culture and Relations Organization." It was interesting to read the numerous footnotes that the Iranian publisher had added. For example, Salman Rushdie's "Satanic Verses" is presented as the latest example of the viciousness of Jewish slanders. (Küntzel 2005)

The Iranian booksellers had planned their exhibit well. There was yet a third anti-Semitic book that glaringly called for Israel's destruction:

A third anti-Semitic screed caught my attention for its gaudy cover: A red Star of David over a gray skull and a yellow map of the world. Its title was "Tale of the 'Chosen People' and the Legend of 'Historical Right,'" written by Mohammad Taqi Taqipour. In his foreword, the author is certain of another "final solution": Given the "global Islamic movement," Israel will soon be destroyed. (Küntzel 2005)

Dr. Küntzel understood that the psychological problem was not only the carelessness of the Book Fair's director, but that it lay deeper in the Iranian and German soul:

The distribution of such texts is prohibited in Germany. The failure of those responsible for the Frankfurt Book Fair is doubly serious because only last year the exhibition made headlines for presenting anti-Semitic texts. Then as now, the fair's directors informed the prosecutor's office only after visitors complained. Perhaps the director of the fair, Jürgen Boos, will be more careful next time. But does more careful supervision address the real problem? (Küntzel 2005)

On the Iranian side, the scholar thought, the problem was a profound hatred of Israel that had nothing to do with its actual character or actions:

At the heart of the real problem is an Iranian policy that could hardly be more authentically represented than through the "Protocols." "We present this book," reads the Iranian foreword, "to expose the real visage of this satanic enemy," to "burn and wholly destroy...this deadly, cancerous tumor." In Iran this pamphlet provides legitimacy to the longed-for destruction of Israel. Iranian state TV instills a delusional hatred of Jews into millions of viewers with anti-Semitic movie series. And it's not just all talk. Billions are spent to advance nuclear programs and the Shahab 3 missile, which could deliver a nuclear payload to Israel. In the meantime, the secret services escalate the terror against Israel by supporting Hamas and Hezbollah. (Küntzel 2005)

In 2006, Iranian anti-Semitism reached a new peak when the Iranian daily *Hamashahri,* which is controlled by the Tehran municipality, announced an international Holocaust-cartoon [*sic!*]competition, cosponsored by the Iranian House of Caricatures, an exhibition hall for political cartoons in Tehran. Over 200 cartoons were selected among 1,100 entries from over 60 countries for the exhibition, which opened that summer. In an insidious inversion of the Holocaust imagery, several cartoons portrayed Israel as having taken the place of the Nazis, with the Palestinians depicted as suffering Nazi-like or even worse treatment by the Israelis (Karimi 2006, Gerstenfeld 2007).

Other anti-Semitic Tehran cartoons in 2006 conveyed the message that Israel exploits the Holocaust, either as a weapon against the Palestinians or as a tool to get sympathy from the world. Still other cartoons indicate that the Holocaust is a hoax or grossly exaggerated. Others exploit classic anti-Semitic motifs such as demonization of the Jews, their deicide, infanticide, conspiracy theories of their world domination, the old blood libel, and portraying the Jews as vermin. Some contained several anti-Semitic or anti-Israeli motifs. Several were not related to the Holocaust. Some cartoons proclaimed that Israel does not want peace, while others attack the West. Abdolhossein Amirizadeh of Iran demonized the Jews by showing a horned devil with vampire fingers reading from a book on which "Holocaust" is written. Next to him is a staff in the form of a seven-branched candelabra topped by a Star of David (Stav 1999; Kotek & Kotek 2003; Karimi 2006; Gerstenfeld 2007).

While the Holocaust-cartoon competition in Tehran was not directly linked to the Ahmadinejad national government, the fact that, as noted earlier, it was sponsored by a paper owned by the Tehran municipality further illustrates how various branches of the government support distortion and manipulation. In late 2006, Iran organized a conference of Holocaust deniers, to which no serious Holocaust historian was invited. UN Secretary-General Kofi Annan expressed his concern about it, but the Iranian Foreign Ministry spokesman Hamid Reza Asefi said that the planned conference would go ahead and, since the Holocaust was a scientific issue, both confirmers and deniers of its historicity could participate. He told reporters: "I have visited the Nazi camps in Eastern Europe. I think it is exaggerated" (Gerstenfeld 2007).

Among those attending the Tehran conference were the German-born Australian "historian" Gerald Fredrick Töben (who had been jailed in Germany for his public Holocaust denial), the virulently anti-Semitic Australian socialite Michele Renouf (a friend of the British Holocaust denier David Irving, who had been jailed in Austria), the French National Front leader Georges Theil (who had been condemned to jail three times in France for breaking the Gayssot law against denying the Holocaust), Veronica Clark from the United States (who thinks that "the Jews made money in Auschwitz"), the anti-Semitic, Ugandan-born, Iranian-Canadian political scientist Shiraz Dossa, the retired French literary scholar Robert Faurisson (who had been jailed in France), and the American former Ku Klux Klan leader David Ernest Duke, who had left the Klan in 1978 to found the National Association for the Advancement of White People. Some ultra-Orthodox Jews of the extreme anti-Israeli *Neturei Karta* sect also attended.

Why is it Iran, of all the dozens of Muslim countries in the world, that hates Israel with such a passion? Why do those who govern Iran, such as Mahmoud Ahmadinejad, unconsciously project all their bad feelings and inner evil on the "satanic" little country west of them? Unlike the Palestinian Arabs, who may have a real "beef" with Israel, Iran has never been hurt by anything Israel or the Jews have ever done. But the unconscious *splitting, projection, externalization,* and *denial,* in the minds of fanatical Muslims are such that any connection between their anti-Semitic fantasies and the reality of the Jews or Israel is coincidental. Deep down, Iran's rulers may feel that they have not been good to their own people. Iran's isolation in the world is increasingly severe. Israel seems to be the psychological "container" for the unconscious projections and externalizations of the Iranian rulers (Volkan 1988).

In 2007, an Israeli Arab Muslim leader seemed to speak up against anti-Semitism. On February 11, Sheikh Abdullah Nimr Darwish, who heads the southern faction of the Islamic Movement in Israel, condemned Holocaust denial in the Muslim world at the meeting of the Global Forum for Combating Anti-Semitism in Jerusalem. Darwish opened his speech by saying, "It was not easy for me to come here today. I thought about what will be said by my clerical colleagues from Indonesia to Morocco, but I decided to come out of duty to Allah." He went on to say that the anti-Semitic texts in the Muslim world did not express the true spirit of Islam. "I know that many of you have read very dark and harsh texts. The people who wrote them have no right to sign off on them in the name of Islam. These are interpretations and not the words of the Prophet," Darwish said, adding that attention should not be paid to Holocaust deniers because "it only gives them something to do. Do you think I suffer less than you when I hear statements by Ahmadinejad or Bin Ladin?" he asked his audience rhetorically. Darwish rejected the Holocaust-denial statements of the Iranian president Ahmadinejad, saying "Tell all who deny the Holocaust to ask the Germans what they did or did not do" (Barkat 2007).

In the same breath, however, the Israeli Muslim Arab leader accused his Jewish audience of not understanding the Muslims and protested Israel's refusal to support the recent Saudi Arabian peace initiative involving the Palestinian parties *Hamas* and *Fatah.* "Why are you trying to distance yourselves from Muslims as if they were the devil?" he said, adding that the Arab world had said yes to the recognition of Israel "but the Jews will run you ragged until they say yes" (Barkat 2007). The sheikh's covert anti-Semitism was showing through his rhetoric. At his side were sitting the former Israeli minister for Diaspora affairs, Rabbi Michael Melchior, and the American chairman of the World Jewish Committee

Policy Council, Rabbi Israel Singer, who hailed Darwish's statements as "historic." Isi Leibler, a right-wing former vice president of the World Jewish Committee who had been ousted from his job, also praised Darwish's comments on the Holocaust (Barkat 2007). The Jewish leaders were denying their Muslim guest's subtle Jew-hatred.

As we have seen, in 1475, the Jews of the Tyrolean town of Trent had been accused of having killed the two-year-old Simonino da Trento (Little Simon of Trent) and used his blood for their Passover ritual (Eckert & Ehrlich 1964, Hsia 1992). Eighteen Jewish men and five Jewish women were arrested, tortured, and tried by the Papal Inquisition. The show trial of the accused Jews became part of the perennial power struggle between the pope and the "holy Roman emperor." The Austrian ruler of Trent, Bishop Johannes von Hinderbach (1418–1486), a proxy for Holy Roman Emperor Friedrich III (1415–1493), fought the bishop of Ventimiglia, Battista dei Giudici, a proxy for Pope Sixtus IV (Francesco della Rovere, 1414–1484). The pope yielded to the emperor, and the German bishop had his way, executing the hapless Jews (Hsia 1992, Kristeller 1993).

In a dramatic footnote to the age-old blood-libel accusation, in February 2007, the Italian-born Israeli Jewish historian Ariel Toaff, son of the former chief rabbi of Rome, Elio Toaff, published a book purporting to "prove" that the ritual-murder accusation in the case of Simonino da Trento was not entirely false, and that some "extreme Ashkenazi Jews" may have practiced ritual child-murder (Toaff 2007). Toaff's colleagues, including the Italian jurist Diego Guaglioni of Trent and the Chinese-American historian Ronnie Pochia Hsia, accused him of flawed scholarship. Toaff, they said, had taken the Inquisition's confession documents at face value, even though they had been obtained under torture or falsified. Worse than that for Ariel Toaff, his 91-year-old father told an Italian newspaper, "If this is so, then he, too, understood. That is, that the criticism that everyone has expressed about his book was justified. His arguments in the book were an insult to the intelligence, to the tradition, to history in general and to the meaning of the Jewish religion. It saddens me that such nonsense was put forward by my son of all people" (Schwartz 2007).

The unfortunate Ariel Toaff, whose book may have been part of his unconscious battle with his father, received anonymous death threats. He withdrew his book from circulation and sought out his elderly father. Toaff, who has two brothers and a sister, told an interviewer, "I am trying to contact my father, but in vain. They won't let me speak to him. Nor can I go to his house: the Jewish quarter [of Rome] would not be safe for me right now. I prefer not to discuss the threats that I have received. I have sought help from my brother Gadi who lives in Salonica, my brother Daniel who is a journalist at the Italian radio and television station RAI, and my sister Miriam who lives in Israel with her husband, Professor [Sergio] della Pergola. I hope soon to be able to speak with my father, to explain myself to him. It is true, I have breached a taboo. But I have not spoken falsely against the family to which I belong, against the Jews" (Cazzullo 2007). In March 2007, the old Elio Toaff made up with his son, who flew back to Rome to see his father (Schwartz 2007).

Sigmund Freud and Anti-Semitism

PSYCHOANALYSIS AND ANTI-SEMITISM

Like most of his Austrian-Jewish contemporaries, the "father of psychoanalysis," Sigmund Freud, suffered personally from anti-Semitism (which, among other things, restricted his academic rank to *Professor extraorinarius,* and which, at the end of his life, in 1938, forced him to flee Austria, annexed to the German Third *Reich* by Adolf Hitler). As his theories developed, Freud gave several different explanations for anti-Semitism. In 1909, in a footnote to his *Analysis of a Phobia in a Five-year-old Boy,* Freud speculated that the universal *fear of castration,* unconsciously provoked in uncircumcised non-Jews by the Jews being circumcised, was "the deepest unconscious root of anti-Semitism" (Freud 1909; Freud 1955, p. 36, note 1; Freud 1957, pp. 95–96, note 3). The five-year-old boy, identified by Freud as "Little Hans," was Herbert Graf (1903–1973), the future New York opera producer. While Freud's "castration theory of anti-Semitism" was adopted by his followers (Fenichel 1946), later scholars thought this theory inadequate because the highly irrational Christian fantasies of the "evil" Jews as children of the Devil had *multiple* unconscious causes and functions, of which the fear of castration was only one, and not necessarily the most powerful one, the unconscious *projection* of unacceptable aspects of the self being a key process (Rubenstein 1966; Stein 1994, p. 44; Ferraroti 1994).

In 1921, Sigmund Freud attributed the "almost insuperable repugnance" that "Aryans" felt for "Semites" to the "narcissism of minor differences" by which closely related groups disdain one another. In 1929, when Hitler's Nazis were already active in Germany but had not yet taken over that country, Freud seems to have realized that anti-Semitism involved the unconscious defensive process of projection: "It is always possible to bind together a considerable number of people in love, so long as there are other people left over to receive the manifestations of their aggressiveness...Neither was it an unaccountable chance that the dream of a Germanic world-dominion called for anti-Semitism as its complement" (Freud 1930; Freud 1961, pp. 114–115).

Until the end of his life in 1939, Freud was obsessed with the father-son conflict and the Oedipus complex, in which the son consciously loves his father but unconsciously wishes to kill him and to possess his mother sexually, and with the universal father-son rivalry. Freud speculated that the ancient Jews who left Egypt in the biblical Exodus had murdered their "great father" Moses, but would not admit their patricidal guilt. The Christians, on the other hand, had killed their "son" Jesus as an unconscious atonement for the murder of the father. To Freud, the murder of "the primal father" was the origin of human civilization. Judaism was a "father religion" while Christianity was "a son religion." His beautiful prose, which won the Goethe Prize for German literature, is worth quoting in full:

> The poor Jewish people, who with their habitual stubbornness continued to disavow the father's murder, atoned heavily for it in the course of time. They were constantly met with the reproach: "You killed our God!" [Jesus Christ] And *this reproach is true,* if it is correctly translated. If it is brought into relation with the history of religions, it runs: "You will not *admit* that you murdered God (the primal picture of God, the primal father, and his later reincarnations)." There should be [a Christian] addition declaring: "We did the same thing, to be sure, but we have *admitted* it and since then we have been absolved." (Freud 1939; Freud 1964, p. 90; some italics added)

The aging and ailing Freud, who was dying from cancer of the jaw caused by his lifelong cigar smoking, understood that his "father-murder" theory was speculative and in any case did not fully explain the irrationality of anti-Semitism. Was Freud aware that he was expressing his own ambivalent feelings about the Jews and being Jewish himself?

> Not all the reproaches with which anti-Semitism persecutes the Jewish people can appeal to a similar justification. A phenomenon of such intensity and permanence as the people's hatred of the Jews must of course have more than one ground. It is possible to find a whole number of grounds, *some of them derived from reality, which call for no interpretation,* and others, lying deeper and derived from hidden sources, which might be regarded as the specific reasons. Of the former, the reproach of being aliens is perhaps the weakest, since in many places dominated by anti-Semitism to-day the Jews were among the oldest portions of the population or had even been there before the present inhabitants. This applies, for instance, to the city of Cologne, to which the Jews came with the Romans, before it was occupied by the Germans. *Other grounds for hating the Jews are stronger— thus the circumstances that they live for the most part as minorities among other peoples,* for the communal feeling of *groups* requires that, in order to complete it,

hostility towards some extraneous minority, and the numerical weakness of this excluded minority encourages its suppression. (Freud 1939; Freud 1964, p. 90; italics added)

Several scholars have studied Freud's lifelong ambivalence about his Judaism (Grollman 1965; Falk 1978; Yerushalmi 1990; Rice 1990; Gilman 1994). In *Moses and Monotheism* (1939), the dying Freud either consciously or unwittingly expressed his ambivalent feelings. In the following paragraph from this work it is not clear whether he was being ironic or serious. Note that Freud kept referring to the Jews as "they" rather than as "we," even though he was a Jew himself:

There are, however, two other characteristics of the Jews which are quite unforgivable. First is the fact that in some respects they are different from their 'host' nations. They are not fundamentally different, for they are not Asiatics of a foreign race, as their enemies maintain, but composed for the most part of remnants of Mediterranean civilization. But they are none the less different, often in an indefinable way different, especially from the Nordic peoples, and *the intolerance of groups is often, strangely enough, exhibited more strongly against small differences than against fundamental ones.* The other point has a still greater effect, namely that they defy all oppression, that the most cruel persecutions have not succeeded in exterminating them, and, indeed, that on the contrary they show a capacity for holding their own in commercial life and, where they are admitted, for making valuable contributions to every form of cultural activity. (Freud 1939; Freud 1964, pp. 90–91; italics added)

By discussing the "unforgivable" characteristics of the Jews, was Freud observing "reality" or expressing his own anti-Semitic or self-hate feelings? (cf. Grollman 1965; Falk 1978; Yerushalmi 1990; Rice 1990; Gilman 1994). In the last sentence, Freud alluded to what he called the "narcissism of minor differences," a major factor in interethnic conflict (Falk 2004, p. 129). He then went on to ascribe Christian Jew-hatred to Jewish group narcissism and to the Jewish practice of circumcision, which aroused the fear of castration among non-Jews:

The deeper motives for hatred of the Jews are rooted in the remotest past ages; they operate from the unconscious of the peoples, and I am prepared to find that at first they will not seem credible. I venture to assert that jealousy of the people which declared itself the first-born, favourite child of God the Father, has not yet been surmounted among other peoples even to-day: it is as though they had thought there was truth in the claim. Further, among the customs by which the Jews made themselves separate, that of circumcision has made a disagreeable, uncanny impression, which is to be explained, no doubt, by its recalling the dreaded castration and along with it a portion of the primaeval past which is gladly forgotten. (Freud 1964, p. 91)

Not content with the foregoing explanations, however, Freud went on to speculate on the further unconscious causes of irrational anti-Semitism, including
unconscious displacement, in which one's early feelings for one's parents are
unconsciously transferred to other, less threatening objects:

> And finally, as the latest motive in this series, we must not forget that all those
> peoples who excel to-day in their hatred of Jews became Christians only in late
> historic times, often driven to it by bloody coercion. It must be said that they are
> all "mis-baptized." They have been left, under a thin veneer of Christianity,
> what their ancestors were, who worshipped a barbarous polytheism. They have
> not got over a grudge against the new religion which was imposed on them; but
> they have displaced the grudge on to the source from which Christianity reached
> them. The fact that the Gospels tell a story which is set among Jews, and in fact
> deals only with Jews, has made this *displacement* easy for them. *Their hatred of
> Jews is at bottom a hatred of Christians,* [italics added] and we need not be surprised
> that in the German National-Socialist [Nazi] revolution this intimate relation
> between the two monotheist religions finds such a clear expression in the hostile
> treatment of both of them. (Freud 1964, pp. 91–92; cf. Loewenberg 1995b,
> pp. 174–176)

Some scholars, who needed to see things in black and white, believed that Freud
was a proud Jew who was greatly influenced by Jewish ideas (Bakan 1958, Szasz
1978). Here is a typical statement from these scholars about Freud's fight against
anti-Semitism:

> Freud believed that anti-Semitism was practically ubiquitous in either latent or
> manifest form; the broad masses in England were anti-Semitic, "as everywhere";
> he was of the opinion that the book on Moses would anger the Jews; he expressed
> a love of Hebrew and Yiddish, according to Freud's son; he refused to accept roy-
> alties on Hebrew and Yiddish translations of his work; he was sympathetic to
> Zionism from the first days of the movement and was acquainted with and
> respected Herzl; he had once sent Herzl a copy of one of his works with a personal
> dedication; Freud's son was a member of the Kadimah, a Zionist organization, and
> Freud himself was an honorary member in it. (Bakan 1958, p. 49; Szasz 1978,
> p. 139)

In fact, Sigmund Freud's feelings about Judaism and Zionism were far more
ambivalent and conflicted, as were his feelings about his Jewish father (Falk 1978;
Yerushalmi 1990; Rice 1990; Gilman 1993a, 1993b).

CRITICIZING AND EXPANDING FREUD'S IDEAS

After Freud's death in 1939, during the Second World War (1939–1945),
some Jewish scholars used his theories on anti-Semitism. One of them was

Maurice Samuel (1895–1972), a Romanian-born and British-educated American Jewish novelist and philosopher who translated Martin Buber's work into English. Some scholars have considered Samuel an anti-Gentile Jewish fascist and racist. Twenty years earlier, Samuel had written, "Jew and Gentile are two worlds, between you Gentiles and us Jews there lies an unbridgeable gulf. . . There are two life-forces in the world I know: Jewish and Gentile, ours and yours. . . I do not believe that this primal difference between Gentile and Jew is reconcilable. You and we may come to an understanding, never to a reconciliation. There will be irritation between us as long as we are in intimate contact. For nature and constitution and vision divide us from all of you forever" (Samuel 1924, pp. 9, 19 , 23).

Maurice Samuel believed that anti-Semites attacked the strictures, notions, and controls of brotherhood in both Judaism and Christianity. The Christians unconsciously yearn for the freedom and license of the pagan world, but cannot attack their own religion. Instead, they unconsciously displace their rage to the Jews, the origin of Jesus Christ, and Christianity. Were it not for the Jews, the Christians believe, they would have remained happily pagan. They blame the Jews for having killed their Christ, which, unconsciously, they wish to do themselves. Like Freud, Samuel saw anti-Semitism as the product of an unconscious Oedipal complex, with the Jews unconsciously standing for the father (Samuel 1943).

Freud's ideas on anti-Semitism have had their critics, even from within psychoanalysis. The American Jewish anthropologist Howard F. Stein believed that Freud's ideas about the unconscious fear of castration, infanticidal feelings, deicide, or the passive surrender of the son to the father as causes of anti-Semitism were a conceptual error, and that unconscious projection was the key issue: "What makes the Jews the perfect dream phantom is the universal process of *condensation* into which historical witches brew [*sic*] Jews emerge as the best and the worst, the most favored and the most condemned, the too proud and the utterly shamed. It is in that fateful convergence that Jews are uncannily available for every historical occasion of mental defeat" (Stein 1994, p. 44). Whether or not Freud was right on every count, however, his highly original and incisive analysis was written prior to the terribly tragic and genocidal Holocaust, in which six million European Jews were murdered by the German Nazis and their collaborators all over Europe and even in North Africa.

After the horrors of the Holocaust, traumatized psychoanalysts took a fresh look at individual and collective anti-Semitism. To deal with their trauma, some of Freud's Jewish followers who had fled to the United States embarked on large-scale psychoanalytic studies of anti-Semitism. Some collections of essays edited by Freud's disciples were published (Simmel 1946). One of them, the Polish-born, German-trained, French-educated, American Jewish psychoanalyst Rudolph Maurice Loewenstein (1898–1976), published a penetrating essay on the historical and cultural roots of anti-Semitism (Loewenstein 1947).

The German philosopher Karl Jaspers had just published a book about Germany's collective genocidal guilt (Jaspers 1946). Wilhelm Reich, a pupil of Freud who became a guru of "orgone therapy," also published his own interpretations of fascism and anti-Semitism (Reich 1946, 1975), but at least two psychoanalysts have considered Reich an illusion-monger (Grunberger & Chasseguet-Smirgel 1976).

In 1950, Nathan Ackerman and Marie Jahoda, who had studied the clinical case reports of 40 anti-Semites who had been in psychotherapy, argued that individual anti-Semitism was directly linked to emotional illness (Ackerman & Jahoda 1950). The main psychological "defense mechanism" in such an illness is *projection,* an unconscious process by which the person attributes what he cannot bear about himself to the object of his hatred. By studying such people psychologically, Ackerman and Jahoda found that anti-Semites—and other people with deep racial, ethnic, or religious prejudice—tend to have suffered from lack of love or rejection in childhood, have little psychological insight about themselves, and their unconscious defenses, including projection, operate massively.

The following year, Loewenstein, who had settled in the United States, expanded his 1947 article into an ambitious book-length psychoanalytic study of anti-Semitism (Loewenstein 1951). One of his chief points was the extreme irrationality of anti-Semitic fantasies about the Jews and their imperviousness to rational argument, which, like Ackerman and Jahoda, he found indicative of "social mental" illness:

> Inaccessibility to reason is also one of the most typical characteristics of the anti-Semite, who is unable to re-evaluate his opinions and prejudices in the light of factual evidence that refutes them. The passions and the unconscious motives and mechanisms involved in his anti-Semitic feelings are too powerful to yield to reason or experience. We find therefore that *although anti-Semitism cannot be placed in any one of the well-known clinical categories it is nevertheless frequently an indication of some sort of mental disturbance* that could be classified among *the social mental diseases.* (Loewenstein 1951, pp. 18–19, italics added)

We shall discuss Loewenstein's ideas below. What characterizes Freud, Loewenstein, and other psychoanalytic thinkers on anti-Semitism is their emphasis on its role as an unconscious defense against unbearable feelings. Let us examine some of the other unconscious aspects of anti-Semitism.

UNCONSCIOUS ASPECTS OF ANTI-SEMITISM

Where do the tragic anti-Jewish fantasies and conspiracy theories spring from? Why are they so popular and widespread? The irrational nature of the hate fantasies and conspiracy theories that anti-Semites have about Jews indicates their unconscious emotional sources. The tragic historical phenomenon of anti-Semitism, which has led to mass murder and genocide, is highly complex and overdetermined, having not only social, cultural, economic, political, ethnic, and religious causes, but also deep psychological causes. However, while the former are relatively easy to see, the psychological ones are often hidden, unconscious, and obscured by rationalizations. While the former have been studied extensively by scholars, the latter are of paramount importance to understanding anti-Semitism. They need to be uncovered in order to be understood. And uncovering their unconscious roots is no easy task. The discipline employed in this book is psychoanalysis, which is not only a method of treating emotional suffering, but also a general theory of human behavior.

It should not be overlooked that psychoanalysis—my primary tool for studying anti-Semitism—has Jewish origins and Jewish aspects, not the least being the Jewish origin of its Austrian Jewish founder, Sigmund Freud, and of many of his disciples (Klein 1981). Another Austrian, the rabidly anti-Semitic Adolf Hitler, who became Germany's *Führer* and, from 1933 to 1945, led it to perpetrating unimaginable horrors and self-destruction, was just as destructive as Freud was creative. Hitler, who was either borderline or psychotic (Erikson 1942, 1963; Langer 1972; Koenigsberg 1975; Stierlin 1975, 1976; Binion 1976; Waite 1977; Bromberg & Small 1983; De Boor 1985; Burrin 1989, 1994, 2004; Schwaab 1992; Bursztein 1996; Young and French 1996; Chamberlain 1997; Victor 1998; Redlich 1999), caused Freud to flee Austria in 1938. Hitler's anti-Semitic German Nazis burned Freud's books publicly, along with those of other Jewish writers. They later gassed the Jews to death in their extermination camps and burned their corpses in their crematoria.

The tragic, age-old, and psychopathological phenomenon of Judeophobia—the hatred and fear of all Jews, which in the late nineteenth century, during the German *Kulturkampf,* acquired the euphemistic appellation of "anti-Semitism"—has attracted the attention of Jewish and non-Jewish psychoanalysts, especially after the incredibly tragic Holocaust in which the German Nazis and their collaborators mass-murdered six million European Jews during World War II (Hilberg 1961; Guttman 1990; Bergen 2003). They also murdered millions of Gypsies and others at the same time. Fear and hatred, naturally, are two different feelings. One German psychoanalyst thought that in xenophobia (the fear of foreigners), fear is transformed into hatred through a complex psychological process (Maciejewski 1994). Some psychoanalysts think that hate and fear of Jews are separate and distinct phenomena (Nicolle 2004, p. 49, note 1). However, it was both fear and hatred of the Jews that led the German Nazis to mass-murder them.

For all its horrors, often too painful to contemplate, the Holocaust was neither the first nor the last genocide in human history (Charny 1982, 1984, 1999; Charny et al. 1988–1994). One of the most difficult questions concerning the Holocaust is why it was the Germans rather than another nation who perpetrated this unthinkable and unprecedented genocide. The common historical wisdom points to the special way, or *Sonderweg*, in which Germany developed, differently from that of other nations, but this is hardly a satisfactory explanation. While the American Jewish historian Daniel Jonah Goldhagen thought that there was a uniquely German "eliminatory anti-Semitism" (Goldhagen 1996), his colleague Richard J. Evans pointed out two unique aspects of the German-perpetrated Holocaust:

> Ever since the full horror of Hitler's death camps dawned upon the world, historians, sociologists, political scientists and philosophers from many countries have been trying to understand how and why it was in Germany rather than anywhere else that antisemitism, one of the longest-lasting and most widespread of ethnic and religious hatreds in European history, led to the deliberate mass murder of Europe's Jews. For *what distinguished Hitler's so-called "Final Solution of the Jewish Question"*—in reality, as many observers have noted, not really a Jewish Question but a German one—*was* not so much its brutality, violence and fanaticism, though this was indeed extreme (similar cruelty and barbarism has been seen in more recent times, in Rwanda, Bosnia and Iraq), but two rather different factors. The first of these was *its mechanized and bureaucratized character*. In no other case of genocide has a state devoted such vast resources of central planning and administration to the total extermination of an ethnic minority. The second factor that made it unique was *the fact that it was intended to eliminate the Jews not just of the country where the policy of extermination originated, but of the whole of Europe, indeed ultimately the world*. (Evans 1997, p. 149; italics added)

Evans may have singled out two unique *aspects* of the German-perpetrated Holocaust, but he did not explain their *causes*. Significantly, Evans cited the efforts of historians, sociologists, political scientists and philosophers to explain the Holocaust, but not those of psychoanalysts. For this is the attitude of many historians, including the majority of Israeli Jewish historians, toward psychoanalysis: a rejection of its explanatory power and of its focus on unconscious motivation. Psychoanalysis is threatening to historians, who like to think that their choice of profession and methods of analysis are rational, indeed that human behavior is rational, while the Holocaust itself is proof that it is not. Therefore, without a psychoanalytic investigation of the unconscious motives for the perpetration of the Holocaust, it is impossible to understand it truly.

Most historians think that the Holocaust had many different causes beside anti-Semitism. The section on the Roots of the Holocaust in *The Columbia Guide to the Holocaust* opens with the following text:

> Several historical trends came together in the early twentieth century to make the Holocaust possible: extreme nationalism, industrialism, antisemitism, racism, Social Darwinism, totalitarianism, and the nature of modern war. This section

begins with a broad survey of developments in modern Europe up to 1933 with emphasis on the situation in Germany. It then focuses more closely on the history of the Jews, Gypsies, and the handicapped in order to understand what made them targets of prejudice. It concludes with an exploration of the prejudice itself. Throughout this section *a central question is whether the Holocaust is better thought of as a culmination of European and German history or as a monstrous aberration.* (Nicosia & Niewyk 2000, p. 53, italics added)

One of the key psychological questions about the Holocaust is how it was possible for a highly civilized European nation like Germany to elect a "psychopathic god" like Adolf Hitler (Waite 1977), who suffered from a severe form of borderline psychiatric disorder (some psychiatrists have even considered him psychotic), as its supreme leader or *Führer* in 1933; to revere him like a god, and to follow him blindly and willingly in murdering six million Jews as well as millions of Gypsies, the physically and mentally handicapped, Soviet prisoners of war, Slavic civilians, political prisoners, religious dissenters, communists, Catholics, homosexuals, and other "inferior people"; and to wage a mad war on the whole world, until Germany itself lost many millions of its own people and was utterly destroyed in what the Germans called *der totale Zusammenbruch* (the total collapse) in 1945.

EVIL: PSYCHOANALYTIC PERSPECTIVES

The word "evil" has religious and moral connotations rather than psychoanalytic ones. Few psychoanalysts have studied evil by this name. They have studied many *aspects* of evil, such as sadism, cruelty, aggression, violence, murder, war, and genocide, but not human evil itself as a broader issue. A few psychological studies of evil were published during the last four decades of the twentieth century (Sanford et al. 1971; Khan 1983; Staub 1989; Bollas 1995; Goldberg 1996, 2000; Oppenheimer 1996; Alford 1997; Baumeister 1997; Victor 1998; Grand 2000). Carl Goldberg's psychoanalytic study of "malevolence" anticipated some of the large-scale evil that was to follow five years later.

One humorous definition of a psychoanalyst in America is "a Jewish doctor who can't stand the sight of blood." Carl Goldberg is one American Jewish psychoanalyst who devoted time and effort to the study of bloody "malevolence"—evil, malicious human behavior that inflicts terrible pain on other human beings. From his clinical psychoanalytic experience, he constructed a theory of the development of the "malevolent personality." Goldberg saw evil as becoming increasingly widespread in our world. He thought that evil was not a pejorative metaphysical concept of historical interest, but a real presence that shaped our lives. Seemingly "senseless" acts of sadistic cruelty, brutality, and destructiveness had become an ubiquitous component of our daily life in every place on this earth (Goldberg 1996).

Goldberg studied "malevolence" not only from the clinical aspect but also from the religious, historical, and moral viewpoints. He defined malevolent behavior as the *deliberate* sadistic infliction of cruel and painful suffering on another living being. Goldberg considered the *intention* of the evil act crucially important, as it distinguished the malevolent personality from other violent criminals. "Malevolence" characterizes serial killers, torturers, terrorists, and genocide perpetrators. It is profoundly evil behavior that we find deeply fascinating, fear greatly, but also find incomprehensible (Goldberg 1996).

The American philosopher Henry David Thoreau (1817–1862) thought that "There are thousands hacking at the branches of evil to one who is striking at its roots." What is the use of a psychoanalytic theory of human "malevolence"? Goldberg thought that to be of real value, any scientific theory of human behavior should have predictive value and enable us to control and change that behavior. A developmental model of "malevolence" should, therefore, recognize specific precursors of malevolent behavior, and would allow early detection and prediction. Strategies of avoidance or amelioration could then be developed. Goldberg believed that psychoanalysis, psychiatry, psychology, sociology, and anthropology lacked a useful behavioral model of "malevolence." He cited two powerful but misleading assumptions that had led to this lack of understanding.

One powerful but misleading assumption is that malevolence is strictly a moral issue and outside the province of psychoanalysis, psychiatry, psychology, or sociology. Moralists believe that individuals *choose* to be evil, and that this choice cannot be explained or even studied scientifically. Moreover, many people have a "moral objection" to psychoanalyzing evil and malevolence. They mistakenly fear that psychological insight into the motivations of evil people could lead to exonerating them from blame for the atrocious acts they commit. People often quote the aphorism "To understand all is to forgive all." They do not wish to forgive Hitler's atrocities by understanding him. The related Latin phrase is *Errare humanum est, perdonare divinum, perseverare diabolicum,* and Alexander Pope wrote, "To err is human, to forgive divine." Psychological understanding, however, does not absolve individuals of their moral or legal responsibility for their own actions.

Goldberg thought that the second powerful but misleading assumption that caused problems in understanding "malevolence" was seeing individuals who exhibit extreme, evil, malevolent, or sadistic behavior as "mentally ill." When such individuals are diagnosed as "paranoid schizophrenics," "criminal psychopaths," or "sociopaths," the problem is diluted, and the "malevolent" individual is "understood" as little as mental illness itself is understood. In addition, the legal defense of "insanity" and "diminished responsibility" carry the implicit assumption that we, being "mentally normal" and rational, cannot really expect to understand such an individual's nonrational motivations. Malevolent behavior remains a mystery, and we sit waiting for it to strike again.

Goldberg discerned several different stages in the early emotional development of the "malevolent personality." They included the individual's early experiences of shame and guilt, the growth of his bad self-image, the internalization of his "bad self," the accumulation of his inner rage, guilt, and emptiness, and the lack of empathy, all potentially leading to the acting out of this "badness" on society. The tragic progression from one stage to the next involves the creation of a uniquely bad internal world in which reasonable and rational choices for good behavior (in terms of the outside world) are no longer available. While malevolence may be an aberrant reaction to life's events, Goldberg believed that the structure of modern society makes it possible (and even necessary) for more and more individuals to follow their own codes. Ties of relationships are often missing, many individuals are alone, and it is this lack of grounding to the "real" world that is most worrying and most tragic.

Carl Goldberg's books were a critique of the current understanding of malevolent behavior in our society, including our modern psychoanalysis. Goldberg stressed the need for understanding on the part of the behavioral sciences. The consequences of malevolence in modern life are devastating, from the localized terror invoked by serial killers or mass murderers, to the worldwide horror at the recent events in Rwanda, Bosnia, Ireland, and elsewhere. All this was written in the last decade of the twentieth century, before the horrors of suicidal murder and terrorism became a global reality.

At the beginning of the twenty-first century, the world discovered a new kind of evil: that of the fanatical fundamentalist Islamic *jihadis* or "holy warriors" of Osama bin Laden's al Qaeda. On September 11, 2001, the Twin Towers of New York's World Trade Center were destroyed by fanatical Muslim Arab suicide murderers who had hijacked American passenger airplanes and flown them into the towers, killing themselves along with thousands of innocent people. The suicidal terrorists were Islamic fundamentalists, and a year earlier, prophetically, the American scholar Karen Armstrong had found fundamentalism in the three monotheistic religions a puzzling and disturbing phenomenon:

> One of the most startling developments of the late twentieth century has been the emergence within every major religious tradition of a militant piety popularly known as "fundamentalism." Its manifestations are sometimes shocking. Fundamentalists have gunned down worshippers in a mosque, have killed doctors and nurses who work in abortion clinics, have shot their presidents, and have even toppled a powerful government. It is only a small minority of fundamentalists who commit such acts of terror, but even the most peaceful and law-abiding are perplexing, because they seem so adamantly opposed to many of the most positive values of modern society. (Armstrong 2000, Introduction)

The New York City horrors of 2001 were indeed committed by that "small minority of fundamentalists," but they shocked all mankind. They also sparked a new study of evil by the American-Israeli Jewish psychoanalyst Ruth Stein, who had moved to New York City, among other reasons, to escape the wars and suicide bombings in Israel. Shocked by the tragedy, Stein tried to overcome her new trauma actively by analyzing the letter written by Mohammed Atta, the leader of the suicide bombers, to his fellow hijackers. Here is the gist of her analysis:

> The letter has a solemn, serene, even joyful tone that is infused with love of God and a strong desire to please Him...incessant incantation of prayers and religious sayings while focusing attention on God led to a depersonalized, trancelike state of mind that enabled the terrorists to function competently while dwelling in a euphoric state...the theme of father-son love is used to explain the ecstatic willingness of the terrorists to do what they saw as God's will and to follow transformations from (self) hate to love (of God), and from anxiety and discontent to the a narrowly focused fear of God. Homoerotic bonding and longing, coupled with repudiation of "femininity," are explained as an inability to "kill" the primal murderous father, as the mythological Primal Horde. Freud's description of sons' (group members') hypnotic love for their father leader (which, that when not reciprocated, turns into masochistic submission), seems pertinent for the understanding of the sons' "return" to an archaic, cruel father imago. "Regression" to the father is compared with classical maternal regression. (Stein 2002, p. 393)

Stein's "Freudian" analysis of the suicide murderers was her way of dealing with the painful emotions evoked in her personally by the suicidal mass murder. She found studying the mind of the fundamentalist mass murderer a very difficult task:

> Thinking about evil requires a tremendous effort of the imagination and a willingness to open one's fold to encompass this phenomenon in one's thinking. Getting deeply into what it feels like to have a violently disinhibited, super-humanly entitled, or radically contemptuous and hateful, or utterly despairing, or ecstatically numbed, state of mind without trying to repudiate it and to split it off and yet without completely identifying with it, is no easy task. It may feel alien and disturbing to one's usual self-states; pursued deeply, it becomes frightening. The shocking absence of compassion in evildoing feels too discontinuous with what we have achieved as a culture in terms of our Western ideals and values of humanism, morality, and compassion (it is by its lack of compassion that religious evil, or what may be called coercive fundamentalism, distinguishes itself from religious thinking, since all religions preach compassion. Against the psychoanalytic imperative that nothing human shall remain alien to us, stands the effort to understand something that is meant precisely to annihilate any understanding as well as any physical (or normal) existence. With all these caveats, it nevertheless seems that psychoanalysts need to urgently seek to understand more the phenomenon gathered under this concept and to incorporate it into their vocabulary. (Stein 2002, p. 396)

A perceptive psychoanalyst, Stein paid special attention to the love of Allah that permeated the terrorist leader's "hate" letter:

> [Mohammed Atta's] letter to the terrorists does not speak of hatred. It is past hatred. Absurdly and perversely, it is about love. It is about love of God. We can palpably sense the confident, intimate discourse of a son close to his father, and the seeking of a love that is given as promised and no longer withheld. If this feeling is innerly sustained, it does not have to be shown externally; the letter is a reminder: "everywhere you go, say that prayer and smile and be calm, for God is with the believers. And the angels protect you without you feeling anything," it says, and "You should feel complete tranquility, because the time between you and your marriage...is very short." Since nothing further is said about that marriage, and particularly whom one will marry (the famous paradisiacal virgins are not mentioned at this point), the idea that the marriage is that of the son(s) to God does not sound absurd at all. (Stein 2002, pp. 398–399)

Evil, however, is not the exclusive province of fanatical religious fundamentalists. The American historian Christopher Browning and the American psychologist James Waller have found that "ordinary people" can become evil and commit atrocities, including genocide (Browning 1992, Waller 2002). After the trial in 1961–1962 of the Nazi mass murderer Adolf Eichmann (1906–1962) by an Israeli court that found him guilty of war crimes and crimes against humanity and condemned him to death by hanging (the only death sentence ever handed down in Israel), the German-born American Jewish scholar Hannah Arendt (1906–1975) wrote an account of the trial subtitled "the banality of evil" (Arendt 1963). Arendt's critics, however, have argued that human evil, though widespread, is far from banal (Robinson 1965; Barnouw 1983, 1990; Rogozinski 1989; Calussen 1995; Bergen 1998; Sharpe 1999; Aschheim 2001; Rabinbach 2004). Evil is a deeply rooted part of human existence, and without trying to understand its psychological roots, we shall never understand ourselves. Arendt herself has not only been the subject of heated controversy but also the subject of a psychoanalytic biography (Kristeva 2001).

Evil, Racism, and Anti-Semitism

THE JEW'S BODY

When Adolf Hitler (1889–1945) was in his early thirties, the German Jewish cultural historian Eduard Fuchs (1870–1940) studied anti-Semitic cartoons in which the body of the Jew was grossly distorted (Fuchs 1921). The ancient Greeks and Romans, the early Christians, and most other non-Jewish groups had portrayed the Jews in their art (and caricature) as ugly, deformed people, horrible demons, horned devils with tails, child-eating monsters, and other fearful creatures, or as the children of the Evil Sow and of the Devil (Trachtenberg 1943; Shachar 1974; Gilman 1991). These psychopathological fantasies eventually led to the wholesale murder of the Jews by the German Nazis. Like the tragic view of some women as "witches," and their subsequent hunting and burning, such portrayals do not derive from reality, but rather from the imagination of their creators, including the unconscious externalization of their "inner demons" (Cohn 1975, Demos 1982).

Sadism and masochism usually go together in the same person, and are known together as sadomasochism. During Hitler's rule in Germany (1933–1945) the disturbed, racist, and sadomasochistic writer Julius Streicher (1885–1946) edited the rabidly anti-Semitic weekly *Der Stürmer,* which published worse cartoon images of Jews, showing them as ugly, diabolical, greedy, murderous, and repulsive creatures, or as rats or sex maniacs (Bytwerk 1983, Imbleau 2005). *Der Stürmer* was controversial even in Nazi circles because of its pornographic obsessions and sensationalism. The cartoons of *Der Stürmer* have become synonymous with vicious anti-Semitism. Some of those notorious cartoons, fascinating by the massive unconscious projection that gave rise to them, have the slogan *Die Juden sind unser Unglück* ("The Jews Are Our Misfortune") at the bottom of the caricature.

One of the best modern scholars of anti-Semitism has been the American Jewish scholar Sander Gilman (Gilman 1986, 1990). Gilman published a collection of his essays on the distorted representation of the body of the Jew—the "Jewish" voice, foot, nose—in Western Christian culture, and on its ideological and social implications (Gilman 1991). He discussed the anti-Jewish stereotypes of the "differences" of the Jew's body from the Christian one that are deeply rooted in Christian theological texts, and their place in modern anti-Semitism. Gilman referred to Sigmund Freud's interpretations of this issue and to the phenomenon of Jewish self-hatred connected to the stigmatization of the image of the Jew. He illustrated this problem in contemporary American culture. Gilman stated that the pseudo-science of race in the late nineteenth century secularized prior Christian religious negative views of the Jews and expressed them in a neutral, "scientific" language.

The modern resurgence of anti-Semitism in Europe, including Germany itself, has preoccupied German psychoanalysts. One of them, Herrmann Beland, studied the "religious roots" of anti-Semitism (Beland 1991). Beland agreed with Freud on the unconscious structure of the anti-Semitism of the Christian church, as well as that of modern racist anti-Semitism, as paranoid projections of unconscious guilt feelings and of a deeper narcissistic illness. Beland also cited Janine Chasseguet-Smirgel's thesis of the perverted character of anti-Semitism and Mortimer Ostow's ideas about the connection of anti-Semitism with apocalyptic thinking.

Many scholars of anti-Semitism have confused individual psychological processes with collective ones. The German sociologist Gunnar Heinsohn used a psychoanalytic theory of infanticide and guilt to explain the irrational nature of anti-Semitism (Heinsohn 1988). He believed that sacrifice to the gods began in the ancient world as a psychological means of reducing the anxiety caused by natural cataclysms. People were convinced that the gods wanted them to sacrifice their children to them in order to appease them. The sacrifice of one's firstborn son was common among the Jews in ancient times (Leviticus 18:21; II Kings 23:10; Jeremiah 32:35). The authors of the Bible sought to replace it with animal sacrifice. Biblical Judaism's renunciation and interdiction of child sacrifice was viewed as alien and threatening by the ancient peoples such as the Greeks and Romans. The act of sacrifice aroused unconscious but powerful guilt feelings in the sacrificers.

Child sacrifice was later repressed, but returned symbolically in Christianity after the execution of Jesus Christ by the Romans. Heinsohn did not say that the Christians had killed their Messiah, but that after his crucifixion by the Romans, they produced the myth that Jesus Christ had been their savior as well the sacrificial lamb who carried the sins of the world. The eating of the Sacred Host, which stands for the flesh of Jesus Christ, unconsciously represents a cannibalistic act that produces unbearable guilt feelings, which are unconsciously projected on the Jew, as though they had themselves sacrificed the Son of God. Anti-Semitic Christians thought that the world's ills could be solved by the sacrifice of Jews—from the medieval massacres to the Nazi Holocaust. To Heinsohn, modern racism was an outgrowth of this psycho-religious process, which Heinsohn thought was again at work in modern Germany, often in the guise of anti-Zionism.

The Hungarian Jewish scholar Imre Hermann, a Marxist and Freudian psychoanalyst, in his work on the psychology of anti-Semitism, written during the Holocaust, did distinguish between individual and collective psychology (Hermann 1945, 1972, 1986). Hermann discussed the unconscious search for a scapegoat and the unconscious projection of guilt onto strangers, the unconscious projection of individual characteristics onto entire peoples, and the desire to eliminate "parasitical communities" from society. He showed how, in Freudian terms, the fear of castration, the Oedipus complex, and clinical paranoia were reflected in anti-Semitism. Hermann surveyed popular anti-Semitism from a Marxist viewpoint, as an endemic collective mental illness that becomes epidemic at times of economic or political crisis. Naturally, Hermann focused on Hungarian anti-Semitism, which led to the Hungarian collaboration with the German Nazis in the extermination of the Jews in 1944.

One of the best-known and most prestigious social science research centers in Weimar Germany (1919–1933) was the *Institut für Sozialforschung* (institute of social research) at the University of Frankfurt on the Main, known as "The Frankfurt School" (Brosio 1980; Bottomore 1984; Wiggershaus 1986, 1994; Bernstein 1994; Schindler 1996). From 1930, the institute was led by Max Horkheimer (1895–1973), and most of its members were German Jews. During Nazi rule in Germany, from early 1933, the institute avoided the subject of anti-Semitism in its research work, perhaps out of fear of Hitler's reprisals on the German Jews (Horkheimer et al. 1936).

In the mid-1930s, after Hitler came to power and began persecuting Germany's Jews, Horkheimer succeeded in moving his institute from Germany to the United States and making it part of Columbia University. He began to write on anti-Semitism (Horkheimer 1939, 1989; Jay 1986). By 1944, Horkheimer and his colleague Theodor Wiesengrund Adorno realized that unconscious projection, in addition to social, economic, political, and religious causes, was a major cause of anti-Semitism (Gilman & Zipes 1997, pp. 571–576). This led them to publish a series of interdisciplinary studies of the authoritarian personality and anti-Semitism, which integrated philosophy, economics, history, sociology, and psychoanalysis (Adorno et al. 1950, Leuschen-Seppel 1987). Horkheimer's and Adorno's theories, however, have been criticized by many serious scholars (Altmeyer 1981, 1996; Schott 1992).

THE INABILITY TO MOURN

The psychoanalyst Rudolph Loewenstein believed that just as the early Christians had rebelled against the "Pharisaic" Jews 2,000 years ago, in the modern Christian unconscious, the Jews were still the stern father against whom they, as the sons, had to rebel against (Loewenstein 1951). Unfortunately, Loewenstein had confused individual psychology with collective psychology. One of his most fascinating psychological points, however, was that the Jews *as a group* had been in a "permanent state of mourning" since the destruction of their Second Temple by the Romans in the year 70 of the Christian Era (Loewenstein 1951, pp. 160–161). Like Freud, Loewenstein believed in the existence of many "unpleasant Jewish character traits" that upset and antagonized non-Jews, and that he laid down to the derision and persecution of the Jews by the Christians, which produced a tragic vicious circle, the Jews internalizing the evil self-image assigned to them and acting it out unconsciously (Gilman 1986). I have amplified this crucial point (Falk 1996, p. 327).

The German psychoanalysts Alexander and Margarete Mitscherlich thought that the collective inability to mourn one's losses was a key factor in human conflict, war, racism, anti-Semitism, persecution, and genocide (Mitscherlich & Mitscherlich 1967, 1975). The Mitscherliches were pessimistic about human nature and about the future of our species. Because the human species, through its families, clans, tribes, and nations, had produced not only great civilizations but also great horrors like organized warfare, suicide, murder, mental illness, mass murder, and genocide, they wondered whether humankind was not the result of one of the most monumental errors in evolution, through which the life principle seeks its own destruction. The reviews of their book ranged from great praise to outright denunciation. They became famous among thinkers but shunned by politicians.

INDIVIDUAL AND COLLECTIVE ANTI-SEMITISM

Ever since the French social psychologist Gustave Le Bon (1841–1931) published his *Psychologie des foules* (Le Bon 1895), we have known that group psychology is *not* individual psychology writ large, that the psychology of the group is different from that of the individual and has its own processes and dynamics. Anti-Semitism has both individual and collective aspects. The psychology of the individual anti-Semite is not the same as that of an anti-Semitic political party or nation. The collective psychology of large human groups, especially nations, preoccupied Freud in 1921, and he cited Le Bon's work (Freud 1921, 1955). Group psychology became the focus of several psychoanalytic studies after Freud's death. In Britain, Wilfred Ruprecht Bion, Siegmund Heinz Foulkes (a German Jew born Fuchs who fled Hitler's Germany to England), John Rickman, and Henry Ezriel studied the psychodynamics of "small" human groups (Ezriel 1950, 1956; Foulkes & Anthony 1957; Rickman 1957; Bion 1961). A few decades later, these studies culminated in the seminal work of the Turkish-Cypriot-born American psychoanalyst Vamık D. Volkan on the psychodynamics of large groups and nations (Volkan 1988, 1997, 2004).

In France, where the government's policies toward the Jewish refugees from Germany and elsewhere became increasingly anti-Semitic from 1933 to 1942 (Caron 1999), which was occupied by the German Nazis from 1940 to 1944 (Burrin 1995, 1996, 2004), whose Vichy government actively collaborated with its German Nazi occupiers in persecuting, rounding up, and murdering the Jews (Marrus & Paxton 1981), and where Georges Mauco (1899–1988) had been the only psychoanalyst who collaborated with the occupying Germans and with the Vichy government (Roudinesco 1995), the Hungarian-born French Jewish psychoanalyst Béla Grunberger (1903–2005) studied individual and group anti-Semitism (Grunberger 1964, 1993; Grunberger & Dessuant 1997; Dessuant 1999), and his colleagues Didier Anzieu and Jacques-Yves Martin studied the psychodynamics of "limited" groups (Anzieu & Martin 1968), while their colleague Jean-Paul Valabrega studied the unconscious meaning of collective myths and fantasies (Valabrega 1980, 2001).

In Germany, which had perpetrated the Holocaust on the Jews (and brought a terrible catastrophe on itself), the sociologist Gunnar Heinsohn studied the interplay of individual and collective psychology in anti-Semitism (Heinsohn 1988). As two well-known German psychoanalysts have shown, the collective *inability to mourn* leads to the group's living in the past, closing itself off from one's present catastrophe, and denying one's losses and humiliations (Mitscherlich & Mitscherlich 1967, 1975). This was also true of the Jews, who could not mourn their historical catastrophes and avoided writing their own history from the first to the sixteenth century (Loewenstein 1951, pp. 160–161; Patai 1976; Yerushalmi 1982b; Falk 1996). The American historian David Olster has shown that this was also true of medieval Byzantine Christians:

> Seventh-century [Christian] literature reveals the Christian preoccupation with the collapse of the imperial world-order in the wake of the Arab, Persian, and Slav invasions. But their preoccupation with defeat did not find primary expression through the historical genres. Classical biography disappears entirely. Theophylact Simocatta is not only the sole extant historian from the seventh century, but the sole known historian, and he chose to narrate the victories that closed the sixth century, not the defeats that opened the seventh. From the Paschal Chronicle at the end of the 620s to Theophanes' Chronicle at the beginning of the ninth century, there is no extant chronicle, and Theophanes' narrative poverty testifies to the Christians' reluctance to face defeat. Christians may have been preoccupied with defeat, but they had no interest in recording it. They had far less interest in what had happened than in how the past would be restored. (Olster 1994, p. 180)

Olster understood that the Europeans Christians had "escaped into the glories of the past" to avoid the pain of their humiliations:

A sudden rejection of classical rhetoric and genres does not explain the disappearance of historical writing from Byzantium. The explanation lies in the Christian Roman rejection of history itself. *Acutely aware of the disaster around them, they sought refuge in the glories of their past and the hope of their return.* Seventh-century disasters firmly fixed the return of the imperial world-order in the Christian Roman psyche, and there it remained until the empire's end. The need to redefine the chaos around them inspired an apologetic of restoration, and they chose literary vehicles with this purpose in mind. This reordering of Christian Roman historical priorities explains the prominence of previously unexploited genres. Apocalyptic was the history of the imperial restoration to come; martyrology achieved the fusion of imperial with Christian victory. And throughout all seventh-century Christian Roman literature, the Christian Romans' sins explained defeat without sacrificing God's love or limiting God's power: a necessary apologetic for Christianity itself. Christians did not turn to such literary themes and genres simply for solace, but for self-justification and future hope. (Olster 1994, p. 180, italics added)

Like Loewenstein and the Mitscherliches, Olster understood that a major psychological reason for the medieval Christian persecution of the Jews was the collective Christian inability to mourn their losses and to come to terms with their defeats. (Olster 1994, pp. 20–21, 83). The hurt self-image was too painful, and its unacceptable aspects were unconsciously projected on the Jews. The persecution and massacres of the Jews relieved the collective Christian emotional pain.

THE INDIVIDUAL, THE FAMILY, AND ANTI-SEMITISM

The British psychoanalyst Donald Woods Winnicott (1896–1971) coined the term "transitional object" for security blankets, teddy bears, and other physical objects used by infants, toddlers, and children to reduce their anxiety as they separate and individuate from their mothers (Winnicott 1971). The German scholar Eberhard Groener applied Winnicott's theories of *individual* psychology to the study of *collective* anti-Semitism (Groener 1994). Extrapolating without adequate justification from individual to collective psychology, Groener speculated that Jesus Christ unconsciously served the Christians as a transitional object, especially during periods of insecurity. The Christians' profound and intense need for this object was one of the causes of their hostility to the Jews, who negated Christ. Like numerous other scholars, however, Groener did not sufficiently distinguish between individual and collective psychological processes.

Some scholars have applied the psychoanalytic approach to dysfunctional families in order to analyze the tragic historical relationship between Christians and Jews. The British family therapist John Launer thought that, as happens in psychologically unhealthy families, the relations of Christianity and Judaism have been characterized by abuse and victimization (Launer 1992). Launer believed that the historical confrontation between Judaism and Christianity was that of two mutually disqualifying beliefs. Both religions demonstrated a mutual process of unconscious projection in their negative stereotyping of each other. The Christian reaction to the challenge of Judaism has often been terror and rage, as seen in the cases of Martin Luther and Adolf Hitler (the latter in a secularized form). Launer thought that the Jewish resistance to seeing Judaism in a continuing dynamic relationship with Christianity also contributed to the perpetuation of this pathological relationship. He suggested ways of resolving the conflict, such as recognizing that both religions were equally legitimate offspring of ancient Judaism, or that there exists a Christian-Jewish symbiosis. Launer's ideas closely resemble those of Howard F. Stein 15 years earlier (Stein 1977). One of the problems with this approach, however, is the assignment of individual or family psychodynamics to large groups like Jewry and Christendom, whose collective psychology is different and special (Volkan 2004).

The Berlin-based journalist, diplomat, and political analyst Paul Hockenos pointed out that after the end of the cold war and the collapse of the Soviet empire "antisemitism is alive and flourishing throughout Eastern Europe, even in the virtual absence of Jews" (Hockenos 1993, p. 272). Hockenos thought that because the nationalist regimes in these formerly communist countries feel guilty for the evils of communism and for what their peoples had done to their Jews during the Holocaust, they "reverse the guilt" and blame the Jews for their people's sufferings (ibid., p. 288).

The American Jewish psychoanthropologist Howard F. Stein linked the resurgent anti-Semitism in the formerly communist Soviet-bloc countries of Eastern Europe to the newly liberated nations' need for boundaries, self-definition, and national identity (Stein 1994). Building on Vamık Volkan's work on the large group's unconscious need for enemies (Volkan 1988), Stein presented a psychoanalytic explanation for the explosion of ethnic hatred, and especially anti-Semitism, in postcommunist Eastern Europe. He thought that the decades of suppression of ethnic identity by the former communist rulers generated an intense quest for identity, which required an image of an ethnic enemy who would serve as a reservoir for all the negated and externalized aspects of the ethnic group. In many instances, the Jews were designated as that enemy, even in countries where there were virtually no more Jews, like Poland. Stein showed how the Jews were unconsciously used as the enemy necessary for self-definition because "Jews remain the final reminder of ambiguity and uncertainty of all human boundaries, between self and other, between good and evil, between clean and unclean, between male and female, between all human distinctions" (Stein 1994, p. 44). Stein also showed that Jew-haters like Vladimir Zhirinovsky in Russia and Louis Farrakhan in the United States harbor deep *ambivalence* toward Jews, which is "played out via personal conversions and a splitting of loving and hating selves into different contexts" (ibid., p. 46). Two years later, the American Jewish political psychiatrist Jerrold Post repeated Stein's ideas (Post 1996).

In 2004, the French Jewish journal *Pardès: Etudes et culture juive* devoted a whole issue to psychoanalytic studies of contemporary anti-Semitism. In the first article, the Lacanian analyst Guy Sapriel pointed out the striking similarities between the anti-Semites' fantasies about their father and their imaginary views of the Jew. In Sapriel's view, everyone was—at least unconsciously—anti-Semitic by virtue of his or her fantasies about their primal father (Sapriel 2004, p. 16). He believed that anti-Semitism was "a permanent, universal phenomenon, linked to the trace of the forgotten memory of the origins of humanity" (ibid., p. 19, my translation). Nevertheless, Sapriel found the continued existence of the Jewish people after the Holocaust a great riddle (ibid., p. 20).

Modern Arabs refer to the Israeli Jews as the "Zionists" and to Israel itself as "occupied Palestine." The French Jewish psychiatrist Georges Gachnochi, who spent a few years in Israel in the 1970s, studied the transition of European anti-Semitism from right-wing fascism to "Islamic leftism." According to Gachnochi, anti-Semitic European Catholics identify what they call the "Zionists" (rather than the Israeli Jews that they really are) with the ancient Jews who "crucified" Jesus Christ, and the Palestinian Arabs with the suffering Jesus Christ, whom the Jews had "sacrificed" on the cross. They accept unquestioningly the Israeli guilt for the tragic death on Saturday, September 30, 2000 of the 11-year-old Palestinian Arab boy Muhammad al-Dura, even though there is great controversy about who shot him, and even after the German TV channel ARD screened a documentary in 2002 by the German Jewish producer Esther Schapira disproving this allegation (Schapira 2002; Lord 2002; Gachnochi 2004, p. 23; Rabonwitz & Abu-Baker 2005, p. 102). Gachnochi found totally irrational the Islamic accusations against the Israeli Jews, in their version of history. Yasser Arafat publicly claimed that there had never been a Jewish temple on Jerusalem's Mount Moriah without discrediting himself with the European public. The European Left was indifferent to history, permeable to anachronisms, and open to dangerous "revisionism" and Holocaust denial (Gachnochi 2004, p. 24). Gachnochi attributed the current resurgence of anti-Semitism in Europe to a "repetition compulsion" with two aspects: the repetition of the same unconscious defenses of projection and scapegoating against the same individual and collective conflicts, and the compulsive repetition of the collective trauma of the Holocaust through attraction to suicide-bombings and mass death (ibid., pp. 31–32).

Jean-Pierre Winter, another French Jewish psychoanalyst, considered anti-Semitism a perversion rather than a phobia or a paranoia (Winter 2004, pp. 35–36). He pointed out that those who fabricated the "proof" of the accusation of treason against the French Jewish officer Alfred Dreyfus in the notorious Dreyfus Affair (1894–1906) knew very well that their evidence was false. If they really believed in a Jewish conspiracy to take over the world, then they were psychotically delusional (ibid., p. 36). Winter found the Muslim anti-Jews' use of epithets like "Judeo-Nazi" for the Israelis, and their own sadomasochistic identification with the Jewish victims of the German Nazis, no less perverse and chilling than the German Nazis' Orwellian use of the words "national social-ism" to describe their own racist and murderous ideology (ibid., pp. 37–38). Winter's colleague Janine Chasseguet-Smirgel also felt that accusing the Jewish survivors of the Holocaust of "lack of repentance" toward "the people who had to pay the price of blood or exile to permit Israel to exist" (the Palestinian Arabs) was "a pure example of perverse thinking" (Chasseguet-Smirgel 2004, p. 57).

Winter recalled Freud's theories about the murder of the father, Moses, by the ancient Jews, and the killing of the son, Jesus, by the early Christians. In Islam, neither murder had occurred. Allah was one of the ancient Arab gods whom Muhammad made into the one and only god of Islam. For the sons, the dead father was even more powerful, psychologically, than the live one. His will con-tinued to dominate his sons, whose superego—the internalized father—forbade them all manner of joys and enjoyments, and the Promise (of the Land of Israel to Abraham) was the will of the dead father (Winter 2004, p. 39). Freud believed that when a little boy sees that his mother had no penis, he thought that she had been castrated, and was filled with panic lest he himself lose his penis. The same panic, Freud thought, took hold of the adult when he heard the cry "the throne and the altar are in danger." We are all imperfect and incomplete. Anti-Jews refuse to accept this fact while at the same time knowing that they are far from perfect (Winter 2004, pp. 40–41).

Olivier Nicolle, another French Jewish psychoanalyst, called the modern dis-course of anti-Semitism a "collective psychic formation" that unconsciously defends anti-Semitic groups against the anxiety of their inner conflicts. Nicolle thought that the current wave of European anti-Semitism was accentuated by collective events of national, international, and even worldwide dimensions, through which it found both forms of expression and a shoring of its dynamics to a clearly-visible object (Nicolle 2004, p. 44). He saw contemporary anti-Semitic slogans as the product of unconscious condensations and displacements of collective fantasy scenes. They range from the most eloquent (the anti-Jewish speech of the former Malaysian premier Mahathir Mohammed in 2003) to the most laconic and schematic (an equation sign between the Star of David and the Nazi swastika), the most inciting ("one Jew—one bullet") and the most allusive ("No to *communautarisme*"), a French code word that alludes to the Jews' "crime" of organizing themselves into communities and betraying their pact with the French Republic. Once proffered and proclaimed, such slogans as "Bush = Sharon = murderer" acquire legitimacy as "public opinion" (ibid., p. 45).

Referring to the French political left, Nicolle thought that the collective anti-Semitic fantasy of all the world's Jews being one huge collective entity, which is responsible for the "American-Zionist war" on Iraq or Afghanistan, helps the anti-Semites imagine themselves as the champions of pacifism, multilateralism, and solidarity with all victims in the world and "the Jews" as traitors who prevent the continued existence of two idealized state collectives—the national French republic and the supranational European Union. During past European crises, the Jews were accused of being a fifth column, the Jewish officer Dreyfus was the traitor, the converted Jews of Spain after the *reconquista* were suspected of cheating, tortured, and persecuted, Christian paschal liturgy called them "the perfidious Jews," and the Christian were sure that the Jews had poisoned their wells (Nicolle 2004, p. 46).

Nicolle found a "projective correspondence" between the distorted representation of the Jews proffered by anti-Semites during first years of the twenty-first century and the effects of those who were its aim: accused of betrayal by the anti-Semites, many French Jews themselves felt abandoned, neglected, even betrayed, by the social and political institutions of France. The creation of the European Union threatens the certainty of the French people about their future. The more the French are apprehensive about their future, the more they idealize their "one and indivisible" republic and denigrate the Jews (Nicolle 2004, p. 47). It should be noted that psychogeographic and psychopolitical entities such as our country, our nation, and our motherland easily lend themselves to the unconscious displacement of our early infantile feelings about our parents—especially our mother (Falk 2004, pp. 99–100, 132–133). Nicolle thought that anti-Jewish accusations of treason conceal deep unconscious jealousy (Nicolle 2004, pp. 48–49).

The French philosopher Jean-Claude Milner has accused democratic Europe of having "criminal tendencies" and of even now seeking to eliminate its Jews (Milner 2003, p. 128). The French Jewish political scientist Alexandre Adler thought that some Jews now "convert" to anti-Zionism as their ancestors converted to Christianity (Adler 2003). Citing them, the French psychoanalyst Janine Chasseguet-Smirgel thought that while anti-Semitism was a highly overdetermined phenomenon, having political, historical, economic, social, cultural, religious, *and* psychological causes, the "new" European anti-Semitism continued the old one in subtle ways. Just before the recent U.S. war on Iraq, for example, fearing chemical-weapons attacks from Iraq, Israel asked Finland to supply it with a sophisticated gas-defense system, only to be told that the European Union forbade arms sales to Israel. No one seemed to remember that millions of European Jews had been gassed to death by the German Nazis (Chasseguet-Smirgel 2004, p. 51).

Like other psychoanalysts, Chasseguet-Smirgel thought that the medieval Christian ritual-murder libel against the Jews was an unconscious projection of Christian guilt feelings for "absorbing" the flesh and blood of Jesus Christ. This blood libel was still very much alive in 1903 Russia and is widely believed in the Arab and Muslim countries of the Middle East (Chasseguet-Smirgel 2004, p. 53). Like her colleague Georges Gachnochi, she pointed out that when, on

September 30, 2000, at the beginning of the Second *Intifada* of the Palestinian Arabs against the Israeli Jews, the boy Muhammad al-Dura was tragically killed, the Israelis were automatically blamed for his murder, and the Jews once again became child murderers to the Europeans, even after the German TV channel ARD had screened a documentary disproving this allegation. Philippe Karsenty, a French Jewish media-rating expert, has accused the French TV channel France 2 of faking the al-Dura murder. France 2 sued Karsenty, and the case is still making its way through the French judicial system.

In 2002, during the Israeli siege of the Church of the Nativity in Bethlehem, where murderous Palestinian terrorists had taken refuge, the Italian newspaper *Corriere della Serra* published a cartoon showing Jesus in his mother Mary's arms saying "Mom, do you think they will kill me a second time?" A Danish Christian pastor publicly compared the Israeli army's actions to Herod's massacre of the innocents, and the atheist left-wing French newspaper *Libération* published cartoons showing Ariel Sharon about to crucify Yassir Arafat and devouring little children. Such myths and fantasies get their emotional power from the archaic sadomasochistic themes of the victim and the victimizer, the sacrifice and the sacrificer, which were so common in the ancient world (Chasseguet-Smirgel 2004, pp. 53–54), and which, one might add, begin in the early life of the infant and child with his or her parents.

COLLECTIVE PSYCHOLOGICAL PROCESSES

During the 1960s and 1970s, the focus of the psychological explanations of racial, ethnic and religious prejudice—including anti-Semitism—began to shift from the individual to the group. In the 1980s, "one began to appreciate that prejudice was inherent in the very structure of all groups" (Ostow 1995, p. 10, quoting Duckitt 1992). This was a major psychological discovery. Individual psychological processes, such as unconscious projection, are not the same as collective psychological processes, such as the human group's needs for boundaries, cohesion, ideology, identity, leaders, and self. Large human groups, especially, such as nations, display such needs ferociously, and threats to them may lead to murderous group violence, and even to genocide (Volkan 2004).

Indeed, during the 1980s, while most of the writers on the psychoanalysis of anti-Semitism had concentrated on unconscious *individual* processes—mainly projection—others began to focus on *group* psychological processes, especially the dire threat to its ideals, ideology, or religion that the majority group has always perceived from the minority group of the Jews. The American psychoanalyst David Terman reviewed the history of anti-Semitism from the perspective of psychoanalytic theory. He explained both ancient and Christian antisemitism as an unconscious psychological mechanism employed by the majority group which feels that its *collective ideology* is threatened:

The fury which may then be unleashed is proportional to so dire a threat . The narcissistic rage of the group, like that the individual, by definition precludes empathy: the offender appears not as an individual or group with needs, motivations, and goals which arise from quite separate or different concerns, but only as a malevolent force whose sole purpose is to destroy one's most precious asset [the majority group's ideology], so the proper response is the obliteration of the danger. All manner of evil is then perceived in the dissenter [the Jew]. Such a phenomenon has often been explained as the projection by the offended party of its own disavowed evil, but in this framework that would be a *secondary* rather than a primary cause. More pertinently, the malevolence attributed to the dissenter of has to do with the narcissistic injury to the group. (Terman 1984, p. 20)

This explanation seems stunning: did the German Nazis murder six million Jews only because their racist ideology was threatened by the "different" Jews, whom they had totally dehumanized, and whose image they had totally distorted out of all proportion to reality? Or did they perhaps develop their racist ideology in response to some other, inner threat that had nothing to do with the Jews themselves? The Nazis opposed Christianity, too, replacing Jesus Christ with Adolf Hitler as their god. Many Roman Catholics were persecuted and even murdered. Heinrich Himmler built great temples to the old Teutonic gods.

The Israeli Jewish historian Jacob Katz believed that many modern historians have misunderstood anti-Semitism (Katz 1983). They ruled out the Jews themselves as a possible cause of anti-Jewish animosity. Rather, these scholars have felt compelled to explain the ongoing hatred and persecution of Jews exclusively in terms of developments within the anti-Semitic camp or in the larger non-Jewish environment. Katz divided such explanations into sociopolitical, psychological, and ideological. He argued that these explanations were inadequate to explain the complex phenomenon of anti-Semitism, which involved a vicious circle in which the Jews themselves played an unwitting part.

The American Jewish historians Dennis Prager and Joseph Telushkin attempted to answer Katz's questions about the causes of anti-Semitism (Prager & Telushkin 1983). They offered a historical survey of anti-Semitism and disputed the most common explanations for "the oldest hatred." These scholars assumed that, regardless of historical period, geographic location, or ideology, the typical anti-Semitic individual or organization believed that Judaism originated "ethical monotheism," that non-Jews opposed this ethical monotheism, and that this is why the "Gentiles" hate the Jews. This neat and logical explanation, however, not only ignores unconscious emotional motives, but also the fact that many anti-Semites are preoccupied not with ethical monotheism, but rather with a host of the evil intentions and bad qualities that they imagine to be typically Jewish.

Moreover, Judaism has rarely been a proselytizing religion. The rabbinic concept of the universal "moral laws of the sons of Noah" binding upon all human beings has never meant that the Jews had actively urged their non-Jewish neighbors to observe even these laws, let alone all of Judaism. The average non-Jew would not even know what Jewish "ethical monotheism" stood for, yet he could hate the Jews. Finally, Prager and Telushkin offered a tempting prescription for ending anti-Semitism, by promoting Judaism's ethical monotheism even more strongly, which seems to contradict their own thesis. If ethical monotheism is the cause of anti-Semitism, could advocating it more assertively and publicly produce even more hatred of Jews? Rational explanations of anti-Semitism tend to run into self-contradiction because the true causes are irrational and unconcsious.

The American Jewish psychoanthropologist Howard F. Stein thought that Judaism and Christianity had been bound up in a reciprocal system of mutual stigmatization based on a shared unconscious father-son conflict that neither group can acknowledge. Each group unconsciously projects onto the other elements that are repressed in its own religion or tradition. Stein believed that Jews defended themselves against their wish to rebel against the Father (God) by their need, in every generation, to offer themselves or their sons as victims. Both Jesus Christ and the Jewish people can be seen as such sacrificial victims. Christians identify the Jews with the onerous conscience (superego) that they reject, and with the Father who kills the son (or Jesus the Son). This is the unconscious origin of the Christian accusation of deicide against the Jews (Stein 1987, pp. 147–179).

In the 1990s, the Israeli Jewish criminologist Shlomo Giora Shoham, who had adopted the name of his fallen-soldier son as his own middle name, published a study of "the German psychological road from Valhalla to Auschwitz" (Shoham 1995). Copying the ideas of Howard F. Stein (Stein 1977, 1978, 1987, 1994), Shoham attributed anti-Semitism and the Holocaust to the conflict between Germanic and Jewish myths, which determine the opposed social character and ethos of the two groups. He stereotyped the Germanic peoples as aggressive and materialistic, the Jews as self-sacrificing and spiritual. Shoham thought that in northern Europe, Christianity was infused with Germanic characteristics. The Jews were its ideal victims because of their refusal to accept Christianity, their foreignness, and their powerlessness, which encouraged demonization and scapegoating. There was always a "macabre symbiosis" between Germanic aggressiveness and the Jewish propensity to self-sacrifice. The Nazis tried to purify the German national character of Jewish-Christian elements. Their propaganda demonized the Jews and prepared ordinary men to commit mass murder. The Jews, by force of circumstance as well as because of their national character, went "like sheep to the slaughter." In my view, Shoham unfortunately used psychological stereotypes and simplifications.

Like most European anti-Semitism, French anti-Semitism has had a centuries-long history (Mehlman 1983; Kingston 1983; Birnbaum 1988, 1992, 2004). Jews were burned alive in France during the fourteenth-century Black Death plague, when the Christians truly believed that the Jews had poisoned their wells. The notorious Dreyfus Affair (1894–1906), in which a French Jewish military officer was falsely accused of treachery and frenzied Frenchmen cried *Mort aus juifs!* (Death to the Jews!), was only one in a series of violent French anti-Jewish outbreaks (Johnson 1966; Marrus 1980; Wilson 1982; Lindemann 1991; Cahm 1994, 1996; Burns 1998). During the occupation of France by Nazi Germany, from 1940 to 1944, many Frenchmen collaborated with their German Nazi occupiers and with their puppet Vichy government, under the *maréchal* Henri-Philippe Pétain (1856–1951) and his prime minister Pierre Laval (1883–1945). The Vichy government, which was anti-Semitic, enacted anti-Jewish statutes that brought about mass Jewish emigration. Its militias rounded up the Jews of France and transported them to the death camps.

The Allies liberated France from its German occupation in the summer of 1944. An informal and spontaneous "purge" (a euphemism for murder or execution without trial) of collaborators, such as Vichy government officials and supporters, began that summer. Summary executions by French Resistance bands exceeded 10,000 people. Charles de Gaulle's provisional French government, which was formally recognized in October by the U.S., British, and Soviet governments, enjoyed unchallenged authority in liberated France. But France had been stripped of raw materials and food by the Germans, its transportation system was severely disrupted by air bombardment and sabotage, 2.5 million French prisoners of war, conscripted workers, and deportees were still in German camps, and the liquidation of the Vichy government's heritage would cause grave domestic stress (Zuccotti 1993).

Formal trials of Vichy officials and other collaborators followed. Special courts set up to try French citizens accused of collaboration with the German occupiers heard 125,000 cases from 1945 to 1947. Some 50,000 offenders were punished by "national degradation"—the loss of civic rights for years—and almost 40,000 received prison terms. Between 700 and 800 Frenchmen were executed. In the summer of 1945, Pétain and Laval were tried for treason, found guilty, and condemned to death. Laval was executed, while Pétain was spared "due to his advanced age." In fact, he was spared because of his judges' ambivalent feelings for him: Pétain had been a French hero of the First World War (Zuccotti 1993).

Who were the men who enlisted in the Vichy government's militias that persecuted the Jews? The French scholar Luc Capdevila studied "the quest for masculinity" in German-occupied France, analyzing the Frenchmen who enrolled in the Vichy government's militias toward the end of the German occupation (Capdevila 2001). Those groups, created mostly in late 1943 and early 1944, acted as subsidiaries to German troops, treating French civilians and partisans with extreme violence. Those men enrolled as a consequence of their political beliefs, notably strong anticommunism, but some were recruited after the Allies had landed in France on June 6, 1944, known as D-Day. Capdevila believed that the behavior of these men was born of despair and shaped according to other cultural patterns, especially an image of masculinity rooted in the memory of the First World War and based on fascist and Nazi ideologies: a "manhood" based on strength, violence, and the military image. Capdevila used judiciary documents from the time of the "purge," carefully reconstructing the men's personal trajectories and self discourse in order to understand the masculine identity that these sometimes very young men tried to realize through political engagement in the guise of warriors (Capdevila 2001).

While many anti-Semitic Frenchmen collaborated with the Vichy government and the German Nazis, the French *résistance* was also active. Some Frenchmen resisted the German occupation at great risk to their lives, and still others saved Jews from being deported to the Nazi death camps. Some French Jews also resisted actively (Michel 1950; Noguères 1967–1981; Latour 1981; Kedward 1985; Zeitoun 1990; Zuccotti 1993; Muracciole 1993, 1998; Lazare 1996). Why did many French people collaborate with the German Nazi evil, while others resisted it, while still others—notably the future French president François Mitterand (1916–1996)—vacillated from one side to the other? The French Jewish film director Marcel Ophuls made a documentary film in the late 1960s which attempted to view this painful story from many different sides, including that of the Germans (Ophuls 1969, 1972). This film created a great controversy in France and was not screened on French television.

In the 1950s the French Jewish historian Jules Isaac (1877–1963), a founder of the French Jewish-Christian friendship movement, had noted the medieval Christian roots of anti-Semitism, claiming that German Nazism imitated the age-old Christian degradation of the Jews (Isaac 1956). French Jewish psychoanalysts have tried to explain French anti-Semitism. Following Freud, the Hungarian-born French Jewish psychoanalyst Béla Grunberger (1903–2005) at first stressed the unconscious role of the Oedipus complex in anti-Semitism (Grunberger 1964), but, 30 years later, focused on the role of narcissism (Grunberger 1993). Grunberger and his colleague Pierre Dessuant published a psychoanalytic study of anti-Semitism based on Grunberger's theories of narcissism (Grunberger & Dessuant 1997). The authors attributed the historical sources of anti-Semitism in history to Judaism's rejection of Jesus as the Messiah. They believed that the "enigma" of Christian anti-Jewish feeling could be solved by viewing Christianity as a "narcissistic religion." They sought the roots of Christian anti-Semitism in the unconscious wish to avoid the Oedipal conflict, which threatens the collective narcissistic illusion on which Christianity is built. Christianity maintained an endemic anti-Semitic culture, which varied in intensity in response to political, social, and religious upheavals.

The Holocaust was the culmination of 2,000 years of disdain for the Jews in the Christian religion. Grunberger and Dessuant used psychoanalytic theory to illustrate how persons like Hitler were prone to become anti-Semitic, based on the inner duality of their personality. They presented examples of this duality, such as the material vs. spiritual, to explain the belief in the existence of Christ in both human and divine form. This paradox led Christians to view Jews as symbols of evil, unredeemable because of their rejection of Jesus as the Christ and of Christian baptism. Grunberger and Dessuant concluded that "Christian narcissism" is what led to the apocalypse, the Holocaust. In confrontation with reality, which breaks his narcissistic illusion of omnipotence, the anti-Semite "pours out" his narcissistic rage on the Jews, rather than face the pain of his own broken dreams. In Part 6 of their book, they analyzed Nazi anti-Semitism (Grunberger & Dessuant 1997, pp. 349–423). However, these psychoanalysts, like many others before them, confused individual psychological processes with group processes.

Three years later, an Italian scholar attempted to integrate the various theories of anti-Semitism (Calimani 2000). He related the history of prejudice against the Jews and stereotypes of Jews from the ancient period to the present, with particular emphasis on the Christian world. Stereotypes are sometimes the only source of knowledge about the Jewish minority, and among many European Christians, the terms "Jew," "Israeli," "Zionist," and "Semite" are often confused and interchanged. Reviewing the historical, philosophical, and psychoanalytic views of anti-Semitism and, above all, of the anti-Semites themselves, this scholar saw in anti-Semitism a projective interpretation by Christian society of its own evils, branding the Jew as a scapegoat. He believed that the Jewish issue did not really exist and the only relevant issue was that of anti-Semitism itself. But as we have seen, the individual unconscious process of projection is only part of the problem, with the collective issue of the threatened "group self" being no less important.

One of the psychological processes that enabled anti-Semites such as the German Nazis to murder Jews (as well as Gypsies, homosexuals, Slavs, and other "inferior" people) without feeling remorse, shame, guilt, or horror at their own actions was that of *dehumanization* and demonization: the killers had convinced themselves that the people they were killing were not human, that they were demons, monsters, or plague-bearing rats, and that they had to be exterminated in order to save the German nation, which was the Nazis' idealized mother. Already in 1967, the scholar Norman Cohn considered the demonization of the Jews as the main psychological factor which led to the Nazi extermination policy (Cohn 1967). Cohn traced the history of the myth of "a Jewish conspiracy to rule the world" as expressed in the fraudulent *Protocols of the Elders of Zion,* which was published in Russia in 1905 and quickly spread around the world, many people believing in its authenticity (Nilus 1905, 1920; Segel 1934; Bernstein 1935; Cohn 1967; Bach 1973; Taguieff 1992; Conan 1999; Bishop 1999; Eisner 2005). The *Protocols* were widely used in anti-Semitic propaganda, and many people still believe them to be true. Cohn viewed the worldwide spread and acceptance of this forgery as a phenomenon of collective psychopathology. The *Protocols* combined medieval and modern elements, reflecting the complex structure of modern anti-Semitism in its most virulent form. In our own time the *Protocols* are being widely circulated in Arab and Muslim countries and presented as authentic proof of Jewish perfidy and monstrousness (Küntzel 2005, 2007).

While the "old" Christian anti-Semitism was religious, the "new" anti-Semitism of the Nazis in the twentieth century was "racial." The Nazis readily adopted all kinds of fantastic racist theories that conveniently divided humanity into superior and inferior races, with the German "race" at the top and the Jewish "race" at the bottom. The "anti-Semitism" of our own time, that of the twenty-first century, does not seem to care whether the Jews are a religion, a people, a nation, a race, or an ethnic group. Fear and hatred of the Jews in France, for example, is not only the province of the extreme right that hates all "foreigners," but also that of the extreme left, which combines its hatred of "the oppressive rule of the fascist government of Israel over the poor Palestinians" with the fact that Israel is "the Jewish state" into a broad anti-Semitism.

Josef Joffe, the German-Jewish editor of the German weekly *Die Zeit* who was also a visiting scholar at Stanford University, has delineated five "elements" of anti-Semitism: stereotyping, denigration, demonization, obsession and elimination (Joffe 2005, p. 2). Joffe believed that while the "new antisemitism" in Europe has given up the fifth "element," which Joffe called "operational anti-semitism"—the physical elimination of the Jews—"classical antisemitism has migrated from the West to the Islamic world," (ibid., p. 3) where the fear and hatred of Jews, and the wish for their annihilation, has become endemic. Whereas anti-Semitism in Europe became "taboo" after the Holocaust, and some European countries—notably Germany—have laws against it, it is not at all so in the Arab and Muslim world. This does not mean that Christian Europe—which now has a sizable Muslim minority, much larger than its Jewish one—has become free of anti-Semitism. One of the countries with the highest number of anti-Semitic incidents in the world is France—which also has several million Arabs and Muslims among its citizens and residents.

"Psychological" Anti-Semitism

THE CASE OF JOHN JAY RAY

Thanks to three notorious Australian anti-Semites, their country has its special place in modern anti-Semitism: the "historian" Gerald Fredrick Töben, the "socialite" Michele Renouf, and the "psychologist" John Jay Ray (Ben-Moshe 2005). Studying their lives and personalities can give us some idea of what makes an anti-Semite "tick."

The German-born Australian "historian" Fredrick Töben, the founder and director of the "revisionist" Adelaide Institute, is one of the world's most vocal Holocaust deniers. The racist and anti-Semitic Töben has called the Holocaust a lie perpetuated by "the Holocaust Racketeers, the corpse peddlers and the *Shoah* Business Merchants" and asserted that "the current U.S. government is influenced by world Zionist considerations to retain the survival of the European colonial, apartheid, Zionist, racist entity of Israel." While Töben denies being an anti-Semite or a white supremacist, he is a favorite among white supremacist organizations, and his Adelaide Institute Web site has an unusual predilection for ubiquitously locating swastikas, often several per page of research or opinion.

In 1999, Töben was jailed for nine months in Germany for his anti-Semitic activities, but he continued them nonetheless. In 2002, a judge of the Federal Court of Australia found that Töben's Web site "vilified Jewish people" and ordered Töben to remove offensive material from his site. The court did not enforce an order made earlier by a commissioner of the Australian Human Rights and Equal Opportunity Commission that he "issue a written apology to the president of the Executive Council of Australian Jewry." While Töben and his associates at the Adelaide Institute have occasionally denied "being Holocaust deniers" in interviews conducted by Australian mass-communication media, in 2005, in an interview with the Iranian state television, he indicated that it was his belief that "Israel is founded on the Holocaust lie." In 2006 Töben attended the revisionist "International Conference to Review the Global Vision of the Holocaust" in Iran.

Michele Renouf is an Australian-born, British-based socialite, who came to public attention when she sat at the side of the British Holocaust denier David Irving during his failed legal action against the American Jewish historian Deborah Lipstadt in 2000. Renouf is known for her open and virulent anti-Semitism. Born Michele Mainwaring in 1946, the daughter of a truck driver, she became a model, dancer, and beauty contestant, winning the title of Miss Newcastle 1968. She married Daniel Griaznoff, a descendant of the Russian aristocracy, which, she claimed, gave her the noble title of countess. In 1991 she entered into her second marriage, to the tennis legend Sir Frank Renouf, when he was 72 and she was 44. The marriage collapsed after a few months when Sir Frank learned of his wife's humble origins. Michele had told Sir Frank that she was the ex-wife of a Russian nobleman and that her father was dead. In fact, her father was a truck driver named Arthur Mainwaring and very much alive. Sir Frank divorced her and described the union as a "nasty accident."

Michele had not only lied to her husband, but also to herself. She could not accept her own origins, her own identity, her own self. Michele's marriage to Sir Frank allowed her to assume the title of "Lady Renouf." Renouf has become increasingly known for her support of prominent anti-Semites. In 2000, she was a daily presence at David Irving's court case, and in 2005, she attended the trial of the anti-Semitic extremist Ernst Zündel in Germany. She has called Judaism "a repugnant and hateful religion." Her attempts to get David Irving invited to London's Reform Club led to Renouf being expelled from that club in 2003. She attended the "revisionist Holocaust conference" in Iran in 2006. Michele Renouf's inability to accept her real self causes her to unconsciously project her self-hate upon the Jews.

One of the most anti-Semitic Australian "scholars" is the psychologist John Jay Ray. Despite Hitler's far-right racist Nazi views and his ties to the Italian fascist tyrant Benito Mussolini, the Australian psychologist John Jay Ray, who describes himself as a "former member of the Australia-Soviet Friendship Society, former anarcho-capitalist [*sic*] and former member of the British Conservative party," has argued that Hitler and his Nazis were left-wing socialists rather than fascists. The word "Nazi," Ray argued, is short for "National Socialist" and *Hitler's* political party was the *National-Sozialistische deutsche Arbeiter-Partei* or National Socialist German Workers Party (Ray 1972, 1973, 1974, 1984). Ray's linguistic argument is like "the Language of the Third Reich" or George Orwell's "doublespeak" (Klemperer 1947; Orwell 1949), which stood reality on its head. It reminds one of some Jew-hating Palestinian Arabs who argue that they cannot be anti-Semitic because they are themselves "Semites." Hitler's Nazis were without doubt far-right fascists, racists, and anti-Semites. Ray believes that political leftists are "haters hiding behind a mask of compassion," that they are just as anti-Semitic as political rightists, and that Adorno's notion of the authoritarian personality has no validity (Ray & Furnham 1984; Ray & Lovejoy 1986).

In the late 1970s and early 1980s, Ray and his colleagues were exposed as racists and anti-Semites by the prominent British social psychologist Michael Billig, who published an English-language pamphlet and a French-language book about the abuse of psychology in the service of racism and anti-Semitism (Billig 1979, 1981). Four years later, Ray publicly and savagely attacked Billig in a scholarly journal as "wacky" and "dishonest," accusing him of "utter perversion of the truth" (Ray 1985). Billig answered Ray in the same issue of the same journal (Billig 1985). The Billig-Ray battle goes on, with the American Jewish scholar Barry Alan Mehler and his Canadian colleague Andrew Winston taking up Billig's sword (Mehler 1988; Winston 1996, 1998). Mehler founded the Institute for the Study of Academic Racism at Ferris State University.

Ray's racist and anti-Semitic attacks on "leftist anti-Semites" were gratuitous. Naturally, some leftists are anti-Semites. The German psychoanalyst Hans Keilson thought that leftist anti-Semitism came from the identification of "Jewish" and "capitalist" in the minds of leftists, and that the political left is just as beset by nationalism, prejudice, and authoritarian character structures as the political right (Keilson 1988). Many scholars examining the relationship between right-wing politics and racial "research" have drawn on Billig's work (Billig 1978, 1979, 1981). Billig exposed the contribution of psychologists and other academics to the racist and neo-Nazi movements after World War II. Billig's work is not widely available in university libraries, and is not known to every scholar of the history of psychology, eugenics, and neofascism. Moreover, some of the individuals described by Billig remain active and dangerous. For example, the journal *Mankind Quarterly*, the major outlet for racial "research," is still being published under the editorship of the racist "scholar" Roger Pearson. Billig's work is very important for students of contemporary "scientific" racism.

"NOT AN ANTISEMITIC BONE IN MY BODY"

Most psychologists, psychiatrists, and psychoanalysts choose their professions because of their own personal psychological troubles, hoping that the study of the profession will help them overcome their own problems as well as help others deal with theirs. Part of a mental-health professional's training is undergoing personal psychotherapy, but in some cases this therapy does not succeed, and psychological professionals may still suffer from serious emotional problems themselves. Ever since the first psychoanalytic studies of anti-Semites demonstrated their emotional problems, disturbed, racist, and anti-Semitic psychological professionals, unaware of the personal causes of their prejudices, have sought to discredit those studies. They have done so in subtle ways, unconsciously rationalizing, denying, or intellectualizing their own racism and anti-Semitism. Some of them have even tried to prove that anti-Semitism did not exist, that it was "a cognitive simplification," or that there was no connection between authoritarianism, fascism, and anti-Semitism.

John Jay Ray is not the only racist psychologist whose anti-Semitism wears an intellectual guise and is rationalized in scientific language. Another such was the infamous Holocaust denier William David McCalden (1951–1990). In 1972, the young McCalden left his hometown of Belfast for London to study at the University of London's Goldsmiths College, where two years later, he obtained a certificate in educational sociology. He was a member of the nationalist, fascist, and racist National Front and hated Jews, homosexuals, and others who unconsciously reminded him of what he could not stand about himself. After getting into trouble in England, McCalden emigrated to the United States and arrived in California in 1978. Here he met the older American neo-Nazi Willis Allison Carto (born 1926), who, among his pearls, had written, "If Satan himself, with all of his super-human genius and diabolical ingenuity at his command, had tried to create a permanent disintegration and force for the destruction of the nations, he could have done no better than to invent the Jews."

Carto had been publishing many far-right nationalist, racist and anti-Semitic journals, including *Right, Western Destiny, Liberty Letter, Washington Observer, American Mercury,* and *The Spotlight.* Sensing that they had found common ground, these two far-right racists, the older Carto and the younger McCalden, founded the infamous "Institute for Historical Review." Carto became the publisher of the new *Journal for Historical Review,* while McCalden was named the institute's director and the editor-in-chief of its journal under the pseudonym of "Lewis Brandon." Carto has also published the racist *IHR Newsletter,* the *American Free Press,* and *The Barnes Review.* McCalden became a tireless advocate of Holocaust denial and the leading figure within the Institute for Historical Review, which could more appropriately be called the "Institute for Holocaust Denial." However, the relations between the older Carto and the younger McCalden became strained. They unwittingly acted out an Oedipal father-son struggle. In 1981, after a dramatic falling out, McCalden left the Institute for Historical Review and set up his own "Truth Mission."

Under the Truth Mission imprint, McCalden published his own anti-Semitic journals—the *Revisionist Reprints, Holocaust News* and *David McCalden's Revisionist Newsletter.* He also published a rabidly anti-Semitic "psychohistorical study of Jewish self-hate" in which he claimed without the slightest self-awareness that he "did not have an antisemitic bone in my body" (McCalden 1982, p. 3). Over two decades later, the anti-Israeli and anti-Semitic far-left mayor of London, Kenneth Robert Livingstone (born 1945), who was suspended from his office by the Adjudication Panel for England in 2006 for comparing a Jewish journalist to a Nazi concentration-camp guard, made the very same statement. The Board of Deputies of British Jews said it regretted the suspension, but added that Mr. Livingstone had been "the architect of his own misfortune." Similarly, McCalden's rabid anti-Semitism made him many sworn enemies, including first and foremost the American Jewish fanatic Irving David Rubin (1946–2002) and his violent Jewish Defense League (JDL), which had been founded in 1968 by the American rabbi Meir David Kahane (1932–1990). On June 7, 1989, McCalden was badly beaten at a Los Angeles meeting, a beating he blamed on Irv Rubin and his JDL. The following year the 68-year-old Rabbi Kahane was tragically assassinated by the 35-year-old El-Sayyid Nosair, an Egyptian Islamic fanatic involved in the 1993 World Trade Center bombing. In that same year the homosexual McCalden died tragically at the age of 39 in his California home from complications of AIDS.

"EVOLUTIONARY" ANTI-SEMITISM

From Wilhelm Marr's invention of the "scientific" euphemism *Antisemitismus* in 1879, many anti-Semites have convinced themselves that their Jew-hatred and Judeophobia had an objective scientific basis. Another form of pseudoscientific anti-Semitism was displayed by the American evolutionary biologist Kevin MacDonald, who called Judaism "a self-interested group evolutionary strategy for survival" (McDonald 1994, p. 1). In his follow-up study, MacDonald rationalized his own anti-Semitism:

> This book builds upon my previous work, *A People That Shall Dwell Alone: Judaism as a Group Evolutionary Strategy* . . . (hereafter *PTSDA*). While *PTSDA* focused on developing a theory of Judaism within an evolutionary framework, the present volume focuses on the phenomenon of anti-Semitism. Judaism and anti-Semitism fairly cry out for an evolutionary interpretation. Anti-Semitism has been a very robust tendency over a very long period of human history and in a wide range of societies with different forms of government, different economic systems, and different dominant religious ideologies. Many anti-Semitic episodes [*sic!*], such as the Iberian inquisitions and the Nazi holocaust, have been characterized by extraordinary intra-societal violence. Moreover, anti-Semitism has sometimes been characterized by a very overt, self-conscious racialism – a phenomenon that immediately suggests the relevance of evolutionary theory. (MacDonald 1998, p. vii)

Like David McCalden and Ken Livingstone, MacDonald believed that he "did not have an antisemitic bone in his body." He was only interested in scientific truth. At the same time, MacDonald expected his book to would provoke an outcry and charges of anti-Semitism, and he prepared himself for the onslaught:

> Nevertheless, as Leslie White (1966, 3) wrote many years ago in his discussion of the Boasian school of anthropology as a politically inspired cult, "One who follows

procedures such as these incurs the risk of being accused of indulging in non-scholarly, personal attacks upon whom he discusses. Such a charge is, in fact, expectable and completely in keeping with the thesis of this essay. We wish to state that no personal attacks are intended." No personal or ethnic attacks are intended here, either. Nevertheless, the charge that this is an anti-Semitic book is, to use White's phrase, expectable and completely in keeping with the thesis of this essay. (MacDonald 1998, p. viii).

Like other anti-Semitic scholars, MacDonald attacked they very concept of anti-Semitism as too broad in scope, adding that "the segregative cultural practices of Judaism have actually resulted in ethnic similarity being of dispro-portionate importance for Jews in regulating their relations with others" (ibid., p. 2). He observed that "people very easily adopt negative stereotypes about outgroups, and these stereotypes are both slow to change and resistant to coun-tervailing examples. Resistance to change is especially robust if the category is one that is highly important to the positive evaluation of the ingroup or the negative evaluation of the outgroup. In terms of the above example, it would be expected that gentiles would change their categorization of Jews as having dark hair far more easily than they would change their categorization of Jews as usurers or potential traitors, because the former category is evaluatively neutral" (ibid., p. 6).

MacDonald showed his true colors in 2000, when he testified for the British Holocaust denier David John Cawdell Irving in his libel suit against the Ameri-can Jewish Holocaust historian Deborah Lipstadt, who had publicly called Irving a liar. Irving acted as his own lawyer, forgetting the old adage, "he who represents himself has a fool for a client and an idiot for a lawyer." Predictably, Irving lost his suit against Lipstadt and had to pay her damages and costs (Evans 2001, Lipstadt 2005). In 2005, the self-destructive Irving went to Austria, where an arrest warrant had been issued against him for his Holocaust-denial speech in 1989. Predictably again, he was arrested and tried for the crime of Holocaust denial, found guilty, and sentenced in 2006 to three years in prison. In the same year, the fascist Serbian leader Solobodan Milošević, who had caused the deaths of countless innocent people in the former Yugoslavia by "ethnic cleansing," and who had also acted as his own lawyer in his war-crimes trial, was found dead in his prison cell. If you think of Adolf Hitler's suicide and of the horrific destruction that he had wrought upon his own country, let alone the Jews, you can see that anti-Semites are self-destructive as well as dangerous.

In addition to the work of Mehler's Institute for the Study of Academic Racism, scholars have studied the history of racism in academic psychology and academic racism in general (Richards 1997, Tucker 1994), the history of "scientific" racism in Germany (Burleigh & Wipperman 1991; Müller-Hill 1987; Proctor 1988; Weindling 1989), and how "scientific" eugenics developed into fanatical racism (Adams 1990; Allen 1997; Barkan 1992; Chase 1979;

Kevles 1985; Haller 1984; Kühl 1994; Mehler 1988). There are popular texts on "scientific" racism for the general audience and a general, scholarly discussion of race, genetics, and anthropology (Kohn 1994; Shipman 1994; Marks 1995). There have also been additional studies of the racist individuals, groups, and publications studied by Billig (Mehler 1983, 1989, 1997; Mintz 1985; Newby 1969; Tucker 1994; Winston 1996, 1998). Tucker provided the most comprehensive and thorough discussion of these issues. The Institute for the Study of Academic Racism at Ferris State University, led by Barry Mehler, publishes bibliographies and biographical information on Billig's subjects.

In fairness to the individuals involved, the Canadian scholar Andrew Spencer Winston has cautioned that in all materials of this kind, due sensitivity to "guilt by association" must be observed, so that innocent scholars are not accused (Winston 1998). Winston, who edited a book on "psychological racism" (Winston 2004), addressed this issue in his introduction to the Internet edition of Michael Billig's pamphlet:

> Scholars examining the relationship between right-wing politics and racial research have drawn on a 1979 work by social psychologist Michael Billig, *Psychology, Racism, and Fascism*. This short pamphlet, along with Billig's (1978) monograph on the social psychology of the neo-fascist National Front, provided the first account of the contribution of psychologists and other academics to racist and neo-Nazi movements of the 1950s to 1970s. This work is not widely available in university libraries. Given the intense interest in these issues, particularly with the 1990s revival of racial research in psychology, it is important that *Psychology, Racism, and Fascism* be available to students of the history of psychology, as well as scholars concerned with eugenics and neo-fascism. However, these are not simply problems of history; some of the individuals described by Billig remain very active. For example, the journal *Mankind Quarterly*, the major outlet for racial research, is still in publication under the editorship of Roger Pearson. Thus Billig's work is also important for students of contemporary scientific racism. With the permission of Michael Billig and Searchlight, I have prepared this on-line version, which reproduces the original as closely as possible...Detailed bibliographies and biographical information on many individuals discussed in Psychology, Racism, and Fascism are available at the web site of the Institute for the Study of Academic Racism... at Ferris State University, directed by Prof. Barry Mehler. In all materials of this kind, due sensitivity to the issue of "guilt by association" must be observed. (Winston 2005)

Not surprisingly, Winston found that, like other people, psychologists, too, can be bigots, racists, and anti-Semites (Winston 1996, 1998). Racism and anti-Semitism are symptoms of emotional trouble, and psychologists are no more immune to emotional illness than other human beings. We shall examine this issue further below, when we discuss the history of psychoanalysis in Germany during Hitler's time.

JAPANESE ANTI-SEMITISM: JUDEOPHOBIA WITHOUT JEWS

The European countries and the United States are by no means the only places where anti-Semitism and Holocaust denial flourish. Several American Jewish scholars have shown that it is not necessary to know any Jews in order to have anti-Jewish fantasies and become a zealous anti-Semite. In Japan, for example, where a handful of Jews live among hundred of millions of Japanese, most people have never seen a Jew, nor do they know anything about the Jews and their history. They have little or no firsthand experience in relating to Jewish people and culture. Nonetheless, Japanese anti-Semitism and Holocaust denial have not only existed, but have also flourished (Rosenman 1977, 1998a, 1998b, 2000; Haberman 1987; Goodman 1987; Shudrich 1987; Golub 1994; Goodman & Miyazawa 1995; Kowner 1997a, 1997b, 2001, 2006).

Japanese Holocaust denial first surfaced in 1989 and reached its peak in 1995, when the Japanese physician Masanori Nishioka published a "historical" article on the Holocaust in a popular Japanese magazine, *Marco Polo,* denying the existence of the Nazi gas chambers (Nishioka 1995; Takahama 1995; Tugend 1995; Anonymous 1995, 1997; Jacobs 1997). *Marco Polo's* editor, Kazuyoshi Hanada, prefaced the article with his own inflammatory denial of the Holocaust:

> On January 27, the Auschwitz concentration camp will observe the 50th anniversary of its "liberation." However, here the greatest taboo of postwar history is being kept a secret...There can be no mistake that Jews died tragically. However, there is scant evidence that they were systematically killed in gas chambers. After the war's end, it was proved that no gas chambers existed in any of the concentration camps situated in the West...Actually, these type of suspicions have been subjected to the scrutiny of journalism in Europe and the U.S....Why is it that [it is] only Japan's mass media that does [*sic*] not write anything on this subject? Here is the new historic truth that a young doctor has taken it upon himself to investigate as an individual. (Hanada 1995)

Nishioka's article was applauded by the Holocaust deniers in Europe and America, but provoked an international storm of protest by prominent Jews, Israelis, Japanese, historians, and politicians, including the Simon Wiesenthal Center, which monitors and fights anti-Semitism and Holocaust denial. This quickly led to a boycott of *Marco Polo* by its advertisers. On January 30, 1995, Kengo Tanaka, the president of the magazine's corporate owner, Bungei Shunju, announced the he would shut down *Marco Polo* and undertook to desist from further anti-Semitic activities (Tugend 1995; Takahama 1995; Goodman & Miyazawa 1995).

This has by no means eradicated Japanese anti-Semitism and Holocaust denial (Jacobs 1997; Anonymous 1997, 1998). In 2005, Rabbi Abraham Cooper, the associate dean of the Simon Wiesenthal Center, urged the Tokyo-based Lawson's chain of bookstores to remove from their shelves copies of a new Japanese book entitled *Yudaya No Seikousha Ga Oshieru Ookanemochi Ni Naru Hito No Houteishiki* (A Successful Jew Teaches the Method for Becoming Fabulously Rich), which was seen by the Japanese Jewish community as an anti-Semitic fraud. Cooper wrote Lawson's CEO, Takeshi Niinami, "The publisher, Nihon Bungeisha, has in the past years issued, and continues to issue, numerous titles that are highly offensive and defamatory to the Jewish people. This current work fosters a stereotyped image of Jews to many young Japanese. We urge your company to review the contents of this work and to permanently remove it from the shelves of all Lawson outlets." The Wiesenthal Center also protested to Bungei Shunju, the former publisher of the now-defunct *Marco Polo,* for running an advertisement for the book in the current issue of *Shukan Bunshun* magazine. "The acceptance of such an ad by Bungei Shunju is a violation of the commitment this company made to the Simon Wiesenthal Center in 1995 to desist from publishing or promoting any antisemitic material," Cooper said. Needless to say, this protest has not ended Japanese antisemitism. The unconscious mind, whether on the individual or collective level, is more powerful than any rational argument. When one needs a scapegoat on whom to project or externalize one's own unacceptable qualities, a group one does not know may serve even better than a group one does.

"Psychoanalytic" Anti-Semitism

It is both ironic and tragic that some prominent psychoanalysts, rather than look into the unconscious causes of anti-Semitism, are themselves anti-Semitic. Many psychologists, psychiatrists, and psychoanalysts have emotional problems themselves, and this, in fact, is what makes them choose their profession. The French call this *Tous les cordonniers sont mal chaussés* (all shoemakers are badly shod). The radical left-wing American Jewish psychiatrist and psychoanalyst Joel Kovel has advocated the abolition of Zionism and the creation of a binational Arab-Jewish state in what are now Israel and the Palestinian Authority (Kovel 2007). For demographic reasons, such a state would almost certainly have an Arab majority, reducing the Israeli Jews to minority status in their own country. Kovel, however, is not the only advocate of this idea: the Israel Jewish historians Meron Benvenisti and Ilan Pappé share his views (Benvenisti 1995, Pappé 1999, 2005), as do many Arabs.

Are anti-Zionism and the wish to replace the Jewish state with a binational one symptoms of anti-Semitism? The answer depends on the individual case. Let us examine a few cases of anti-Semitic psychoanalysts and the personal causes of their anti-Semitism.

THE CASE OF CARL GUSTAV JUNG

The Swiss psychiatrist and psychoanalyst Carl Gustav Jung (1875–1961) claimed to have "saved psychoanalysis from the Nazis" (Serrano Fernández 1966). In fact, during the 1930s and early 1940s, Jung was an anti-Semitic Nazi collaborator. In his case, too, his hatred of the Jews may have been unconsciously displaced from his rage and disappointment with his father during his early life. Jung's father was a mentally ill Lutheran pastor. Carl's childhood was lonely, and he escaped his reality by developing vivid fantasies. From an early age, he observed the behavior of his parents and teachers, whose conflicts he wished to understand and resolve. Concerned with his father's failing belief in religion, Jung tried to communicate to his father his own experience of God. Though the father could be kind and tolerant, he and his son never understood each other. Jung's father had occasional psychotic breakdowns. Carl was deeply disappointed in his father and enraged at him. He later acted out his conflict with his father in his relationship with Sigmund Freud, which led to a bitter falling-out in 1913 (Rieff 1964; Maidenbaum & Martin 1991; Bengesser & Sokoloff 1992; Samuels 1993, 1994, 1996; Roudinesco 1998; Erlenmeyer 2001; Maidenbaum 2002).

In his youth, Carl Jung seemed destined to become a Lutheran minister, for there were a number of clergymen on both sides of his family. In his teens, he discovered philosophy and read widely, and this, together with the disappointment with his father, led him to forsake the family tradition, to study medicine and become a psychiatrist. As a young physician, Jung studied with the eminent Swiss psychiatrist Eugen Bleuler at the Burghölzli psychiatric hospital and clinic in Zurich (Loewenberg 1995a). Jung became a follower of Sigmund Freud, who treated Jung like a son and thought of making him his successor, but in 1909, Jung was forced to leave the Burghölzli and broke with his "father" Freud after having had an unethical love affair with his female patient Sabina Spielrein (1886–1941). While the Italian scholar Aldo Carotenuto denied the sexual nature of Carl's relations with Sabina, the American scholar Peter Loewenberg saw it very clearly (Carotenuto 1982; Loewenberg 1995a, pp. 71–76). Jung then founded his own "Jungian" school of psychoanalysis, thus declaring his independence of both Freud and Bleuler. His breaks with Bleuler in 1909 and with Freud in 1913 were an acting out of his disappointment and rage at his father. After his break with Freud, Jung went through a prolonged depression.

To replace Freud's concept of the "unconscious," Jung had coined the term "shadow." The Jungian "shadow" is the diametrical opposite of the conscious self, everything that it does not wish to acknowledge about itself. A person who sees himself as kind has a shadow that is unkind. Conversely, an individual who is brutal has a kind shadow. The shadow of persons who are convinced that they are ugly appears to be beautiful. The Jungian "shadow" is neither good nor bad. It is meant to counterbalance our one-sided "character traits." Jung emphasized the importance of being aware of one's shadow and incorporating it into one's conscious awareness, to avoid unconsciously projecting these attributes onto others. The shadow in dreams is often represented by dark figures of the same gender as the dreamer, such as gangsters, prostitutes, beggars, or liars.

Jung believed in the existence of "psychic archetypes" and a "collective unconscious" in each ethnic and religious group. During the Nazi era in Germany (1933–1945), Jung gladly collaborated with Hitler's Nazis, believing, like them, that the Germans were the superior race. In 1934, he published an article that included the following astounding statement: "The Aryan unconscious has a greater potential than the Jewish unconscious...In my opinion, current psychology has made an error by applying categories, not even applicable to all Jews, to German Christians as well as to slaves...Medical psychology has claimed that the greatest secret of the Germans, the creative and fantastic depths of their soul, is only an infantile and banal swamp. I have spoken out against this, and have been suspected as an antisemite. The source of this suspicion is Sigmund Freud. He knows nothing of the German soul, nor do his followers" (Jung 1934, 1970). Jung's terrible rage at his father and at himself had been transferred not only to Freud, but also to all Jews.

Jung's anti-Semitic article of 1934 was only a beginning. Though psychoanalysis was dominated by Jewish practitioners, and Jung had many Jewish friends and colleagues, Jung edited the anti-Semitic *Zentralblatt fur Psychotherapie,* a publication that endorsed Hitler's *Mein Kampf* as required reading for all psychoanalysts. Jung later claimed that he had done so in order to save psychoanalysis from the Nazis: psychoanalysis would not otherwise have survived, because the Nazis considered it to be a "Jewish science." He also claimed that he did it with the help and support of his Jewish friends and colleagues. Jung also served as the president of the Nazi-dominated International General Medical Society for Psychotherapy and worked at the Nazi-created Göring Institute of Psychotherapy (Cocks 1985, Rickels 2002).

While there, Jung published several articles that expanded his 1934 claim about the superiority of the "Aryan race" over the "Jewish race," stating that the Aryan race had a more "creative unconscious" than the Jewish race. Jung also published an anti-Semitic commentary that read as follows: "The Jew, who is something of a nomad, has never yet created a cultural form of his own and as far as we can see never will, since all his instincts and talents require a more or less civilized nation to act as host for their development...In my opinion, it has been a grave error in medical psychology up to now to apply Jewish categories...to German and Slavic Christendom" (Cocks 1985, Elshtain 2004). From 1934 to 1943, Jung actively collaborated with Hitler's Nazi regime. In 1941, his former patient and lover Sabina Spielrein was murdered in a Nazi death camp. Later in the war, however, when Germany's fortunes began to decline, the turncoat Jung defected to the United States, resigned from the German-dominated International General Medical Society for Psychotherapy, and joined the Allied cause. In 1943, he helped the U.S. Office of Strategic Services by "psychoanalyzing" Nazi leaders for them. Nonetheless, in 1946, an American Jewish Holocaust survivor named Maurice Léon sent a formal lawsuit against Jung to the "British War Crimes Executive" at Nuremberg, which, however, was never acted upon (Léon 1946).

Jung's mid-war reversal from Nazi anti-Semitism to anti-Nazi activity and his claims of having "saved psychoanalysis" from the Nazis and of not having really believed in Nazism are a topic of ferocious debate among scholars (Rieff 1964; Slochower 1981; Maidenbaum & Martin 1991; Bengesser & Sokoloff 1992; Samuels 1993, 1994, 1996; Roudinesco 1998; Erlenmeyer 2001; Maidenbaum 2002). Some scholars have argued that Jung's reversal did not exonerate him from his complicity in the "Nazification" of psychoanalysis. While many of Jung's followers deny his sympathies for Nazism, Jung himself admitted them in a 1946 interview with Leo Baeck (1873–1956), a former leader of German Jewry who had survived the Nazi concentration camp at Theresienstadt (Terezin).

After the war, Jung tried to defend his views and to shift the blame for his "errors" onto the Germans and their collective psychopathology, but he also admitted that he had "been mistaken." Jung gave a series of interviews to his Chilean friend Miguel Joaquín Diego del Carmen Serrano Fernández (born 1917), the self-styled "esoteric Hitlerist" (Serrano 1966; Noll 1994, 1997). Nevertheless, even in the last years before his death in 1961, Jung never really distanced himself from his earlier thinking and from its parallels with Nazi propaganda. In the 1990s, two Austrian Jungian psychoanalysts thought that Jung's concept of the "collective unconscious" explained "the transgenerational transmission of antisemitism" (Bengesser & Sokoloff 1992, 1993). The American Jewish psychoanalyst Mortimer Ostow disagreed, pointing out the difference between murderous Christian antisemitism and "non-murderous" Islamic anti-Semitism, which "does not distinguish between Jews and other infidels" (Ostow 1993). Unfortunately, as we know by now, Islamic anti-Semitism has also become murderous. Other Austrian psychoanalysts, however, have had more sophisticated and complex explanations for the intergenerational "transmission" of anti-Semitic feelings and fantasies (Brainin et al. 1993).

THE CASE OF MASUD KHAN

Some psychoanalysts have been openly anti-Semitic. One of them was the well-known and charismatic Pakistani-British psychoanalyst Masud Khan (1924–1989), whose full name was Mohammed Masud Raza Khan, and who signed his publications "M. Masud R. Khan." Born to a wealthy landowner in British India, Khan came to England as young man falsely claiming to be an Indian prince. He had a gold nameplate affixed to his door that read, "His Royal Highness Masud Khan" (Boynton 2002; Willoughby 2005; Hopkins 2006). For 15 years, Khan was a patient of the psychoanalyst Donald Woods Winnicott (1896–1971), the pediatrician who founded child psychiatry without being a psychiatrist. Unfortunately, in violation of the basic rules of psychoanalysis, Winnicott also made Khan his secretary, pupil, and editor (Hopkins 1998, 2006; Boynton 2002; Rodman 2003). Naturally, the "psychoanalysis" of Khan by Winnicott was a total failure.

In 1947, with the bloody partition of India, the 23-year-old Khan became a Pakistani. "Tall, darkly handsome, and impeccably tailored (Savile Row with a dash of the Raj)" (Boynton 2002), he became notorious for his flamboyant personality and lifestyle, at first, widely acknowledged as a brilliant clinician. He was close to some of the best-known people of his time, including his former analyst (and employer) Winnicott, his colleagues Anna Freud and Robert Stoller, and the celebrities Francois Truffaut, Princess Margaret, Michael Redgrave, Julie Andrews, Rudolph Nureyev, Julie Christie, Peter O'Toole, and Mike Nichols. A prolific writer, Khan authored many books, including, not accidentally, a psychoanalytic study of evil (Khan 1983).

Tragically for himself, however, the self-destructive and sadomasochistic Khan not only hated Jews, he also abused his patients and, after Winnicott's death, violated almost every code of his professional ethics (Godley 2001; Boynton 2002; Willoughby 2005; Hopkins 2006). This may have been in part Masud's reaction to the loss of his beloved father figure Winnicott, whom he could not mourn. "Khan's behavior was always eccentric, but his descent into madness only began when his mother and Winnicott died within a few months of one another in 1971. The final blow came when Winnicott's will was read and Khan learned that Winnicott had appointed his wife, not Khan, as his literary executor. After years of selfless editorial service, Khan felt cruelly cast out" (Boynton 2002). Before his death, Khan caused his own ejection from the psychoanalytic establishment by publicly documenting his abuse of his patients, his contempt for his colleagues, and his anti-Semitism in a scandalous book (Khan 1988). Its central case study, "A Dismaying Homosexual," was viciously anti-Semitic. A terminally ill, alcoholic, and deranged Masud Khan was expelled from the British Psychoanalytical Society, after which the enraged Khan sent anonymous bomb threats to its president. Masud Khan was his own worst enemy.

Masud Khan's anti-Semitism has been documented by several scholars as well as by himself (Khan 1988; Cooper 1994; Godley 2001; Boynton 2002, 2003; Hopkins 1998, 2002, 2004, 2006; Willoughby 2005). Exploiting his patients' transference in the psychoanalytic situation, the disturbed "Prince Khan" turned many of his female patients into his lovers and messed up the lives of other patients. The American psychoanalyst Linda Hopkins thought that Khan had a multifaceted personality: "Khan often referred to himself as a paradox and people who knew him well tend to agree. He was a living example of Winnicott's theory that when we get access to the deeper parts of a person's self, we find multiple selves which are incompatible with each other. As Khan [himself] wrote, 'one can explicate a paradox, but one cannot resolve it thereby.'" (Hopkins 2001a). Hopkins called Masud Khan's personality "false self" (Hopkins 2006). Khan wore many psychological masks and guises to conceal his unbearably painful lack of self-esteem. Hopkins understood Khan's anti-Semitism better than his other biographers:

When Spring Comes: Awakenings in Clinical Psychoanalysis was published in 1988. (In the same year, a paperback edition was published in the United States under the title *The Long Wait.*) The declaration of war [against his colleagues] was most obvious in a chapter entitled "A Dismaying Homosexual" that described an analysis Khan had done years earlier...The patient was a Jewish man who came to Khan as a last resort before killing himself. An anti-Semitic tirade by Khan shocked the man out of his narcissistic self-absorption—and indeed, this is a report of an apparently successful analysis. The technique of mirroring the self-attack of a severely ill patient has a theoretical rationale, but Khan provided no such explanation. It seems clear that the account, which may not even be truthful, was meant to shock. (Hopkins 2006, p. 364)

The well-known American Jewish psychoanalyst Robert Stoller, a great scholar of human sexuality and its vicissitudes, who had been a close friend of Masud Khan, understood that Khan was committing psychological suicide:

Robert Stoller was horrified. He wrote to [his colleague Victor Nikolayevich] Smirnoff, "I found reading [the book] to be a most interesting experience—interesting in the way it is interesting to watch a kamikaze pilot in his final plunge." Smirnoff wrote back that he thought that Khan was out of his mind and not responsible for what he had done. Stoller agreed only that Khan was out of his mind—he was outraged at his friend, despite the sorry state of his mental health: "[Masud's] damnable book, with its gross, gauche, nasty-little-boy-piss-on-you scurrility, is a joke out of control." (Hopkins 2006, p. 366)

What was the psychological connection between Masud Khan's self-destructiveness and his anti-Semitism? Here's what the perceptive Linda Hopkins thought about it:

Most analysts whom I interviewed agree with Stoller that the book was inexcusable: "People in the British [Psychoanalytical] Society said goodbye to Masud when he wrote the book, not when he died. We thought, 'We've forgiven Masud a lot, but this we won't forgive.'" (Pearl King). Khan had prejudices against many groups in addition to Jews—his targets included Americans, the British, Hindus, feminists, and psychoanalysts in general. Anti-Semitism, however, is so central to his legacy that it deserves separate consideration. (Hopkins 2006, p. 366)

The British literary scholar Anthony Julius studied the anti-Semitism of the American-British homosexual poet Thomas Stearns Eliot (Julius 1995). Linda Hopkins compared Eliot's anti-Semitism with that of Masud Khan:

Anthony Julius suggests that in calling a person an anti-Semite, we should address the question of what kind of anti-Semite they are. Speaking of T.S. Eliot, he writes: "Anti-Semites are not all the same. Some break Jewish bones, others wound Jewish sensibilities. Eliot falls into the second category. He was civil to Jews he knew, offensive to those who merely knew him through his work." Khan's anti-Semitism was of the wounding variety rather than the bone-breaking variety, similar to Eliot's. A friend who was not an analyst said that Khan's anti-Semitism was "curiously unconvincing" and another friend commented: "Masud's anti-Semitism was a red herring. He was actually very interested in Jews – they were a fascinating subject that he wanted to understand. He used his apparent anti-Semitism to provoke people into talking about their Jewishness." An analysand remembers that Khan supported the existence of Israel and "often used to main-tain that there was nothing more impressive than a cultured Jew." And an anony-mous British analyst (who is Jewish) told me: "Anti-Semitism was not a central issue for Khan, he just went on about it sometimes. Had his patient in the final book not been Jewish, he would have been just as abusive about some other topic, in all likelihood." (Hopkins 2006, pp. 367–368)

If Masud Khan's anti-Semitism was "a red herring," what were the uncoinscious emotional conflicts that motivated it? Did it have to do with his Jewish colleagues? Hopkins discussed the widespread anti-Semitism among British psychoanalysts and how Khan reacted to it:

As a child, Khan had not known Jews, and the racism he saw involved Hindus and Muslims. Several anonymous British analysts suggested to me that his anti-Semitism developed in England as an exaggerated mirroring of bigotry that he observed and experienced within the [British Psychoanalytical Society]. An anony-mous Jewish peer said: "The British analysts used Masud to act out their own prejudices—they needed a Satan, and they chose a wonderful actor for their script." And a Protestant analyst told me that anti-Semitism still thrives in Britain and in the [British Psychoanalytical Society]. "There is a high degree of tolerance for anti-Semitism in Britain and in the Society, whatever people may pretend." (Hopkins 2006, p. 368)

But why did the Pakistani-born Khan become an exaggerated mirror of the anti-Semitism of his British colleagues? Had he been discriminated against in England because of his Muslim religion or his dark skin? Did he "identify with the aggressor" or did he unconsciously externalize his self-hatred? And how much anti-Semitism was there in the British Psychoanalytical Society? Here again is Linda Hopkins's view of the situation:

It is very difficult to know to what extent anti-Semitism (and its opposite) truly exists at the [British Psychoanalytical Society] because it is not a topic of open dis-cussion. My own experience is that, in comparison to other analytic/psychological groups, the [British Psychoanalytical Society] is characterized by more thoughtful-ness and tolerance than is average. Nevertheless, there is a history of Jewish-Protestant tension that can be documented. The tension roughly overlaps the clash between the [followers of Melanie Klein] who historically had predominantly Jew-ish identities, and the Middle Group/Independents, who were mostly Protestant.

Certainly the [British Psychoanalytical Society] that Khan entered was quite aware of the Jewish or non-Jewish identity of its members. So Khan may have spoken in part for [his] colleagues when he expressed anti-Semitism. (Hopkins 2006, p. 368)

Khan's anti-Semitism, however, was much more self-destructive than that of his colleagues. It was of a kind that was not and would not be tolerated:

> But even if that is the case, open disrespect for Jews is something that has never been characteristic of any group of British analysts. Khan's lack of thoughtfulness about his bigotry is something that is totally unacceptable in an analyst, as he well knew. The offensive (vs. playful) quality of Khan's anti-Semitism increased over the years. In 1976, when he was disciplined by the Society, he developed a paranoid belief that the Jews in the group were purposely targeting him. With this belief in mind, he began to voice his prejudices with the single goal of being offensive. André Green told me: "In the early 70s, Masud wasn't openly anti-Semitic. That came only at the end after his cancer and after his loss of training status. Then he became anti-Semitic mostly against Hanna Segal." Barrie Cooper made a similar comment: "You don't find overt anti-Semitism [from Masud] before the Institute rejected him. The anti-Semitism was meant as an attack on his colleagues and the Institute. It was a "professional anti-Semitism." (Hopkins 2006, p. 369)

Masud Khan's anti-Semitism was the result of several unconscious psychological forces that operated in him at the same time. As an unconscious defense of externalization, it protected him against the unbearably painful sense of his own "bad self." As an unconscious "identification with the aggressor," it defended him against the hostility or discrimination that he may have felt (justifiably or not) from his British colleagues. As an unconscious sadomasochistic process, it enabled him to commit psychological suicide. It also expressed his unconscious murderous rage against his Jewish colleagues who, he felt, had injured him. And, as a "playful" provocation that got out of hand, it was also an expression of his "false self." In the last analysis, anti-Semitism always is an unconscious attempt to deal with unbearable aspects of one's own self.

THE CASE OF ANNEMARIE DÜHRSSEN

In addition to the "historical scholarship" and "journal" of the "Institute for Historical Review," which specialize in Holocaust denial, many racist "psychological journals" and books have been published to minimize anti-Semitism or to prove that it did not exist. One painful issue in this connection is the history of German psychoanalysis, which began in 1894 and goes on in two different and separate societies. In 1910, the *Deustche Psychoanlytische Gesellschaft* or *DPG* (German psychoanalytic society), was formally established. After Hitler came to power in 1933, however, Nazi Germany dissolved the *DPG* and created the notorious Göring Institute of Psychotherapy (Cocks 1985). German Jewish psychoanalysts fled overseas, mainly to the United States. Many non-Jewish German psychoanalysts, however, including the well-known Alexander Mitscherlich, remained in Germany during the Nazi period (Cocks 1996, p. 207). While not as painful as the history of the Holocaust, this is a painful chapter in German history, which some German psychoanalysts need to deny.

After Hitler's suicide and Germany's surrender to the Allies in 1945, the *Deutsche Psychoanlytische Gesellschaft* was revived. In 1950, however, there was a schism in the *DPG*. The new *Deutsche Psychoanlytische Vereinigung* or *DPV* (German psychoanalytic association) seceded from the *DPG,* and in 1951, the *DPV* was recognized as a member by the International Psychoanalytical Association in London. Since the 1970s, there has been conflict and turmoil between the *DPG* and the *DPV.* The latter claimed to have recovered the Freudian psychoanalytic tradition that had been lost in Hitler's Third Reich (Eickhoff 1995; Cocks 1996, p. 208). As part of this conflict, in 1994, on the centenary of the *DPG* , its 78-year-old honorary member Annemarie Dührssen (1916–1988) published a "revisionist" book on the history of the psychoanalytic movement in Germany which sought to rewrite German Nazi history and exonerate Hitler and his Nazis of having destroyed German psychoanalysis along with Germany's Jews (Dührssen 1994). As could be expected, Dührssen's book caused an uproar among her colleagues and was labeled anti-Semitic by several German and American scholars (Kreuzer-Haustein & Schmidt 1996; Rensmann 1996; Cocks 1996).

THE CASE OF JACQUELINE ROSE

Another anti-Zionist and anti-Semitic psychoanalytic scholar is Jacqueline Rose (born 1949), a British literary critic whose anti-Zionist book is a striking example of intellectualized anti-Semitism (Rose 2005). Rose is a professor of English at Queen Mary College, University of London, and the author of a book on modern psychoanalysis (Rose 2003). While she may be a brilliant scholar in her field, Rose lacks adequate knowledge of Judaism, Jewish history, and Zionism. She does not seem aware of her own anti-Semitism. Her prestigious publisher, Princeton University Press, presented her book glowingly:

Zionism was inspired as a movement—one driven by the search for a homeland for the stateless and persecuted Jewish people. Yet it trampled the rights of the Arabs in Palestine. Today it has become so controversial that it defies understanding and trumps reasoned public debate. So argues prominent British writer Jacqueline Rose, who uses her political and psychoanalytic skills in this book to take an unprecedented look at Zionism—one of the most powerful ideologies of modern times. Rose enters the inner world of the movement and asks a new set of questions. How did Zionism take shape as an identity? And why does it seem so immutable? Analyzing the messianic fervor of Zionism, she argues that it colors Israel's most profound self-image to this day. Rose also explores the message of

[Jewish] dissidents, who, while believing themselves the true Zionists, warned at the outset against the dangers of statehood for the Jewish people. She suggests that these dissidents were prescient in their recognition of the legitimate claims of the Palestinian Arabs. In fact, she writes, their thinking holds the knowledge the Jewish state needs today in order to transform itself. In perhaps the most provocative part of her analysis, Rose proposes that the link between the Holocaust and the founding of the Jewish state, so often used to justify Israel's policies, needs to be rethought in terms of the shame felt by the first leaders of the nation toward their own European history. For anyone concerned with the conflict in Israel-Palestine, this timely book offers a unique understanding of Zionism as an unavoidable psychic and historical force. (Rose 2005, dust jacket)

Emanuele Ottolenghi, the Italian Jewish executive director of the Transatlantic Institute in Brussels, had some scathing comments for Rose's publisher as well as for Rose herself: "While the reader may be left to wonder who should lose their jobs at the prestigious publishing house for this little oversight, one should not judge this book by the blissful ignorance of PUP's public relations personnel, which perhaps is just a welcome indication of how this book made it into print. In fact, their little stretch of imagination is reality television compared to Rose's reach for the stars. Rose's argument has little to do with the reality of Zionism or indeed of the current state of the Arab-Israeli conflict. It is more a reflection of the state of mind of Jews who—like Rose and other radical Jewish intellectuals opposed to Israel's existence—do not want to be Jews, are ashamed to be Jewish, and take pride in saying it out loud—in short, her own state of mind" (Ottolenghi 2006, p. 194).

Indeed, Rose's scholarship is flawed. In the very first paragraph of her book, she demonstrated her ignorance of a basic term of Jewish religion. Rose stated—quoting the German-born Israeli Jewish scholar Gerhard Gershom Scholem—that the seventeenth-century Jewish "Messiah" Shabtai Zvi (Sabbatai Sevi) "preached a blasphemous sermon, exempted the congregation from the duty of prayer, and announced that the Pentateuch was holier than the Torah" (Rose 2005, p. 2). In fact, the Pentateuch (the Greek name for the five books of Moses) *is* the Torah. What the mentally ill "Messiah" had actually declared was that *his printed copy* of the Torah was holier than *the handwritten scroll* (Scholem 1973, p. 397). Even the British Jewish writer Simon Louvish, who is sympathetic to Rose's political views, felt compelled to point out her errors:

[T]here are serious flaws in this work. The main problem is an overriding shallow-ness. Rose does not access the primary sources, and relies on translations from the Hebrew. This need not cripple a researcher. But it does require a greater rigour and caution than is demonstrated in this book. An over-reliance on certain dissident Israeli historians [Benny Morris, Ilan Pappé and Avi Shlaim], and avoidance of others, skews the analysis. Rose has visited Jewish rightist settlers and interviewed their defender, "Bibi" Netanyahu, but she appears to have little grounding in the religious iconography that informs their thought. Who might blame her? Much of the material in that field is so extreme and racist as to feed the most rabid anti-Semites. The mad Rabbi [Meir] Kahane's Kach movement is mentioned but its influential fascist rhetoric is not properly analysed. As elsewhere in our 21st-century chaos, religion, in fundamentalist format, has flowed in where secular ideas have foundered. In modern Israel, Jewish vandals deface the tomb of Herzl with Nazi signs. (Louvish 2005)

Rose's ignorance of Jewish religion and mysticism was not her only problem. She also failed to understand that which she did know:

But even if omission is inevitable, lack of basic understanding is not. Rose has bought into the idea that the Holocaust "fully enters the [Israeli] national memory only after the 1967 Six Day War." This is nonsense. The Holocaust, and the "illegal" immigration of [survivor] refugees, galvanised the Jewish resistance in Palestine in the aftermath of the Second World War. It fiercely fed the polemic of the new state from 1948. The ethos of a rebirth from the ashes was paramount, as I can personally attest from primary and secondary schools in Jerusalem in the 1950s and 1960s. In 1961, the Eichmann trial gripped Israel in a frenzy of relived agony. There is no mention of this in Rose's book. She is fixated on the Word, eschewing lived experience, condemning herself to the closed circle of the neo-Marxist neverland, obsessed with finding a Freudian, Lacanian or Hegelian term to fit the decline of the "non-violent" Zionist dream. "I approached two distinguished Hegelian philosophers," for the solution, she writes. She should have approached Abd el-Jawad X, on any street corner in Ramallah or Gaza, or Mrs Frieda Y, née of Dachau. They, like countless victims of the 20th century's ideological certainties, can bear witness to the result when force is deployed to achieve the ideas of polemicists and thinkers. (Louvish 2005)

There have been many other reviews of Rose's book, some of them positive, most of them negative. It seems that Rose's personal feelings against the Jews caused her to write a book that any serious scholar would not have published. In my own book on the same subject, I had tried to be emotionally objective and to understand the Arab-Israeli conflict from a truly psychoanalytic, nonpartisan, nonjudgmental viewpoint—even though I am an Israeli Jew (Falk 2004).

How did Jacqueline Rose acquire her anti-Semitic anti-Zionism? For some years before she wrote her book, Rose had been living with the Welsh Jewish psychoanalyst Adam Phillips, one of the best-known psychotherapists in Britain, who is not, however, a member of the British Psychoanalytical Society. They adopted a Chinese orphan, whom they named Mia, and raised her together. The relationship, however, soured. Finally, Phillips left Rose and married the fashion curator Judith Clark, with whom he has a three-year-old daughter, Marianne. Hell hath no fury like a woman scorned. Rose's book may be her revenge against her former lover and partner.

One piece of evidence for this hypothesis is Rose's closeness to the British Psychoanalytical Society, which excludes Phillips. Despite Rose's anti-Semitism, the British Psychoanalytical Society awarded her the unlimited use of its library facilities for her "services to psychoanalysis." The librarian of the British Psychoanalytical Society, Andrea Chandler, boasts on its Web site that her library "houses the finest collection of psychoanalytic material in the world. Our stock of nearly 22,000 volumes ranges from the mid-19th century to the present day. The library contains an extensive and valuable collection of psychoanalytic works ever published in the UK, related foreign materials, and donations of the private collections of many leading psychoanalysts, notably Ernest Jones, James Strachey, and Donald Winnicott. We hold roughly 1600 catalogued monographs and nearly 300 serial titles—50 of which are active. It also houses unpublished material associated with the British Psychoanalytical Society." Why did the British Psychoanalytical Society make such an award to an anti-Semitic scholar?

A "FEROCIOUS SILENCE"?

The British psychologist Stephen Frosh recently studied the complex quadrangular relationship between Sigmund Freud, anti-Semitism, Judaism, and psychoanalysis (Frosh 2003, 2004, 2005). Frosh thought that "the history of psychoanalysis in Germany during the Nazi period has been a source of some controversy and heart-searching within the analytic community over the past twenty years. Prior to that, with the exception of early revelations concerning C.G. Jung's collaboration with the Nazis ... and a rather negative report to Ernest Jones from John Rickman in 1946 ... there had been *a ferocious silence* over events between 1933 and 1945" (Frosh 2003, p. 1315, citing Léon 1946 and Brecht et al. 1985, 1992; italics added). The "early revelations" about Jung were contained in a private report on Jung's Nazi past, which the American Jewish Holocaust survivor Maurice Léon sent in 1946 to the "British War Crimes Executive" at Nuremberg. It was received by the International Military Tribunal at Nuremberg but never acted on (Léon 1946).

Had Frosh read his colleagues' work carefully? Many scholars had studied Jung's anti-Semitism and his collaboration with the Nazis, showing that Frosh's "ferocious silence" had been broken decades earlier (Rieff 1964; Maidenbaum & Martin 1991; Bengesser & Sokoloff 1992; Samuels 1993, 1994, 1996; Roudinesco 1998; Goggin & Goggin 2001; Maidenbaum 2002; Rickels 2002). Freud's ambivalence about his Judaism had also been studied by several scholars (Falk 1978; Yerushalmi 1990; Rice 1990; Gilman 1993a, 1993b), and Frosh's "controversy and heart-searching within the analytic community" had been studied by the German scholar Regine Lockot and by the American scholar Geoffrey Cocks (Lockot 1985, 1994; Cocks 1985, 1996, 2001).

Frosh thought that the science that Freud had created, psychoanalysis, had become closely associated with the Jewish identity, a situation that the psychoanalytic profession in Germany had to defend when confronted with Nazism, that some Jewish psychoanalysts saw an advantages in assimilation and an abandonment of their Judaism, while some German "Gentiles," who had chosen a field in which Jews dominated, were caught in a double-bind of "collaboration" and, therefore, "betrayal," and that psychoanalysis, the frequent target of anti-Semitism, had *not* succeeded in explaining it (Frosh 2005). As the reader knows by now, this book is an attempt to prove that it has.

ABUSING PSYCHOHISTORY

The American "psychohistorian" Lloyd DeMause rejected Goldhagen's notion of "eliminatory antisemitism" because it ascribed to the Germans and Austrians the "inherited" trait of anti-Semitism. In a lecture at the Austrian University of Klagenfurt, DeMause said, "I hope you will find that my psychohistorical view of the origins of the Holocaust makes better sense than views like that of Daniel Goldhagen, who recently portrayed Germans and Austrians not only accurately as 'Hitler's Willing Executioners' but also as mysteriously containing seemingly *inherited* antisemitic personalities" (DeMause 2005, p. 205). DeMause himself attributed the Holocaust to pathological child-rearing practices in Germany and Austria before Hitler's time. Unfortunately, DeMause's "scholarship" lacks caution, rigor, and serious evidence, giving psychohistory a bad name. He called the Holocaust a "phobic group fantasy" triggered by the "leap into modernity" in Germany and Austria and their democratization in the 1920s "when the new psychoclass [*sic*] began to experiment with all kinds of new freedoms that violated every rule most people had learned as children" (DeMause 2005, p. 215).

DeMause saw the Holocaust as the result of the acting out of unconscious infanticidal and matricidal wishes and "phobic group fantasies":

> If the Killer Parent alter [*sic*] deep in your unconscious hated you for your new independence, rather than lose her approval you fused with her and punished scapegoats who could be accused of being smelly shit-babies full of poisonous lice. What was needed was "a national enema," a purging that would "cleanse" people of their independence as their mothers had used the purging enema to cleanse them as infants. Even before Jews were designated to be the main scapegoats that were declared impure and diseased, the Weimar period spawned powerful racial hygiene movements that feared pollution by others. Doctors spontaneously began arguing for euthanasia of "the unfit who were a burden on the fit," people who were "useless eaters"—a term all children were familiar with from their parents' accusations against them. These "lice" were thought to be responsible for spreading typhus, syphilis and other infectious diseases, and it was said to be a major problem in sanitation management (called "house-cleaning") to get rid of the

"filthy lice" polluting the national blood. Symbolic lice-covered shit-babies were seen as the cause of all kinds of disease. (DeMause 2005, p. 216)

To DeMause, the psychological origins of the Holocaust began and ended with the German mother's death wishes for her baby and with the son's wish to kill his mother, personified in the motherland. Using the simplistic "traumatic reliving" notion of the controversial "psychohistorian" Rudolph Binion (born 1927), an oversimplification and misrepresentation of Freud's key concept of unconscious repetition compulsion (Binion 1976, 2005), DeMause believed that "every detail of traumatic German and Austrian childrearing was restaged during the Holocaust." The Jews were made to live in their own filth (feces and urine) because German and Austrian infants had been made to do this by their parents, and the "cattle-car trips" and "death marches" of the Jews unconsciously restaged the endless movement from family to family of turn-of-the-century German and Austrian children (DeMause 2005, p. 219).

> Killing German Jews meant, of course, that they would not contribute to the winning of the war for Germany. That starting a war against nations whose combined power was far superior to that of Germany and Austria was suicidal was obvious to anyone not caught up in the war trance. Early on, the slogan of the Hitler Youth was "We were born to die for Germany," and Hitler promised that "ten million German youth would experience sacrificial deaths" under his leadership. He often considered suicide himself, saying "Germans do not deserve to live" at the end of the war, and finally issuing orders to destroy Germany as he killed himself. Ultimately, shit-babies deserve death—no more, but also no less, since even in death they fantasied that they were returning to their mothers, to their Motherland. (DeMause 2005, p. 220)

While it is true that mothers may unconsciously wish the death of their babies, especially if the baby is very demanding or disturbing, or if the mother herself is emotionally disturbed, or if she wishes herself to be taken care of like a baby, or if the baby is born at a time when the mother is depressed, anxious, preoccupied with other matters, or having serious personal troubles of her own; and while it is also true that the motherland unconsciously symbolizes the mother, explaining an extremely complex phenomenon like the Holocaust on that basis alone, or using Binion's oversimplified notion of "traumatic reliving" to explain it, is the kind of psychohistorical reductionism justly derided by serious historians and psychologists.

So much for "psychohistorians" like Lloyd DeMause. Now to some more serious scholars. The German Jewish philosopher and sociologist Helmuth Plessner (1892–1985), who had lost his university position when Hitler's Nazis came to power in 1933, considered Germany a "belated nation" (Plessner 1935). Germany only became one nation after Prussia united it in 1871—later than most other European nations. In an allusion to Plessner's idea of the "belated nation," the Swiss Jewish scholar Raphael Gross described the German historical research of the Holocaust as "belated Holocaust research" (Gross 2001). Gross noted that in comparison to Israel, the United States, and Poland, Holocaust studies had hardly been conducted in Germany, where they just seemed to be getting under way. In view of this tardiness Gross doubted that the history of the Holocaust could have been written earlier by German scholars, for it was clear that German historians who were personally enmeshed in the Nazi past could not produce scholarly Holocaust studies matching the quality of Reitlinger's, Hilberg's, Browning's or Goldhagen's studies (Reitlinger 1953, Hilberg 1961, Browning 1992, Goldhagen 1996). Because of the emotional pain it caused them, the German historians had avoided studying their nation's destruction of the Jews.

The idea of the uniqueness of the Holocaust, its being essentially different from all other mass murders and genocides, has been one of the most debated issues among its historians (Katz 1994). Gross put the term in quotation marks:

> This, however, does not mean that German historians did not exert their influence on the [discourse on the Holocaust]. This influence may be noted in other fields, namely in the "politics of memory," where the remembrance of the Holocaust becomes more and more abstract. In similar evasive words, with which German historians shied away after the war from empirical Holocaust research, they now dabble in the "politics of memory" by producing a highly abstract consensus, ritualistically stressing the "uniqueness" of the Holocaust, insisting that it cannot be compared to any other genocide and that it constitutes everlasting shame etc. (Gross 2001, p. 11, Fred Kautz's translation)

Kautz noted that even the Holocaust research conducted in Germany today gave Gross much cause for concern, because it was isolated from any real emotion. Gross perceived in German Holocaust research "a strange emotional distance to the horrendous event under investigation...and the absence of value judgments" (Gross 2001, p. 11; Kautz 2003). In psychoanalytic terms, this "strange emotional distance" is the unconscious defense of isolation, which also operated in many Nazi mass murderers and extermination-camp troops. This theme was also studied by the Israeli historian Yaacov Lozowick and by the British scholar Ian Kershaw (Lozowick 2000, 2002; Kershaw 2001).

Beside a storm of historical controversy, Goldhagen's book provoked several German psychoanalytic studies of anti-Semitism and the Holocaust, most of which were published in the leading German psychoanalytic journal *Psyche: Zeitschrift für Psychoanalyse und ihre Anwendungen* in 1997. The German psychoanalyst Werner Bohleber tried to integrate Anderson's idea of the nation as an "imagined community" (Anderson 1983) with Goldhagen's "cultural model" of German anti-Semitism (Goldhagen 1996) to further clarify German nationalism and anti-Semitism (Bohleber 1997). Bohleber investigated the inter-dependence and mutual reinforcement of German anti-Semitism and national-ism from both the psychoanalytic and historical viewpoints. He analyzed some of the collective German nationalistic and anti-Semitic fantasies that were shared in this process, as well as the complicated interchangeability of collective mental-ities and individual psyche in nationalist German anti-Semitism. Through their historical development, Bohleber showed that such anti-Semitic and nationalist fantasies tended to become radicalized and to erase the boundaries between imagination and action. These tendencies found their most tragic high point under Hitler, whom Bohleber described as an example of the psychic influence of the Nazi perpetrators through their anti-Semitic ideology.

Goldhagen's book provoked another psychoanalytic study by two German scholars (Brede & Karp 1997). While these authors accepted Goldhagen's basic thesis that most Nazi-era Germans carried out Hitler's murderous orders volun-tarily, they distinguished between his willingly motivated German anti-Semitism and his specific type of Nazi "eliminatory" anti-Semitism. Brede and Karp made their argument in four steps: 1. That Goldhagen's book had forced German Holocaust researchers to deal with the question of the Germans' willingness to obey Hitler and placed the burden of proving otherwise on them. 2. That the thesis of a German "eliminatory" anti-Semitism requires a distinc-tion between common-sense meaning structures and cultural obviousness. 3. With the help of this distinction, it becomes possible to detach the problem of German social integration during the Nazi era from that of "eliminatory" anti-Semitism. 4. They introduced the concept of aggression, which Goldhagen did not use theoretically, and used it in the framework of Freud's theory of drives and culture, to explain Goldhagen's "eliminatory anti-Semitism."

Goldhagen's book also provoked a study by the old German psychoanalyst Margarete Nielsen Mitscherlich (born 1917) who, together with her husband Alexander Mitscherlich (1908–1982), had coauthored *The Inability to Mourn,* a key text on group psychological processes, and in particular on the collective inability to mourn group losses and catastrophes and its unhealthy emotional results (Mitscherlich & Mitscherlich 1967, 1975; cf. Falk 1996). Mitscherlich borrowed the title of her study—*Erinnern, Wiederholen, Durcharbeiten* (remem-bering, repeating, working through)—from a psychoanalytic book published five years earlier about the collective psychological processes in Germany after its reunification (Rauschenbach 1992; Mitscherlich 1997). She pointed out that it had taken two or three generations for the Germans to be able to discuss publicly the part taken by their army, police, and other "normal" state organizations in the Nazi genocide of the Jews. The German publication of Goldhagen's book, which brought to light a key aspect of the German extermination wishes, the "elimina-tory" anti-Semitism of the Germans, was part and parcel of this process, which could unfold only in the second or third generation after the Nazi era.

Mitscherlich thought that Goldhagen's "eliminatory anti-Semitism" had been embedded in a multitude of German historical and social conditions—Germany as Plessner's "belated nation" that sought to find its precarious identity and its ethically-defined unity through specific exclusion maneuvers against "foreigners" and through the unconscious projection of self-hatred—which, at least in hindsight, let it appear as such. She believed that only if the Germans succeeded in breaking the vicious cycle of self-hatred, idealization of authority, readiness to subjugate, and sadism, and to recognize others (non-Germans) as human beings, would it be possible for Germany to renounce violence inwardly as well as outwardly (Mitscherlich 1997).

Goldhagen's book also provoked a study by a couple of German psychoanalysts, Rolf and Barbara Vogt (Vogt & Vogt 1997). These authors examined Goldhagen's basic hypothesis, that the historically traditional anti-Semitism of the Germans was responsible for the extermination of the Jews in the Third Reich, on three levels: the micro level of the individual, the meso level of the institutions, and the macro level of German society. In the collective German criticism of Goldhagen's conclusions (which partly confirmed them), the Vogts saw classical unconscious defense mechanisms at work, such as reversal, reaction formation, projection, denial, rationalization, and derealization, whose chief motive lay in a collective, unconscious, dissociated guilt feeling. The German philosopher Karl Japsers (1883–1969) had discussed this German guilt right after the Holocaust (Jaspers 1946, 1947). The Vogts thought that this collective dissociated guilt feeling was, beside true insight processes, also responsible for Goldhagen's enormous success in Germany, because it promoted the idealizations directed upon him personally, in the sense of unconscious hopes for redemption and positive identifications.

ANTI-SEMITISM AND "THE JEWISH SCIENCE"

Ever since the Austrian Jewish physician Sigmund Freud "invented" psychoanalysis, the relationship between anti-Semitism and "the Jewish science" of psychoanalysis has been complicated and uneasy. The Austrian Jewish psychoanalyst Elisabeth Brainin and her colleagues discussed the Jewish identity and that of Austrian psychoanalysts (Brainin et al. 1989). In modern Austria, they thought, Jewish Holocaust survivors and other living Jews did not only unconsciously symbolize for non-Jews (including non-Jewish psychoanalysts) the "uncanny" in Freud's sense of the term, because of one's own dangerous and repressed drives or wishes, but also the memory of the mass murder of the Jews, in which the older Austrian generation was directly implicated. This situation led to a reinforcement of Austrian anti-Semitic prejudices rather than to their weakening.

Like other people, psychologists, psychiatrists, and psychoanalysts are not immune to anti-Semitic feelings. However aware they may be of their deeper feelings, having undergone their own "training analysis," psychoanalysts often have anti-Semitic feelings or ambivalent feelings about Jews. Brainin and her colleagues believed that non-Jewish German and Austrian psychoanalysts have developed a "cover identity" that has helped them "sort out" their emotional relationship with their Nazi parents (Brainin et al. 1989, 1993, pp. 47–48). Brainin and her colleagues saw anti-Semitic fantasies as defensive "deindividualized and depersonalized" transference fantasies *unconsciously displaced* from one's early parents to the Jews.

This is even truer of politicians, who tend to project their feelings and externalize their self-image. The twentieth-century British statesman Winston Leonard Spencer Churchill (1874–1965), who hated both the Russian Bolsheviks and the German Nazis with a passion—he called the latter "Huns," after the "barbarian" tribes who had invaded the Roman Empire and its great civilization in the fifth century—had deeply ambivalent feelings about the Jews. After the Russian Revolution, Churchill published a scathing attack on the "International Jews" and "Terrorist Jews" while praising Zionism as a "simpler, truer and far more attainable goal" (Churchill 1920). Churchill's feelings for the Jews may have been unconsciously displaced to them from his beautiful but narcissistic American Jewish mother, Jenny Jacobson, a promiscuous woman who neglected and rejected him when he was a child. He was emotionally saved by the love of his nanny, but he was on the verge of suicide at least twice after losing his posts (Rintala 1984, 1995).

The unconscious displacement of feelings and fantasies from one's parents to the Jews helps people relieve the anxiety caused by their conflict between their bad feelings for their parents and their love for them. Thus, the dangerous fantasies of the *Protocols of the Elders of Zion,* in which the Jews secretly conspire to rule the world (Nilus 1905, 1920; Segel 1934; Bernstein 1935; Cohn 1967; Bach 1973; Taguieff 1992; Conan 1999; Bishop 1999; Eisner 2005), may be the result of an unconscious displacement of childhood fantasies about the sexual or other secrets of the parents, combined with an unconscious projection of the anti-Semites' wishes for power and control.

One source of confusion in such discussions is that the word "psychoanalysis" has two different meanings: it is a general theory of human behavior, but also a clinical psychological method for treating emotional pain and mental illness. Ackerman and Jahoda, as well as Ostow, used the clinical setting of the psychoanalytic treatment to gain insights into the unconscious processes operating in anti-Jewish patients. Like Elisabeth Brainin, the Moroccan-born American Jewish psychoanalyst Danielle Knafo believed that in psychoanalytic treatment, the emotional conflicts of the patient are often conveyed in terms of religious, racial, or ethnic stereotypes (Knafo 1999). Some patients bring up their anti-Semitic feelings at critical times during their psychotherapy. Knafo presented three clinical cases (one of a non-Jewish patient, another of a Jewish one, and a third of a half-Jewish one) showing that anti-Semitism is a psychological defense that serves various unconscious defensive purposes, involving split-off or projected aspects of the personality. On the basis of her experience as a Jewish psychoanalyst in New York, she concluded that Jewish psychoanalysts need to confront their own ambivalence about anti-Semitic patients rather than remain silent about their anti-Semitism, which challenges their own identity. Thus, potentially anxiety-producing information or situations can help establish peace between analyst and patient, as well as within each of them. Knafo also discussed the self-hatred of the Jewish patient, which several scholars have studied as a collective Jewish phenomenon (Lewin 1941; Gilman 1986; Marcus & Rosenberg 1989; Booker 1991; Finlay 2004). Psychoanalysts must make themselves aware of their own anti-Semitic or anti-anti-Semitic feelings, and those of their patients.

Nazi Anti-Semitism and
the Holocaust

The murder of six million European Jews, along with millions of Slavs, homosexuals, communists, gypsies, and other "inferior races" by the German Nazis from 1933 to 1945 is one of the greatest tragedies in all of human history. Psychoanalysts have studied the deeper causes of this tragedy, and we shall now take a critical look at what they have found. The Canadian Jewish historian Michael Robert Marrus, who edited a monumental nine-volume study of the Holocaust (Marrus 1989), believed that we need to integrate the history of the Holocaust into the general European historical context in order to be able to answer the crucial historical questions: "How did Nazi policy evolve to mass murder?" "What was the role and responsibility of the individual in Nazi Germany?" "How are we to evaluate the role of the various bystanders to the Holocaust?" Marrus felt that in order to answer these questions, we must view the Holocaust as part of the overall historical process and study the dynamics of previous historical situations. Moreover, while this approach acknowledges the uniqueness of the Holocaust, Marrus thought, it also requires investigation and comparison with other incidents of persecution and genocide (Marrus 1988). In order to understand how such an incredible tragedy could come about, we shall examine the history of Germany and of its Jews, how Hitler's Nazi Party and extermination machine came about, and what made them psychologically possible.

A "GERMAN-JEWISH SYMBIOSIS"?

Common historical wisdom holds that the eighteenth century brought the "enlightenment" (known as the *lumières* in France and as the *Aufklärung* in

Germany) to Europe. One of the best-known German Jewish intellectuals and community leaders at that time was the great Prussian Jewish philosopher Moses Mendelssohn (1729–1786), a scholar esteemed by his Christian contemporaries as much as by his Jewish ones (Arkush 1994; Sorkin 1996; Falk 1996, pp. 600–604; Simon 2003; Bourel 2004). Jewish tradition compares Mendelssohn to the biblical Moses and to the medieval sage Moses Maimonides. Mendelssohn introduced the German language and *Aufklärung* into Jewish culture, which had feared Christian culture and had sealed itself off from it. He translated the Hebrew-and-Aramaic Bible into German, but wrote it in Hebrew characters to make it easier for his fellow Jews to read his translation and to learn the German language.

After Mendelssohn's death in 1786 (he died in the same year as his king, Friedrich II), Mendelssohn was succeeded as the leader of Berlin's Jewish community by his pupil David Friedländer (1750–1834), who sought to "modernize" Judaism. Friedländer had been born in the East Prussian city of Königsberg (now the Russian city of Kaliningrad) and moved to Berlin in 1771 after marrying a daughter of Daniel Itzig (1723–1799), a *Hofjude* and banker to King Friedrich II. The ambitious and upwardly mobile Friedländer occupied a prominent social position in both Jewish and non-Jewish Berlin circles. He was a Jewish community leader, politician, writer, and educator. In 1778, he cofounded the *Freie Schule für Juden* (free school for Jews), which he directed together with his brother-in-law, Isaac Daniel Itzig. In this school, exclusively Jewish subjects were crowded out in favor of general subjects. Friedländer also wrote school textbooks, and was one of the first to translate the Hebrew prayerbook into German. In spite of all this, unlike his mentor Mendelssohn, he was more concerned with endeavors to facilitate the entry into Christian circles for himself and other Jews than with the spirit of Judaism.

While most Prussian Jews were not allowed to live in the capital of Berlin, Friedländer gradually achieved the emancipation of the Jews of Berlin and a few other minor reforms. King Friedrich Wilhelm II, who succeeded Friedrich II to the throne of Prussia upon the latter's death in 1786 (the year of Mendelssohn's death), created a committee to acquaint him with the grievances of his Jews, naming Friedländer and Itzig to it. Its recommendations, however, were unacceptable to the Jews. In 1799, Friedländer, who had a powerful desire to fuse with the Christians, sent an anonymous letter to the Lutheran *Propst* of Berlin, Wilhelm Abraham Teller (1734–1804), entitled *Sendschreiben an Seine Hochwürden Herrn Oberconsistorialrath und Probst Teller zu Berlin, von einigen Hausvätern Jüdischer Religion* (An Epistle to the Reverend High Consistorial Counsellor and Probst Teller of Berlin, from Some Jewish Heads of Households), in which he offered in their name *"to accept Christianity and even baptism, if they were not required to believe in Jesus* [sic] and might evade certain ceremonies." The "epistle" was patently absurd and betrayed Friedländer's profound ambivalence. Teller, who had not expected Friedländer to show such "lack of character," rejected his appeal outright with due severity, urging the Jews to convert to Christianity (Friedländer 1799, 1812, 2004).

It was not until 1812, well after the French Revolution, when Friedländer was 62 years old, that the Prussian Jews finally obtained equal rights to the Christians from King Friedrich Wilhelm III. Friedländer and his friends in the Berlin Jewish community turned their energy and attention to the reform of the Jewish religion in line with modern ideas and the new social and political position of the Jews. Once again, the reforms of Friedländer, who in 1813 was a delegate to the conference on the reorganization of the Jewish religion in the Jewish consistory at the Westphalian capital of Cassel, were unacceptable to even the most radical Jews, as they tended to reduce Judaism to a Christian-like code of ethics. In 1816, when the government of Friedrich Wilhelm III decided to improve the situation of the Polish Jews in East Prussia (now divided between Poland, Lithuania, Latvia, and Russia), it asked the Polish bishop of the northeastern Prussian region of Kujawia (now in Poland) to help formulate the reforms. The bishop consulted Friedländer, who gave him a circumstantial account of the material and intellectual condition of the Jews, and indicated the means by which it might be ameliorated (namely, assimilation).

During Mendelssohn's life, the young Friedländer translated into German parts of the Hebrew Bible according to Mendelssohn's commentary, as well as Mendelssohn's *Sefer ha-Nefesh* (The Book of the Soul). After Mendelssohn's death, together with his younger pupil Joel Löwe (1762–1802), Friedländer published Mendelssohn's German translation of the biblical *Megillat Kohelet* (The Scroll of Ecclesiastes). After the French Revolution, following the practice of the French Jews, Friedländer renamed the Jews *Israeliten*. He wrote a Hebrew commentary to a key portion of the *Mishnah* and translated it into German as *Reden der Erbauung gebildeten Israeliten gewidmet* (Words of Edification Dedicated to Educated Israelites). Friedländer also published a book about his mentor, *Moses Mendelssohn, von Ihm und über Ihn* (Moses Mendelssohn, by Him and about Him); *Über die Verbesserung der Israeliten im Königreich Polen* (On the Improvement of the Israelites in the Kingdom of Poland), his 1816 answer to the query of the bishop of Kujawia; and *Beiträge zur Geschichte der Judenverfolgung im XIX. Jahrhundert durch Schriftsteller* (Contributions to the History of the Persecution of the Jews in the 19th Century by Writers). Friedländer was also an assessor of the royal Prussian college of manufacture and commerce in Berlin, and the first Jew to sit in the municipal council of that city. His wealth enabled him to be a patron of science and art, and among those he encouraged were the brothers Alexander and Wilhelm von Humboldt (Lowenstein 1994).

All this may give the reader a good feeling about Christian-Jewish relations and the situation of the Jews in Prussia, if not in the rest of Germany. Indeed, the German Jewish philosopher Hermann Cohen (1842–1918) thought that Jews and Germans lived in a happy "symbiosis" in which the best elements of

German and Jewish culture were fused. (Cohen 1919, 1924, 1971). Cohen founded the Marburg school of neo-Kantian philosophy, which emphasized "pure thought" and ethics over metaphysics. In later life, however, he shifted his thinking from man-centered to God-centered. (Cohen 1919). Several decades later, the German-born Israeli scholar Gershom Scholem (1897–1982) accused Cohen's "dangerous delusion of German-Jewish Symbiosis" of having misled the Jews of Weimar Germany between the two world wars into thinking that they could live peacefully with the Germans, only to find Hitler's German Nazis persecuting and annihilating them. However, Steven Schwarzchild, an American Jewish scholar, angrily denounced Scholem's "unjustified" attack on Cohen (Schwarzchild 1979).

Scholem was a special kind of German Jew. When it was time for him to serve in *Kaiser* Wilhelm II's German army, he feigned madness to avoid it. A few years later, shortly after getting his PhD degree, he left Germany for Palestine, against his father's wishes. He became a librarian at the newly founded Jewish National and University Library at the Hebrew University of Jerusalem. Four years later, a vacancy occurred for a lecturer in Jewish mysticism at the new university, and Scholem won that job, beginning his academic career. His father, who had wanted him to be a professor in a German university, could hardly have imagined the international renown his son would achieve as a scholar of Jewish mysticism at the Hebrew University. The British-Jewish scholar Hyam Maccoby thought that, having scorned German academic success, rejecting Hermann Cohen's concept of "German-Jewish symbiosis," and immigrating to Palestine, Scholem was vindicated by the subsequent course of events (Maccoby 1983).

Gershom Scholem corresponded with many of his contemporaries. One of his corespondents from 1932 to 1940 was Walter Benjamin (1892–1940), a German Jewish Marxist philosopher and literary critic. Benjamin's brother, Georg, a communist physician, had married Hilde Lange (1902–1989), a future infamous judge in the "German Democratic Republic" of East Germany, known as "Red Hilde," "Bloody Hilde" and "Red Guillotine." Walter Benjamin was associated with the *Institut für Sozialforschung* (Institute of Social Research) at the University of Frankfurt on the Main, also known as "The Frankfurt School" of critical theory, and was also inspired by the Marxism of Bertolt Brecht and by Scholem's Jewish-mysticism scholarship.

Having published many important scholarly works in German, Walter Benjamin stayed in Germany until the late 1930s, when Hitler made life impossible for the Jews. Benjamin committed suicide at the age of 48 in the Catalan town of Port Bou, on the Spanish-French border, while attempting to escape from the Nazis, when it appeared that his party would be denied passage across the border to freedom. However, the rest of Benjamin's group was allowed to cross the border the next day, possibly because their desperation was made clear to the Spanish officials by Benjamin's suicide. A completed manuscript that

Benjamin had carried in his suitcase, which some critics speculate was his ambitious "Arcades Project" in its final form, disappeared after his death but was later recovered and published (Benjamin 1999).

In 1932, then, these two brilliant German Jewish scholars, Walter Benjamin in Germany and Gershom Scholem in Palestine, began corresponding (Benjamin & Scholem 1980, 1989). Relations between Germans and Jews were still relatively good (Mosse 1970). After Hitler's rise to power in January 1933, their main subject, naturally, was the fast-deteriorating situation of the Jews in Germany. In February 1939, Benjamin complained to Scholem about the false trend in academic Jewish studies which presented German-Jewish relations in an "edifying and vindicatory" light. Scholem agreed, calling those relations "an alliance built on deception." Citing the Benjamin-Scholem correspondence, the Italian-born French historian Enzo Traverso questioned Hermann Cohen's rosy view of the situation of the Jews in Germany as a happy "symbiosis":

> The Jewish entry into German culture was often understood in terms of symbiosis. Did Central Europe, between the times of Moses Mendelssohn and Adolf Hitler, between the long and agonizing process of emancipation and the rise to power of National Socialism, experience a Germano-Jewish symbiosis? How is [Jewish] assimilation [into German culture] to be defined? Modernity's assault on the suspended, frozen world of Judaism? A fusion of Judeity [*sic*] with the German world, based on the abandonment of a past and of a distinct identity, or rather on the encounter and dialogue between two distinct elements? Or, on the other hand, a synthesis engendered by the secularization of the Jewish world, a metamorphosis due to the absorption of Germanic culture by the Jewish tradition? These questions have given rise to a wide-ranging controversy, which can be approached via an observation taken from one of the richest and most fascinating correspondences of this century [the Benjamin-Scholem correspondence] . . . This mystification [of German-Jewish relations] is in danger of carrying over into the present, fifty years after Auschwitz. Benjamin's and Scholem's observations make it possible for us to avoid the trap of retrospectively idealizing these relations, reminding us of the need, without denying or underestimating their significance, to point out their contradictions. (Traverso 1995, p. 3)

Indeed, Hermann Cohen's happy "German-Jewish symbiosis" was a dangerous delusion that was shattered by the mass expulsion or emigration of Germany's Jews and the wholesale murder of those who stayed in Hitler's Germany.

THE LANGUAGE OF THE THIRD REICH

Hitler's Nazis used a special German language, full of acronyms and euphemisms, to discuss the murderous work of their terror organizations (Klemperer 1947, 1997). For example, *Gestapo* was the German acronym for *Geheime Staatspolizei* (secret state police), the dreaded Nazi organization that arrested people without a court warrant, tortured them, killed them, or sent them to extermination camps. More dreaded still was the *SS,* the German acronym for *Schutzstaffel* (protection echelon), a euphemism for the "elite" corps of the Nazi party, a murderous organization (or, rather, an organization of professional murderers) whose members killed Jewish babies in front of their mothers by smashing their heads against the wall and mass-murdered Jews in labor camps, concentration camps, and extermination camps. Of all the German Nazi terror organizations, the *SS* was the most infamous and the least understood by historians. From 1925 to 1945, the initials *SS* increasingly struck terror in the hearts of Germans and, after Germany invaded its neighbors, of all Europeans.

The Nazis also had the acronyms *SD* for *Sicherheitsdienst* (security service) and *SA* for *Sturmabteilung* (Storm Division) and many other innocent-sounding acronyms for terror organizations. The acronym *KZ* stood for *Konzentrationslager* (concentration camp), itself a euphemism for an extermination camp. This Orwellian "language of the Third Reich" (Klemperer 1947, 1997) alleviated the painful feelings of horror, shame, and guilt aroused in the perpetrators of the crimes by their own murderous actions through the obsessional unconscious defense of *isolation.* The Nazis deceived their victims, who believed they were going to take a shower when they walked into the gas chamber. They also lied to the whole world about their "concentration camps." The Nazis also deceived themselves about what they were doing, thinking that they were "purifying the German nation" when they were, in fact, committing unprecedented massacres, mass murder, and genocide.

The *SA* had been created by Hitler in 1921 out of disturbed, violent former members of the right-wing *Freikorps.* The brown-shirted storm troopers of the *SA* marched in Nazi Party rallies, protected Nazi Party meetings and violently assaulted their left-wing political rivals. From 1931, the *SA* was led by Ernst Julius Röhm (1887–1934), the charismatic former leader of the *Freikorps,* a notorious homosexual who had amassed great wealth and power. From 1931 to 1934, Röhm's *SA* grew to some two million members. Röhm provoked the envy and hatred of the German army leaders, of wealthy German industrialists, of the *SS,* and of Hitler himself. In 1934, the tensions, intrigues, and plots within the Nazi Party leadership came to a head. Hitler had been led to believe that Röhm and his *SA* were about to stage a *Putsch* against him and overthrow him. Losing his power was unthinkable to Hitler. Without his illusion of omnipotence, he would have felt helpless

Like a panting panther, an agitated Hitler pounced on Röhm. The *SS* secretly trained for its attack on *SA* headquarters. On the night of June 29–30, 1936—the so-called *Nacht der langen Messer* (Night of the Long Knives)—and on the following days, the *SS* attacked the *SA* headquarters in Bavaria and mass-murdered the entire leadership of the *SA,* from Röhm on down, a total of 83 people including an innocent Bavarian musician and journalist named Willi

Schmid, who had nothing to do with the *SA* and was a victim of mistaken identity (the real "culprit" was one Willi Schmidt). Schmid was seized while playing Bach on his cello and murdered at Dachau. Hitler and his *SS* escort personally drove to the Bavarian resort of Bad Wiessee to arrest Röhm, who was murdered on July 2. Others murdered were Kurt von Schleicher, Hitler's predecessor as chancellor of Germany. Hitler had personally carried out a bloody "purge" of the *SA* leadership. Germany was deeply traumatized and terrorized. Any remaining resistance to the Nazi regime became unthinkable. The *SS* would always murder anyone Hitler wanted dead, incredibly and perversely believing that what they did was honorable because "their honor was their loyalty."

The black-uniformed *SS* was not a monolithic "black corps" of goose-stepping Gestapo men, as it is depicted in the popular mass-communication media and in third-rate historical works. The *SS* was a complex political and military organization made up of two distinct branches, related to one another, but each unique in its functions and goals: the *Allgemeine-SS* (General *SS*) and the *Waffen-SS* (Armed *SS*). The *Allgemeine-SS,* the main branch of this complex organization, had political and administrative roles. The *Waffen-SS,* formed in 1940 after the German invasion of France, was the military part of the *SS,* which fought on the battlefield (Pappas 2006).

The *Waffen-SS* was made up of three major subgroups: the *SS-Leibstandarte*, the *SS-Totenkopfverbände,* and the *SS-Verfügungstruppen.* The *Leibstandarte* (Flesh Standards) were Hitler's personal bodyguards, the *Totenkopfverbände* (Death's-Head Associations) administered the extermination camps, and the *Verfügungstruppen* (Disposition Troops) was a fighting force that swelled to 39 divisions and 600,000 men by the end of World War II and that, in serving as elite combat troops alongside the regular army, gained a reputation as fanatical fighters. The *Waffen-SS* spearheaded some of the most crucial battles of World War II while its men shouldered some of the most difficult and daunting combat operations of all units in the German military (Pappas 2006).

SS men were schooled in racial hatred and admonished to harden their hearts to human suffering. They were forced to kill children in front of their mothers as a test of their "manhood" and "valor." Their chief "virtue" was their absolute loyalty to the *Führer* (Hitler), who gave them the motto *Meine Ehre heißt Treue* (my honor is loyalty). During World War II, the *SS* carried out massive executions of Hitler's political opponents, Gypsies, Jews, Polish leaders, Communists, Catholics, partisans, and Russian prisoners of war. Following the defeat of Nazi Germany by the Allies in 1945, the Allied War-Crimes Tribunal in Nuremberg declared the *SS* a criminal organization. The *Waffen-SS* is sometimes described as the fourth branch of the German Nazi *Wehrmacht* (defense force), along with the *Heer* (army), *Luftwaffe* (air force), and *Kriegsmarine* (navy). When fighting in battle, the *Waffen-SS* came under the tactical control of the *Oberkommando der Wehrmacht* or *OKW* (high command of the defense force). This, however, is inaccurate, as the strategic control of the *Waffen-SS* remained within the *SS*. The *Waffen-SS* and its former members are often vilified for being a part of the larger terror organization. Some historians, however, think that the *Waffen-SS* was primarily a frontline combat organization (Williamson 1995).

"ORDINARY MEN" AND "ELIMINATORY ANTI-SEMITISM"

From the mid-1940s, the conventional psychological wisdom was that members of the *SS* and other German anti-Semites were emotionally disturbed (Simmel 1946; Ackerman & Jahoda 1950; Adorno et al. 1950; Dicks 1972). Almost five decades later, however, the distinguished American historian Christopher Browning published a groundbreaking book in the social psychology of genocide research, showing that, under extreme circumstances, ordinary men who had not been trained to commit murderous acts—as had "elite" German forces like the *SS*—could commit horrendous mass murder against Jews (Browning 1992). However, Browning's book took a social-psychological, rather than a psychoanalytic, viewpoint. It dealt with the conscious rather than with the unconscious mind, and it begged a key psychological question: how normal or abnormal the German Nazis (and other Germans during the Nazis period) were, whether the human species and human civilization themselves were "normal" and mentally healthy.

Four years after Browning's book, the young American Jewish scholar Daniel Jonah Goldhagen, himself the son of a distinguished Holocaust scholar at Harvard University, scored an Oedipal victory on his father by publishing his award-winning doctoral dissertation as a sensational book entitled *Hitler's Willing Executioners: Ordinary Germans and the Holocaust* (Goldhagen 1996). Goldhagen argued that because of the deeply anti-Semitic German culture before Hitler, and due to the special social and cultural character of German anti-Semitism, which was a key part of German culture, millions of Germans went along with Hitler's mass murder of the Jews willingly, even enthusiastically. They were not forced to commit their murderous acts. They hated and feared the Jews and wanted to kill them. It may be significant that Goldhagen used the word "executioners" rather than "murderers" in the title of his book, even though in the case of the German Nazi mass murders, "execution" was a euphemism for murder.

Despite his claims to originality and "revolutionary thinking," Goldhagen accepted the conventional historical wisdom that the German nation had developed in a *Sonderweg* (special way), differently from the Western democracies; and that in the course of this *Sonderweg,* it had embraced a vicious kind of anti-Semitism, which explains its insane and single-minded extermination of European Jewry. Goldhagen called this German phenomenon "eliminatory anti-Semitism," a term which he believed describes a uniquely German attitude that was pervasive in German society from the nineteenth century and led to the great popularity in Germany of the Nazi measures to eliminate the Jews.

Goldhagen's book was published in German translation in the same year as its English publication (Goldhagen 1996a). It gave rise to a great scholarly and popular controversy both in the United States and in Germany. Some considered the book revolutionary, riveting, original, illuminating, and fascinating. Others found it conventional, simplistic, distorted, biased, and repetitious. Many Germans embraced Goldhagen with enthusiasm, while others felt unjustly attacked by him and furiously denounced him as anti-German (Becker 1997; Mitscherlich 1997; Schneider 1997; Vogt & Vogt 1997; Shandley 1998; Zank 1998; Kött 1999; Eley 2000; Feldkamp 2003). One German journalist called the book "a thorn in the flesh" of the German historians (Wehler 1996), while one German historian denied that there was any Goldhagen controversy in Germany (Wippermann 1999). The German-Canadian historian Fred Kautz thought that Goldhagen's book had upset the German historians, most of whom had avoided doing Holocaust research (Kautz 2002, 2003, 2004). While one cannot speak of all German historians as a monolithic group, most of them closed ranks against Goldhagen and rejected his book and its conclusions. Ten years after his groundbreaking book was published, Christopher Browning returned to the social psychology of the Holocaust with two of his colleagues (Newman et al. 2002).

Also 10 years after Browning's groundbreaking study, the American social psychologist James Waller returned to the subject of how "ordinary men" can commit atrocities (Waller 2002). Waller cited psychological experiments, ethnological field studies, and evolutionary theory to support his thesis that we are *genetically predisposed* to divide into groups, value our in-group over other human groups, and treat those within the group more "ethically" than those outside the group. This predisposition has encouraged ethnocentrism, xenophobia, bigotry, and hatred. Our biological heritage also influences our response to authority and our desire to exert authority over others.

Waller thought that there are also "social forces" that help prepare "ordinary people" to commit genocide. One such "force" is cultural beliefs, like nationalism, racism, or "manifest destiny." Another evil-disposing "social force" is disengaging morality from conduct by displacing responsibility, deploying euphemisms, seeking moral justification, looking for advantageous comparisons, or minimizing, distorting, or distancing ourselves from the consequences of our actions (such as not broadcasting the disturbing images of war, concentration camps, or mass killing; calling torture "abuse"; and calling the destruction of a village "liberation").

Waller believed that the more highly regarded one's self-interest becomes, the easier it is to justify evil done to others. At the same time, having a self-identity that is distinct from one's group identity is essential to maintaining moral norms.

Psychoanalytic Studies of Nazism

The Holocaust, in which six million Jews were brutally murdered by the German Nazis and their collaborators during the Second World War of 1939–1945, is so horrifying to contemplate that it takes a great degree of self-control, if not psychic numbing and denial of feelings, to study it objectively and scientifically. In fact, one wonders whether any scholar or psychoanalyst can study the Holocaust without feelings of horror. While the general literature on Hitler, German National Socialism and the Holocaust is vast, there are not very many studies that may be labeled truly psychological. In 1944, while the war was still raging, and the Holocaust was at its worst, a group of American psychoanalysts and social scientists held a conference on anti-Semitism in San Francisco. They called it "a social disease" (Simmel 1946). As we have seen above, the horrors of the Holocaust prompted psychoanalytic studies of the authoritarian personality (Adorno et al. 1950), of anti-Semitism (Ackerman and Jahoda 1950, Loewenstein 1951) and of the Holocaust itself. Raoul Hilberg's chilling chronicle of the Nazi bureaucratic mind at its murderous work (Hilberg 1961) is not a psychological work; but to psychoanalysts, it does offer psychological insight into the unconscious splitting and isolation of feeling in the Nazi mind. Lucy Dawidowicz's studies of the Holocaust and of its historians (Dawidowicz 1975, 1981) are similarly historical rather than psychological (Kren & Rappoport 1980, Luel & Marcus 1984). We shall now review some of these studies.

HEINRICH HIMMLER: BUREAUCRATIZED MASS MURDER

The German acronym *SS* stands for *Schutzstaffel* (Defense Squad). Hitler's black-shirted private army was one of the most dreaded entities of the Nazi regime. Its very name struck terror throughout Germany and all over Europe. The *SS* began as Hitler's private bodyguard in 1923, 10 years before the Nazis took over Germany's government. An *SA* commander named Julius Schreck (the name means "terror") picked eight men to serve as Hitler's personal bodyguard, his *Stabswache* (Staff Guard). In late 1923, the *Stabswache* took part in Hitler's failed Beer Hall *Putsch* in Munich. Hitler was briefly imprisoned. In 1926, a journalist of the racist German newspaper *Völkischer Beobachter* (Popular Observer) named Joseph Berchthold took over the *Stabswache,* which was renamed *Schutzstaffel.* Hitler publicly proclaimed the *SS* his "elite organization." In 1927, Berchthold was replaced by Erhard Heiden, "a former police stool pigeon of unsavory reputation" (Shirer 1960, p. 121), who became the *Reichsführer SS.*

From 1929 to 1945, the *Reichsführer SS* was a fanatical Bavarian racist named Heinrich Himmler (1900–1945). Hitler appointed Himmler to the post because of his blind loyalty, and Himmler kept enlarging his *SS.* By 1933, the *SS* membership had grown from eight bodyguards to 50,000 "elite" troops. Himmler personally screened applicants, seeking to recruit the "elite" of the German people. It was the *SS* that ran the Nazi extermination camps and gassed to death millions of Jews, Gypsies, Slavs, homosexuals, and other "enemies of the Aryan race." Himmler was a fanatical pagan, vegetarian, and fantasist who truly believed that his *SS* were the great new order of German knights. Psychologically, he lived not in the present but in the past, in the tenth century, seeking to revive the mythical glory of his namesake, King Heinrich I of Germany (876–936), of whom Himmler seriously believed himself to be the reincarnation.

Like Hitler, Himmler wanted to replace the German Christian religion with the old German pagan religion and its fierce gods such as Wotan and Donner. He rebuilt the old Westphalian castle of Wewelsburg, using slave labor, into the ritual center of the *SS.* The Wewelsburg castle had been built from 1603 to 1609 by the German Prince of Paderborn. It lies near what was believed to be the site of the ancient battle of the Teutoburg Forest between the Romans and the Germans. German legend suggests that the castle held thousands of accused witches during the seventeenth century, who were tortured and executed within its walls. In 1802, the Wewelsburg castle fell to the ownership of the Prussian state, and in 1815, it fell victim to a fire that gutted the North Tower. In 1925, the castle had been renovated into a museum, banquet hall and hostel, and in 1931, the North Tower again proved to be the weak point of the architecture, and had to be supported by guy wires.

Himmler wanted to restore the ancient glory of the Wewelsburg castle. In 1934, at the suggestion of Karl Maria Wiligut (1866–1946), a strange man of many aliases who was a major influence on Nazi mysticism and on Germanic neopaganism, Himmler signed a 100-mark, 100-year lease with the Paderborn district government, initially intending to renovate and redesign the castle as the *SS Führerkorps,* a school for Nazi leadership. He created a forced-labor camp nearby to carry out the huge work. In 1938, Siegfried Taubert was in charge of developing the castle, when Himmler inquired about the cost of installing a planetarium. From 1939 to 1943, Himmler used inmates from the nearby concentration camps as laborers to perform much of the construction work on Wewelsburg under the design of the Nazi architect Hermann Bartels (1900–1989). The design of floor mosaic laid in the Marble Hall of Wewelsburg Castle during that time became known as the *Schwarze Sonne* (Black Sun) and is now used by the German neo-Nazis as their symbol. The castle contained a room dubbed the Himmler Crypt, dedicated to Himmler's "previous incarnation" King Heinrich I of Germany, where Himmler hoped to be interred after his death. Himmler's plans included making Wewelsburg the center of a new German-dominated world following Germany's "final victory" over its enemies. He planned a huge installation of a one-kilometer diameter in accordance with secular Nazi principles, including a representational figure for the *Führerkorps* .

Perhaps confusing the legendary King Arthur with the real King Heinrich, Himmler imagined the *SS* castle at Wewelsburg as a reincarnation of the castle of the mythical Knights of the Round Table and appointed 12 *SS* officers as his followers, who would gather at various rooms throughout the castle and perform unknown rites. He would be King Heinrich and they would be his loyal knights. There is only one documented meeting of Himmler with his 12 "knights" in June 1941, though they are assumed to have been held regularly. When one of the officers died, his ashes would be interred in the castle. Similarly, any recipient of one of Himmler's personally signed *Totenkopfringen* (Death's Head Rings) was to arrange to have the ring returned to the castle upon his death.

Himmler's loyalty to Hitler was blind and total. He imagined his murderous *SS,* which killed some 10 million innocent people, as an honorable chivalric order. In 1945, when Germany's "final victory" failed to materialize, Himmler ordered his subordinate Heinz Macher, with 15 of his men, to destroy the Wewelsburg castle, two days before the U.S. Army seized its grounds. Reports of the castle's destruction vary from near-complete damage to only the North Tower suffering damage. Be that as it may, the damage was soon restored after Macher's company ran out of explosives. Himmler himself escaped the Allies and tried to make his way back home to Bavaria with the false papers of a farmer, but was arrested and identified by British troops. He committed suicide in jail.

What made a pedantic Bavarian farmer into a bureaucratic mass murderer? The British psychoanalyst Harry Guntrip used Himmler as a prime example of the "schizoid personality" (Guntrip 1968, p. 47), and the American Jewish psychoanalyst Peter Loewenberg diagnosed Himmler as "an obsessive-compulsive character" in whose unconscious mind the defense mechanisms of isolation and denial warded off his unbearable feelings (Loewenberg 1971, p. 616; Loewenberg 1983, p. 213). Loewenberg studied Himmler's adolescent diaries in order to describe his "unsuccessful adolescence." For Himmler, manhood was the ability to control one's feelings, to be hard, cold, and unfeeling.

The American psychoanalyst Robert Jay Lifton (born 1926) studied the psychological processes that made it possible for Nazi physicians to murder their "patients" (Lifton 1986). The Nazi doctors did more than conduct bizarre experiments on concentration-camp inmates. They supervised the entire process of medical mass murder, from selecting those who were to be exterminated to disposing of corpses. In his earlier books, Lifton showed that this medically supervised killing was done in the name of "healing," as part of a racist program to cleanse the Aryan body politic in which the Nazis fervently believed. After the German eugenics campaign of the 1920s to force-sterilize the "unfit," it was a small step to "euthanasia," which, in the Nazi context, meant the systematic murder of the Jews. Building on interviews with former Nazi physicians and their prisoners, Lifton presented a disturbing portrait of career doctors who killed others to overcome their own unbearable feelings of powerlessness. He included chapters on the infamous Josef Mengele and on Eduard Wirths—the "kind" and "decent" doctor, as some inmates incredibly described him—who set up the Auschwitz death machinery. Lifton also collectively psychoanalyzed the German people, scarred by the devastation of World War I and mystically seeking regeneration.

Lifton analyzed the terrible and seemingly contradictory phenomenon of medical doctors, who have vowed to save human life, becoming agents of mass murder. With chilling power, Lifton delineated the Nazi transmutation of values that allowed medical killing to be seen as a therapeutic healing of "the body politic." Based on arresting historical scholarship and personal interviews with Nazi and prisoner doctors, Lifton traced the inexorable logic leading from early German Nazi sterilization and euthanasia of German citizens to mass extermination of the European Jews and other "racial undesirables." Lifton wondered how the Nazi doctors rationalized being "killer-healers." His reply was a multifaceted evaluation of genocide, of the seductive power of Nazi ideology, and of the defensive psychological processes of "numbing" and "doubling." These were also the unconscious defenses of many nonmedical Nazi murderers (Lifton 1986).

The American scholars George Kren and Leon Rappoport felt that the scientific psychological "study of the SS leads one into a bottomless pit of contradictions...rational study of the SS seems impossible because the organization was never really based upon consistent principles defining either its structure or its function" (Kren & Rappoport 1980, p. 39). As an organization, the SS was characterized by paradox, diversity, contradiction, disunity, and irrationality. Kren and Rappoport thought that only two methods were appropriate for understanding the SS: the Alice in Wonderland principle and the Psychiatric Model one (ibid., p. 40) The first principle suggests that in the world of the SS, everything was the reverse of the normal world. A man was killed not because there was a reason to kill him, but because the SS found no reason to keep him alive.

The second principle suggests that only psychiatry (and psychoanalysis) can really explain the gross irrationality of the *SS* behavior. Life in the extermination camps was psychotic-like. The slogans on the gates of the death camps such as *Arbeit macht frei* (Work Makes Free) and *Jedem das Seine* (To Each His Own) were similarly irrational.

Himmler, an emotionally disturbed German who unconsciously isolated his painful feelings and became ruthlessly sadistic, was the supreme *SS* commander. The American Jewish historian and psychoanalyst Peter Loewenberg explored the unhappy circumstances of Himmler's early life and diagnosed him as schizoid and obsessional (Loewenberg 1971). Henry Dicks found that all the *SS* killers suffered from unhappy childhoods, stern fathers and corporal punishment (Dicks 1972). Robert Waite (1919–1999), one of the best psychological historians of Nazi Germany, thought the sadistic *SS* men were intentionally inured to suffering, blood, and death, their human feelings of compassion being numbed or destroyed:

> In Hitler's Germany, medical doctors of the SS were required to perform, or to watch, "medical experiments" such as skin grafts and abdominal surgery on the unanesthesized bodies of Jewish or Polish "patients." Other initiates of the *SS* were forced to kill Jewish babies before the eyes of their mothers. Hitler's theory was that after members of his *SS* had participated in such activity, they would feel drawn together by the bonds of a common experience. The technique seems to have worked rather well. (Waite 1977, p. 24)

As we have seen, the German acronym *Gestapo* stood for *Geheime Staatspolizei* (secret state police), the word *Sipo* for *Sicherhgeitspolizei* (security police), and the acronym *SD* for *Sicherheitsdienst* (security service). Like the *SS,* in Hitler's Germany, this name struck terror in all Germans (Shirer 1960, p. 273). The *SD* was set up by Himmler in 1932 as the intelligence wing of the *SS*. Its leader was Reinhard Tristan Eugen Heydrich (1904–1942), "an arrogant, icy and ruthless character" (Shirer, 1960, p. 273) Like many other top Nazis, Heydrich was a disturbed, murderous, paranoid man known as "Hangman Heydrich." His net of informers all over Germany spied on every German and reported his most casual remarks to *SD* headquarters. People no longer dared speak freely. Anyone near you could be an *SD* informer. The obsessional psychopathology of the SD was remarkable. "Among these professional spies there was always the bizarre atmosphere of pedantry. They had a grotesque interest in such side lines as the study of Teutonic archeology, the skulls of the inferior races and the eugenics of a master race" (Shirer 1960, p. 273). After causing the death of millions, Heydrich was assassinated in Prague in 1942. The Nazis took terrible vengeance, killing thousands of Czechs and Jews. The entire male population of the Czech village of Lidice was murdered. The women and children were carted off to the Nazi death camps. Lidice itself was wiped off the face of the earth.

WERE THE NAZI MURDERERS "NORMAL"?

The question of how normal or abnormal the members of the German Nazi organizations (and other Germans during the Nazi era) were, which had been raised by Browning (1992) and Goldhagen (1996), was tackled by the German Jewish psychoanalyst Isidor Jehuda Kaminer while his non-Jewish colleagues were trying to understand and explain German anti-Semitism (Kaminer 1997). Five years later, another Jewish scholar picked up this theme (Waller 2002). German historians often describe the Nazi era from 1933 to 1945 as a "barbarian aberration" in highly cultured German history, which, before and after Hitler, was greatly civilized. Yet, as one can see from the Brothers Grimm's fairy tales and from such cartoon strips as *Max und Moritz,* which are fraught with violence and sadism, this is a superficial view of German culture. Based on a series of "historical and psychosocial indicators," Kaminer concluded that German National Socialism was no aberration, no accidental "derailing of German history"; rather, it brought to light the hidden part of a specific German "normality."

Kaminer found this "normality" of the German perpetrators of the Holocaust, with which they carried out the "business" of the mass extermination of the Jews, Gypsies, homosexuals, and mentally ill very alarming. He believed that it was due to "an expanded psychic basic structure" whose nucleus was "an internalized world of annihilation," which, during the Nazi era, was externalized and acted out on others. The rejection of weakness, impotence, and helplessness, which was preached by the Nazis, and which is also found in the German pedagogic and psychiatric literature of the 1920s, 1930s, and 1940s, points to unconsciously defended parts of the self, which were projected upon the "foreign." The "people's body" had to be purified of the "foreign," and the "vermin" that had infested it had to be exterminated. There is strong evidence that an education that, by means of "soul murder," turns children into unfeeling perpetrators of mass murder, is as effective before the Holocaust as after it, and that behind the façade of a seemingly harmless normality lies a murderous potential.

As Bohleber has shown, racism, anti-Semitism, and xenophobia often go together. Xenophobia is widespread in modern Germany, where millions of Turks, Gypsies, and other non-German minorities live amid the 80 million "native" Germans. The fear and hatred of the "Gypsies" (the Sinti and Roma migrants) in Germany, were studied by the German psychoanalyst Franz Maciejewski, himself of Polish origin. (Maciejewski 1994). Like the Jews, the Sinti and Roma people were mass-murdered by Hitler's Nazis, who believed them to be inferior and subhuman. The name "Gypsy" indicates the fantasy that the Sinti and Roma came from Egypt, whereas in fact, their ethnic origins are in India— whence the Nazis took their symbol of the swastika.

Unlike the fear and hatred of the Jews, the xenophobia directed at the Gypsies has received little attention from psychoanalysts. Maciejewski drew on Freud's work on the uncanny and on Fenichel's work on anti-Semitism to explain the transformation of the *fear* of the foreign into the *hatred* of the foreign. As for the difference between anti-Semitism and Gypsy-hatred as operative factors in Western civilization, the author argued that whereas both anti-Semitism and Gypsy-hatred derive from the unconscious projection of unacceptable aspects of the self onto others, the conscious hatred of the Jews derives from the son's unconscious hatred of the *father*, representing civilizational progress, while the conscious hatred of the Gypsies unconsciously comes from the son's hatred of the *mother*, because the Gypsies symbolize the archaic world by their adherence to the pleasure principle of matriarchy and their corresponding evasion of the constraints of patriarchy.

The Israeli-German Jewish psychoanalyst Yigal Blumenberg studied what he called "the crux of anti-Semitism" (Blumenberg 1997). Citing the work of Alexander and Margarete Mitscherlich on the German "inability to mourn," Blumenberg focused on what he saw as "the German inability to remember and to work through anti-Semitism," which, even though in a distorted image, as in what Freud called a "counter-cathexis," expresses the ambivalent German relationship to Judaism. Blumenberg thought that the German difficulties in deciphering this counter-cathexis and of putting oneself into a relationship with "the Jew" while remembering German anti-Semitism come from a threefold German tradition of cultural-historical repression of Judaism—through the institutionalization of Christianity, through the Enlightenment, and through National Socialism. German Christian culture, having denied its Jewish roots, flees into purifying, ambivalence-raising tendencies, and carries within itself the germ of its own destruction. Blumenberg thought that the extinction of the memory of the assumed self-origin, which represents a central dimension of Jewish thought, was the point of origin of anti-Semitism, and that only through the working through of anti-Semitism—that is, in the restoration of its memory—is it possible to write cultural history.

One of the first scholars to undertake a full-scale psychohistorical study of anti-Semitism was the Austrian-born American Jewish psychoanalyst Ernest Rappaport (1903–1974), who had been interned in the German Nazi concentration camp at Buchenwald before managing to be liberated and making it to the United States. Rappaport's posthumously-published book included chapters on the "collective psychosis" of anti-Judaism, the psychopathological aspects of Christianity, the projective myth of the Wandering Jew (whose unconscious purpose was to dispel Christian doubts about the myth of Jesus Christ's crucifixion), the psychopathology of the ritual-murder libel (in which the Jews were accused of murdering Christian children and of drinking their blood or using it for their unleavened Passover bread), the medieval persecution and massacres of Jews by Christian monks, popes, and crusaders, and the paranoid Spanish Inquisition and the *auto da fé* (Act of Faith) ritual, in which Christians burned Jews alive to prove their faith (Rappaport 1975). Twenty years later, the American Jewish psychoanalyst Mortimer Ostow devoted a chapter in his book on anti-Semitism to a review of the history of "antisemitic myths" (1996, pp. 95–149).

Rappaport's book includes separate chapters on the individual psychopathology of Jew-haters like St. Paul, St. Augustine, Martin Luther, Adolf Hitler—to whom Rappaport devoted three out of his 14 chapters—Adolf Eichmann, and Joseph Stalin. On Hitler, for example, after describing the obstacles and humiliations of his disturbed mother, Klara Poelzl, before marrying his equally disturbed father, Alois Schicklgruber (who had changed his last name to Hiedler, Hüttler, and Hitler), Rappaport wrote, "I have intentionally started my chapters on Hitler with the frustrations that his mother suffered prior to her so much desired marriage to her diol, Hitler's father. In the voluminous literature on Hitler the finger is always pointed at the father... *The key to the understanding of Adolf Hitler is his mother*" (Rappaport 1975, p. 160, italics added).

Indeed, the psychopathology of Hitler's mother and its profound effect on his own severe psychopathology—whether borderline or psychotic—were emphasized in all the psychoanalytic studies of Hitler's life and personality, both before and after Rappaport's book was published (Erikson 1942, 1963; Langer 1972; Koenigsberg 1975; Stierlin 1975, 1976; Binion 1976; Waite 1977; Bromberg & Small 1983; De Boor 1985; Burrin 1989, 1994, 2004; Schwaab 1992; Bursztein 1996; Young and French 1996; Chamberlain 1997; Victor 1998; Rosenbaum 1998; Redlich 1999). Hitler's mother died of breast cancer when he was 18 years old. She had been treated by a Jewish physician. It was the most formative—and traumatic—experience of Hitler's youth (Waite 1977, pp. 208–213). Hitler made the war on cancer a key part of his ideology and called the Jews a poison and a cancer in "the body of the German nation" (Kitzing 1941, p. 41; Proctor 1999, p. 46). The word "nation" comes from the Latin word for birth, and, unconsciously, as we have seen, the nation is the mother.

In the final chapter of his posthumously published book, Rappaport had these incisive things to say about Christian Jew-haters:

> The historical facts are that the anti-Jew, trying to free himself from the pangs of anxiety, turned the tree of life into the tree of death, the cross, nailed his Christ onto it, and transferred his anxiety to this product of his perverse, sado-masochistic imagination. It added only guilt to his anxiety and made the story even less believable; but the compulsive individual is rigid and inflexible. Then came the final maneuver: the Jew, already uncanny because of his disbelief, was accused of acting out the fantasy of the cross and of perpetrating in actuality the crime of deicide which existed only in the distorted mind of the anti-Jew. Not enough with that, the Jew was accused of addiction to crucifixion by persistent repetition of the act in ritual murder or rape of the Host or Eucharist. (Rappaport 1975, pp. 282–283)

Following Sigmund Freud, Rappaport saw Judaism as "a father religion" and Christianity as "a son religion." The early Jews imagined their father-god

Yahweh as a little child imagines his father, an omnipotent giant who can be both benevolent and malevolent, who is both loved and feared, both revered and hated. The Christians made God's son, Jesus Christ, their new god. Here Rappaport used the term "survivor guilt," which had been coined by his colleagues Henry Krystal and William Niederland (Krystal & Niederland 1968). "Survivor guilt" is a key concept in the psychoanalytic literature on survivors of war, genocide, natural disaster, and any other catastrophe in which people die. "Survivor guilt," however, is a *feeling* or a *fantasy* of guilt rather than actual guilt (Buber 1957; Améry 1966, 1980; Rosenbloom 1995). In discussing Freud's theory of religion, Rappaport strangely attributed "survivor guilt" to the father who has survived the son's attempt to replace him:

> In Christianity, as a son religion, the son has dethroned the father and done away with him, but the father has survived and owing allegiance now to the son he suffers from survivor guilt. Of course, the father could also have been killed by the son. In that case the son projected his own guilt of deicide on the father so that it appeared the father killed the son, then the filicide was also designated as deicide. Since the Jew represents the father god the guilt for filicide and for deicide including the guilt for survival are projected upon him as the Christ killer. Jew hatred is a pre-channelized generalization which makes the individual feel important as the chosen victim of a conspiracy, the conspiracy of the Jews against Christ. Indoctrinated with the passion of Christ in early childhood, the individual empathized and identified with the seemingly helpless persecuted innocent Christ and subsequently feels himself persecuted and threatened by the bad Jews. (Rappaport 1975, p. 283)

In the early twentieth century, the age-old European Christian fantasy of a Jewish conspiracy against Jesus Christ spawned many other conspiracy theories. The most notorious of them was that of an international Jewish plot to take over the world, put forth in the infamous *Protocols of the Elders of Zion,* a rabidly anti-Semitic forgery plagiarized for the *Okhranka* (the tsarist Russian secret police) from a French political satire. (Nilus 1905, 1920; Segel 1934; Bernstein 1935; Cohn 1967; Bach 1973; Taguieff 1992; Conan 1999; Bishop 1999; Eisner 2005). The forger was Matvei Vasilyevich Golovinski (1865–1920), a reactionary Russian aristocrat exile in France who was known there as comte Mathieu Golovinski. He wrote the forgery to convince the Russian tsar Nikolai II that the Jews were to blame for the political unrest in Russia and to persuade him to abandon his liberal reforms. Golovinski plagiarized the *Dialogue aux enfers entre Machiavel et Montesquieu* (Joly 1864, 2002), a satirical essay by the French attorney and publicist Maurice Joly (1829–1878) against Emperor Napoleon III, by replacing every instance of "France" by "the world" and every instance of "Napoleon" by "the Jews." Joly himself had been arrested by Napoleon III's police shortly after the publication of his book in Belgium and was sentenced to 15 months in jail. All copies of his book were confiscated. Golovinski may also have borrowed from an anti-Semitic chapter in the novel *Biarritz* (Goedsche 1868) by the German writer Hermann Ottomar Friedrich Goedsche (1815–1878).

In 1921, at a time of pro-Jewish sentiment in Great Britain, the *Times* of London published series of articles showing that much of *The Protocols of the Elders of Zion* was directly plagiarized from Joly's *Dialogue* (Graves 1921). This, however, did not stop those who believed in a Jewish conspiracy to rule the world from holding fervently to their beliefs, proving that anti-Semitism has nothing to do with rational thought or objective reality. Despite the revelation in the *Times*, the *Protocols* continued to be used, from the Nazis to Henry Ford to more contemporary hate groups and governments (Cohn 1967). The American Jewish political cartoonist William Erwin Eisner (1917–2005) compared sections of the *Dialogues* and the *Protocols* side by side (Eisner 2005). His book was well researched and, for the most part, accomplishes Eisner's goal of making the information available to a wider audience by using a graphic format.

The Austrian Jewish psychoanalyst Elisabeth Brainin and her colleagues believed that such fantasies are unconsciously *transferred* from feelings originally felt by the child for the parents and later *displaced* to the Jews (Brainin et al. 1993). Adopting the important theories of the Austrian-British Jewish psychoanalyst Melanie Klein about our early relationship with our mother and its profound effect on our adult life (Klein 1948, 1957, 1971), Ernest Rappaport thought that the anti-Jew's painful infantile feelings about his mother and her menstrual blood had to do with his paranoid accusations against the Jews via unconscious splitting and projection:

> The paranoid schizophrenic *splitting* of the personality begins with the distinction between the good breast and the bad breast, the madonna and the whore. The Church skillfully utilizes and unscrupulously exploits these primitive alternatives in teaching small children her stereotypes of heaven and hell, a loving Christ and a wrathful father-god, a most cruelly sacrificed Christ and a Satanic anti-Christ or perfidious Jew. The education to racial anti-Judaism only adds synonyms, such as, *Mensch* and *Untermensch* , Aryan and Jew. (Rappaport 1975, p. 285)

Did the Christian Church *consciously* and *intentionally* "utilize and exploit these primitive alternatives," or was this a collective unconscious process? Be that as it may, Rappaport saw the Christian obsession with the crucifixion of Jesus Christ "by the Jews"—actually, it was the Romans who crucified him, if he actually existed—and with his blood as the source of their guilt feelings projected upon the Jews:

> In spite of some attempts at modification and modernization it is obvious that Christendom is not ready yet to de-Christianize Christianity, but there is no urgency that it give up the messianic idea, since the pathology derives from the fantasy of the crucifixion and it would be sufficient if Christianity would only relinquish the

cross [*sic*]. When Christ was riding on his donkey into Jerusalem on Palm Sunday he carried the branch of a palm tree, the symbol of peace. The compulsively repetitive show of the blood dripping from the cross lifts the child's vague memories of the primal scene and the monthly bleeding of the "suffering" mother out of repression and stimulates his lustful bloody fantasies. "There is no redemption without the shedding of blood. We can hear the marching Hitler Youth chanting:

> *Wenn Judenblut vom Messer spritzt,*
> *geht's uns nochmal so gut.*

> (When Jewish blood spurts from the knife,
> then twice as much do we enjoy life.)

Every stereotype of friend and enemy including believers and non-believers in the cross, depends fundamentally on the preparation by the first educator, the mother, who only too often was restricted in her mentality to what the Germans called the three K's: *Kirche, Küche* and *Kinder* (church, kitchen and children). (Rappaport 1975, pp. 285–286)

Naturally, Rappaport's wish that Christianity would give up the cross was pure fantasy and wishful thinking. Rappaport's study was unique in that it was psychoanalytic and historical at the same time. In the same year as Rappaport's book was published, the Czech-born, French-trained Israeli Jewish historian Saul Friedländer, who as a child had been a victim of Nazi persecution, reviewed the psychoanalytic studies of anti-Semitism without being aware of Rappaport's book (Friedländer 1975, pp. 162–168; Friedländer 1978, pp. 92–95). Friedländer repeated Freud's view that *we are dealing with an overdetermined phenomenon, one which has many different causes.* Somewhat inaccurately for a careful historian, Friedländer called anti-Semitism a "collective psychosis." He pointed out that the Jew, like witches and demons, served the Christian psyche as "the most enduring symbol of Evil known to Christianity" (Friedländer 1978, p. 92) The Jew, he said, "fulfills a single function from the sociological and the psychological point of view: he allows the society in question to distinguish Good from Evil, the Pure from the Impure, what is itself from what is 'other'. . .the Jews represent above all the deviant group that allows a society to define its own limits." In psychoanalytic terms, this unconscious process is known as "splitting."

Like Freud and Loewenstein, Friedländer pointed out the obvious element of *unconscious projection* in anti-Semitism. The Christians hate the Jews because they unconsciously project upon the Jews everything they cannot stand about themselves. This is what Freud meant when he wrote that the Christian hatred of Jews was, at bottom, a hatred of Christians. Furthermore, wrote Friedländer, the religious self-segregation of the Jews helped to arouse Christian hostility, as did the Jews' belief in their being God's Chosen People. The Christians imagined the Jews to be foreign and attributed all manner of treason to them. The concentration of

Jews in the most visible sectors of society, such as finance in the Middle Ages, their unusually rapid upward social mobility and their participation in extremist ideological movements reinforced the Christian hatred for them (Friedländer 1978, p. 93)

The Jews, added Friedländer, also served to reinforce the social cohesion and integration of their Christian persecutors, especially at times of political or social crisis in Christian society. During such crises, the tension between Jews and non-Jews becomes exacerbated, and the role of the Jew seems more threatening to the non-Jewish society. Friedländer added the psychoanalytic notion that the Jew was the symbol of God the Father in the collective unconscious of the Christians, whereas the Christian child identified with God the Son [Jesus Christ] whom the Jews had killed, or so he was told. "The Christian imagination sees... in the conflict between Jews and Christ a reflection of old personal conflicts with the father." Friedländer cited the studies by Ackerman and Jahoda (1950), Adorno et al. (1950, pp. 57–101), Gough (1951), and Loewenstein (1951) showing the psychopathology of the anti-Semitic mind. (Friedländer 1978, p. 94)

Friedländer, however, thought that all the above sociological and psychological explanations did not constitute a true *psychohistorical* study of anti-Semitism because "the diachronic element is still missing... *one must study the transformation of the general functions in specific, and changing, historical contexts*" (ibid., p. 94). Friedländer made no mention of Ernest Rappaport's psychohistory of anti-Judaism (Rappaport 1975), either because it was published before the original French-language version of Friedländer's book in the same year, or because Friedländer's translator, Susan Suleiman, was not aware of Rappaport's book, or because she did not make Friedländer aware of it. A social or economic crisis in a given society may give rise to a sharp increase in anti-Semitism. The manifestations of anti-Semitism have ranged from laws prohibiting Jewish ownership of Christian slaves in the early Middle Ages to the genocide and mass murder of six million Jews by the German Nazis and their collaborators in the twentieth century. The common psychological unconscious defensive processes of projection, splitting, scapegoating, and cohesion by exclusion have operated throughout, but the historical contexts were different.

Echoing Sigmund Freud, Howard Stein thought that "the underlying core of the conflict lies in Christian *ambivalence* toward the heavy conscience derived from Judaism... the Jews in turn recoil against... the successful Christian revolt against the repressive moral burden... that Jews dare not admit to be *their* wish" (Stein 1987, p. 149) Stein argued that Judaism never abolished the original sacrifice of the son, moving instead to animal sacrifice and then to self-sacrifice (ibid., p. 156) The Jews themselves, identifying with the sacrificial Son, became the sacrifice. Dying, martyrdom, and sacrifice became part of the Jewish "group self"—a term that includes self-image, self-respect, self-love, self-hate, and everything else that has to do with the group's attitudes and feelings about itself.

Holocaust Denial Disguised as "Historical Revision"

On November 1, 2005, the United Nations General Assembly adopted an Israeli-initiated resolution designating January 27, 1945—the day of the liberation of the Auschwitz-Birkenau extermination camp from the German Nazis by soldiers of the Soviet Union in the First Army of the Ukrainian Front under the command of Marshal Ivan Stepanovich Koniev (1897–1973)—International Holocaust Remembrance Day. The resolution was supported by 104 UN member states. On January 26, 2007, the day before the International Holocaust Memorial Day that year, the General Assembly adopted a U.S.-initiated resolution condemning the denial of the Holocaust, which was supported by 103 member countries. The U.S. representative declared that denying the Holocaust was tantamount to approval of genocide in all its forms. This resolution was approved by consensus, without a vote. The resolution condemned without reservation any denial of the Holocaust and urged UN member states "unreservedly to reject any denial of the Holocaust as a historical event." Some countries, like France, Germany, and Austria, have enacted laws making Holocaust denial a criminal offense.

One of the members of the United Nations, however, namely Iran, which had hosted an international Holocaust-denial conference a few months earlier, rejected the UN resolution as an attempt by the United States and Israel to exploit the Holocaust for their own political interests. At the General Assembly, Iran stood by its stance that the Holocaust should be "closely examined" to determine its scope. "Only by studying objectively what happened in the past, can we ensure that such crimes will never be repeated again," said the Iranian delegate, Hossein Gharibi. "The seriousness and sincerity of this endeavor would be indeed undermined by rendering political judgments on such events and closing the door to any inquiry on their characteristics, scope and extent," he earnestly said.

Despite its specific meaning, or perhaps because of it, the word "Holocaust" has been used by some people to describe other genocides, such as that of the "American Indians," or native Americans, by the white European settlers of North America in the nineteenth century. The term "American Indian" is both an egregious error and a fascinating psychological phenomenon. When the Italian-born Spanish explorer Cristoforo Colombo (1451–1506), known in Spanish as Cristóbal Colón and in English as Christopher Columbus, "discovered" America in 1492 after a long voyage to the "east" (which actually took him to the west), he mistook it for India, and its natives thenceforth became known for centuries as "Indians."

In the United States, the native tribes are called "Indian nations" and their members "native Americans," while in Canada they are called "First Nations." The "American Indian" scholar Ward Leroy Churchill has called the genocide of the "American Indians" by the white European immigrants "Holocaust," and has accused "White America" of denying it for over five centuries (Churchill 1997). However, Churchill, who was born in 1947 in Elmwood, Illinois, claims "American Indian" ancestry from both his parents, and has presented himself as a member of the United Keetoowah Band of Cherokee Indians, while the United Keetoowah Band itself has stated that it had accepted Churchill only as an "honorary associate member." Ward Churchill has been a member of the "American Indian Movement" since 1972, and he has led its Colorado chapter. In 2005, however, he was widely criticized in the American mass-communication media, stimulated by the publicity given to an essay in which he questioned the innocence of many of the people killed in the World Trade Center massacre of 2001, labeling them "technocrats" and "little Eichmanns." In the psychological sense, Ward Churchill himself is a racist Holocaust denier.

The genocide of the European Jews by the German Nazis and their collaborators during the Second World War, which the world calls "Holocaust," is known to the Israelis Jews by the biblical Hebrew word *shoah,* which means catastrophe, calamity, desolation, destruction, and disaster (Isaiah 47:11; Psalms 35:8; Job 30:14; Ben-Sasson 1976, pp. 1017–1039; Falk 1996, pp. 703–721). This word has a special and powerful meaning in modern Israeli Hebrew, and the general feeling in Israel is that the *shoah* is unique in human history, and that it cannot be compared to any other genocide or human catastrophe. I have personally heard a former Israeli supreme-court justice exclaim in public that the Armenian genocide of 1915 and all other genocides cannot be compared to the *shoah,* and that there has been one and only one *shoah* in all of history (meaning ours). Yet the Israeli Christian Arab priest Emile Shoufani (born 1947), the Melkite Greek Catholic archimandrite of Nazareth, has led large groups of Christians,

Muslims, and Jews to Auschwitz. He and the Christian Indian-French writer Jean Mouttapa believe that non-Jews can empathize with the Jewish tragedy, and that treating the *shoah* as "incomparable" is a dangerous psychological barrier that must be breached (Mouttapa 2004).

The enormity of the tragedy of the Holocaust overwhelms our feelings and defies our imagination. As Ruth Stein felt about the evil of the fanatical Muslim suicide murderers who destroyed the twin towers of New York's World Trade Center and killed several thousand innocent souls in them (Stein 2002), we tend to avoid thinking about the Holocaust, avoid feeling the unbearable grief of our terrible loss and our impotent rage at its perpetrators. During the first two decades after the Holocaust, the psychological problems of the survivors were not confronted by Israeli mental-health professionals. This avoidance of unbearable reality is known as *denial,* and the denial of the Holocaust is a special case.

The world center for Holocaust denial is the "Institute for Historical Review" in California, founded in 1976. But already in September 1944, at the German death camp of Janowska, in the Polish city of Lwow (formerly the Austrian city of Lemberg, now the Ukrainian city of Lviv), a German *SS* corporal named Merz told his Jewish prisoner Simon Wiesenthal (1908–2005) that the Americans would never believe him if he ever survived the camp, reached the United States and told them what the German Nazis had done to the Jews. "You would tell the truth to the people in America...And you know what would happen, Wiesenthal?" Merz asked, smiling. "They wouldn't believe you. They'd say you were crazy. They might even put you into a madhouse. How can anyone believe this terrible business—unless they lived through it?" (Wiesenthal 1967).

HOLOCAUST DENIAL AND "HISTORICAL REVISION"

Nazi war criminals are not the only ones denying the enormity of the tragedy they had perpetrated. The standard euphemism for Holocaust denial has been "historical revision," a term which, like "anti-Semitism," is itself a form of denial. One of the early "revisionists" was the German-American "historian" Austin Joseph App (1902–1984), an anti-Semite and a racist Nazi. In 1973, App "laid out" eight patently-absurd "axioms": 1. Emigration, not extermination, was the German Nazi plan for dealing with Germany's "Jewish problem." 2. No Jews were gassed in any German concentration camps, and probably not at Auschwitz, either. 3. Jews who disappeared during the years of World War II and have not been accounted for did so in territories under Soviet, rather than German, control. 4. The majority of Jews who were killed by the Nazis were people whom the Nazis had every right to "execute" as subversives, spies, and criminals. 5. If the Holocaust claims have any truth, Israel would have opened its archives to historians. 6. All evidence to support the "hoax" of six million dead rests upon misquotes of Nazis and Nazi documents. 7. It is incumbent upon the accusers to prove the six million figure. 8. Jewish historians and other scholars have great discrepancies in their calculations of the number of victims (App 1973, 1977).

In 1978 App's absurd "scholarship" spawned the notorious "Institute for Historical Review," the California center for Holocaust denial founded by Willis Allison Carto and the late David McCalden and currently directed by the neo-Nazi American "historian" Mark Weber, who also edits the *Journal for Historical Review,* which could more appropriately be called the *Journal for Holocaust Denial.* The "Institute's" chief spokesmen in the United Kingdom is the British Holocaust denier and "revisionist historian" David John Cawdell Irving, a great admirer of Adolf Hitler (Irving 1977). Irving's nemesis has been the courageous American Jewish historian Deborah Lipstadt, who has spearheaded the scholarly battle against Holocaust deniers. In 2000, Irving lost his libel suit against Lipstadt and her publisher (Lipstadt 1993, 2005; Evans 2001). In early 2006, he was tried in Austria for the crime of Holocaust denial, found guilty, and sentenced to a three-year prison term, but was released and expelled from Austria "forever" later that year.

Another American Jewish scholar, Edward Alexander, had these incisive words to say about Holocaust denial:

> Among the various forms of travesty and exploitation of the Holocaust—relativization, mitigation, appropriation—the crudest but also most highly publicized is the outright denial that the destruction of European Jewry ever took place at all. It used to be said that Stalinism was a more sophisticated totalitarianism than Hitlerism because whereas Hitler ordered books to be burnt, Stalin had them rewritten. The Holocaust deniers are mainly followers, latter-day disciples, and adulators of Adolf Hitler rather than of Stalin. But since the documents bearing witness to the systematic destruction of European Jewry at the hands of National Socialism by now mount into the thousands, burning them would be a formidable task indeed; and so these "neo-Nazis" (as the deniers are usually called) have had to resort to some of the methods of their erstwhile rivals in mass murder, the Stalinists, in order to clear their political ideal of the taint of genocide. Deborah Lipstadt's book, *Denying the Holocaust,* provides a detailed and incisive account of the antecedents, origins, and development of Holocaust denial, starting with "revisionist" polemics against American involvement in World War I and proceeding through the initial steps taken in France by Maurice Bardèche and Paul Rassinier and in America by a variety of Nazi sympathizers starting with Austin J. App. It is to App, a professor of English at the University of Scranton and La Salle College (Philadelphia), that Lipstadt assigns the dubious credit for enumerating the eight assertions that would form the credo of all subsequent deniers. (Alexander 1996, pp. 152–153, citing Lipstadt 1993)

In France, which has the world's third-largest Jewish community (after Israel and the United States), anti-Semitism and Holocaust denial have flourished. In 1982 the young French Jewish intellectual Alain Finkielkraut published a book about Holocaust denial which called it *négation* (negation) rather than *déni* (denial), but his book was translated into English only 16 years later, after the notorious affair of Roger Garaudy and "l'Abbé Pierre" (Finkielkraut 1982, 1998, 2003; see below). The word *négationnisme* was coined in 1987 by the Egyptian-born French historian Henry Rousso to distinguish *révisionnisme,* which, as Rousso argues, refers to "a normal phase in the evolution of historical scholarship," from denial of the Holocaust, where "what is at issue is a system of thought, an ideology, and not a scientific or even critical approach to the subject" (Rousso 1987, p. 176; Fresco 1990; Rousso 1991, p. 151). Rousso sought to expose the false, euphemistic, and misleading nature of the term "historical revisionism" for dangerous anti-Semitic denial of the Holocaust. The usefulness of his distinction between revisionism and *négationnisme,* however, has been questioned by at least one scholar (Fresco 1990; Redeker 1996; see below).

Some of the most prominent and notorious French *négationnistes* have been Paul Rassinier (1906–1967), Maurice Bardèche (1907–1998), Henri Grouès, also known as l'Abbé Pierre (1912–2007), Roger Garaudy (born 1913), and Robert Faurisson (born 1929), the most active surviving Holocaust denier (Bardèche 1948, 1961; Rassinier 1955, 1964; Faurisson 1980, 1982, 1994, 2000; Grouès & Kouchner 1993; Garaudy 1996, 1997). Bardèche was the brother-in-law of Robert Brassilach (1909–1945), a rabidly anti-Jewish writer who collaborated with the German Nazi occupiers of France from 1940 to 1944, advocated the extermination of the Jews, and was the only French intellectual executed for treason after France's liberation from Nazi rule (Kaplan 2000). These *négationnistes* have denied the existence of the Nazi gas chambers, described their extermination camps as vacation resorts, and accused Israel of "inventing the myth of the Holocaust" to further its own political ends, portraying itself as the victim and getting money from Germany.

THE GARAUDY AFFAIR

The importance of Rousso's distinction between "revisionism" and *négationnisme* became clear in 1995, when Pierre Guillaume (born 1940), owner of the far-left French anti-Semitic and *négationniste* publishing house *La Vieille Taupe,* which had begun as a Paris bookshop in 1965, published a virulently anti-Semitic, *négationniste,* and anti-Israeli book by the prolific but Communist-turned-Muslim 82-year-old French "eclectic intellectual" Roger Garaudy. The old man claimed that Israel had "invented the myth of the Holocaust" to finance its own construction (Garaudy 1995, 1997). To escape the punishment of the French law that outlaws antisemitic, racist and xenophobic acts, and in particular acts of *négationnisme* (the Gayssot law), the book was sold off the general market as a "confidential tract reserved for Friends of *La Vieille Taupe.*"

Garaudy's book was a sloppy piece of plagiarism. Its *négationniste* part was heavily borrowed without any credit from Rassinier and Faurisson, the latter's name appearing only once in the entire book as that of "a victim of anti-revisionist repression" (Garaudy 1995, p. 119). Its anti-Semitic and anti-Israeli parts rehashed old themes. But Garaudy's book made waves when it was applauded by his 83-year-old friend Henri Grouès (1912–2007), better known as *l'Abbé Pierre,* a former *résistant* who had saved Jews from the German Nazi occupiers of France and had been revered for helping drug addicts and other emotionally afflicted people. L'Abbé Pierre publicly compared modern Israel's treatment of the Palestinian Arabs to the Biblical Joshua's "massacre" of the Canaanites over 3,000 years ago.

Garaudy seemed like a psychiatrically borderline chameleon-like charlatan. He had changed his religion and political affiliation several times, from Protestant Christian to Stalinist communist to staunch Catholic to Muslim. Without any mention of his sources, he had shamelessly plagiarized his *négationniste* predecessors such as Rassinnier and Faurisson and various extreme-right publications. L'Abbé Pierre fell from his pedestal as national relief worker for the "wretched of the earth," was verbally lynched by the French mass-communication media, castigated by the Jewish-born Jean-Marie Cardinal Lustiger (1926–2007), and expelled from the LICRA (*Ligue internationale contre le racisme et l'antisémitisme*) of which he had been a leader. On April 29, 1996, the left-wing French daily *Libération* wrote that l'Abbé Pierre seemed to have "the mental baggage of a 19th-century village priest, steeped in antisemitism."

After a series of provocative pronouncements, which were often attributed to senility (even though he had been advocating these ideas for years), the old Abbé Pierre publicly withdrew his anti-Semitic statements and asked for forgiveness from those whom he had hurt. With this act, it appeared that the Garaudy-Pierre case was closed. It was nevertheless remarkable that a well-meaning French Jewish intellectual like the present foreign-affairs minister Bernard Kouchner, the founder of *Médecins sans frontières* and a fighter for human rights, a man "above any suspicion of antisemitism," had believed in l'Abbé Pierre's good intentions and published a book of "dialogues" with him (Abbé Pierre & Kouchner 1993). But the two French journalists who compiled the book revealed in 1997 that, in consultation with Kouchner, they had kept out a number of anti-Jewish and anti-Israeli pronouncements by the Abbé Pierre that seem identical to those he would express three years later (Burnier & Romane 1997). The whole affair makes one wonder whether the fear of their approaching death had derailed these two old men, Roger Garaudy and Henri Grouès (l'Abbé Pierre).

Rousso's distinction between historical revisionism and *négationnismne* is not without its critics. During the Garaudy affair, the French scholar Robert Redeker argued that, although some in France still insist on a distinction between the two terms in discussing the Holocaust, the differentiation is a false one and serves the purposes of the deniers. Redeker argued that the end pursued in both cases was the same—the denial of the tragic reality of Jewish history during World War II —the only difference being that *négationnisme* moves directly toward its goal, whereas revisionism adopts the more subtle strategy of minimization rather than outright denial (Redeker 1996, p. 1).

As might be expected, the Roger Garaudy–"Abbé Pierre" affair was exploited by the French mass-communication media to advance their sales. In June 1996, publicity posters appeared in French book shop windows and newsstands announcing the upcoming issue of the popular weekly newsmagazine *L'Evénement du jeudi* (which would cease to exist the following year to be succeeded by *Marianne*). The poster for the June 27 to July 3 issue announced in large, bold, red, black, and white letters, "The Holocaust: The Victory of the Revisionists." This sensational headline was superimposed on a crisp color photograph of the familiar bearded face of the old Abbé Pierre. When that issue of *L'Evénement du jeudi* appeared on the newsstands the following week, it sold out within hours. While the headline alone was certainly shocking enough to attract a large readership, it was the juxtaposition of the announcement of the victory of the "revisionists" with the photograph of l'Abbé Pierre that brought into sharp focus the latest episode of what has come to be known in France as *le négationnisme*— the denial of the Holocaust. As we have seen, however, shocking as it may have been in 1996, such *négationnisme* had already been identified in 1982 by the young French Jewish intellectual Alain Finkielkraut, whose book was translated into English only after the Garaudy affair (Finkielkraut 1982, 1998, 2003).

Jewish Scholars and the Holocaust

THE HANNAH ARENDT CONTROVERSY

In February and March 1963, less than two years after Hilberg's book was published, the German-born American Jewish scholar Hannah Arendt (1906–1975), an expert on political theory and the history of totalitarianism and anti-Semitism (Arendt 1951, 1968), published a five-part series of articles in the *New Yorker* about the trial in Jerusalem of the Nazi mass murderer Adolf Eichmann by an Israeli court that condemned him to death by hanging. Soon thereafter, those articles were published in book form with the provocative subtitle *A Report on the Banality of Evil* (Arendt 1963). Arendt depicted the deeply disturbed Nazi war criminal as a "banal" or "normal" bureaucrat whose "routine" extermination of the Jews epitomized "the fearsome, word-and-thought-defying banality of evil" that had spread across Europe at the time. Arendt *seemed* to blame the European Jews themselves—the Nazi-appointed *Judenräte* (Jewish councils) and other European Jewish bodies that functioned during the war—for their own horrendous fate at the hands of the German Nazis.

Our emotions do not always fit our ideas. The young Hannah Arendt had been the lover of the German philosopher Martin Heidegger (1889–1976), who was 17 years her senior and married—despite the latter's Nazi sympathies and despite Arendt's hatred of totalitarianism (Ettinger 1995). Arendt's book on Eichmann provoked a highly emotional controversy among her fellow intellectuals that still rages years after her death (Robinson 1965; Laqueur 1965; Arendt 1966; Laqueur 1966; Barnouw 1983, 1990; Bergen 1998; Sharpe 1999; Kristeva 2001; Rabinbach 2004; Cesarani 2004, 2006). The Zionist historian Walter Laqueur thought that "the Arendt debate" had provoked both violent denunciation and emphatic assent, that it generated more heat than light, and that because passions had run so high, historical truth had suffered (Laqueur 1965). Arendt's venomous reply to Robinson's book, which listed her numerous errors and distortions, threw more oil into the fire, and Laqueur answered her soon thereafter (Robinson 1965, Arendt 1966, Laqueur 1966). The perceptive American Jewish scholar Anson Rabinbach reviewed the early controversy between Arendt and her critics that raged from 1963 to 1966:

> The Eichmann controversy [actually the Arendt controversy], occasioned by Hannah Arendt's five-part series that appeared in *The New Yorker* from February 16 to March 16, 1963, was certainly the most bitter public dispute among intellectuals and scholars concerning the Holocaust that has ever taken place. It was also the first time that both Jews and non-Jews were witness to a controversy over Jewish memory, an affair that took place largely, but not exclusively, among Jews. The controversy elicited over a thousand published responses. It lasted almost three years from the initial burst of reactions to Arendt's articles and book in 1963, gradually subsiding only after her response to Jacob Robinson's book-length disputation, *And the Crooked Shall Be Made Straight,* more than two years later. The animosity and rancor of the dispute was so extreme that more than two decades later Irving Howe could write that "within the New York intellectual world Arendt's book provoked divisions that would never be entirely healed." (Rabinbach 2004, p. 97; cf. Robinson 1965, Laqueur 1965, Arendt 1966, Laqueur 1966, and Howe 1986)

Robinson's book was a point-by-point refutation of Arendt's theses and arguments. Arendt thought that he had made numerous errors and believed that she had "stumbled on what in fact was a hornets' nest because she had touched upon what seemed an intricate problem and is indeed a painful one" (Arendt 1966). But the Austrian-born American Jewish psychiatrist and psychoanalyst Ernest Rappaport was "taken aback" by Arendt's "naivete" and by her "lack of awareness that her statements could be interpreted as expressions of sympathy for Adolf Eichmann, the first member of our unhappy species to exterminate people en masse with insect exterminators" (Rappaport 1975, p. 238). Rappaport himself diagnosed Eichmann as "an ambulatory schizophrenic." (ibid., p. 239).

Thirty years after Rappaport, the British Jewish historian David Cesarani (born 1956), who had spent some time in his youth on an Israeli kibbutz, published a full-scale scholarly biography of Adolf Eichmann (Cesarani 2004, 2006). Cesarani sought to dispel the myth of Eichmann's unhappy childhood, placing him against the normal but selective background of Austrian Calvinism, very different from the previous picture of an embittered man who turned Nazi on grounds of social disgrace and economic hardship or out of resentment against Jewish employers. As Cesarani saw it, Eichmann, a diligent worker and dutiful son, grew up in a milieu where dislike of Jews was unremarkable; where little animosity was displayed towards individual Jews but "Jewry" was viewed as an alien body in the German "national organism." It was a fantasy to which he became increasingly susceptible, but he was not driven in the first instance by racial hatred (Petit 2004).

At the same time, Cesarani viewed Eichmann as a man suffering from psychotic paranoid delusions. His undoing was his deep humorlessness and his inflexibility of mind. His lethal delusion was exemplified, on the one hand, by his insistence on himself as a referent, carrying out orders approved by his superiors; and, on the other hand, by his profound disappointment when a book that he had written in May 1942, with an anticipated print run of 50,000, was banned by his bosses. Its subject was the statistical data of Jewish transports. Of his work, he commented without irony: "Time just flew by" (Petit 2004).

Whatever Cesarani's views of Eichmann's mental health, he seemed to hate Hannah Arendt more than Adolf Eichmann. He believed that Arendt's judgments were "wayward," that her depiction of Eichmann was "self-serving, prejudiced and ultimately wrong." Arendt could be infuriatingly arrogant and, to impugn her objectivity and blacken her character, Cesarani cited disparaging comments that she had made about Eastern European Jews in her private letters. He went even further in this scathing statement: "She had much in common with Eichmann. There were two people in the courtroom who looked up to the German-born judges as the best of Germany and looked down on the prosecutor as a miserable *Ostjude*: one was Eichmann and the other was Hannah Arendt" (Gewen 2006, citing Cesarani 2006).

Cesarani's unprecedented attack on Arendt as Eichmann's double reminds one of the anti-Zionist Israeli Jewish filmmaker Eyal Sivan (born 1964), who in his film *The Specialist* (1999), sought to equate Eichmann with his prosecutor, Gideon Hausner (1915–1990). Sivan manipulated the documentary evidence from Eichmann's trial to create a similarity between Hausner's and Eichmann's external appearance and character. In one scene in the film, Eichmann is seen asking permission to leave his protective booth to take a close look at a map hanging outside. In the background music is heard, and the camera focuses on the prosecutor, Hausner, who turns his gaze towards the panel of judges. The judge approves, and Eichmann leaves the booth. The quality of the picture begins to deteriorate, the music becomes louder. Hausner joins Eichmann next to the map, and the two of them are seen standing side by side, with their backs to the camera. The picture becomes even fuzzier, and at that same moment, the two bald men, dressed in black, look almost identical. In the original videotape of the trial, however, the judge and Hausner were not even filmed at that moment. The pictures were taken from another part of the trial. The deterioration in the quality of the picture, which emphasizes the great similarity between the men, is deliberate.

The Hannah Arendt controversy also involved the American Jewish writer Irving Howe, who in the mid-1980s observed (as the Israeli-American psychoanalyst Ruth Stein would find 20 years later) that the subject of evil in general, and of the Holocaust in particular, "resists the usual capacities of the mind" (Howe 1986, Stein 2002). In dealing with this terrible subject, we become entangled in very difficult intellectual and emotional problems, wrote Howe, "for which no aesthetic can prepare us." Howe agreed with Arendt and with the American Jewish scholar Richard Rubenstein that it was a conceptual error to "elevate" the Holocaust to an event "outside history," to see it as an occult, mystical, or nonhuman phenomenon, even if, as Howe put it, "we lack adequate categories for comprehending how such a sequence of events could occur" (Arendt 1963; Rubenstein 1966; Howe 1986). Irving Howe had lost some of his friends due to the Arendt controversy. In fact, psychoanalysis does offer us "adequate categories for comprehending how such a sequence of events could occur."

ZYGMUNT BAUMAN: PERSONAL HISTORY AND NAZISM

Three years later, the Polish-British Jewish sociologist Zygmunt Bauman (born 1925) added the notion of the "modernity" of the Holocaust evil to the "banality" and "normality" ideas of Arendt, Rubenstein, and Howe (Bauman 1989). Bauman ignored the powerful and irrational emotional forces that were at the heart of the tragedy. The criticism leveled by the Austrian-born American-Jewish psychoanalyst Ernest Rappaport at Rubenstein's and Arendt's ideas (Rappaport 1975, pp. 236–238) can be applied to Bauman's notions. The most common claim against Bauman's ideas is that his emphasis on the role of bureaucratization and instrumental rationality, in his interpretation of the Holocaust, paid little or no attention to the ideological factors in Nazism that were necessary to bring it about.

This criticism may not be quite fair, since Bauman himself had written, "Modernity meant, among other things, a new role for ideas—because of the state relying for its functional efficiency on ideological mobilization, because of its pronounced tendency to uniformity...because of its 'civilizing' mission and sharp proselytizing edge, and because of the attempt to bring previously peripheral classes and localities into an intimate spiritual contact with the idea-generating centre of the body politic" (Bauman 1989, p. 44). Bauman's focus on the increasing rationalization of modernity is itself ideological, yet Bauman tended to disregard or to leave without explanation the irrational ideological factors that were crucial to German Nazism and the Holocaust. In other words, like many other social scientists, Bauman overlooked the irrational and unconscious emotional motives of the German Nazi horrors that are precisely the focus of psychoanalysis. He rationalized and intellectualized the Holocaust into his sociological notions.

The life story of Zygmunt Bauman, one of the most important sociologists of our time, who in 1998 won the Theodor W. Adorno Award from the city of Frankfurt (named after Theodor Ludwig Wiesengrund Adorno, the famous German-Jewish social scientist), is a fascinating illustration of anti-Semitism and the variety of the Jewish reactions to it. Here is an interview he gave to a perceptive British journalist:

> [Bauman] bats away questions about his early life with self-deprecating comments: "I don't have the capacity to present my life as a story," he claims. Over the years, he has given a few details: his birth in the provincial town of Posnan [Poznan] in west Poland to a family of very modest means; his struggle for an education as a poor Jew; the flight to Soviet Russia when the Germans invaded and how he joined the Red Army. He was posted to a remote town (westerners were not allowed in big cities) in northern Russia and whiled away his free time by studying for a physics degree. To these bare outlines, he adds a few new details: "I was brought up in the kitchen. My mother was a woman of great ambition, inventiveness and imagination, but we were relatively poor and she was confined to the housewife role. My father came back from work in the evening and immediately fell asleep, he was so tired. But I hold him in very high esteem; he was a self-made man. He never went to any schools, but he learnt to read several languages and was an avid reader of wide horizons. Above all, he was amazingly honest. In fact, we almost lost our lives because of his honesty. In 1939, we were running away from Posnan as the Germans were invading—the town was almost on the German border. We took the last train east, but we were stopped at a station which was being bombed by the Germans. We should have run away from the station because that was the object of the bombing, but he wanted to find a ticket inspector to pay for our tickets." (Bunting 2003)

Bauman's personal story unfolded in the interview as the perceptive journalist managed to gain the scholar's confidence and get him to talk about his past:

> Although aware of being a Jew, Bauman was brought up speaking only Polish, eating Polish food and mixing only with Poles. His grandfather tried to inculcate some Judaism into the small Zygmunt, to no effect. But his wife Janina is adamant on one aspect of Bauman which is quintessentially Jewish: *he is a Jewish mother* and, since his retirement, does all the cooking. He presses visitors to try the little cakes, strawberries and canapés spread out on the coffee table with napkins, forks and sideplates and offers coffee and tea with solicitous eastern European hospitality. (Bunting 2003, italics added)

Like many other Polish Jews, Zygmunt Bauman escaped certain death at the hands of the German Nazis by fleeing to Russian-occupied eastern Poland after the Germans occupied western Poland in September 1939. He later joined a "free" Polish military unit in the Soviet Red Army and returned to Poland in 1945 as a 20-year-old Soviet officer. He and his future wife, Janina Lewinson, who had survived the horrors of the Warsaw ghetto, met in their early twenties at a lecture at the University of Warsaw and married after a whirlwind courtship. Bauman first had an academic career in Poland, but in 1968, an anti-Semitic "purge" in Poland drove most of the surviving Polish Jews out of the country, including many intellectuals who had fallen from grace with the communist Polish government. Bauman, who had lost his chair at the University of Warsaw, was one of them. He first went to Israel to teach at Tel Aviv University, and later accepted a chair in sociology at the British University of Leeds, where he intermittently also served as head of department. Since then, he has published mostly in English.

It was only after his beloved wife Janina published her Holocaust memoirs (Bauman 1986, 1988) that Zygmunt Bauman published his own Holocaust book augmenting the ideas of Hannah Arendt and Richard Rubenstein about the "banality" and "normality" of the Holocaust's perpetrators by adding the notion of their "modernity" (Bauman 1989). Richard Kilminster, a Leeds colleague of Bauman's, said: "When the book was published in Germany, it caused a sensation. [Bauman] argued that the Holocaust could only happen because of modernity's technology and bureaucracy. What modernity did was to generate unintended consequences of bureaucratic complexity and created the conditions in which moral responsibility disappeared" (Bunting 2003). The British journalist had this to add:

> The escape to Soviet Russia saved him from the worst experiences of wartime Poland: the ghettos, concentration camps and the Holocaust. Indeed, he says that *it was not until his wife wrote her own memoirs of life as a young Jewish girl in the Warsaw ghetto that the enormity of the suffering hit home.* Janina's account, *Winter in the Morning,* which was published in 1985 [*sic*], describes how she was hidden and survived while much of her extended family perished. It influenced enormously Bauman's *Modernity and the Holocaust* published four years later [*sic*]. The book received great critical acclaim in Germany, and provoked controversy elsewhere for "letting Germany off the hook". Bauman's thesis was that the Holocaust was a product of modernity rather than being specific to German nationalism. (Bunting 2003, italics added)

In fact, Janina Bauman's memoirs were published in 1986–1988 and Zygmunt Bauman's Holocaust book in 1989. For all his brilliance, the Polish Jewish scholar avoided the subject of the Holocaust for over 40 years, dealing with it only after he was forced to deal with it by his wife's memoirs—and then missed its key psychological aspects. Zygmunt Bauman's ideas about the Holocaust are as controversial as Arendt's, Rubenstein's, and Howe's. Like them, he not only seems to exonerate the German Nazi perpetrators of their horrendous genocide (an ethical judgment rather than an explanatory theory), but also to ignore the powerful unconscious emotions that fueled the perpetrators of the Holocaust tragedy:

> Bauman argues that to blame Germany effectively exonerates everyone else, whereas *the ideas of eugenics were adopted and received scientific credibility in many countries including the US and Scandinavia.* The Holocaust triggered the ethical

preoccupations of his books of the early to mid-90s: "What is it in our society which makes this sort of thing possible? The real problem is why, under certain circumstances, decent people who are good husbands, neighbours and so on, participate in atrocities. That's the real heart of the problem. There are not so many psychologically corrupted people in the world to account for all the many atrocities around the world. So that was my problem: people who, under other circumstances, would be exemplary members of society, participate in monstrous things—though it's difficult to say if they become monsters. (Bunting 2003, italics added)

Did Bauman confuse eugenics with racism? Bauman saw eugenics as the origin of Nazi racism. He refused to blame Germany alone for the Holocaust and insisted on individual rather than collective responsibility. Bauman believed that there were as many people in Europe who helped Jews as those who killed them: "It all boils down to a person and personal responsibility. I was fascinated by sociologists' research into the people who helped the victims: these people were a cross-section of the population. None of the factors which sociologists believe to be the determinants of human behaviour—education, religious belief, political attachment—correlated with the incidents of heroic resistance against evil. Somehow, the ability to resist is not fully dependent on social conditioning" (Bunting 2003).

Did Bauman effectively deal with his wartime trauma? From the scholarly criticisms leveled at his work, he seems to have rationalized and intellectualized the experience. It was no accident that he wrote his book about the Holocaust only after the publication of his wife's Holocaust memoir. Perhaps he felt guilty for not having suffered as much as his wife had. Here is the account given by the perceptive British journalist:

After the war, Bauman returned to Warsaw as a Red Army officer, a position which gave him a decent flat and access to a university education. He described in one interview how he and Janina sometimes play a game over a drink in the evening, speculating on how Hitler changed the course of both their lives. Paradoxically, he owes his education indirectly to the Nazis; in inter-war Poland, severe quotas on Jews would have ruled out a Polish university, and the option of studying abroad—pursued by well-off Jews—would never have been open to him. Bauman also acknowledged that he owed his marriage to Hitler; the enormous gap in social status between the poor provincial Baumans and Janina's wealthy, cosmopolitan [Warsaw] family would have made a relationship impossible. But by the time the two met in their early 20s in a lecture theatre in Warsaw University, Janina was living in genteel poverty with her mother and younger sister. "Immediately I saw her, I knew I didn't have to look further and within nine days, I'd proposed. Why did I know I didn't need to look any further? I'm not a poet," says Bauman shortly, though he adds that she has been the most important woman in his life. Janina's wry comment on their 55 years of marriage is obviously a familiar joke: "We're Poles apart." (Bunting 2003)

The British journalist thought that Zygmunt Bauman had found happiness in his marriage despite his wartime sufferings. His wife Janina had suffered much more than he as a child in the Warsaw ghetto. He and Janina still love one another:

> Their every gesture expresses their mutual respect and love. Although she admits her reading of his work can't keep up with his writing, she accompanies him on all his lecture tours. In her second volume of memoirs, *A Dream of Belonging*, Janina describes with tenderness their whirlwind courtship and the happy early years of marriage with the arrival of a daughter, Anna, now a mathematics professor in Israel, then Bauman's assiduous care of Janina after the birth of their twin daughters, Lydia, now a painter, and Irena, an architect. These were good years despite the small flats and shortages of postwar Poland; their lives were full of family and friends and their careers flourished as they were both drawn into the dream of creating a new communist society. Janina worked as a film script editor while Bauman was forging a career in sociology, an academic discipline which was then at the centre of public debate. He founded and edited a journal, *Sociological Studies*, which sold out on its first day of publication. (Bunting 2003)

Despite his credentials as a sociologist, Zygmunt Bauman—along with Hannah Arendt, Richard Rubenstein and Irving Howe, each for his own personal reasons—ignored the crucial importance of the unconscious psychology of the Nazi perpetrators of the Holocaust. Arendt's critics were not only American Jewish intellectuals. The French Jewish philosopher Jacob Rogozinski reviewed and criticized Arendt's theories on totalitarianism, Nazi ideology, and the Holocaust, including her interpretation of the concentration camp as the essence of total domination and the "inferno" (Rogozinski 1989). He claimed that Arendt's theory of the "banality of evil" as an "explanation" of the Nazi psyche was erroneously based on the analysis of an executor (Eichmann) and not on that of the decision maker (Hitler). Rogozinski compared Arendt's views with the psychoanalytic interpretation of modern and Nazi anti-Semitism, focusing on myths such as Jewish "world domination," a Jewish "conspiracy," and the idea of a "chosen people," and the use of these myths by Adolf Hitler. He concluded that Arendt's explanations failed to take into account the religious roots of anti-Semitism, as well as the role of the collective unconscious mind. The same may be true of Rubenstein, Howe, and Bauman.

Contemporary Anti-Semitism

RECENT PSYCHOANALYTIC STUDIES

In a recent book on the unconscious psychodynamics of anti-Semitism by a group of New York psychoanalysts, Mortimer Ostow and his colleagues made case studies of anti-Semites in psychotherapy in a method similar to that of Ackerman and Jahoda many years earlier (Ostow 1995). Curiously, Ostow described the anti-religious Nazis—who persecuted Jews and Catholics—as a religious apocalyptic movement of the millenarian type (ibid., pp. 164–165). While some millenarian and apocalyptic movements engage in mass suicide (Falk 2004, pp. 163–168), the Nazis engaged in mass murder:

> There can be no question but that the Holocaust was such a religious, millenarian movement [sic], intended to eradicate the cosmic enemy, the Jews, to make way for the "Thousand-year Reich"...Hitler's irrational behavior, sacrificing the entire [German] nation and finally himself in response to his delusions about Jews, leaves no doubt that he saw himself as a divinely inspired leader...It is ironic that the apocalyptic violence that is intended to achieve his own rebirth by the aggressor, does so by imposing apocalyptic destruction upon the designated enemy. On the other hand, given its origin as an attempt to avoid suicide by displacing the violence outward, the attack is often so [unconsciously] contrived as to result in the ultimate defeat and demise of its instigator. The Nazi Holocaust destroyed six million Jews but in the end destroyed itself. (Ostow 1995, pp. 165–166)

It is strange to see a respected colleague referring to the supremely-tragic Holocaust as a "movement." The Holocaust was not a "movement" by any definition: it was the systematic genocidal mass murder of six million European Jews by an obsessively-systematic extermination machine. Did Ostow confuse German Nazism with the Holocaust?

Most psychoanalysts agree that the rabid and murderous anti-Semitism of the German Nazis was an extremely irrational and pathological racist ideology, deriving from the primitive primary processes of unconscious projection and splitting. All bad aspects of the individual and group self were unconsciously split off, externalized, and projected upon the Jews. Anti-Semitism and the belief in the superiority of the Germans as a *Herrenvolk* (master race), along with the song *Deutschland über alles* (Germany above All), both cornerstones of National Socialism, were a collective paranoid illness.

Let us take a closer look at the psychological aspects of Nazi ideology and of the mass murder of the European Jews by the German Nazis. The German-American Jewish social scientist Theodor Ludwig Wiesengrund Adorno (1903–1969) had replaced his father's last name of Wiesengrund with his mother's maiden name of Adorno. His study with Max Horkheimer (1895–1973) and his other colleagues of the psychodynamics of the authoritarian personality (Adorno et al. 1950) was brought forth by the horrors of the Second World War, of the Nazi regime, and of the Holocaust of European Jewry. The scholars, some of whom had been forced by German Nazi persecution to emigrate from Europe to the United States, unconsciously sublimated their painful feelings of grief and rage about their losses, about the war, fascism, Nazism, and Hitler, and their "survivor guilt" feelings into the creative and constructive field of scientific study. These scholars sought to understand how and why such an extreme, racist, fanatic, irrational, violent, murderous, destructive, and dangerous right-wing political party as the *Nationalsozialistische deutsche Arbeiterpartei* or *NSDAP* (known to the world as the Nazi Party), had come to power in Germany and brought about such a terrible catastrophe both upon Germany itself and upon the rest of the world.

Adorno and his colleagues' postwar study was the first to combine the insights of psychoanalysis with those of social psychology. They found that those who became Nazis, those who collaborated with the Nazis and who submitted to them, were characterized by inner insecurity, by a longing for a domineering, aggressive, and tyrannical leader, and by having "resolved" their Oedipal conflict negatively by surrendering to an authoritarian father, repressing their jealousy and their rage at him. The scholars thought that this was often a homosexual solution, confusing sadism with sexual potency. Freud had thought that unconscious denial and projection of homosexual feelings produced paranoid delusions of persecution. The leadership of the Nazi Party and of its dread "security" forces, the *SA, SD, SS,* and Gestapo, certainly showed much homosexual, obsessional, sadomasochistic, and paranoid psychopathology. The doubts and *ambivalence* of the obsessional patient often become the suspicions and delusions of the paranoid. Projective paranoid rage, suspicion, intrigue, homosexuality, plots, and murders were quite common among the Nazi leaders.

MASTERING THE PAST?

In Germany and Austria, the countries of the Holocaust's perpetrators, the collective psychological process of working through the nation's guilt feelings over its mass-murderous acts is known as *Vergangenheitsbewältigung* or "mastery of the past" (Rosenkötter 1979; Adorno 1986; Adler 1990; Mohler 1991; Gruber 1995; Von Dirke 1996; Jesse and Löw 1997). This process is commonly thought to involve an *Auseinandersetzung,* or "sorting out" of the collective past for oneself as a way of mastering the trauma, guilt feelings, shame, rage and disappointment about the deeds of one's parents, and the unhappiness about belonging to a nation that could perpetrate such crimes. However, two German psychoanalysts had argued that the Germans "had not been able to mourn their losses" (Mitscherlich & Mitscherlich 1975), and that they did not go through a true emotional working through of their past. An Israeli psychoanalyst is supposed to have quipped, "The Germans will never forgive the Jews for Auschwitz." This sad "quip" has an obvious and terrible truth to it.

Theodor Adorno's lectures included *Was bedeutet Aufarbeitung der Vergangenheit?* ("What does working through the past mean?"), a subject related to his thinking of "after Auschwitz" in his later work. (Adorno 1986). Adorno criticized the German philosopher Martin Heidegger, whose ties to the Nazi Party are well known. Heidegger, distinct from his role in the Nazi Party during the Third Reich, made up a historical conception of *Germania* as a philosophy of German origin and destiny (he later replaced *Germania* with the West). The Spanish-German philosopher Alexander Garcia Düttman attempted to treat the philosophical value of the two seemingly-opposed and incompatible terms "Auschwitz" and "*Germania*" in the philosophy of both men in a manner that was not simply comparative (Düttmann 1991, 2002).

The erection of monuments to Holocaust victims has been a theme in Germany's *Vergangenheitsbewältigung.* Nazi death camps in Germany like Dachau, Buchenwald, Bergen-Belsen, and Flossenbürg are open to visitors as memorials and museums. Most German towns have plaques on walls marking the spots where particular atrocities took place. When the seat of the German government was moved from Bonn to Berlin in 1999, an extensive "Holocaust Memorial," designed by the American Jewish architect Peter Eisenman, became part of the vast development of new official buildings in the district of *Berlin-Mitte* (central Berlin). The museum was opened in 2005. It is officially called *Das Denkmal für die ermordeten Juden Europas* (The Memorial for the Murdered Jews of Europe). Some controversy attaches to this museum both because of this formal name and because of its exclusive emphasis on Jewish victims rather than including the Gypsies, homosexuals, Catholics, and others. As Eisenman acknowledged at the opening ceremony, "It is clear that we won't have solved all the problems—architecture is not a panacea for evil—nor will we have satisfied all those present today, but this cannot have been our intention." The museum's informal but common German name, *Holocaust-Mahnmal,* is also significant. The German noun *Mahnmal,* which is distinct from *Denkmal* (monument or memorial), connotes "a warning to future generations" rather than "remembrance" or "memorial."

The German Holocaust memorial museum is part of the collective German effort not to forget what Hitler's generation perpetrated upon the Jews, a very painful but integral part of German history. But have the Germans been able to mourn their own enormous losses during the Second World War? One of the two German authors of *The Inability to Mourn* wondered whether anti-Semitism was a male disease (Mitscherlich 1983). The social-prejudice disease called "anti-Semitism" had been treated by Freud and his successors as a developmental-psychological issue, almost purely a result of the psychosexual development of the male. Margarete Mitscherlich-Nielsen thought that there was no direct connection between normal female socialization, in which the fear of loss of love replaces the male's castration anxiety, and anti-Semitism. Women usually become anti-Semitic through their accommodation to the ideologies of men, whose love, sexuality, and support they need.

Another German scholar, Detlev Claussen, reviewed the literature on anti-Semitism until the mid 1980s and tried to combine social theory with psychoanalysis (Claussen 1987a). Based on the critical social theory of Marx, Horkheimer, and Adorno, Claussen saw anti-Semitism as an economic-social-psychological phenomenon, which rests on the twisting of the unconscious into false consciousness. One must clarify the process through which this false consciousness arises, and here critical social theory and psychoanalysis can combine their explanatory powers. The author saw a connection between the social passage from marginal precapitalistic anti-Semitism to the universal modern kind and the economic universalization of the production of goods and of exchange value in a world of goods and services. Claussen believed that, historically, "Jew" and "value" were experienced as identical in developed capitalism. He thought that the universalization of the production of goods and exchange value remains unacknowledged, while instead the fetishism of goods and anti-Semitism come to light as a false consciousness.

Tragically, Hitler's German Nazis not only killed tens of millions of non-German people, but also brought about the deaths of tens of millions of their own people. The result was millions of German war widows with millions of orphaned children as well as millions of traumatized German survivors who severely damaged their own children emotionally (Bruhns 2004). Incredible as this may seem, therefore, the systematic mass murder of the European Jews by the German Nazis and their collaborators was not only traumatic and tragic for the few Jewish survivors—and for their offspring, who were in turn traumatized by their own traumatized parents—but also for the German perpetrators and for their offspring, who still suffer from psychic trauma, rage, guilt, and shame.

Born of Hitler's own psychopathology, itself a product of that of his disturbed parents (Waite 1977), the Holocaust was an incredible mass tragedy that has affected several generations in Israel, in Germany, and in all the countries where Jewish survivors have found refuge.

For the latter, *Vergangenheitsbewältigung,* or "mastering the past," is an impossible task. Many of them—and their children—suffer from lifelong posttraumatic stress disorders, which involve emotional pain and suffering, anxiety, depression, and suicidal ideation. One of the questions about the German *Vergangenheitsbewältigung,* therefore, is whether it is psychologically possible, whether it is real or a mirage. How can one "master" a past so traumatic and horrible? Can one forget the horrific past? Can one let it go? Can one work it through? Does one need to repress it, project it, or deny it unconsciously? As we have seen, the German-Canadian historian Fred Kautz believes that most of the German historians have denied the Holocaust by not studying its history and by treating the Nazi era as an aberration or derailing of German history.

Indeed, denial of the Holocaust is frequent in Germany—and understandably so. Coming to terms with what their nation did to the Jews is very painful for Germans. During the last decades of the twentieth century, the incidence of neo-Nazism, anti-Semitism, and Holocaust denial increased in Germany (Bergmann & Erb 1996; Kurthen et al. 1997). Among the notorious German Holocaust deniers were Thies Christophersen (1918–1997), a neo-Nazi farmer who had served during the war years as an officer in the Nazi extermination camps, and Wilhelm Stäglich (1916–2006), a neo-Nazi judge (Christophersen 1973, 1979; Stäglich 1979, 1986). Incredibly, as an Israeli psychoanalyst is supposed to have said, these Jew-haters accused the Jews of crimes against Germany (Broder 1986a). Christophersen and Stäglich were tried for their crimes by the German authorities, who, like France and several other European countries, had made it a crime to deny the Holocaust and to spread Nazi propaganda and racial hatred. Their neo-Nazis' "research" was refuted by serious German historians (Bastian 1994, 1997).

The fall of the Berlin Wall in 1989, Germany's reunification soon thereafter, and the fall of the "iron curtain" between Western and Eastern Europe triggered a fresh wave of anti-Semitism and Holocaust denial. The Israeli Jewish historian Jonathan Frankel had this view of East German and West German anti-Semitism during the last decade of the twentieth century:

> The wave of xenophobic violence and antisemitic incidents that erupted in Germany between 1991 and 1994 focused an uncomfortable spotlight on that country, souring the euphoria that followed the sudden fall of the Berlin Wall and the seemingly smooth unification of East and West Germany. With alarmists sounding warnings, survey researchers combed the country and returned with gratifying data. Contrary to expectations, "Ossis" proved less antisemitic than their "Wessi" counterparts (one 1990 survey found 4 to 6 percent hard-core

antisemites in the east as compared to 12 to 16 percent in the west). At the same time, easterners were more uncomfortable with the 1 percent of the population who were foreigners in the GDR than were West Germans with the 10 percent of foreigners in their midst. Moreover, many easterners resented the transition from an ethnically homogeneous to a more diverse society, and the rate of xenophobia was 15 percent higher in the east than in the west. (Frankel 2000, p. 323)

Frankel criticized the German scholar Hermann Kurthen and his colleagues (Kurthen et al. 1997) for being too optimistic about German anti-Semitism and for their "inadvertent or unconscious conflation of xenophobia and anti-semitism." (Frankel 2000, p. 323). However, as we have seen, many German psychoanalysts think that xenophobia, racism, and anti-Semitism often go hand in hand (Bohleber 1992, 1997).

MODERN FRENCH ANTI-SEMITISM

In the Middle Ages, the Christians forced the Jews into high-risk usurious money lending, having barred them from other trades, and then accused them of blood-sucking usury. In the second half of the nineteenth century, the anti-Semites, with great violence, accused the Jews of loving only money. German speakers called them *Geldjuden* (money Jews). Money has deep unconscious emotional significance, symbolizing, among other things, blood, feces, parts of the human body, love, milk, omnipotence, and even life itself. Money replaced human and animal sacrifice (Faber 1981, pp. 104–124). The Jewish philosopher Karl Marx (1818–1883), himself the grandson of rabbis on both sides of his parents, wrote an anti-Jewish text entitled *Zur Judenfrage* (On the Jewish Question), in which he said that "money is the jealous God of Israel" and imagined the world without Jews (Marx 1844, 1959).

The rabidly anti-Jewish French journalist Edouard Drumont (1844–1917) echoed his German colleagues in *La France juive* (Jewish France), which he subtitled "a political and social-economic newspaper" when it began publication in 1886. Six years later, Drumont began publishing *La Libre Parole* (Free Speech). Allegedly founded with Jesuit involvement, the newspaper denounced French Jewish military officers as being future traitors. This led a brave (or hotheaded) young Jewish captain of dragoons, André Crémieu-Foa (1857–1892), to declare the slanderous assault made upon the body of Jewish officers a personal insult to himself. Crémieu-Foa fought pistol duels, first with Drumont, then with a Comte de Lamase, under whose name the anti-Semitic articles had appeared. Drumont was slightly hurt in the first duel, and all the bullets went wide in the second. Crémieu-Foa died in Africa later that year.

It had been agreed between the parties to the duels that they would not be made public. In a tragic and unconsciously fratricidal move, Crémieu-Foa's brother, following the treacherous advice of the Captain Ferdinand Walsin

Esterhazy (1847–1923)—the real traitor of the Dreyfus affair, who was secretly selling military secrets to the Germans, and who was one of the Jewish captain's seconds—leaked the information about the duels to the newspaper *Le Matin*. The furious Marquis de Morès, who had been the chief second of Monsieur de Lamase and was a well-known anti-Semite and a famous duelist, held Captain Mayer, Crémieu-Foa's chief second, responsible for the breach of confidentiality. Though innocent of the matter, Mayer tragically accepted a duel challenge from the marquis. The duel was fought on June 23, 1892, and the Jewish captain was mortally wounded at the first attack and died a few days later.

Crushed by Mayer's death, and exposed to still more violent insults on the part of the anti-Semitic French press, the impetuous Captain Crémieu-Foa was about to issue more duel challenges when Charles Louis de Saulces de Freycinet (1828–1923), the French war minister, ordered him to Tunis to organize one of the two squadrons of Sudanese spahis destined for Dahomey in West Africa, which had risen up against France. In the ensuing expedition, Crémieu-Foa distinguished himself in several combats prior to the taking of Abomey, was mentioned for bravery in the order of the day, and received in the presence of the troops the congratulations of the commander-in-chief. He died at Porto Novo in North Africa in November 1892 of a wound sustained while reconnoitering, and of tropical fever. Owing to the sensation caused by the death of Captain Mayer, *La Libre Parole* thought it wise to stop its campaign against Jewish officers until the storm had abated.

The notorious *affaire Dreyfus* broke out in 1894 when a French spy in the German embassy in Paris discovered a handwritten *bordereau* (list or schedule) received by Major Max von Schwartzkoppen, the German military *attaché* in Paris, which listed secret French military documents. The *bordereau* had been written by Major Esterhazy, who had been selling military secrets to the Germans to pay his debts. Instead, Captain Alfred Dreyfus was put on trial, falsely accused of espionage, found guilty and sentenced to life imprisonment on Devil's Island. In 1896, Theodor Herzl published *Der Judenstaat* (The Jewish State), his Zionist manifesto (or fantasy). On January 13, 1898, Emile Zola published his famous accusation of the French state in the liberal *l'Aurore*. Zola himself was tried for treason. Five years later, Dreyfus accepted a pardon from the new president of France, which brought his release but implied a tacit admission of guilt. It was not until 1906 that Dreyfus was fully exonerated of the charges against him and readmitted into the army. He was also made a knight in the French Legion of Honor. Dreyfus served behind the lines of the Western Front during the Great War of 1914–1918 (Reinach 1901–1911, Burns 1998).

Two years before Adolf Hitler came to power in Germany in 1933, the racist and anti-Semitic French Catholic writer Georges Bernanos praised Drumont and bitterly attacked the Jews (Bernanos 1931). The French Jewish psychoanalyst Janine Chasseguet-Smirgel thought that child sacrifice, torture, and blood-sucking were the age-old themes of most Christian anti-Jewish accusations and fantasies (Chasseguet-Smirgel 2004, p. 55). The ritual-murder libel, the accusations of deicide and usurious blood-sucking, from the child Jesus through Shakespeare's Shylock to the child Muhammad al-Dura, are all variations on this theme (Chasseguet-Smirgel 2004, pp. 55–56). Today, in a complete inversion, rather than being seen as the victims of Nazi racism, the Jews themselves are perversely accused of unrepentant colonialism, imperialism, and racism—even Nazism. Just as perversely, the French Catholic writer Georges Bernanos accused the Jews themselves of racism and nationalism, believed that "the Jews" had paid for Céline's rabidly anti-Jewish book (Céline 1937) and compared the ancient kings of Israel to the Nazi propagandist Alfred Rosenberg (Bernanos 1938, 1944). The French rebel leader José Bové (born 1953) has absurdly accused the Israeli *Mossad* (foreign intelligence service) of having engineered the anti-Semitic attacks in France (Chasseguet-Smirgel 2004, p. 59).

The anti-Semitic accusation of "Jewish nationalism and racism" is based, among other things, on the Jews' "arrogant" belief in being God's chosen people and having a covenant with Yahweh, and on their looking down upon the non-Jews or *goyim* (gentiles) as inferior. The fact is, however, that the Hebrew word *goyim* (like the Latin word *gentes*) originally meant "nations," that it later took on the derogatory meaning of "foreigners." Moreover, every human clan, stock, tribe, people, and nation has had "myths of election," a form of group narcissism in which the human group thinks of itself as special, unique, and superior to all other groups (Falk 1996, pp. 10–11, 311–312). The Japanese have thought of themselves as the world's smartest and ablest people, and the United States believes itself to be God's Chosen Nation (Hughes 2003). Evangelical Christians believe that the Jews are indeed God's chosen people and that the rebirth of the Jewish state proves the veracity of their faith (Burge 1993). Other Christians still hope for the Second Coming of Jesus Christ and for the conversion of all the world's Jews to Christianity. The seventeenth-century English poet Andrew Marvell, in his ironic love poem *To His Coy Mistress,* wrote, "And you should, if you please, refuse / Till the conversion of the Jews." Still, as the scholar Howard F. Stein has pointed out, Christian anti-Semitism and Jewish "anti-Gentilism" have created a tragic vicious circle (Stein 1977, 1978, 1984, 1994).

The American Jewish scholar William Brustein studied the history of anti-Semitism in Europe before the Nazi Holocaust (Brustein 2003). Here are his conclusions:

> I have examined the rise of European anti-Semitism through the lens of the religious, economic, racial, and political roots of anti-Semitism. These four roots of anti-Semitism appear to have been instrumental in the formation of anti-Jewish narratives emerging between 1879 and 1939. The four anti-Jewish narratives gained credence from the effects of declining economic well-being, increased Jewish immigration, growth of leftist support, and identification of Jews with the

leadership of the political left. However, popular support for anti-Semitism varied temporally and spatially. Anti-Semitism, as measured by acts and attitudes, reached its highest points between the two world wars, particularly in Germany and Romania. Anti-Semitic levels in both Great Britain and France were significantly lower than those in Germany and Romania. The case of France may come as a surprise to many, in light of France's Dreyfus Affair experience and the oft-cited writings of many of France's rightist intellectuals. The conventional wisdom would have it that France, notably during the mid-1930s, with the circulation of the popular slogan vaut mieux Hitler que Blum (better Hitler than Blum), was a hotbed of anti-Semitism. The empirical data do not support this contention, however, at least as it may apply to the French middle and lower classes. Italy remained relatively untouched by anti-Semitism, at least until 1936. We have seen that in the case of Italy, the immigration of Eastern European Jews and the identification of Jews with the Italian revolutionary left never materialized as significant issues. (Brustein 2003, p. 337)

Another problem with anti-Semitism is that "the kernel of truth" or "germ of reality" that Freud thought to discern in the projective fantasies of Jew-haters (Freud 1964, p. 90) sometimes exists. The fantasies of Jew-haters, who demonize the Jews and attribute all evil to them, at times coincide with reality, such as when Israeli Jews tragically inflict unnecessary or unintentional suffering on Palestinian Arabs. "Thanks, Sharon," wrote Janine Chasseguet-Smirgel with a sad irony (Chasseguet-Smirgel 2004, p. 60). On the other hand, this "kernel of truth" is often totally absent. In 2004 a German politician, followed by a general, blamed the Jews for the fatal consequences of the October 1917 revolution in Russia. Both were dismissed: German law prohibits anti-Semitic acts. The French-born Jewish philosopher George Steiner, whose family fled German-occupied France when he was a boy in 1940, thought that Jewish morality was the root of anti-Semitism (Steiner 1971). The French Jewish psychoanalyst thought that human sacrifice was only part of the problem: the Jews had brought a whole new morality to the world, which has not forgiven them for it (Chasseguet-Smirgel 2004, pp. 60–61).

The Polish-born French Jewish psychoanalyst Elisabeth Bizouard-Reicher quoted the work of the Polish scholars Sergiusz Kowalski and Magdalena Tulli about how indifferent contemporary Polish society is to anti-Semitism, and how anti-Semitic some of it still is, even after more than three million Polish Jews have been killed by the German Nazis and by their Polish Catholic collaborators. Even though contemporary Poland has no more than a few thousand Jews, as opposed to some 3.5 million before 1939, anti-Semitism is rampant, and fantasies about the evil Jews flourish everywhere. Jews are accused of being communist, pagan, anti-Catholic, anti-Polish. Unlike the past, the Polish Catholics do not wish to convert or integrate the Jews: they want to get rid of them (Kowalski & Tulli 2004, quoted in Bizouard-Reicher 2004, pp. 76–78).

Bizouard-Reicher sided with the French Jewish sociologist Pierre Birnbaum in his controversy with the American Jewish historian Yosef Hayim Yerushalmi about the life of the Jews in Europe during the early modern era (Yerushalmi 1997, Birnbaum 2004). Yerushalmi had thought that Jewish life in exile did not necessarily involve persecution and assimilation. He believed that the European Jews had "domiciles assimilated to ancient Israel" in which life flowed peacefully, where synagogues defined private quarters, with voluntary Jewish segregation from the host society being deemed indispensable to the observation of the law (Yerushalmi 1997, pp. 10–11, quoted by Birnbaum 2004, p. 360, then quoted in Bizouard-Reicher 2004, p. 79). Bizouard-Reicher thought that Yerushalmi's was "a false vision" that betrayed "a stunning lack of knowledge of Jewish diaspora life." Already in the fifteenth, sixteenth, and seventeenth centuries, the "Judaization of exile" was impossible. Jewish villages and towns were systematically burned by Poles and Cossacks, and their inhabitants massacred (Bizouard-Reicher 2004, p. 79). In 1648–1649, Bohdan Khmelnitsky's Cossacks massacred hundreds of thousands of Jews in Polish Ukraine. Khmelnitsky, a name akin to Hitler in Jewish memory, became a Ukrainian national hero, with a town named after him and his equestrian statue in the center of the Ukrainian capital of Kiev.

Like the Cypriot-Turkish-born American psychoanalyst Vamık Volkan and the Canadian-American historian Gavin Langmuir, the younger Swiss historian Philippe Burrin believed that anti-Semitism was "a weapon in the collective battle for *identity*. It is a [psychological] construction through which the majority society, usually a part of that society, expresses its anxieties and its tensions and seeks to overcome its doubts about its group identity" (Burrin 2004b, p. 18). Burrin's series of lectures at the *Collège de France* was better at asking probing questions about the Nazi period than at answering them. Burrin's answers were provocative. He used the latest scholarship to explore the core of Nazi ideology and why the German people accepted it. He was persuasive in tracing *the multiple origins of Nazi anti-Semitism,* noting that it combined traditional beliefs, Christian anti-Semitism, and modern racial theories. Burrin located anti-Semitism at the heart of Nazi ideology. As to why Germans followed Hitler, Burrin disagreed with Goldhagen's idea of a long-standing German "eliminatory anti-Semitism." Burrin believed that Judeophobia, as he calls it, became more than a prejudice; it was "an interpretive grid by which to make sense of what was happening" and thus became a core part of the German national identity. Burrin gave a brief account of the latest scholarship on the origins of the Nazi policies toward the Jews.

Elisabeth Bizouard-Reicher thought that modern Poland is beset by a virulent nationalism (Bizouard-Reicher 2004, p. 81). Foreigners in general, and Jews in particular, are perceived as dangerous. In 2002, the German psychoanalyst Gemma Jappe had criticized her own idea that "all Jews were alike" because it was "incompatible with psychoanalysis...but in accord with national feeling."

She added, "we hate the Jews because they remind us of our guilt" (Jappe 2002). Bizouard-Reicher thought that the deeper problem was the unfavorable collective German narcissistic image which the Germans unconsciously projected on the Jews. In a lecture in the Israeli Christian Arab city of Nazareth, Dr. Jappe expressed her mortal fear of the Jewish vengeance for the Holocaust, imagining her hotel as a concentration camp in which the Jews had locked up the Germans in order to kill them all (Jappe 2002).

Bizouard-Reicher attributed such collective projections to what she called "the narcissism of belonging," which she defined as "the narcissistic investment, by the Ego, in a collective" (Bizouard-Reicher 2004, p. 83). Nationalism satisfies the individual's need for belonging, but also his destructive impulses. (ibid., pp. 81–83). The idea of nationalism as satisfying the individual's need for belonging was expressed by the German philosopher Johann Gottfried von Herder before the French Revolution (Herder 1784, 1968). The French Jewish sociologist Pierre Birnbaum thought that the human need for belonging to a large group was as powerful as the need for food, drink, warmth, love, and security (Birnbaum 2004, p. 254, as quoted in Bizouard-Reicher 2004, p. 82). In fact, nationalism is a very complex psychological phenomenon on both the individual and group levels, involving splitting, group narcissism, the inability to mourn collective losses, chosen historical trauma, chosen glories, and other unconscious processes (Falk 2004, pp. 87–102).

Narcissism can be high-level and healthy, or it can be pathological and maladaptive. In the latter case, the narcissist's self boundaries are not clearly defined, because of his inadequate separation and differentiation from the mother in his early life. Bizouard-Reicher saw a direct unconscious link between pathological narcissism and anti-Semitism. The Jews serve as an unflattering mirror to the self-hating narcissist, and this is too painful. He must smash that mirror. The Germans tried to de-Germanize their Jews, and the Poles wish to de-Polonize theirs. The Jews must be totally different from their host society so that the latter can have a safe sense of identity. What besets the anti-Semite is "Who am I?" That is because the narcissistic anti-Semite has an undifferentiated self and is fearful of losing the boundaries of his self. The complex "undifferentiated" identity of the Jew, who is both Jewish and Polish, for example, unconsciously threatens the anti-Semite's lack of clear self boundaries (Bizouard-Reicher 2004, p. 85).

Bizouard-Reicher thought that to the anti-Semite, the Jew plays the unconscious role of a "monstrous double" who must be destroyed if the anti-Semite is not to be overwhelmed by his own anxiety. The projection of one's own hated feelings and wishes is not enough: the "monstrous double" must be eliminated to gain relief from anxiety and depression. Burrin thought that Nazi anti-Semitism was the fusion of two ambitions for universal empire: one imaginary, which was attributed to the Jews, the other caressed, that of the Nazis themselves (Burrin 2004b, p. 50). The Poles accuse the Jews of "paganism," while the whole world accuses them of greed, with money being their only criterion for evaluating anything. Bizouard-Reicher thought that this was the case with our entire current civilization, and that envy played a deep role in the attitude toward the Jews (Bizouard-Reicher 2004, p. 86). Melanie Klein thought that hateful and guiltless envy is a very powerful early feeling that we experience toward our mother's breast (Klein 1957). The infant splits the mother's breast into a "good breast" and a "bad breast" and wishes to destroy "the bad breast" despite its rich nourishment, because it feels that the "bad breast" turns away from him for its own benefit. The same feelings in disguise are displayed by anti-Semites toward the Jew, whom they accuse of ingratitude and even treachery toward those who have done so much for him. In addition to unconscious projection, denial and splitting are paramount in anti-Semites. This is the most dangerous kind of anti-Semitism, which leads to murder (Bizouard-Reicher 2004, p. 87).

Holocaust Survivors: "Jean Améry," Simon Wiesenthal, Leon Wieslicer

It is impossible within the scope of this book to study the vast psychological problem of Holocaust survivors, their massive trauma, their struggle for physical and psychological survival, their very painful life after the Holocaust, their families, their children and grandchildren and their own psychological sufferings. The horrors that those courageous and resilient survivors went through are painful to contemplate and hard to heal. Often their physical and psychological survival seem nothing short of miraculous. I have chosen to discuss three very special cases here, those of "Jean Améry" (Hans Maier, 1912–1978), an Austrian Jewish survivor of the Auschwitz death camp, and of Simon Wiesenthal (1908–2005) and Leon Wieliczker (born 1925), both of them Polish Jewish survivors of the Janowska death camp near Lwów.

After Austria's annexation by Hitler's Germany in 1938, fleeing to France, joining the *Résistance intérieure française,* being arrested and tortured, and surviving Auschwitz, writing in German under the French name of "Jean Améry," was part of Hans Maier's strategy of psychological survival. Hans Maier was Jewish, but his mother was Christian and his Jewish father was much more Austrian than Jewish. "The picture of him did not show me a bearded sage," Maier later wrote, "but rather a Tyrolean Imperial Rifleman in the First World War." The father died in battle during the Great War, in 1916, when his son was too young to remember him. Maier's mother, who supported her only child and herself by keeping an inn, was a Roman Catholic. "Several times a day she invoked Jesus, Mary, and Joseph," he recalled. As a young man, Hans Maier was powerfully drawn to his mother's Christianity, even to Nazism and racism (Myers 2002, quoting Améry 1980).

By the time of Austria's annexation to Hitler's Third Reich in 1938, the young Hans Maier harbored an ambivalent mixture of pro-Jewish and anti-Jewish feelings. He fled to France and, after its occupation by Hitler's Germany, to occupied Belgium, where he joined the *Résistance*. His reasons, however, were complicated: he later acknowledged that this was merely his last unconscious attempt to evade his Jewish identity. "The Jews were hunted, cornered, arrested, deported because they were Jews," he writes, underlining every word, "and only because of that. Looking back, it appears to me that I didn't want to be detained by the enemy as a Jew but rather as a resistance member" (Myers 2002, quoting Améry 1980). Indeed, in 1943, he was arrested by the *Gestapo* for spreading anti-Nazi propaganda among the German occupation forces in Belgium.

Traumatized survivors need to tell their trauma over and over again all their lives. The telling is an attempt to relive the trauma actively rather than passively, to relieve the pain, to get it off one's chest, to master the overwhelming suffering. The 31-year-old Hans Maier was tortured by the *Gestapo* sadists in ways that are too horrible to contemplate, but which he later described vividly in his book (Améry 1966, 1980). The torture was so bad that, like other *Gestapo* victims, Hans Maier confessed to everything, including imaginary "crimes" that he had never committed. He knew only the aliases or *noms de guerre* of his comrades in the *résistance* and had no real information to divulge. Once the *Gestapo* torturers realized he was useless to them—once they realized that he was a Jew and not just a political prisoner—the Gestapo shipped him off to Auschwitz.

In 1943–1944, Hans Maier "miraculously" survived a year in "Auschwitz III," the Buna-Monowitz labor camp. It was a sub-camp of Auschwitz, where synthetic rubber was manufactured for the German military. During 1942–1944, the German Nazis created hundreds of sub-camps for each of their concentration camps. Sub-camps were located near factories or sites where labor was needed to collect raw materials (such as mines, quarries, etc.). The Nazis sent thousands of prisoners from various countries to Buna-Monowitz. There were approximately 10,000 prisoners in this camp in 1944, most of them Jewish. A large percentage of the prisoners died from starvation, beatings, the difficult labor, and executions. A prisoner who was unable to work was taken to the gas chambers in nearby Birkenau and gassed to death.

Lacking a manual skill, the young Viennese Jew Hans Maier was assigned to a labor detail at the German *I. G. Farben* site, digging dirt, laying cables, lugging heavy sacks of cement and iron crossbeams. He survived "somehow" (Myers 2002). How can one possibly survive such trauma? It took a tremendous amount of psychological strength and resilience not to succumb to the traumatic daily torture, constant and very real fear of being killed, and the excruciatingly hard labor. The Viennese Jewish psychologist Viktor Emil Frankl (1905–1977), another Auschwitz survivor, derived an existential psychological theory from his trauma (Frankl 1959, 1997). Not so Hans Maier, who became "Jean Améry."

Unlike Frankl, he refused to derive any theory, psychological or otherwise, from his survival.

Many years later "Jean Améry" agreed that the "religiously or politically committed," such as Orthodox Jews or orthodox Marxists, had a better chance of surviving the death camps, or at least of dying with dignity. They were able to look beyond the basic reality of Auschwitz. For them, the horrors were weakened by being reinterpreted as a renewal of creation when evil was released into the world or as natural political martyrdom. They had a psychological mode of transcendence that was anchored to a reality that the Nazis could not reach, because it existed in faith. "Whoever is, in the broadest sense, a believing person, whether his belief be metaphysical or bound to concrete reality, transcends himself," Hans Maier wrote. "He is not the captive of his individuality; rather he is part of a spiritual continuity that is interrupted nowhere, not even in Auschwitz" (Myers 2002, quoting Améry 1980).

But Hans Maier was an unbeliever. Emotionally, he had nothing but himself to fall back upon. He was an intellectual, but, confronted by a reality that could not be interpreted as anything other than horror, he found that his intellect had lost its fundamental quality of transcendence. There was no other reality to which a mere intellectual could appeal. The incredible terror of Auschwitz was total and overwhelming (Myers 2002). How did Hans Maier survive the horrors perpetrated on him, not only physically (which was no mean feat even for a strong young man), but, above all, psychologically? After all, many weaker inmates were either murdered or committed suicide out of total despair at escaping the hell in which they were living. Was it an inner strength derived from his strong, believing mother?

In November 1944, the gas chambers of Birkenau, where millions of innocent people had been gassed to death, were blown up by the Germans in an attempt to hide their crimes from the advancing Soviet troops and from the entire world. On January 17, 1945, German Nazi personnel began to evacuate the camp. Most of the surviving prisoners were marched west. Those too weak or sick to walk were left behind. About 7,500 prisoners were liberated by the Red Army 10 days later. Hans Maier was evacuated by his German captors first to Buchenwald and then to Bergen-Belsen, ahead of the advancing Red Army, and it was at Bergen-Belsen that he was liberated in April 1945.

Returning to Brussels, the traumatized survivor passed the rest of his life outside the cultural mainstream. When he began to write for the German-language press of Switzerland, he chose a French-sounding pen name, "Jean Améry," Jean being the French translation of his first name, Hans (Johannes), and Améry being an anagram for Mayer, a common variant of his surname, Maier. The pseudonym supposedly signified his ambivalent "rejection" of German culture, and his identification with French, yet Améry continued to write in German. Even so, he avoided Germany for two decades after the war (Myers 2002). But "Jean Améry" later returned to Vienna and spent the rest of his life there, writing many articles and books in German. He died at the age of 66 (Myers 2002).

In recent years, it has become fashionable among academic and political circles to accuse the Jews of exploiting the Holocaust for their "victimhood needs," or for political or financial gain. Some Jews, including Jewish historians, have also embraced this accusation. The American Jewish historian Peter Novick believed that the Holocaust encouraged contemporary Jews to adopt a "victim identity based on the Holocaust," which he called a "fashionable victimhood," and which he derogated as "exploitive and phony" (Novick 1999, pp. 190–202). "Jean Améry" had other ideas about the survivors and victims of the German Nazi Holocaust:

> For Améry, then, the Holocaust is central to human self-understanding because it represents not an accidental function of the Nazi regime, but its essence. Améry would have liked to "introduce certain Auschwitz books into the upper classes of secondary school as compulsory reading," because these books would introduce students to an idea that is indispensable to any humanistic curriculum in a post-Holocaust era—the idea of the victim, the "dead man on leave." If dignity is the right to live granted by society, then the Third Reich demonstrates how easily the grant can be revoked. (Myers 2002)

Hans Maier did derive a *Lebensanschauung* from his massive traumatization at Auschwitz. He believed that ordinary morality played no role in such a place:

> Améry is not particularly interested in the perpetrators of the Holocaust. "The crimes of National Socialism had no moral quality for the doer," Améry explains. "The monster, who is not chained by his conscience to his deed, sees it from his viewpoint only as an objectification of his will, not as a moral event." Améry's literary ambition in *At the Mind's Limits* [Améry 1980] is to speak from the viewpoint of the victim, for whom the National Socialism had a moral quality. He seeks to understand suffering from the inside rather than extorting pity and special consideration for victims. Améry thus stands as a challenge to the increasingly common view, of which the historian Peter Novick is merely one representative, that the Holocaust encourages contemporary Jews to adopt a "victim identity based on the Holocaust," a "fashionable victimhood" which is exploitative and phony...While Améry certainly agrees that the existence of the Jews has been forever determined by the Holocaust, *At the Mind's Limits* does not celebrate victimization. Instead, the book engages in a fundamental redefinition of victimhood. To be a victim is no longer to be the object of other people's designs. In the sort of post-Holocaust thinking practiced by Améry, the Jewish victim makes himself the subject of his own history. (Myers 2002)

In a sense, Hans Maier, who had become "Jean Améry," was able to master his incredible trauma in the death camp through his intellectual and literary abilities. Many other survivors were not so fortunate, and their life after the Holocaust was a living nightmare. Many became inmates of psychiatric hospitals. A few were successfully treated and "cured" by mental-health professionals. Those who created families often transmitted their trauma to their children, and an entire psychiatric literature has grown up around the treatment of the second and third generations of Holocaust survivors.

The biography of Simon Wiesenthal (1908–2005) may give us a glimpse into the murderous anti-Semitic Nazi mind and into the massive collective and individual trauma that it inflicted on the Jews (Wiesenthal 1967). The "Nazi hunter" and "Conscience of the Holocaust" was born Szymon Wiesenthal on the last day of 1908 in the Eastern Galician town of Buczacz, Austro-Hungary (now in the Ukraine), which was also the birthplace of the Israeli Nobel prize winner in literature, S.J. Agnon. The little boy Szymon lost his father as a child when the father was killed in World War I. He then also lost his hometown, when his mother fled to Vienna with her children, returning to Buczacz (then a Polish town) after she remarried. Wiesenthal graduated from a Viennese high school in 1928 and applied for admission to the Lwów polytechnic institute, then in Polish Galicia, but was turned down due to the Polish antisemitic quota restrictions on Jews. He then attended the technical university of the Czech capital of Prague, from which he received his architectural engineering degree in 1932 and went back to Poland. In 1936 Wiesenthal married Cyla Müller. They had a daughter, Paulina, who later immigrated to Israel.

The Wiesenthals were living in the Polish city of Lwów when World War II broke out in 1939. As agreed in the Molotov-Ribbentrop Pact, Lwów was occupied by Stalin's Soviet troops on September 17 along with the rest of eastern Poland and annexed to the Soviet Union, while western Poland was annexed to Hitler's *Reich*. Wiesenthal's stepfather and stepbrother were killed by agents of the Soviet secret police as part of Stalin's anti-Polish repressions, designed to eliminate the anti-Soviet Polish intelligentsia. Wiesenthal was forced to close his private firm and work in a Soviet factory. In June 1941, when Hitler abrogated his pact with Stalin and invaded the Soviet Union, Wiesenthal and his family were captured and imprisoned by the Germans. The following month, a Ukrainian auxiliary policeman saved Wiesenthal from certain "execution" by the German Nazis occupying Lwów. Many years later, when asked about the Ukrainians on a popular U.S. television show, Wiesenthal forgot this fact and agreed with his interviewer that the Ukrainian police were worse than the Germans. For this, he was publicly excoriated by some outraged Ukrainians.

Shortly after being saved by the Ukranian policeman, however, Wiesenthal was taken to the Janowska forced-labor camp near Lwów, which later became a notorious German Nazi concentration and extermination camp. This may be a good time to take a close look at Janowska, an example of the Nazi labor, concentration, and extermination camps during World War II (Wells 1966; Gilbert 1986; Gutman 1990; Kahane 1991). The camp began in September 1941 when the Germans set up an arms factory at 134 ulica Janowska in the Lwów suburbs to serve the needs of the German army in Poland and Russia. Soon thereafter, the Germans expanded the factory into a large network of arms and munitions factories as part of the *Deutsche Ausrüstungwerke* (German armament works) or *DAW,* a division of the *SS.* The Jews of Lwów were forced to work in these factories, and by the end of October 1941, some 600 Jews were working there.

In November 1941, the Nazis turned the Janowska munitions factories into a *Judenzwangsarbeitslager* (Jewish forced-labor camp). The area became a restricted camp, enclosed by barbed wire, which the Jews were not permitted to leave. It was called the Janowska "labor camp." The Janowska camp complex was divided into three sections. The first comprised the garages, workshops, and offices, with a separate villa for the camp staff, *SS, SD,* and the Ukrainian guards, many of whom hated both Poles and Jews. At the center of this section stood the villa of the camp commander. The second section was the camp proper. Here barracks, each housing 2,000 inmates, were erected for the Jewish laborers. The conditions in the barracks were appalling. Prisoners slept on the ground or on planks. Sanitation was primitive, resulting in permanent conditions of disease and sporadic outbreaks of epidemics. The diet was a black coffee substitute in the morning, a midday meal of watery soup containing unpeeled potatoes, and 200 grams of bread in the evening. Many inmates died of disease or starvation. The third section of the camp consisted of the *DAW* factories. Barbed-wire fences separated the three camp sections from each other, and the entire camp was surrounded with a double barbed-wire fence illuminated with searchlights. Watchtowers were placed all around the camp at 50-meter intervals, with armed Ukrainians and German *SS* men patrolling the perimeter.

The first commandant of the Janwoska camp was Fritz Gebauer. His deputies were Gustav Wilhaus and Wilhelm Rokita. In May 1942, Gebauer took over the command of the *DAW* camp, and Wilhaus was appointed commandant of Janowska. A staff of 12 to 15 *SS* officers, who were replaced from time to time, administered the camp. The guards at the camp were Russian POWs who had volunteered for service with the *SS.* The camp had originally been planned exclusively for Jews, but after several months, a special section was set up for Poles. They were separated from the Jews, received better treatment, and were often released from the camp after a period of detention. In the first months of Janowska's history, only Jews from Lwów were brought to the camp, but later on Jews were sent to the camp from other Polish districts, including the Western Galician capital of Krakow. Most of the Jews in the camp came from Eastern Galicia, and from the sub-districts of Rawa-Ruska, Kamionka Strumilowa, Sambor, Brzezany, and Kaluz. The *SS* from the camp visited these districts from time to time for extermination actions. Sub-branches of the Janowska camp were also established in Laski Kurowice, Jaktarowe, and other places to which the Jewish laborers of the Janowska camp were transferred.

The Jews who were brought to the Janowska camp had to surrender all their valuables on arrival. The Jewish prisoners were divided into *Sonderkommandos* (special commandos, a Nazi euphemism for forced-labor groups) of 20 to 30 persons. They worked a 12-hour day, both in the camp and in Lwów, where they were forced to break up the tombstones in the Jewish graveyards. The *SS* and the Ukrainian militia constantly and brutally supervised them. The prisoners also worked on various projects organized by the *SS*. There was a special Jewish "commando" engaged in the burying of the Jewish dead in the camp, particularly those Jews murdered on the sandhills behind the camp. This "commando" was also used to sort the clothing and property of the dead.

The living conditions in the Janowska camp were exceptionally harsh and barbaric. Unable to stand their terrible pain and suffering, many Jewish prisoners committed suicide by hanging themselves in the barracks, rather than face another day of torture. When they returned from work, the prisoners were made to run into the camp. Wilhaus and his deputy Rokita singled out those Jews who showed signs of fatigue for immediate death. These Jews were placed between the wire rows and left there to die. Each morning there was a roll call for all prisoners, who were personally inspected by an *SS* officer. Any prisoner failing the inspection was immediately shot dead. Rokita had a special practice when passing through the rows of prisoners on the parade ground. If he did not like a prisoner, he would shoot him in the back of the neck.

Every *SS* man at Janowska had his personal reasons for and ways of killing Jews. Jews in the camp were murdered for the slightest misdemeanor: for working slowly, for not paying attention, or for no reason at all except the whims of the *SS* men. The sadistic manner in which a Jew was killed varied, depending on the murderer: shooting, flogging, choking, hanging, fixing to crosses with the head down, cutting to pieces with knives or axes. Distinctive methods were adopted when killing women. They were mostly flogged to death or killed by stabbing. To soothe their own feelings, the German Nazis conducted their tortures, beatings, and shootings to the accompaniment of music. For this purpose they organized a prisoners' orchestra. Composers were ordered to write a special tune, which was called "The Death Tango." Shortly before the camp was liquidated, the Nazis shot all members of the orchestra dead.

On March 2, 1942, the first day of the Jewish holiday of Purim, six Jews at Janowska were forced to spend the night outside the barracks, on the grounds that they "looked sick" and should not infect the others. The temperature was below freezing. "In the morning," the former inmate Leon Wieliczker, who escaped the Janowska death camp in November 1943 and later immigrated to the United States (where he changed his last name to Weliczker Wells), recalled, "all six people were frozen [dead] lying down where they were put out the night before; completely white like long balls of snow." Two days later, *Kommandant* Gebauer ordered a barrel of water to be brought and picked out eight more laborers from Janowska. The eight Jews were forced to undress and were then placed in the barrel. They remained in the barrel all night. In the morning Wieliczker recalled, "we had to cut the ice away. The men were frozen to death." (Union of Soviet Socialist Republics 1946; Wells 1966, 1995; State of Israel Ministry of Justice 1992).

In March 1942, when the mass deportation of Jews from Eastern Galicia to the Belzec extermination camp began, the Janowska camp became a transit camp for Jews from towns and villages in the area. Inside the camp, selections of those considered fit for labor took place: those not selected were transported to Belzec. Later in the spring of that year, the Janowska labor camp was enlarged and took on the character of a concentration camp. Following "actions" in Lwów in the summer of 1942, thousands more Polish Jews were sent to the camp. Most of them were killed by the *SS*.

Barrack No. 5 at the Janowska camp, which was occupied by the *Ostbahn-Brigade* (east-railroad brigade), Jews scrubbing and cleaning locomotives at Lwów's east railroad station, was the subject of intense *SS* brutality. This "brigade" supplied the largest quotas for murders or "executions." On March 16, 1943, following the killing of an *SS* man by a Polish Jew, 30 members of the "brigade" were shot dead as a reprisal, and 11 Jewish policemen were hanged from balconies in the main street of the Lwów ghetto. Nearly 1,000 Jews were taken out of other working groups outside the camp and shot dead. A further 200 Jews in Janowska itself were also murdered.

On April 20, 1943, Hitler's 54th birthday, Wilhaus picked out 54 prisoners and personally shot them. In the camp there was a so-called hospital for prisoners. The Nazi executioners Brambauer and Birmann examined the patients on the first and 15th of every month. If they found any patients who had been in hospital over a fortnight, they shot them on the spot. Six or seven people were murdered during each such examination. Miraculously, the former inmate Leon Wieliczker survived internment in Janowska twice, once as a prisoner condemned to death and then as a member of the *Sonderkommando 1005,* forced to exhume and cremate the corpses of the murdered.

By mid-1943, while still functioning as a labor and concentration camp, Janowska was becoming an extermination camp. Fewer prisoners were employed in the factories inside the camp and in Lwów, and the length of stay of newcomers was shortened. The murders or "executions" took place in the Piaski sandhills behind the camp. There were two slopes on which Jews were shot and then buried in pits. In mid-May 1943 alone, over 6,000 Jews were murdered there. Under *Kommandant* Gebauer, a savage system of extermination was instituted at the Janowska camp. After Gebauer's appointment to another post, this system was "perfected" by Commandant Gustav Wilhaus and his new deputy Friedrich Warzok. From the testimony of many Soviet POWs as well as French subjects held in German camps, it was ascertained that the Nazis "invented" most "refined" methods for the extermination of human beings. This initiative was regarded as a matter of special merit at Janowska.

Horrific sadistic atrocities were an everyday occurrence at Janowska. One witness told the Soviet special commission that investigated the German Nazi war crimes: "I saw Gebauer strangle women and children with my own eyes. I saw them place men in barrels of water to freeze in the depth of winter. The barrels were filled with water and then the victims were tied hand and foot and put into the water. The doomed people remained in the barrels until they froze to death" (Union of Soviet Socialist Republics 1946). Wilhaus, partly for sport, and partly to amuse his wife and daughter, used to fire a machine gun from the balcony of the camp office at prisoners occupied in the workshops. Then he would pass the machine gun to his wife, who also shot at them. On one occasion, to please his nine-year-old daughter, Wilhaus had two four-year-old children tossed into the air, while he fired at them. His daughter applauded and cried, "Papa, do it again, papa, do it again!" He did.

Deputy *Kommandant* Warzok liked to hang prisoners on poles by their feet, and leave them in this position until they died. His colleague Rokita personally ripped open prisoners' stomachs. The chief of the investigation department of the Janowska camp, a German named Heine, used to perforate the bodies of prisoners with a spike or iron rod. He would pull out the fingernails of women prisoners with pliers, then undress his victims, hang them by the hair, and set them swinging, before shooting at the "moving target." At Janowska, as in other Nazi death camps, prisoners were murdered on any pretext, often for a bet between two *SS* men.

The victims at Janowska were not only Jewish. A Janowska survivor named Kirschner informed the Soviet special commission after the war that Wepke, a *Gestapo* commissar, had boasted to other camp executioners that he could cut a boy in two parts with one blow of a hatchet. His colleagues did not believe him, so he caught a 10-year-old boy in the street, forced him to his knees, then made the boy put his palms together to hide his face. Wepke made a trial stroke, adjusted the boy's head, and with a single blow of the hatchet slashed him in two. The Nazis congratulated Wepke warmly, and shook him by the hand. A week later, *Kommandant* Gebauer and his deputy Wilhaus began a game whereby they used the Jewish laborers, who were walking in the camp, as target practice. In the evening, the same officers selected sick Jews and shot them. Gebauer was known for his sadistic strangling abilities. He would select a Jew and strangle him with his bare hands (Union of Soviet Socialist Republics 1946).

In his 1961 testimony at Eichmann's trial in Jerusalem, the former Janowska inmate Leon Wieliczker described how, having first dug his own grave in the sandhills of Piaski, near Lwów, he was ordered to fetch the body of a prisoner who had been shot in the camp. Despite a raging fever, which caused him to lag behind his guard, he dragged the body of the dead man towards the execution site. There was a moment when the guard's back was turned. Wieliczker seized the opportunity to drop the body and disappear into the camp. The guard knew that he had lost Wieliczker, and was afraid of the reactions of his superiors. Anyone taken to Piaski could never return to the camp. And so the dead man was buried as if he were Wieliczker. The numbers tallied and Wieliczker was officially dead. This was of vital importance. At that time, escaping from the camp was easy, but if one prisoner escaped, the *SS* shot 10 people from that person's "brigade" dead and the family and relatives of the escapee were hanged. Now that he was officially dead, Wieliczker understood that he could escape without endangering any of his fellow prisoners or his family. Escape he did, only to be subsequently recaptured and returned to Janowska.

In June 1943, when Hitler's Germans began to suffer reverses in the war, they decided to eliminate the traces of their murderous acts at Janowska so they could not be discovered by the Allies. The 126-man Jewish "brigade" of *Sonderkommando 1005* was made to exhume and cremate the corpses of all Jews who had been murdered and buried in the Lwów district. The German *Sicherheitspolizei* (security police) and *Sicherheitsdienst* (security service) were put in charge of this, and the officers supervising this "commando" were *Sipo-SD Scharführer* Rauch and *Sipo-SD Oberwachtmeister* Kepick. The bodies recovered from the pits were laid on special platforms in stacks, each containing 1,200 to 1,600 corpses. Tar and petrol were poured over the bodies and they were burned. The ashes and bones were sifted in order to collect articles of value—gold fillings, teeth, rings, watches, etc. Eyewitness accounts testify that during the five months' activity of this "death commando," 110 kilograms of gold were sifted out of the ashes and dispatched to Germany. The ashes were scattered on the fields or buried; large bones were collected separately and crushed in a bone-crusher, which was specially designed to speed up the "work." The bone-crusher supervisor was *Sipo-SD Scharführer* Elitko. The Germans failed to destroy this bone-crusher, which was later recovered by the Soviets and used as material evidence in war crimes trials in the Soviet Union.

Leon Wieliczker was a member of the *Sonderkommando,* and he described the procedure in his testimony at Eichmann's trial of 1961–1962:

> We used to uncover all the graves where there were people who had been killed during the past three years, take out the bodies, pile them up in tiers and burn these bodies; grind the bones, take out all the valuables in the ashes such as gold teeth, rings and so on—separate them. After grinding the bones we used to throw the ashes up in the air so that they would disappear, replace the earth on the graves and plant seeds, so that nobody could recognize that there was ever a grave there. In addition to this they used to bring new people—new victims; they were shot there—undressed beforehand—we had to burn these new bodies too. When on Tuesday, 29 June 1943, 275 people arrived, they were shot with a machine gun in groups of 25. After the first 25 stepped into the pit and were shot, the next 25

followed. The 275 that were shot that day explained something that we had found before. There were some graves where it didn't seem to us that the people had been shot...Their mouths were open with their tongues protruding. They were more like people who had suffocated. This told us that these people were buried alive, because when we came to burn the bodies we found that some of them were only slightly injured due to the machine gun shooting 25 people in one burst...So some of them were only slightly injured in the arm and they fell down and were buried beneath the bodies above them. So it happened that this night when we picked up a body and put it in the fire, at the last moment the person started to scream—yell aloud because they were still alive. (State of Israel Ministry of Justice 1992; cf. Wells 1966, 1987, 1995)

Official Allied estimates of the number of Jews, Poles, Russians, and others murdered at Janowska from 1941 to 1945 range from 100,000 to 200,000. On October 25, 1943, the SS began murdering members of the corpse-burning squad, so that no witnesses to their crimes would be left. When the final 30-odd Jews of the *Sonderkommando* left in Janowska realized their intended fate, they understood that they had nothing to lose and planned an escape. Some Germans were killed during the course of the breakout on November 20, 1943. Their number, and that of the Jews who succeeded in fleeing alive, is unknown. Leon Wieliczker, who managed to escape without being killed or recaptured, gave this chilling account of the horrific physical and mental torture inflicted by the *SS* on their victims at Janowska:

The "brigade" was divided into corps. There were one, then two *Brandmeister* (burn masters), two *Zähler* (counters), an "ash commander," carriers, pullers and cleaners. The *Brandmeister* were in charge of the fire. When they put up a heap like a pyramid, sometimes up to 2,000 bodies—one had to watch out so that the fire didn't go out. They were in charge of the fire, while the *Zähler* was keeping a count of how many bodies were burnt to check out with the original list—how many were killed, because if we uncovered a grave we were sometimes looking for hours for one body or more if it was buried on the side; there was an exact list of how many people were killed. So the *Zähler* kept the number of bodies burned and taken out of each grave. The report was made with pencil and paper—it was forbidden for anybody to mention the number, and the *Zähler* himself had to forget. So that if the *Hauptscharführer* or *Untersturmführer* next morning asked: "How many were burned yesterday?" the *Zähler* couldn't say. He had to reply: "I forgot." (State of Israel Ministry of Justice 1992; cf. Wells 1966)

Thus the German Nazis, who systematically lied to and cheated the Jews throughout their murderous work, made their Jewish victims lie and cheat as well. As Wieliczker testified, *the world of the extermination camps was psychotic:*

We had to make up songs and sing while we were going to work, and also the *Brandmeister* would march in front, he was clothed like a devil; he had a special uniform with a hook in his hand and we had to march after him and sing. Afterwards we were also joined by an orchestra which would play as we sang and accompany us on our march to work. We were told that after eight to ten days we had to be exchanged—we would be shot and another group would come; so when visiting *SD* men came over to the death brigade and asked us how long we had been there it was forbidden for us to say that we had been longer than six, eight, up to eight or ten days—no longer." (State of Israel Ministry of Justice 1992; cf. Wells 1966)

The Soviet special commission that investigated the German Nazi war crimes in 1945–1946 found a number of pits in the earth around Janowska full of the corpses of prisoners shot during the second half of July 1944. According to the testimony of surviving witnesses and relatives of the murdered people, the Nazis used this place as an execution site for people brought from various *Gestapo* prisons. Contrary to their usual practice, the Nazis did not search the clothes of the murdered people. The commission found identification papers in the pockets of the clothes of those shot. From these papers, the identity of many of the victims was established (Union of Soviet Socialist Republics 1946).

The Soviet special investigative commission found that mass murders of civilians were carried out in the Janowska camp and that most of the murders were effected by the standard German method of shooting through the back of the head. Some were murdered by a shot through the roof of the skull. On the territory adjoining Janowska camp, the Germans carried out the mass burying and subsequent burning of bodies. The burnings were spread over a period, and the sites were scattered over the territory of the camp, but mostly they took place at Piaski, where the earth proved to be saturated to a considerable depth with corpse fluid and fats, together with the smell of decay and burning. The nature of the ashes discovered, consisting of small pieces of bone, and the brittleness of the larger bone fragments, testify that the burning of the bodies was carried out at a high temperature. The ashes remaining after the bodies were burnt were buried in various places on the territory of the camp at a depth of three to six feet. In all, 59 corpse-burning sites were discovered.

Ashes and bones were found on the surface of the soil over nearly all of the Janowska camp territory examined by the Soviet commission. Since the total area of burials and scattering of ashes and bones occupied nearly two square kilometers, the Soviet commission calculated that over 200,000 people were exterminated in Janowska (Union of Soviet Socialist Republics 1946). This may have been an overestimate. As with all of the German Nazi killing sites, it is impossible to know the exact the number of victims killed at Janowska. The official U.S. and Soviet commissions investigating these sites immediately after World War II tended to overestimate the numbers of people murdered. The survivor Leon Wieliczker, who had escaped from Janowska on November 20, 1943, testified to the Soviet special commission:

I was a former inmate of the Janowska camp who was ordered to work in the *Blobel Kommando 1005,* compelled to work in this team engaged in exhuming and burning bodies. I worked from 6 June 1943, to 20 November 1943. During this time the team burned more than 310,000 bodies, including about 170,000 on the sandstone of the Janowska camp, and over 140,000 in the Lisincki forest. This number includes bodies which were exhumed by the *Kommando,* as well as those which were not buried, and burned directly after shooting. On 20 November 1943 our whole team escaped. Only a few remained alive—most of us were killed while trying to escape. The Germans formed another team of prisoners, who continued with the work of burning bodies. I do not know how many bodies were burned after my escape, but I know that burning of bodies continued in the Lisincki forest until January 1944. (Union of Soviet Socialist Republics 1946; cf. Wells 1966)

Another survivor named Manussevich testified as follows: "After burning the bodies in the gully, near the Janowska camp, we were taken at night on trucks to the Lisincki forest, where we opened forty-five pits full of the bodies of people who had been shot. From the uniforms, marks of distinction, buttons, medals and orders we identified among the bodies Red Army men, French, Belgian and Italian war prisoners. There were also bodies of civilians among them" (Union of Soviet Socialist Republics 1946). The Soviet Red Army liberated Lwów on July 26, 1944, but by that time the Germans had sent Janowska's 34 surviving Jews on a death march to the Mauthausen extermination camp, the central Nazi extermination camp for all of Austria. *Kommandant* Gebauer was later tried by a West German court and sentenced to life imprisonment. In the postwar years, Janowska remained a prison—Soviet Camp No. 30. It still serves the same function in the Ukraine today.

By now the reader will have gained a horrific feel for the pure hell that was an inmate's daily life in the Janowska concentration camp. In the fall of 1941, along with other Lwów Jews, Simon Wiesenthal and his wife Cyla were imprisoned at Janowska, where they were forced to work on the local railroad as part of the *Ostbahn-Brigade* in Barrack No. 5. Members of the Polish underground army helped Cyla Wiesenthal escape from the camp and provided her with false papers in exchange for diagrams of railroad junctions drawn by Simon. Cyla Wiesenthal was able to hide her Jewish identity from the Nazis because of her blond hair and survived the war as a forced-laborer in the German Rhineland. Not knowing this, Simon Wiesenthal believed that she had escaped to her home in Warsaw, and after the Warsaw ghetto uprising of April 1943, he believed that she had perished in the uprising.

Simon Wiesenthal himself was not as fortunate as his wife Cyla. Although, incredibly, with the help of the deputy commander of the Janowska camp, he escaped from the camp in October 1943, just before the *SS* began killing all of the camp's inmates, he was recaptured in June 1944 (a month before Lwów's liberation by the Soviet army), tortured by the *SS,* and attempted to kill himself several times, first by slashing his wrists, then by trying to overdose on sleeping pills, and finally by hanging himself with his trousers. He was hospitalized for five weeks, and his life was saved. When he recovered, he was taken back to Janowska death camp.

By late 1944, the Allied forces were closing in on the Germans. Wiesenthal and 33 other survivors—out of an original 100,000 prisoners—who had not died or been moved out of the camp were lined up to be shot. For a third time, Wiesenthal's life was saved when Commandant Warzok decided to let the prisoners live so they would need guarding: then Warzok and his men would not have to go to the eastern front to fight the Russians and get killed. "We 34 Jews," Wiesenthal wrote, "became the life insurance for almost 200 SS men."

Kommandant Warzok moved his prisoners west. Some were shot. It was then that Wiesenthal had his famous conversation with *SS-Corporal* Merz, who told him that no one would ever believe him if he survived to tell the world what the Nazis had done. Just before Lwów's liberation by the Allies, the *SS* sent Wiesenthal among the remaining 34 Janowska survivors on the death march to the Mauthausen concentration camp in Austria. The deeply traumatized Simon Wiesenthal was liberated from Mauthausen by the Americans on May 5, 1945. He had been an inmate in 12 labor and concentration camps (five of which were extermination camps) and had barely escaped execution several times. Between them, Cyla and Simon Wiesenthal lost 89 relatives during the Holocaust.

After the Nuremberg trials, Wiesenthal fought his incredible trauma by hunting down the surviving Nazi mass murderers, who had scattered around the world, for 60 years and running an anti-Nazi Jewish Documentation Center in Vienna. In his autobiography, Wiesenthal claimed to have been instrumental in Israel's capture of Hitler's top lieutenant Adolf Eichmann, who had been kidnaped in Argentina, taken to Israel, tried, found guilty, condemned to death, and hanged in 1962 (Wiesenthal 1967). Israel's foreign-intelligence chief, however, denied this claim and even accused Wiesenthal of having nearly botched his Eichmann operation (Harel 1975). In 1977, a Holocaust memorial agency was named the Simon Wiesenthal Center. Its headquarters are in Los Angeles, California, but it also has offices in major Jewish population centers like New York, Miami, Toronto, Jerusalem, Paris, and Buenos Aires. The Simon Wiesenthal Center promotes awareness of anti-Semitism, monitors neo-Nazi groups, operates Museums of Tolerance in Los Angeles and Jerusalem, and helps bring surviving Nazi war criminals to justice.

Related Issues

Several other social and political issues related to anti-Semitism have also been studied by psychoanalysts. I shall now review some of these studies.

JEWS, WOMEN, AND HOMOSEXUALS

Misogyny—the hatred and fear of women—whether conscious or unconscious, has afflicted men for millennia, has often caused them to kill the women they saw as "witches," and has preoccupied historians and psychoanalysts for decades (Cohn 1975; Demos 1982; Beck 1990; Gilmore 2001; Lotto 2001; Moss 2001). Misogyny has to do with a man's earliest relationship to his mother and goes deep into men's souls. Many women were labeled "witches" and burned alive over the centuries as a result of misogyny. Some scholars have connected Judeophobia and xenophobia to misogyny and homophobia, claiming that those who hate and fear Jews and foreigners are often also those who hate and fear women and homosexuals. The American Catholic homosexual scholar John Boswell (1947–1994), who died of AIDS, thought that homophobia was not an essential aspect of Christianity until the late Middle Ages (Boswell 1980). Hitler's Nazis persecuted and exterminated Jews, Gypsies, and homosexuals. When the Garaudy–Abbé Pierre affair broke out in France, another affair broke out with the homosexual Jews in Austria. Here is the story as told by Matti Bunzl, an Austrian-born American Jewish scholar:

> On June 29, 1996, a small group of lesbian and gay Jews took to the streets of Vienna to join the city's first-ever Gay Pride Parade. *Re'uth,* as the group called itself after the Hebrew word for friendship, had come into existence in 1991 . . . the organization hoped to provide an affirmative space for Vienna's queer Jews. But *Re'uth* not only

functioned as a social group for lesbian/gay Jews and their friends; the organization also saw itself as a crucial bridge between two minority communities. Indeed, ever since its founding, *Re'uth's* members endeavored to raise awareness for Jewish concerns among queers and for lesbian/gay issues among Jews. So when a group of queer activists organized Vienna's inaugural Gay Pride Parade under the name *Regenbogen Parade* (Rainbow Parade), *Re'uth's* members were eager to participate. The event would present a unique opportunity to showcase the existence of lesbian/gay Jewish life and publicize the group's activities. To maximize visibility during the parade, *Re'uth* designed a banner that symbolized the interarticulation of the group's ethnic and sexual identification. Recalling the design of Israel's national flag, the banner featured a prominent Star of David, a powerful and ambivalent sign in the context of Central Europe's recent past. While historically a sign of affirmative Jewish nationness, Austria's Jews were required to wear the star of David as a means of abject identification during the Nazi period. (Bunzl 2004, p. 1)

Does Bunzl's story prove that misogyny always goes with anti-Semitism, racism, xenophobia, and homophobia? This is an important psychological question, as the unconscious processes involved in each of these phenomena may not be identical. Perhaps one should not too easily put in the same bag different psychological processes and phenomena.

Guilt feelings and shame are painful emotions. It is very painful for most Germans and Austrians to think of their own people as having murdered millions of human beings. This pain leads to unconscious denial and projection. "Historians" such as Arthur R. Butz, David Irving, and Ernst Nolte have denied or minimized the enormity of the Holocaust and of the German people's actions, likening the Holocaust to other mass executions in history such as Stalin's "purges" in the Soviet Union. Nolte has argued that the Nazis were not more wicked than many other groups in the twentieth century, and in particular the Soviet Communists, and that we should not be overly upset by the Holocaust, in which fewer people were killed than in Stalin's "purges" (Nolte 1985, 1991, 1995). The American-Israeli historian Steven Katz wrote a big tome to refute such ideas (Katz 1994).

The fact that millions of Jews were seized, deported to camps, abused, tortured, starved, shot dead, gassed to death, and their corpses burned to ashes is being denied by an entire "school" of "revisionist" history. The American scholar Bradley Smith called these efforts "alibis for the inhumanities" (Smith 1978). In 1993, as the Holocaust-denial literature was multiplying and gaining more anti-Jewish followers, the Jewish-American historian Deborah Lipstadt published a book about the deniers of the Holocaust (Lipstadt 1993). The British "historian" David Irving lost his libel suit against Lipstadt, who had accused him of falsifying history, and her British publisher (Lipstadt 2005).

Modern France has laws against racism and anti-Semitism. In 1972, the Pleven law made it a criminal act to incite to racial hatred, discrimination, defamation, and injury. In 1990, the Gayssot law outlawed all anti-Semitic, racist, and xenophobic acts, and in particular acts of Holocaust denial (*négation-nisme*). French historians, especially Jewish ones, have published an impressive scholarly literature on *négationnisme* (Rousso 1987; Vidal-Naquet 1987; Comte 1990; Fresco 1990, 1999, 2004; Grynberg 1995; Bridonneau 1997; Bihr et al. 1997; Igounet 2000). In 2000, an Algerian-born French-Jewish scholar, Jacques Tarnero, made a documentary film entitled *Autopsie d'un mensonge: le négation-nisme* (Autopsy of a Lie: Holocaust Denial) about this subject, which he had written about earlier (Tarnero 1999). As I have told Tarnero in public, however, "autopsy" means a postmortem, whereas the lie in question is far from dead.

AMERICAN ANTI-SEMITISM

At about the same time as Tarnero's film, an American sociologist named Spencer Blakeslee sought to prove that anti-Semitism was dead in the United States (Blakeslee 2000). As he put it, "This book is not about individual incidents of anti-Semitism, as appalling as they may have been, but about the overall safety of America's Jews at the beginning of the twenty-first century. It examines the emotional significance antisemitism continues to exert on the consciousness of substantial numbers of American Jews and the political necessity anti-Semitism continues to exert on *a small group of Jewish advocacy organizations...* that *purport to represent Jewish interests* [italics added]. All of this emotion and political necessity in spite of the statistical reality that since the end of World War II anti-Jewish beliefs have almost disappeared from the American cultural scene. The vast majority of Americans are simply not antisemitic!" (ibid., p. ix).

Unfortunately, however, anti-Semitism has not died in the United States. Jews have been called "kikes" and "sheenies," accused of being power-hungry and money-mad, and excluded from clubs, hotels, restaurants and other facilities. One of the rabidly anti-Semitic American organizations is the racist Ku Klux Klan (KKK), the name of a number of past and present "fraternal orders" in the United States that have advocated white supremacy, anti-Semitism, racism, anti-Catholicism, homophobia, and nativism. These "orders" have used terrorism, violence, and acts of intimidation such as cross burning to oppress African Americans and other hated groups.

The Ku Klux Klan was founded in 1866, after the end of the American Civil War, by veterans of the Confederate army. Its main purpose was to resist Reconstruction, and it focused as much on intimidating "carpetbaggers" and "scalawags" as on putting down the freed slaves. The KKK quickly adopted violent methods. A backlash against the Klan set in, with the Klan's leadership disowning violence, and Southern elites seeing the Klan as an excuse for federal troops to continue their activities in the South. The organization was in decline from 1868 to 1870 and was destroyed in the early 1870s by President Ulysses

S. Grant's vigorous action under the Civil Rights Act of 1871 (also known as the Ku Klux Klan Act). Some Southerners, however, are still fighting the Civil War in the guise of their battles for the Confederate flag and their "heritage."

In 1915 William Joseph Simmons founded the second Ku Klux Klan, a distinct group using the same name that was inspired by the newfound power of the modern mass-communication media, by D. W. Griffith's film *The Birth of a Nation* and by inflammatory anti-Semitic newspaper accounts surrounding the trial and lynching of the accused murderer Leo Frank. The second KKK was a formal membership organization, with a national and state structure, that paid thousands of men to organize local chapters all over the country. At its peak in the early 1920s, the organization included about 15 percent of the nation's voting population, approximately 4–5 million men. The second KKK preached racism, anti-Catholicism, anticommunism, nativism, and anti-Semitism, and some local groups took part in lynchings and other violent activities. Its popularity fell during the Great Depression (1929–1939), and its membership fell further during World War II (1939–1945) due to scandals resulting from prominent members' crimes and its support of the Nazis.

The name "Ku Klux Klan" has since been used by several different groups, including many who opposed the U.S. Civil Rights Act and desegregation in the 1950s and 1960s, with members of these groups eventually being convicted of murder and manslaughter in the deaths of civil rights workers and children (such as in the bombing of the 16th Street Baptist Church in Alabama). Today, it is estimated that there is as many as 150 Klan chapters with up to 8,000 members nationwide. These groups, with operations in separated small local units, are considered extreme hate groups.

The charismatic and narcissistic Ku Klux Klan leader David Ernest Duke (born 1950) was active in South Boston during the school-busing crisis of 1974. Duke also made efforts to update the Klan's image, urging Klansmen to "get out of the cow pasture and into hotel meeting rooms." Duke was the leader of the Knights of the Ku Klux Klan from 1974 to 1978, when he resigned from the Klan and in 1980 formed the National Association for the Advancement of White People, a white-supremacist nationalist political organization. He was elected to the Louisiana State House of Representatives in 1989 as a Republican, even though the Republican Party threw its support to another candidate. The modern KKK has been repudiated by all mainstream U.S. media and political and religious leaders.

During the Great Depression of the 1930s, the American Catholic "radio priest" Father Charles E. Coughlin (1891–1979) constantly maligned the Jews on his national radio program that reached millions of listeners (Coughlin 1939; General Jewish Council 1939; Athans 1991). In 1935, Father Coughlin founded the National Union for Social Justice, a fascist, racist, anticommunist, and anti-Semitic group with a violent hatred of President Franklin Delano

Roosevelt's social-welfare policies. Actively fueling extreme anti-Semitism, in the June 12, 1936, issue of his newspaper *Social Justice,* Father Coughlin assaulted Jews as "Christ killers," "Shylocks," and "Bolsheviks" (General Jewish Council 1939). Nor has American anti-Semitism "died" after World War II. It is still widespread among American white-supremacist and Christian-supremacist groups such as the John Birch Society and Christian Identity (Dinnerstein 1971, 1994; Aho 1990). Even the well-meaning scholar Blakeslee acknowledged that anti-Semitism was thriving—in other countries: "A careful examination of the sociocultural fabric of several European countries (not to mention the Arab countries) quickly reveals the tenacity and persistence of anti-Semitism in these parts of the globe" (Blakeslee 2000).

The problem with most of the current literature on Holocaust denial is that while it attacks the deniers and exposes their historical falsifications, it does not explain their psychological underpinnings and unconscious motivations. Just as we need to understand the individual and collective psychological processes that cause anti-Semitism, and those that made it possible for ordinary Germans to become mass murderers (Browning 1992, Waller 2002), so we also need to understand what it is about the Holocaust deniers like Mark Weber that makes them stake their entire reputation on absurd and irrational claims. Without considering the unconscious feelings of guilt and shame, and the unconscious defenses of projection and externalization, without examining the problematic self-image of those deniers, it may be impossible to understand them.

The country in which most of the European Jews were murdered by the German Nazis and by their collaborators during the Second World War was Poland. It was home to most of Europe's Jews, most of the Nazi extermination camps were there, and Catholic Poland had a long history of anti-Semitism. While some Poles fought the Germans, and some even saved Jews from certain death at the risk of their own lives, many Poles helped the German Nazis kill the Jews. In 1941, Poles massacred Jews in the small Polish town of Jedwabne, and even after the Holocaust, in 1946, another massacre of Jews took place at the Polish town of Kielce. Polish memories of what happened during the war are often very different from Jewish ones—yet more proof of how everything is in the eye of the beholder. (Zimmerman 2003, Krajewski 2005).

In a very different way, the unconscious denial of the Holocaust has occurred not only among the Nazi perpetrators and anti-Semites, but also among the victims—those deeply traumatized Jewish survivors who could not think about the unthinkable, and those Israeli Jews who were supposed to help them, but who instead accused them of having gone like lambs to the slaughter—as if they had any choice. To illustrate the point, I will permit myself a personal example of my own denial of the Holocaust in my youth. My father was born in Germany in 1913 and died in Israel in 1992. My mother was born in Poland in 1916 and died in Israel in 2004. Both of them immigrated to Palestine during the first two years of Hitler's rule in Germany—my father in 1933 and my mother in 1935. My paternal grandfather was interned at Buchenwald but was released before the "final solution," when Germany was still letting its Jews leave, and came to Palestine as well. My father's family survived, although his father had become seriously ill. Most of my mother's family was being murdered in Poland's Lodz ghetto and Auschwitz-Birkenau concentration camps around the time of my birth in 1943. I was born to a mother absorbed in a very complicated mourning of the family she had left behind. My mother lost all her grandparents, both her parents, all her uncles and aunts, and six out of her nine siblings. All this became clear to her only after the war, when her surviving younger brother arrived in Palestine. All her life, she felt irrationally guilty for the deaths of her immediate family.

In 1957, as an adolescent boy in Tel Aviv, I saw my first Holocaust film. It was a 32-minute French documentary film made by the 33-year-old French film director Alain Resnais in 1955 from footage taken by the Nazi *SS* men themselves in their extermination camps of Auschwitz and Birkenau and entitled *Nuit et Brouillard* (Night and Fog). The title is the French rendering of Hitler's *Nacht-und Nebel-Erlass* (Night and Fog Decree), issued on December 7, 1941, whose purpose was to seize persons deemed to endanger German security, who were not to be immediately executed, and to make them vanish without a trace into the "night and fog" of Germany (Shirer 1960, p. 957). No information was given to the vanished person's family or friends. The *SD,* or Security Service of the *SS,* was charged with carrying out this decree. *Nuit et brouillard* had a running commentary by its scriptwriter, the 44-year-old French poet Jean-Raphaël-Marie-Noël Cayrol, a former *Résistant* who had been captured by the Germans in 1943 and survived two years in their Mauthausen concentration camp. Cayrol spoke of "the concentrationary beast slumbering within us all."

Nuit et Brouillard may be the best noncommercial film about the Holocaust, next to Claude Lanzmann's documentary film *Shoah,* made 20 years later (Lanzmann 1985a, 1985b; Hazan et al. 1990). One film critic called *Nuit et Brouillard* "an official film of great dignity" (Halliwell 1989, p. 725). To me, *Nuit et Brouillard* was horrifying and traumatic. For the first time in my life, I saw the inmates at Auschwitz herded into gas chambers and let out dead, the corpses of women and children piled up before the crematoria, Jews being shot to death and dumped into mass graves they had just dug themselves. For several nights following this film, I could barely sleep. The horrors kept coming back to me. After a while, I calmed down and the memories abated. For a long time thereafter, however, I avoided contact with Holocaust literature and films. It was not until many years later, when I became a psychotherapist and saw Holocaust survivors in therapy—a painful experience in itself—that I actively read about the subject. In 1997, after a scholarly meeting in Poland, I also visited the abandoned extermination camps of Auschwitz-Birkenau and Treblinka, which was a very important experience.

Mourning is a painful and prolonged emotional process, which most people naturally try to avoid. Those who have lost their dearest ones tend to avoid feeling grief over their losses because grief is too painful. In Shakespeare's tragedy *Macbeth,* the good doctor called to heal the mad Lady Macbeth says, "My mind she has mated, and amaz'd my sight. I think, but dare not speak" (Shakespeare, *Macbeth,* Act V, Scene 1). It may be more accurate to say that he dares not feel. During Hitler's rule in Germany, many German doctors became Nazis and took part in the mass extermination of the Jews without feeling the horror of what they were doing. The psychology of these physicians was studied by the American psychiatrist Robert Jay Lifton (Lifton 1986). Lifton called the unconscious processes of ceasing to feel *psychic closing-off* and *psychic numbing,* which he distinguished from Freud's *denial* (Lifton 1967, p. 32). However that may be, the pain of feeling the horrors of the Holocaust is so great that even we, its victims, the Jews, did not wish to think about it and never wanted to feel it. We denied both the external reality and our own unbearable feelings. From 1945 until the Eichmann trial in 1961–1962, almost no Israeli psychiatric studies of Holocaust survivors were published anywhere. It was not until the 1960s that Israeli psychiatrists, psychologists, and psychoanalysts began studying and treating Holocaust survivors and their offspring (Solomon 1995, Chaitin 2000).

LITERATURE AND ANTI-SEMITISM

During the thirteenth, fourteenth, fifteenth, and sixteenth centuries, the burning of books often preceded the burning alive of Jews in an *auto da fé* (act of faith), the ritual of public penance of condemned heretics and apostates that took place after the Spanish or Portuguese Inquisition had decided their punishment. Similarly, the publication of anti-Semitic literature has often preceded the actual persecution and massacre of the Jews (Brainin et al. 1993). The German scholar Jens Malte Fischer studied anti-Semitic stereotypes in European literature (Fischer 1987). Fischer quoted an anonymous German anti-Semitic pamphlet published in the 1920s as a supplement to the notorious *Protocols of the Elders of Zion* (Nilus 1905, 1920; Segel 1934; Bernstein 1935; Cohn 1967; Bach 1973; Taguieff 1992; Conan 1999; Bishop 1999; Eisner 2005). A study of the Jewish stereotype in German anti-Semitic cartoons showed that anti-Jewish sexual fantasies were present in German folklore as early as the Renaissance (Fuchs 1921).

Another racist stereotype of the Jews was expressed by the German writer Artur Dinter (1876–1948), who portrayed the Jews as contaminating "Aryan" blood (Dinter 1927). Fischer compared this work with passages from Adolf Hitler's notorious *Mein Kampf* (Hitler 1925–1927, 1939). Fischer also analyzed the works of the anti-Semitic and racist French writer Louis-Ferdinand Céline (Céline 1937) using some of Erich Fromm's psychoanalytic theories (Fromm 1973) to explain Céline's violent hatred of the Jews, an unconscious projection of his own self-hatred. Céline, who was born Destouches, took his mother's first name as his own last name and suffered from deep psychopathology (Szafran 1976). Fischer concluded that perverse anti-Semitic literary depictions arise from the disturbed minds of their authors via unconscious projection.

Ambivalent about their own Judaism, some Jewish writers have idealized their own "race," projecting their own narcissistic grandiosity on their ethnic or religious group, while at the same time blaming the Jews for conspiring to rule the world. One such Jew was the nineteenth-century British statesman Benjamin Disraeli (1804–1881), the Earl of Beaconsfield, Viscount Hughenden of Hughenden. Disraeli was the grandson of an Italian Jew who had immigrated to England from Venice, and the son of the British Jewish writer Isaac d'Israeli (1766–1848). In 1813, when Benjamin Disraeli was nine years old, his father fell out with the head of his synagogue, the oldest Jewish synagogue in London, established in the London neighborhood of Bevis Marks by Portuguese and Spanish Jews in 1698. In 1817, when Benjamin was 13 years old and would normally have had his Jewish *bar-mitzvah* initiation ceremony, his father Isaac d'Israeli had him and his other children baptized Christians in the Anglican Church, opening the way for Disraeli's extraordinary political career, which would never have been possible had he remained a Jew. The young Disraeli entered British politics, rose in the ranks, and became a favorite of Queen Victoria of Great Britain and Ireland, who made him her prime minister. He in turn made her empress of India (Meynell 1903; Levine 1968; Schwarz 1979; Rather 1986; Weintraub 1993; Glassman 2003; Flavin 2005).

The British writer Andrew Norman Wilson recently "discovered" that Disraeli was a racist (Wilson 2005). Disraeli's "racism," however, was not rare for his time, and the American literary scholar Patrick Brantlinger has called it "positive racism" (Brantlinger 2005). Disraeli believed that the superior British "race" should rule over inferior "races" such as the Indians. A racist statement attributed by the German Nazis to Disraeli was "No one may treat the race principle, the race question, indifferently. It is the key to world history. And therefore history is so frequently confused because it was written by people who did not understand the race question and likewise few of the circumstances appertaining to it. Race is everything and every race that gives away its blood by careless interbreeding must perish. Language and religion do not make a race, the blood makes it" (NSDAP 1942).

Disraeli was as ambivalent about his Jewishness as he was about his father. In 1835, he and the older Irish MP Daniel O'Connell (1775–1847), who may have played the role of the father in Disraeli's unconscious mind, quarreled publicly over false press reports that Disraeli had called O'Connell "a traitor and incendiary." The pair were to fight a duel, but the British police intervened and Disraeli undertook to keep the peace. Later, in a heated debate in parliament, O'Connell taunted Disraeli about being a Jew, and Disraeli famously replied, "Yes, I am a Jew, and when the ancestors of the right honorable gentleman were brutal savages in an unknown island, mine were priests in the Temple of Solomon." Yet at the same time Disraeli denounced "secret Jewish conspiracies to rule Europe."

Disraeli's novels were political statements (Schwarz 1979; Flavin 2005). One of his historical novels, about the medieval crusader prince Tancrède de Haute-ville (1075–1112), idealized "the chosen Hebrew race" (Disraeli 1847). Disraeli is called "the father of British imperialism." Like many other politicians, whose chief unconscious defense mechanism is projection, and who tend to be paranoid (Robins & Post 1997), Disraeli entertained many conspiracy theories. In 1856, he said in Parliament, "It is useless to deny, because it is impossible to conceal, that a great part of Europe—the whole of Italy and France and a great portion of Germany, to say nothing of other countries—is covered with a network of... secret societies...They do not want constitutional government...They want to change the tenure of land, to drive out the present owners of the soil and to put an end to ecclesiastical establishments" (Rather 1986).

Did Disraeli think that those "secret societies" were Jewish? Once, in a moment of unguarded candor, he said, "The world is governed by far different personages than what is imagined by those not behind the scenes." Disraeli made several other statements, both in his books and on the floor of the British House of Commons, about a secret conspiracy to control Europe. While he was proud of his Jewish origins, he also said that there was a Jewish conspiracy to rule Europe and the whole world. The Stanford pathologist Lelland Joseph Rather believed that Disraeli's "racist" Jewish-conspiracy theories anticipated the notori-ous *Protocols of the Elders of Zion* in projecting upon the Jews and "secret soci-eties" his own unconscious wish for world domination (Rather 1986).

Disraeli's ambivalence about his own Jewishness (and no less about his own father) has characterized other members of the Jewish "diaspora" and "exile," as we Israeli Jews fantastically call all countries other than Israel, which we call "The Land." Some Jews have even displayed a hatred of their own people. On the other hand, some anti-Semites have presented us with psychological riddles. One of these was the extreme-right-wing British political leader Arthur Kenneth Chesterton (1896–1973), founder of the fascist and racist British National Front and a cousin of the British writer Gilbert Keith Chesterton (1874–1936). Some scholars concluded from Chesterton's extreme anti-Semitism that his character had a deep psychological defect. The American scholar David Baker thought that the case of Chesterton suggests that not all fascist leaders have authoritarian per-sonalities, nor are they all crazed genocidal Nazis. Baker thought that the histori-cal, social, and intellectual—rather than psychological—forces in Chesterton's upbringing and experiences during World War I had impelled him towards cul-tural and ethnocentric fascism. He was attracted to the fascist and racist British leader Oswald Mosley (1896–1980) and to British fascism in general because of their camaraderie and sense of purpose. Despite his belief in a world Jewish conspiracy, Chesterton condemned the Nazi genocide of the Jews and joined the British army against Germany (Baker 1986). Chesterton's ambivalence toward the Jews, however, does not necessarily disprove his psychopathology.

Another puzzling case of ambivalence was that of the German Catholic writer Carl Schmitt (1888–1985), a racist anti-Semite with close ties to Hitler's Nazi party. The German sociologist and writer Nicolaus Sombart (born 1923) analyzed the life and work of Schmitt, placing him in the historical context of a generation of antiliberal, antifeminist, and anti-Semitic German men (Sombart 1991). Sombart thought that Jews became the archenemy of the German people when they continued to fight for the ideals of emancipation after the Germans had abandoned them. Ultimately, however, Sombart agreed with Freud that the psychic roots of anti-Semitism lay in the unconscious castration fear of the uncircumcised, their envy of Jewish political and sexual superiority, and their fantastic interpretation of contemporary history as the rise of the Jews to world domination, exemplified in Benjamin Disraeli's inordinate influence over Queen Victoria. Sombart thought that Hitler's German nationalism defined itself as the fight against world Jewry to the point of its extinction. Like Hitler himself, Schmitt, though a pronounced anti-Semite, was fascinated by Jewish thinkers, especially by Disraeli and his idea of the chosen race. Ironically, Disraeli had been baptized a Christian at age 13, Disraeli himself had complained about the Jewish conspiracy to dominate the world, and his chosen race was the "Hebrew" one. Sombart believed that for these German anti-Semites, the Jewish enemy unconsciously represented a bad part of their selves that they had to destroy—hardly a new idea.

Conclusion

Judeophobia, Jew-hatred, and anti-Judaism, known by the "scientific" euphemism of "anti-Semitism," are highly complex psychological phenomena on both the individual and collective levels. In addition to the economic, political, social, historical, religious, and conscious-psychological causes of anti-Semitism, there are also unconscious defensive psychological processes, such as the individual's splitting, projection, and externalization, and the majority group's collective needs for identity, boundaries, and enemies. Anti-Semitism, including Judeophobia and the hatred of Jews, is one of the oldest psychopathological collective phenomena in human history, one that has not disappeared, and has recently intensified, even after six million European Jews were murdered by the German Nazis and their collaborators during the Second World War. Anti-Semitism intensifies in times of social, political, or economic crisis in the majority society, in times of heightened anxiety, when the Jews unconsciously become the scapegoat for all the society's ills and all manner of fantastic evil qualities are attributed to them. We have seen that anti-Semitism flourishes even in countries that have few Jews or none at all, and that the irrational nature of the fantasies that anti-Jews have about Jews is an indication of their paranoid psychopathology. It is only by considering both the conscious and unconscious, individual and collective psychological processes active in anti-Semitism that this most pernicious and dangerous phenomenon can be understood.

Jerusalem, May 2008

References and Bibliography

Abel, Ernest L. (1975). *The Roots of Anti-Semitism.* Rutherford, NJ: Fairleigh Dickinson University Press.

Abel, Theodore Fred (1938). *Why Hitler Came into Power.* New York: Prentice Hall. Reprinted (1981). New York: Ams Press.

Abella, Irving (1987). Antisemitism in Canada in the Interwar Years. In Rischin, Moses (Ed.), *The Jews of North America.* Detroit, MI: Wayne State University Press.

Abraham, Gary A. (1992). *Max Weber and the Jewish Question: A Study of the Social Outlook of His Sociology.* Urbana and Chicago: University of Illinois Press.

Abraham, Karl (1955). The Day of Atonement: Some Observations on Reik's *Problems in the Psychology of Religion.* In Abraham, Karl, *Clinical Papers and Essays on Psychoanalysis.* Tr. H.C. Abraham & D.R. Ellison. Ed. H. C. Abraham. New York: Basic Books.

Abrahams, Israel (1961). *Jewish Life in the Middle Ages.* Cleveland and New York: World Publishing Company. Philadelphia: Jewish Publication Society of America.

Abulafia, Anna Sapir (1995). *Christians and Jews in the Twelfth-Century Renaissance.* New York: Routledge.

Abulafia, Anna Sapir (Ed.). (2002). *Religious Violence Between Christians and Jews: Medieval Roots, Modern Perspectives.* New York: Palgrave.

Ackerman, Nathan W. (1947). Antisemitic Motivation in a Psychopathic Personality: A Case Study. *The Psychoanalytic Review,* vol. 34, pp. 76–101.

Ackerman, Nathan W., & Jahoda, Marie Lazarsfeld (1950). *Anti-Semitism and Emotional Disorder: A Psychoanalytic Interpretation.* New York: Harper & Row.

Adam, Barry D. (1978). Inferiorization and "Self-esteem." *Social Psychology,* vol. 41, no. 1, March, pp. 47–53.

Adams, Mark B. (Ed.). (1990). *The Wellborn Science: Eugenics in Germany, France, and Russia.* New York: Oxford University Press.

Adler, Alexandre et al. (2003). *Le sionisme expliqué à nos potes.* Paris: La Martinière. [French].

Adler, Meinhard (1990). *Vergangenheitsbewältigung in Deutschland: eine kulturpsychiatrische Studie über die Faschismusverarbeitung, gesehen aus dem Blickwinkel der zwei Kulturen.* Frankfurt am Main and New York: Peter Lang. [German].

Adorno, Theodor Wiesengrund (1944). Letter to Max Horkheimer. Max Horkheimer Archive, Frankfurt am Main. [German].

Adorno, Theodor Wiesengrund (1946). Anti-Semitism and Fascist Propaganda. In Simmel, Ernst (Ed.), *Anti-Semitism: A Social Disease.* New York: International Universities Press. New edition (1948). New York: International Universities Press.

Adorno, Theodor Wiesengrund (1981). Das Schema der Massenkultur. In Adorno, Theodor Wiesengrund, *Gesammelte Schriften,* vol. 3, pp. 299–335. Frankfurt am Main: Suhrkamp Verlag. [German].

Adorno, Theodor Wiesengrund (1986). What Does Coming to Terms with the Past Mean? In Hartman, Geoffrey (Ed.). *Bitburg and Beyond: Encounters in American, German, and Jewish History,* pp. 114–130. New York: Shapolsky Publishers.

Adorno, Theodor Wiesengrund (1990). Theorie der Halbbildung. In Adorno, Theodor Wiesengrund, *Gesammelte Schriften,* vol. 8, pp. 93–121. Frankfurt am Main.: Suhrkamp Verlag. [German].

Adorno, Theodor Wiesengrund, & Horkheimer, Max (1968). Ideologie. In Adorno, Theodor Wiesengrund, & Dirks, Walter (Eds.). *Soziologische Exkurse: nach Vorträgen und Diskussionen,* pp. 162–181. Frankfurt am Main: Europäische Verlagsanstalt. [German].

Adorno, Theodor Wiesengrund, et al. (1950). *The Authoritarian Personality.* Eds. Max Horkheimer & Samuel H. Flowerman. New York: Harper & Row. New edition (1952). New York: Harper & Bros. New edition (1969). New York: W.W. Norton. New edition (1982). New York: W.W. Norton.

Agobard of Lyon, Saint (1981). *Agobardi Lugdunensis Opera Omnia.* Tr. W.L. North. Ed. L. Van Acker. Turnhoult: Brepols.

Aho, James A. (1990). *The Politics of Righteousness: Idaho Christian Patriotism.* Seattle and London: University of Washington Press.

Alba, Richard, et al. (Eds.). (2003). *Germans or Foreigners? Attitudes Toward Ethnic Minorities in Post-unification Germany.* New York: Palgrave Macmillan.

Albert, Phyllis Cohen (1992). The Right to Be Different: Interpretations of the French Revolution's Promises to the Jews. *Modern Judaism,* vol. 12, no. 3 (October), pp. 243–257.

Alexander, Edward (1996). *The Jewish Wars: Reflections by One of the Belligerents.* Carbondale and Edwardsville, IL: Southern Illinois University Press.

Alexander, I.E., & Blackman, S. (1957). Castration, Circumcision, and Anti-semitism. *Journal of Abnormal Psychology,* vol. 55, no. 1, pp. 143–144.

Alford, C. Fred (1997). *What Evil Means to Us.* Ithaca, NY: Cornell University Press.

Allen, G.E. (1986). The Eugenics Record Office at Cold Spring Harbor, 1910–1940: An Essay in Institutional History. *Osiris,* Vol. 2.

Allport, Gordon W. (1954). *The Nature of Prejudice.* Reading. MA: Addison-Wesley.

Allswang, Bradley Benzion (1989). *The Final Resolution: Combating Anti-Jewish Hostility.* Jerusalem: Feldheim.

Almog, Shmuel (1988). The Racial Motif in Renan's Attitude to Jews and Judaism. In Almog, Shmuel (Ed.) (1988), *Antisemitism Through the Ages,* tr. Nathan H. Reisner, pp. 255–278. Oxford and New York: Published for the Vidal Sassoon International

Center for the Study of Antisemitism, The Hebrew University of Jerusalem, by the Pergamon Press.

Almog, Shmuel (Ed.). (1990). *Nationalism and Antisemitism in Europe, 1815–1945.* Oxford and New York: Pergamon Press.

Altemeyer, Bob (1981). *Right-wing Authoritarianism.* Winnipeg: University of Manitoba Press.

Altemeyer, Bob (1988). *Enemies of Freedom: Understanding Right-wing Authoritarianism.* Foreword by M. Brewster Smith. San Francisco: Jossey-Bass.

Altemeyer, Bob (1996). *The Authoritarian Specter.* Cambridge, MA: Harvard University Press.

Altman, Linda Jacobs (2003). *Hitler's Rise to Power and the Holocaust.* Berkeley Heights, NJ: Enslow Publishers.

Altman, Linda Jacobs (2004). *Impact of the Holocaust.* Berkeley Heights, NJ: Enslow Publishers.

Ambrose, Stephen E. (2001). *Band of Brothers.* London: Pocket Books.

Améry, Jean (1966). *Jenseits von Schuld und Sühne: Bewältigungsversuche eines Überwältigen.* Munich: Szczezny. Reprinted (1970). Munich: Deutscher Taschgenbuch-verlag. New edition (1977). Stuttgart: Klett-cotta. [German].

Améry, Jean (1980). *At the Mind's Limits: Contemplations by a Survivor on Auschwitz and its Realities.* Tr. Sidney Rosenfeld and Stella P. Rosenfeld. Bloomington: Indiana University Press. Reprinted (1986). New York: Schocken Books.

Ammerman, N. (1989). *Bible Believers: Fundamentalists in the Modern World.* New Brunswick, NJ: Rutgers University Press.

Amsee, Andreas (1939). *Die Judenfrage.* Luzern: Raeber & Cie. [German].

Anctil, Pierre (1992). Interlude of Hostility: Judeo-Chriostian Relations in Quebec in the Interwar Period, 1919–1939. In Davies, Alan (Ed.), *Antisemitism in Canada: History and Interpretation.* Waterloo, Ontario: Wilfred Laurier University Press.

Anderson, Benedict (1983). *Imagined Communities: Reflections on the Origin and Spread of Nationalism.* London and New York: Verso. Revised and expanded edition (1991). London and New York: Verso.

Angenot, Marc (1984). *Ce Que L'on Dit Des Juifs En 1889: Antisémitisme et Discours Social.* Montréal: Centre Interuniversitaire D'études Européennes. Reprinted (1989). Saint-Denis: Presses Universitaires de Vincennes.

Anzieu, Didier (1975). *Le Groupe et L'inconscient.* Paris: Dunod. [French].

Anzieu, Didier, & Martin, Jacques-Yves (1968). *La Dynamique des groupes restreints.* Paris: Presses Universitaires de France. 3rd edition (1971). Paris: Presses Universitaires de France. 4th edition (1973). Paris: Presses Universitaires de France. 5th edition (1976). Paris: Presses Universitaires de France. 6th edition (1979). Paris: Presses Universitaires de France. 7th revised edition (1982). Paris: Presses Universitaires de France. 8th edition (1986). Paris: Presses Universitaires de France. 9th edition (1990). Paris: Presses Universitaires de France. 10th edition (1994). Paris: Presses Universitaires de France. 11th edition (1997). Paris: Presses Universitaires de France. [French].

App, Austin Joseph (1973). *The Six Million Swindle: Blackmailing the German People for Hard Marks with Fabricated Corpses.* Takoma Park, MD: Boniface Press. New edition (1976). Takoma Park, MD: Boniface Press.

App, Austin Joseph (1977). *German-American Voice for Truth and Justice: Autobiography.* Takoma Park, MD: Boniface Press.

Appelfeld, Aron (1980). *Badenheim 1939.* Tr. Dalya Bilu. Boston: D.R. Godine. Reprinted (1981). Boston: G.K. Hall. New edition (2001). Tr. Betsy Rosenberg. Ed. Ken Frieden. New York: Syracuse University Press.

Arendt, Hannah (1951). *The Origins of Totalitarianism.* New York: Harcourt, Brace. 2nd edition (1958). New York: Meridian Books. New edition (1966). New York: Harcourt, Brace & World. New edition (1968). New York: Harcourt, Brace & World. New edition (1973). New York: Harcourt Brace Jovanovich. New edition (2004). Intro. by Samantha Power. New York: Schocken Books.

Arendt, Hannah (1963). *Eichmann in Jerusalem: A Report on the Banality of Evil.* New York: Viking Press. Revised and enlarged edition (1964). New York: Viking Press. New edition (1976). New York: Penguin Books. New edition (1994). New York: Penguin Books.

Arendt, Hannah (1966). The Formidable Dr. Robinson: A Reply. *New York Review of Books,* vol. 5, No. 12, January 20.

Arendt, Hannah (1968). Antisemitism. In Arendt, Hannah, *The Origins of Totalitarianism,* Part 1. New York: Harcourt, Brace & World.

Arendt, Hannah (1994). *Essays in Understanding, 1930–1954.* Ed. Jerome Kohn. New York: Harcourt, Brace & Co. New edition (2005). *Essays in Understanding, 1930–1954: Formation, Exile, and Totalitarianism.* New York: Schocken Books.

Arendt, Hannah, & Jaspers, Karl (1992). *Correspondence, 1926–1969.* Trans. Hans Saner. New York: Harcourt Brace & Co.

Arens, Katherine (1986). Schnitzler and Characterology: From Empire to Third Reich. *Modern Austrian Literature,* vol. 19, nos. 3–4, pp. 97–127.

Arkush, Allan (1994). *Moses Mendelssohn and the Enlightenment.* Albany: State University of New York Press.

Arlow, Jacob A. (1992). Aggression und Vorurteil: psychoanalytische betrachtungen zur Ritualmordbeschuldigung gegen die Juden. *Psyche: Zeitschrift für Psychoanalyse und ihre Anwendungen,* vol. 46, pp. 1122–1132. [German].

Arlow, Jacob A. (1994). Aggression and Prejudice: Some Psychoanalytic Observations on the Blood Libel Accusation Against the Jews. In Richards, Arlene Kramer, & Richards, Arnold D. (Eds.). *The Spectrum of Psychoanalysis: Essays in Honor of Martin S. Bergmann,* pp. 283–294. Madison, CT: International Universities Press.

Armstrong, Karen (2000). *The Battle for God.* New York: Alfred A. Knopf. Reprinted (2001). New York: Ballantine Books.

Aschheim, Steven E. (1982a). *Brothers and Strangers: The East European Jew in German and German Jewish Consciousness, 1800–1923.* Madison: University of Wisconsin Press.

Aschheim, Steven E. (1982b). Caftan and Cravat: The *Ostjude* as a Cultural Symbol in the Development of German Anti-Semitism. In Drescher, Seymour, et al. (Eds.) *Political Symbolism in Modern Europe.* New Brunswick, NJ: Transaction Books.

Aschheim, Steven E. (Ed.) (2001). *Hannah Arendt in Jerusalem.* Berkeley: University of California Press.

Ashmore, Richard D., & Del Boca, Francis K. (1976). Psychological Approaches to Understanding Intergroup Conflict. In Katz, Phyllis A. (Ed.) *Towards the Elimination of Racism.* Oxford and New York: Pergamon Press.

Assmann, J. (1995). Ancient Egyptian AntiJudaism: A Case of Distorted Memory. In Schacter, Daniel L., et al. (Eds.), *Memory Distortions: How Minds, Brains, and Societies Reconstruct the Past.* Cambridge, MA: Harvard University Press.

Ateek, Naim, et al. (Eds.) (1992). *Faith and the Intifada: Palestinian Christian Voices.* Markyknoll, NY: Orbis Books.

Athans, Mary Christine (1991a). *The Coughlin-Fahey Connection: Father Charles E. Coughlin, Father Denis Fahey, C. S. Sp. , and Religious Anti-semitism in the United States, 1938–1954.* New York: Peter Lang.

Athans, Mary Christine (1991b). Antisemitism? Or Anti-Judaism? In Shermis, Michael, & Zannoni, Arthur E. (Eds.). *Introduction to Jewish-Christian Relations.* New York: Paulist Press.

Atran, Scott (2002). *In Gods We Trust: The Evolutionary Landscape of Religion.* Oxford and New York: Oxford University Press.

Attali, Jacques, Boniface, Pascal, Houziaux, Alain, & Israël, Gérard (2005). *Israël, Les Juifs, L'antisémitisme.* Paris: Les Editions De L'atelier. [French].

Bach, Hans Israel (1973). Projections of the "Protocols": The Guilt Feeling in Antisemitism. *Patterns of Prejudice,* vol. 7, no. 4, pp. 24–31.

Baeyer-Katte, W. von (1962). Nachträgliche Gedanken zu einem Symposium über die psychologischen und sozialen Voraussetzungen des Antisemitismus. *Psyche: Zeitschrift für Psychoanalyse und ihre Anwendungen,* vol. 16, pp. 312–317. [German].

Baird, W. (1990). *To Die for Germany: Heroes in the Nazi Pantheon.* Bloomington: Indiana University Press.

Bakan, David (1958). *Sigmund Freud and the Jewish Mystical Tradition.* Boston: Beacon Press.

Baker, David L. (1985). A. K. Chesterton, the Strasser Brothers, and the Politics of the National Front. *Patterns of Prejudice,* vol. 19, No. 3.

Baker, David L. (1986). The Appeal of Fascism: Pathological Fantasy or Intellectual Coherence? *Patterns of Prejudice,* vol. 20, no. 3, pp. 3–12.

Baldwin, Neil (2001). *Henry Ford and the Jews: The Mass Production of Hate.* New York: Public Affairs Books.

Bankier, David (Ed.). (2000). *Probing the Depths of German Antisemitism: German Society and the Persecution of the Jews, 1933–1941.* New York: Berghahn Books.

Banton, Michael (1983). *Racial and Ethnic Competition.* Cambridge and New York: Cambridge University Press.

Bar-Tal, Daniel, & Teichman, Yona (2005). *Stereotypes and Prejudice in Conflict.* New York: Cambridge University Press.

Bar-Zvi, Mickaël, et al. (2003). *Le Sionisme face à ses détracteurs.* Ed. Shmuel Trigano. Paris: Raphaël. [French].

Bardèche, Maurice (1948). *Nuremberg, ou la terre promise.* Paris: Les Sept Couleurs. [French].

Bardèche, Maurice (1961). *Qu'est-ce que le fascisme?* Paris: Les Sept Couleurs. [French].

Barkan, E. (1992). *The Retreat of Scientific Racism: Changing Concepts of Race in Britain and the United States between the World Wars.* New York: Cambridge University Press.

Barkat, Amiram (2007). Founder of Islamic Movement in Israel Slams Holocaust Denial at Global Forum Against Anti-Semitism Conference in Jerusalem. *Ha'aretz,* February 12.

Barkun, Michael (1974). *Disaster and the Millennium*. New Haven, CT: Yale University Press.

Barnouw, Dagmar (1983). The Secularity of Evil: Hannah Arendt and the Eichmann Controversy. *Modern Judaism,* vol. 3, pp. 75–94.

Barnouw, Dagmar (1990). *Visible Spaces: Hannah Arendt and the German-Jewish Experience.* Baltimore: Johns Hopkins University Press.

Baron, Salo Wittmayer (1937). *A Social and Religious History of the Jews,* 3 vols. New York: Columbia University Press. 2nd edition (1952–1983). 18 vols. New York: Columbia University Press. 3rd edition (1993). 23 vols. New York: Columbia University Press.

Baron, Salo Wittmayer (1976). Changing Patterns of Antisemitism: a Survey. *Jewish Social Studies,* vol. 38, pp. 5–38.

Baron, Salo Wittmayer, & Wise, G. (1977). *Violence and Defense in Jewish Experience.* Philadelphia: Jewish Publication Society of America.

Bartchy, S. Scott (2005). Where Is the History in Mel Gibson's *The Passion of the Christ? Pastoral Psychology,* vol. 53, no. 4, pp. 313–328.

Bass, Helene (1987). *Annihilation Anxiety as a Factor in the Development of the Antisemitic Personality.* PhD dissertation, Union for Experimenting Colleges and Universities (now the Union Institute and University).

Bastian, Till (1994). *Auschwitz und die "Auschwitz-lüge": Massenmord und Geschichtsfälschung.* Munich: C.H. Beck. [German].

Bastian, Till (1997). *Furchtbare Soldaten: deutsche Kriegsverbrechen im zweiten Weltkrieg.* Munich: C.H. Beck. [German].

Bat Ye'or (1985). *The Dhimmi: Jews and Christians under Islam.* Pref. Jacques Ellul. Tr. David Maisel, Paul Fenton & David Littman. Madison, NJ: Fairleigh Dickinson University Press. Cranbury, NJ: Associated University Presses. New edition (1996). Madison, NJ: Fairleigh Dickinson University Press. Cranbury, NJ: Associated University Presses.

Bat Ye'or (1996). *The Decline of Eastern Christianity under Islam: From Jihad to Dhimmitude, Seventh to Twentieth Century.* Fwd. by Jacques Ellul. Tr. Miriam Kochan & David Littman. Madison, NJ: Fairleigh Dickinson University Press. Cranbury, NJ: Associated University Presses.

Bat Ye'or (2002). *Islam and Dhimmitude: Where Civilizations Collide.* Tr. Miriam Kochan & David Littman. Madison, NJ: Fairleigh Dickinson University Press. Cranbury, NJ: Associated University Presses.

Bat Ye'or (2005). *Eurabia: The Euro-Arab Axis.* Madison, NJ: Fairleigh Dickinson University Press.

Bataille, Georges (1947). Review of Jean-Paul Sartre: "Réflexions sur la question juive." *Critique,* vol. 2, no. 12, pp. 471–473. [French].

Bataille, Georges (1954). *Inner Experience.* Tr. L.A. Boldt. Albany: State University of New York Press.

Bataille, Georges (1962). *Death and Sensuality: A Study of Eroticism and the Taboo.* New York: Walker. New edition (1977). New York: Arno Press.

Bataille, Georges (1987). Rezension von Jean-Paul Sartre: "Réflexions sur la question juive." *Babylon: Beiträge zur jüdischen Gegenwart,* no. 2, July, pp. 80–81. [German].

Bataille, Georges (2001). *The Unfinished System of Nonknowledge.* Ed. Stuart Kendall. Tr. Michelle Kendall & Stuart Kendall. Minneapolis: University of Minnesota Press.

Bauer, Bruno (1843a). Die Fähigkeit Der Heutigen Juden und Christen, Frei Zu Werden. In Herwegh, Georg (Ed.), *Einundzwanzig Bogen Aus Der Schweiz,* vol. 5, pp. 56–71. Zürich Und Winterthur: n.p. [German].

Bauer, Bruno (1843b). *Die Judenfrage.* Braunschweig: F. Otto. [German].

Bauer, Yehuda (1985). *Antisemitism Today: Myth and Reality.* Jerusalem: Shazar Library, Institute of Contemporary Jewry, and Vidal Sassoon International Center for the Study of Antisemitism, The Hebrew University of Jerusalem.

Bauer, Yehuda (2001). *Rethinking the Holocaust.* New Haven, CT: Yale University Press.

Bauer, Yehuda (Ed.) (1988). *Present-Day Antisemitism.* Jerusalem: The Vidal Sassoon International Center for the Study of Antisemitism, The Hebrew University of Jerusalem.

Baum, Steven K. (2004). A Bell Curve of Hate? *Journal of Genocidal Research,* 6, no. 4 (December), pp. 567–577.

Baum, Stephen K. (2008). *The Psychology of Genocide: Perpetrators, Bystanders and Rescuers.* Cambridge and New York: Cambridge University Press.

Bauman, Janina (1986). *Winter in the Morning: A Young Girl's Life in the Warsaw Ghetto and Beyond, 1939–1945.* London: Virago. New York: The Free Press. Reprinted (1987). Bath: Chivers. Reprinted (1991). London: Virago.

Bauman, Janina (1988). *A Dream of Belonging: My Years in Postwar Poland.* London: Virago.

Bauman, Zygmunt (1989). *Modernity and the Holocaust.* Ithaca, NY: Cornell University Press. New edition (2000). Ithaca, NY: Cornell University Press.

Baumeister, Roy F. (1997). *Evil: Inside Human Cruelty and Violence.* New York: W.H. Freeman.

Bayme, Steven (1997). *Understanding Jewish History: Texts and Commentaries.* Hoboken, NJ: Ktav Publishing House in Association with the American Jewish Committee.

Bayton, James Arthur, et al. (1956). Race-Class Stereotypes. *Journal of Negro Education,* vol. 25, pp. 75–78.

Beck, Evelyn Torton (1990). Therapy's Double Dilemma: Anti-Semitism and Misogyny. *Women and Therapy,* vol. 10, no. 4, pp. 19–30.

Becker, Ulrike, et al. (Eds.). (1997). *Goldhagen und die deutsche Linke, oder, die Gegenwart des Holocaust.* Berlin: Elefanten Press. [German].

Beddock, Francine (1990). Le temps de voir, le temps de dire. In Hazan, Barbara, et al. (1990). *Shoah, le film: des psychanalystes écrivent,* pp. 65–75. Paris: Jacques Grancher. [French].

Beisel, David R. (1997). Europe's Killing Frenzy. *The Journal of Psychohistory,* vol. 25.

Beland, Herrmann (1991). Religiöse Wurzeln des Antisemitismus: Bemerkungen zu Freuds "Der Mann Moses und die Monotheistische Religion" und zu einigen neueren psychoanalytischen Beiträgen. *Psyche: Zeitschrift für Psychoanalyse und ihre Anwendungen,* vol. 45, pp. 17–37. [German].

Bellah, Robert Neelly (2003). *Imagining Japan: The Japanese Tradition and its Modern Interpretation.* Berkeley and Los Angeles: University of California Press.

Bellamy, Elizabeth J. (1997). *Affective Genealogies: Psychoanalysis, Postmodernism, and the "Jewish Question" after Auschwitz.* Lincoln: University of Nebraska Press.

Belloc, Hilaire (1904). *Emmanuel Burden.* New York: C. Scribner's Sons.

Belloc, Hilaire (1908). *Mr. Chutterbuck's Election.* London: E. Nash.

Belloc, Hilaire (1910). *Pongo and the Bull.* London: Constable & Co.

Ben-Moshe, Danny (2005). Holocaust Denial in Australia. In *Analysis of Current Trends in Antisemitism.* Jerusalem: The Vidal Sassoon International Center for the Study of Antisemitism, The Hebrew University of Jerusalem.

Ben-Sasson, Haim Hillel (1974). *Trial and Achievement: Currents in Jewish History.* Jerusalem: Keter Publishing House.

Ben-Sasson, Haim Hillel (Ed.). (1976). *A History of the Jewish People.* Contributors: Abraham Malamat, Hayim Tadmor, Menahem Stern, Samuel Safrai, Haim Hilell Ben-Sasson and Samuel Ettinger. Cambridge, MA: Harvard University Press.

Bendersky, Joseph W. (2000). *The Jewish Threat: Anti-Semitic Politics of the American Army.* New York: Basic Books.

Bengesser, Gerhard, & Sokoloff, Stephen (1992). Antisemitism and Jung's Concept of the Collective Unconscious. Letter to the Editor. *American Journal of Psychiatry,* vol. 149, no. 3, pp. 414–415.

Bengesser, Gerhard, & Sokoloff, Stephen (1993). Reply to Mortimer Ostow. Letter to the Editor. *American Journal of Psychiatry,* vol. 150, no. 1, p. 173.

Benjamin, Jessica (1995). *Like Subjects, Love Objects: Essays on Recognition and Sexual Difference.* New Haven, CT: Yale University Press.

Benjamin, Walter (1994). *The Correspondence of Walter Benjamin, 1910–1940.* Ed. Gershom Scholem and Theodor W. Adorno. Tr. Manfred R. Jacobson and Evelyn M. Jacobson. Chicago: University of Chicago Press.

Benjamin, Walter (1999). *The Arcades Project.* Tr. Howard Eiland & Kevin McLaughlin. Cambridge, MA: The Belknap Press.

Benjamin, Walter, & Scholem, Gershom Gerhard (1980). *Briefwechsel 1933–1940.* Ed. Gershom Scholem. Frankfurt am Main: Suhrkamp. [German].

Benjamin, Walter, & Scholem, Gershom Gerhard (1989). *The Correspondence of Walter Benjamin and Gershom Scholem, 1932–1940.* Ed. Gershom Scholem. Tr. Gary Smith and Andre Lefevere. Intro. by Anson Rabinbach. New York: Schocken Books. New edition (1992). Cambridge, MA: Harvard University Press.

Bensoussan, Georges (2006). *Europe, une passion génocidaire: essai d'histoire culturelle.* Paris: Éditions Mille et une nuits. [French].

Benvenisti, Meron (1995). *Intimate Enemies: Jews and Arabs in a Shared Land.* Berkeley: University of California Press.

Benz, Wolfgang (1995). *Der Holocaust.* Munich: C.H. Beck. [German].

Benz, Wolfgang (2001). *Bilder vom Juden: Studien zum alltäglichen Antisemitismus.* Munich: C.H. Beck. [German].

Benz, Wolfgang (2004). *Was ist Antisemitismus?* Munich: C.H. Beck. [German].

Benz, Wolfgang (2006). *A Concise History of the Third Reich.* Tr. Thomas Dunlap. Berkeley: University of California Press.

Benz, Wolfgang (Ed.). (1995). *Antisemitismus in Deutschland: Zur Aktualität Eines Vorurteils.* Munich: Deutscher Taschenbuch Verlag.

Benz, Wolfgang, & Königseder, Angelika (Eds.). (2002). *Judenfeindschaft als Paradigma: Studien zur Vorurteilsforschung.* Im Auftrag des Zentrums für Antisemitismusforschung. Berlin: Metropol. [German].

Beradt, Charlotte (1966). *Das dritte Reich des Traums.* Munich: Nymphenburger Verlag-shandlung. New edition (1981). Mit Einem Nachwort von Reinhart Koselleck. Frankfurt am Main: Suhrkamp. [German].

Beradt, Charlotte (1968). *The Third Reich of Dreams.* Tr. Adriane Gottwald. With an Essay by Bruno Bettelheim. Chicago: Quadrangle Books. New edition (1985). *The Third Reich of Dreams: the Nightmares of a Nation, 1933–1939.* Wellingborough, Northamptonshire, England: Aquarian Press.

Berdyayev, Nikolai Aleksandrovich (1952). *Christianity and Anti-Semitism.* Ed. Alan A. Spears. Tr. Alan A. Spears and Victor B. Kanter. Aldington, Kent: Hand and Flower Press.

Berenbaum, Michael (1993). *The World Must Know: The History of the Holocaust as Told in the United States Holocaust Memorial Museum.* Arnold Kramer, editor of photographs. Boston and Washington, DC: Little, Brown and United States Holocaust Memorial Museum.

Berenbaum, Michael (1994). *Vision of the Void: Elie Wiesel, God, the Holocaust, and the Children of Israel.* West Orange, New Jersey: Behrman House.

Berenbaum, Michael (Ed.) (1990). *A Mosaic of Victims: Non-Jews Persecuted and Murdered by the Nazis.* New York: New York University Press.

Berenbaum, Michael (Ed.) (1997). *Witness to the Holocaust.* New York: HarperCollins Publishers.

Berenbaum, Michael (Ed.) (2003). *A Promise to Remember: The Holocaust in the Words and Voices of Its Survivors.* Boston: Bulfinch Press/AOL Time Warner Book Group.

Berenbaum, Michael, & Peck, Abraham J. (Eds.) (1998). *The Holocaust and History: The Known, the Unknown, the Disputed, and the Reexamined.* Bloomington: Indiana University Press.

Bergen, Bernard J. (1998). *The Banality of Evil: Hannah Arendt and "The Final Solution."* Lanham, MD: Rowman & Littlefield.

Bergen, Doris L. (1996). *Twisted Cross: the German Christian Movement in the Third Reich.* Chapel Hill: University of North Carolina Press.

Bergen, Doris L. (2003). *War & Genocide: A Concise History of the Holocaust.* Lanham. MD: Rowman & Littlefield.

Berger, Alan L. (Ed.). (1991). *Bearing Witness to the Holocaust, 1939–1989.* Lewiston, NY: Edwin Mellen Press.

Berger, David (Ed.). (1986). *History and Hate: The Dimensions of Anti-Semitism.* Philadelphia: Jewish Publication Society. New edition (1997). Philadelphia: Jewish Publication Society.

Bergmann, Martin S. (1992). *In the Shadow of the Moloch: The Sacrifice of Children and its Impact on Western Religion.* New York: Columbia University Press.

Bergmann, Martin S. (1995). The Jewish and German Roots of Psychoanalysis and the Impact of the Holocaust. *American Imago,* vol. 52, no. 3, pp. 243–259.

Bergmann, Martin S., & Jucovy, Milton E. (Eds.). (1982). *Generations of the Holocaust.* New York: Basic Books. New edition (1990). New York: Columbia University Press.

Bergmann, Werner (1988) Approaches to Antisemitism Based on Psychodynamics and Personality Theory. In Bergmann, Werner (Ed.) *Error Without Trial: Psychological Research on Antisemitism.* Berlin and New York: Walter De Gruyter.

Bergmann, Werner (1992). Psychological and Sociological Theories of Antisemitism. *Patterns of Prejudice,* vol. 26 [20], nos. 1–2, pp. 37–47.

Bergmann, Werner (2002). Exclusionary Riots: Some Theoretical Considerations. In Hoffmann, Christhard, et al. (Eds.), *Exclusionary Violence: Antisemitic Riots in Modern German History.* Ann Arbor: University of Michigan Press.

Bergmann, Werner, & Erb, Rainer (1996). *Anti-Semitism in Germany: The Post-Nazi Epoch since 1945.* Tr. Belinda Cooper and Allison Brown. New Brunswick, NJ: Transaction Publishers.

Bergmann, Werner, & Erb, Rainer (2003). Antisemitism in the Later 1990s. In Alba, Richard, Schmidt, Peter, & Wasmer, Martina (Eds.). *Germans or Foreigners? Attitudes Toward Ethnic Minorities in Post-Unification Germany.* New York: Palgrave Macmillan.

Bergmann, Werner, & Heitmeyer, Wilhelm (2005). Communicating Antisemitism: Are the Boundaries of Speaking Shifting? *Tel Aviver Jahrbuch Für Deutsche Geschichte,* Vol. 33, *Antisemitismus, Antizionismus, Israelkritik,* Ed. Moshe Zuckermann, Minerva-institut Für Deutsche Geschichte, Tel Aviv University. Göttingen: Wallstein-verlag.

Bering, Dietz (1992). *The Stigma of Names: Antisemitism in German Daily Life, 1812–1933.* Tr. Neville Plaice. Ann Arbor: University of Michigan Press.

Berke, Joseph H. (1988). *The Tyranny of Malice: Exploring the Dark Side of Character and Culture.* New York: Summit Books.

Berke, Joseph H. (1991). Psychosis and Malice. *The Psychoanalytic Review,* vol. 78, no. 1.

Berke, Joseph H., & Schneider, Stanley (2006). A Psychological Understanding of Muslim Terrorism. *Free Associations* Psychoanalysis and Psychotherapy Web site, http://www.psychoanalysis-and-therapy.com/human_nature/free-associations/berke schneider.dwt (accessed May 3, 2008).

Berkovits, Eliezer (1973). *Faith after the Holocaust.* New York: Ktav Publishing House.

Berkowitz, Leonard (1959). Anti-Semitism and the Displacement of Aggression. *Journal of Abnormal and Social Psychology,* vol. 59, pp. 182–187.

Bernanos, Georges (1931). *La grande peur des bien-pensants: Édouard Drumont.* Paris: B. Grasset. Reprinted (1949). Paris: B. Grasset. New edition (1969). Postface De Michel Estève, Suivie De Trois Textes De Georges Bernanos: *a propos de l'antisémitisme de Drumont; encore la question juive; l'honneur est ce qui nous rassemble.* Paris: Le Livre De Poche. New edition (1998). Préface De Bernard Frank, Postface De Michel Estève. Paris: Le Livre De Poche. [French].

Bernanos, Georges (1938). *Les grands cimetières sous la lune.* Paris: Plon. New edition (1969). Paris: Plon. New edition (1971). With *Les Chrétiens et les révolutions* by Jacques Madaule. Préface De Hélder Câmara. Saint-Cloud: Éditions du Burin. [French].

Berneri, Camillo (1936). *Le juif anti-sémite.* Paris: Éditions Vita. [French].

Bernhardt, Heike, & Lockot, Regine (Eds.). (2000). *Mit ohne Freud: zur Geschichte der Psychoanalyse in Ostdeutschland.* Giessen: Psychosozial-verlag. [German].

Bernstein, Herman (1935). *The Truth about "The Protocols of Zion": A Complete Exposure.* New York, Covici, Friede. New edition (1971). (1972). Intro. by Norman Cohn. New York, Ktav Publishing House.

Bernstein, Jay (Ed.). (1994). *The Frankfurt School: Critical Assessments.* 6 vols. London and New York: Routledge.

Bernstein, Richard J. (1998). *Freud and the Legacy of Moses.* Cambridge: Cambridge University Press.

Bertani, Mauro, & Ranchetti, Michele (Eds.). (1999). *La Psicoanalisi e L'antisemitismo.* Turin: Einaudi. [Italian].

Beswick, D.C., & Hills, M.D. (1972). A Survey of Ethnocentrism in Australia. *Australian Journal of Psychology,* vol. 24, pp. 153–163.

Betcherman, Lita-Rose (1975). *The Swastika and the Maple Leaf.* Toronto: Fitzhenry & Whiteside.

Bettelheim, Bruno (1986). *Surviving the Holocaust.* London: Flamingo.

Bettelheim, Bruno, & Janowitz, Morris (1950). *Dynamics of Prejudice: A Psychological and Sociological Study of Veterans.* New York: Harper & Row. Reprinted (1964). In Bettelheim, Bruno, & Janowitz, Morris, *Social Change and Prejudice, Including Dynamics of Prejudice.* New York: The Free Press of Glencoe.

Bettelheim, Peter, et al. (Eds.). (1992). *Antisemitismus in Osteuropa: Aspekte einer historischen Kontinuität.* Contributors Wolfgang Benz et al. Vienna: Picus Verlag. [German].

Biale, David (1994). The Blood Libel. *Tikkun,* July–August.

Biddiss, Michael (1977). *The Age of the Masses.* Harmondsworth: Penguin Books.

Bieringer, R., et al. (Eds.). (2001). *Anti-Judaism and the Fourth Gospel.* Louisville, KY: Westminster John Knox Press.

Bihr, Alain, et al. (1997). *Négationnistes: les chiffonniers de l'histoire.* Villeurbane: Éditions Golias. Paris: Éditions Syllepse.

Billig, Michael (1978). *Fascists: A Social Psychological View of the National Front.* London and New York: Academic Press, in Cooperation with European Association of Experimental Social Psychology. New York: Harcourt, Brace, Jovanovich.

Billig, Michael (1979). *Psychology, Racism, and Fascism: A Searchlight Pamphlet.* Birmingham: A. F. & R. Publications.

Billig, Michael (1981).*L'internationale raciste: de la psychologie à la science des races.* Paris: F. Maspero. [French].

Billig, Michael (1985). The Unobservant Participator: Nazism, Antisemitism and Ray's Reply. *Ethnic and Racial Studies,* vol. 8, pp. 444–449.

Billig, Michael (1990). Psychological Aspects of Fascism. *Patterns of Prejudice,* vol. 24, no. 1, pp. 19–31.

Binion, Rudolph (1976). *Hitler among the Germans.* New York: Elsevier. New edition (1984). Dekalb, IL: Northern Illinois University Press.

Binion, Rudolph (2005). *Past Impersonal: Group Process in Human History.* Dekalb, IL: Northern Illinois University Press.

Bion, Wilfred Ruprecht (1961). *Experiences in Groups, and Other Papers.* New York: Basic Books. New edition (1989). London: Tavistock/Routledge.

Birnbaum, Pierre (1988). *Un mythe politique, "la République juive": de Léon Blum à Pierre Mendès France.* Paris: Fayard. [French].

Birnbaum, Pierre (1992). *Anti-Semitism in France: A Political History from Léon Blum to the Present.* Oxford, England, and Cambridge, MA: Basil Blackwell.

Birnbaum, Pierre (1996). *The Jews of the Republic.* Stanford, CA: Stanford University Press.

Birnbaum, Pierre (2004). *Géographie de l'espoir: l'exil, les lumières, la désassimilation.* Paris: Gallimard. [French].

Bishop, Patrick (1999). The Protocols of the Elders of Zion. *The Washington Times,* November 21, p. C10.

Bizouard-Reicher, Elisabeth (2004). Les Murs de Varsovie: quelques aspects psychanalytiques de l'antisémitisme. *Pardès: Études et Culture Juives,* no. 37, *Psychanalyse de L'antisémitisme Contemporain,* pp. 75–89.

Blakeslee, Spencer (2000). *The Death of American Antisemitism.* Westport, CT: Praeger.

Bloom, Harold (Ed.). (1991). *Shylock.* New York: Chelsea House Publishers.

Blum, Harold P. (1994). Dora's Conversion Syndrome: A Contribution to the Prehistory of the Holocaust. *The Psychoanalytic Quarterly,* vol. 63, no. 3, pp. 518–535.

Blumenberg, Yigal (1997). "Die Crux Mit Dem Antisemitismus": Zur Gegenbesetzung von Erinnerung, Herkommen Und Tradition. *Psyche: Zeitschrift für Psychoanalyse und ihre Anwendungen,* vol. 51, pp. 1115–1160. [German].

Blümner (1863). Voltaire im Prozesse mit Abraham Hirsch. *Deutsches Museum,* No. 43, D. [German].

Bohleber, Werner (1992). Nationalismus, Fremdenhaß und Antisemitismus: psychoanalytische Überlegungen. *Psyche: Zeitschrift für Psychoanalyse und ihre Anwendungen,* vol. 46, no. 8, pp. 689–709. [German].

Bohleber, Werner (1997). Die Konstruktion imaginärer Gemeinschaften und das Bild von den juden—unbewußte Determinanten des Antisemitismus in Deutschland. *Psyche: Zeitschrift für Psychoanalyse und ihre Anwendungen,* vol. 51, pp. 570–605. [German].

Bohleber, Werner, & Drews, Jörg (Eds.). (1991). *Gift, das du unbewusst Eintrinkst: der Nationalsozialismus und die deutsche Sprache.* Bielefeld: Aisthesis.

Bohleber, Werner, & Kafka, John S. (Eds.). (1992). *Antisemitismus.* Bielefeld: Aisthesis. [German].

Bohm-Duchen, Monica (Ed.). (1995). *After Auschwitz: Responses to the Holocaust in Contemporary Art.* Sunderland: Northern Centre for Contemporary Art. London: Lund Humphries.

Bollas, Christopher (1995). The Structure of Evil. In Bolas, Christopher, *Cracking Up: The Work of Unconscious Experience.* New York: Hill & Wang.

Bonacich, Edna (1973). A Theory of Middleman Minorities. *American Sociological Review,* vol. 38, no. 5, pp. 583–594.

Bonaparte, Marie (1951). Des causes psychologiques de l'antisémitisme. *Revue Française de psychanalyse,* vol. 15, no. 4, Pp. 479–491. [French].

Bonaparte, Marie (1992). Psychologische Ursachen des Antisemitismus (aus dem Archiv der Psychoanalyse). *Psyche: Zeitschrift für Psychoanalyse und ihre Anwendungen,* vol. 46, pp. 1137–1151. [German].

Bonfil, Robert (1980). *The Devil and the Jews in the Christian Consciousness of the Middle Ages.* Jerusalem: International Center for University Teaching of Jewish Civilization, Office of the President of Israel. Tel Aviv: Everyman's University. Reprinted (1988) in Almog, Shmuel (Ed.), *Antisemitism Through the Ages.* Tr. Nathan H. Reisner. Oxford and New York: Published for the Vidal Sassoon International Center for the Study of Antisemitism, The Hebrew University of Jerusalem, by Pergamon Press.

Booker, Janice L. (1991). *The Jewish American Princess and Other Myths: The Many Faces of Self-hatred.* New York: Shapolsky Publishers. New edition (1992). New York: S.P.I. Books.

Boswell, John (1980). *Christianity, Social Tolerance, and Homosexuality: Gay People in Western Europe from the Beginning of the Christian Era to the Fourteenth Century.* Chicago: University of Chicago Press.

Bottomore, Thomas B. (1984). *The Frankfurt School.* Chichester: E. Horwood. London and New York: Tavistock Publications.

Bourel, Dominique (2004). *Moses Mendelssohn: la naissance du judaïsme moderne.* Paris: Gallimard. [French].

Boynton, Robert (2002). The Interpretation of Khan. *The Boston Globe,* December 15.

Boynton, Robert S. (2002–2003). The Return of the Repressed: the Strange Case of Masud Khan. *The Boston Review,* vol. 27, no. 6.

Brager, Bruce L. (1999). *The Trial of Adolf Eichmann: The Holocaust on Trial.* San Diego, CA: Lucent Books.

Braham, Randolph L. (Ed.). (1986). *The Origins of the Holocaust: Christian Anti-Semitism.* Boulder: Social Science Monographs. New York: Institute for Holocaust Studies, City University of New York.

Brainin, Elisabeth (1986). Psychoanalyse des Antisemitismus nach 1945. In Silbermann, Alphons, & Schoeps, Julius Hans (Eds.), *Antisemitismus nach dem Holocaust: Bestandsaufnahme und Erscheinungsformen in Deutschsprachigen Ländern,* pp. 105–113. Cologne: Wissenschaft Und Politik. [German].

Brainin, Elisabeth, & Kaminer, Isidor Jehdua (1982). Psychoanalyse und Nationalsozialismus. *Psyche: Zeitschrift für Psychoanalyse und ihre Anwendungen,* vol. 36, pp. 989–1012. [German].

Brainin, Elisabeth, et al. (1989). Antisemitismus in Psychoanalysen: zur Identität österreichischer Psychoanalytiker heute. *Psyche: Zeitschrift für Psychoanalyse und ihre Anwendungen,* vol. 43, no. 1, pp. 1–19. Expanded Version (1993). Antisemitismus in Psychoanalysen: Zur Identität Österreichischer und Deutscher Psychoanalytiker Heute, in Brainin, Elisabeth, et al. (1993). *Vom Gedanken zur Tat: zur Psychoanalyse des Antisemitismus,* pp. 45–65. Frankfurt am Main: Brandes and Apsel. [German].

Brainin, Elisabeth, et al. (1993). *Vom Gedanken Zur Tat: Zur Psychoanalyse Des Antisemitismus.* Frankfurt am Main: Brandes and Apsel. [German].

Brantlinger, Patrick (2005). Review of Bernard Glassman's *Benjamin Disraeli: The Fabricated Jew in Myth and Memory* (2003). In *Shofar: An Interdisciplinary Journal of Jewish Studies,* vol. 23, no. 4, pp. 157–159.

Brearley, Margaret (2007). The Anglican Church, Jews and British Multiculturalism. In *Posen Papers in Contemporary Antisemitism,* No. 6. Jerusalem: The Vidal Sassoon International Study for the Study of Antisemitism, The Hebrew University of Jerusalem.

Brecht, Karen, et al. (Eds.). (1985). *"Hier Geht das Leben auf eine sehr merkwürdige Weise weiter..." Zur Geschichte der Psychoanalyse in Deutschland.* Hamburg: M. Kellner Verlag. [German].

Brecht, Karen, et al. (Eds.). (1992). *"Here Life Goes On in a Most Peculiar Way..." Psychoanalysis Before and after 1933.* Tr. Christine Trollope & Joyce Crick. Ed. Hella Ehlers. Hamburg: M. Kellner Verlag. London: Goethe-institut.

Brede, Karola, & Karp, Alexander C. (1997). Eliminatorischer Antisemitismus: wie ist die These zu Halten? *Psyche: Zeitschrift für Psychoanalyse und ihre Anwendungen,* vol. 51, pp. 606–628. [German].

Brenner, Arthur B. (1948). Some Psychoanalytic Speculations on Anti-Semitism. *The Psychoanalytic Review,* vol. 35, pp. 20–32.

Breslauer, S. Daniel (Ed.). (1997). *The Seductiveness of Jewish Myth: Challenge or Response?* Albany: State University of New York Press.

Brewer, M.B., & Kramer, R.M. (1985). The Psychology of Intergroup Attitudes and Behavior. *Annual Review of Psychology,* vol. 36, pp. 219–243.

Bridonneau, Pierre (1997). *Oui, il faut parler des négationnistes.* Paris: Editions du Cerf. [French].

Brill, Abraham A. (1918). The Adjustment of the Jew to the American Environment. *Mental Hygiene,* vol. 2, pp. 219–231.

British Ministry of Economic Warfare (1944). *Who's Who in Nazi Germany.* 4th Ed. London: Ministry of Economic Warfare.

Broder, Henryk M. (1986a). *Der ewige Antisemit: über Sinn und Funktion eines beständigen Gefühls.* Frankfurt am Main: Fischer Taschenbuch. [German].

Broder, Henryk M. (1986b). "It Thinks Inside Me...": Fassbinder, Germans and Jews. *Encounter,* vol. 66, pp. 64–68.

Broder, Henryk M. (2004). *A Jew in the New Germany.* Tr. Broder Translators' Collective. Eds. Sander L. Gilman and Lilian M. Friedberg. Urbana: University of Illinois Press.

Bromberg, Norbert, & Small, Verna Volz (1983). *Hitler's Psychopathology.* New York: International Universities Press.

Brosio, Richard A. (1980). *The Frankfurt School: An Analysis of the Contradictions and Crises of Liberal Capitalist Societies.* Muncie, IN: Ball State University.

Browder, G.C. (2003). Perpetrator Character and Motivation: an Emerging Consensus? *Holocaust and Genocide Studies,* vol. 17, pp. 480–497.

Brown, K.M. (1985). Turning a Blind Eye: Racial Oppression and the Unintended Consequences of White "Non-racism." *The Sociological Review,* vol. 33, pp. 670–690.

Brown, Michael (1987). *Jew or Juif? Jews, French Canadians and Anglo-Canadians, 1759–1914.* Philadelphia: Jewish Publication Society.

Brown, Michael (1992). From Stereotype to Scapegoat: Antisemitism in French Canada from Confederation to World War I. In Davies, Alan (Ed.), *Antisemitism in Canada: History and Interpretation.* Waterloo, Ontario: Wilfred Laurier University Press.

Brown, Michael (Ed.). (1994). *Approaches to Antisemitism: Context and Curriculum.* New York: American Jewish Committee. Jerusalem: International Center for University Teaching of Jewish Civilization, Office of the President of Israel.

Browning, Christopher R. (1985). *Fateful Months: Essays on the Emergence of the Final Solution.* New York: Holmes & Meier. New edition (1992). *The Path to Genocide: Essays on Launching the Final Solution.* Cambridge and New York: Cambridge University Press. New edition (2003) *Initiating the Final Solution: The Fateful Months of September–October 1941.* Washington, DC: United States Holocaust Memorial Museum, Center for Advanced Holocaust Studies.

Browning, Christopher R. (1992). *Ordinary Men: Reserve Police Battalion 101 and the Final Solution in Poland.* New York: HarperCollins and Aaron Asher Books.

Bruhns, Wibke (2004). *Meines Vaters Land: Geschichte einer deutschen Familie.* Munich: Econ. [German].

Brumlik, Micha (1987). Das verkörperte "Sein für die Anderen": zu Sartres Theorie des Judentums. *Babylon: Beiträge zur jüdischen Gegenwart,* no. 2, July, pp. 89–98. [German].

Brustein, William (2003). *Roots of Hate: Anti-Semitism in Europe Before the Holocaust.* Cambridge and New York: Cambridge University Press.

Brym, R.J., & Lenton, R.L. (1991). The Distribution of Antisemitism in Canada in 1984. *Canadian Journal of Sociology,* vol. 16, pp. 411–418.

Buber, Martin (1957). Guilt and Guilt Feelings. Tr. Maurice Friedman. *Psychiatry,* vol. 20, no. 2, pp. 114–129. Reprinted in Buber, Martin (1965). *The Knowledge of Man,* pp. 116–126. Tr. Maurice Friedman & Ronald Gregor Smith. Ed. & Intro. Maurice Friedman. London: George Allen and Unwin. New York: Harper & Row. Reprinted (1988). Atlantic Highlands, NJ: Humanities Press International.

Bullock, Alan (1952). *Hitler: A Study in Tyranny.* New York: Harper. New edition (1971). New York: Harper & Row. New edition (1990). Harmondsworth: Penguin Books.

Bunting, Madeleine (2003). *Profile: Passion and Pessimism.* Zygmunt Bauman Has Known the Terror of War and the Trauma of Exile. These Experiences Have Made Him a Champion of the Underdog and a Caustic Critic of the Status Quo. Yet for All His International Popularity—He Is One of Europe's Most Influential Sociologists—He Remains a Loner and a Maverick. *The Guardian,* Saturday, April 5.

Bunzl, John, & Marin, Bernd (1983). *Antisemitismus in Österreich.* Innsbruck: Inn-Verlag. [German].

Bunzl, Matti (2004). *Symptoms of Modernity: Jews and Queers in Late-Twentieth-Century Vienna.* Berkeley: University of California Press.

Burge, Gary M. (1993). *Who Are God's People in the Middle East?* Grand Rapids, MI: Zondervan Publishing House.

Burghardt, Walter J. (1977). Response to Rosemary Ruether. In Fleischner, Eva (Ed.), *Auschwitz: Beginning of a New Era? Reflections on the Holocaust.* New York: Ktav Publishing Co.

Burleigh, Michael, & Wipperman, Wolfgang (1991). *The Racial State: Germany 1933–1945.* New York: Cambridge University Press.

Burnier, Michel-Antoine, & Romane, Cécile (1997). *Le Secert de l'abbé Pierre.* Paris: Editions Mille et Une Nuits. [French].

Burns, Michael (1998). *France and the Dreyfus Affair: A Documentary History.* New York: Farrar, Straus, and Giroux. Reprinted (1999). Boston: Bedford and St. Martin's.

Burrin, Philippe (1986). *La Dérive fasciste: Doriot, Déat, Bergery, 1933–1945.* Paris: Editions du Seuil. [French].

Burrin, Philippe (1989). *Hitler et les Juifs: genèse d'un génocide.* Paris: Editions du Seuil. [French].

Burrin, Philippe (1994). *Hitler and the Jews: The Genesis of the Holocaust.* Tr. Patsy Southgate. Intro. by Saul Friedländer. London: Edward Arnold.

Burrin, Philippe (1995). *La France à l'heure allemande: 1940–1944.* Paris: Editions du Seuil. [French].

Burrin, Philippe (1996). *France under the Germans: Collaboration and Compromise.* Tr. Janet Lloyd. New York: the New Press.

Burrin, Philippe (2000). *Fascisme, nazisme, autoritarisme.* Paris: Editions du Seuil. [French].

Burrin, Philippe (2004a). *Nazi Anti-Semitism: From Prejudice to the Holocaust.* Tr. Janet Lloyd. New York: the New Press.

Burrin, Philippe (2004b). *Ressentiment et apocalypse: essai sur l'antisémitisme nazi.* Paris: Editions du Seuil. [French].

Bursztein, Jean-Gérard (1996). *Hitler, La Tyrannie et La Psychanalyse: Essai Sur La Destruction de la Civilisation.* Aulnay-sous-bois: Nouvelles Études Freudiennes. [French].

Butnaru, Ion C. (1992). *The Silent Holocaust: Romania and its Jews.* Foreword by Elie Wiesel. New York: Greenwood Press.

Bytwerk, Randall L. (1983). *Julius Streicher.* New York: Stein and Day. New edition (2001). *Julius Streicher: Nazi Editor of the Notorious Anti-semitic Newspaper Der Stürmer.* New York: Cooper Square Press.

Cahalan, D., & Trager, F.N. (1949). Free Answer Stereotypes and Anti-semitism. *Public Opinion Quarterly,* vol. 13, pp. 93–104.

Cahm, Eric (1994). *L'affaire Dreyfus: histoire, politique, société.* Paris: Librairie Générale Française. [French].

Cahm, Eric (1996). *The Dreyfus Affair in French Society and Politics.* London: Longman.

Cahneman, Werner J. (1957). Socio-Economic Causes of Anti-Semitism. *Social Problems,* vol. 5, no. 1.

Cala, Alina (1995). *The Image of the Jew in Polish Folk Culture.* Jerusalem: Magnes Press.

Calais, Etienne (1996). Voltaire et Les Juifs. In Calais, Etienne, *Petit bréviaire voltairien,* chapter 13. Paris: Calpet. [French].

Calimani, Riccardo (2000). *Ebrei e pregiudizio: introduzione alla dinamica dell'odio.* Milan: Oscar Mondadori. [Italian].

Capdevila, Luc (2001). The Quest for Masculinity in a Defeated France, 1940–1945. *Contemporary European History,* vol. 10, pp. 423–445.

Carlebach, Elisheva, et al. (Eds.). (1998). *Jewish History and Jewish Memory: Essays in Honor of Yosef Hayim Yerushalmi.* Hanover, NH: University Press of New England for Brandeis University Press.

Carmichael, Joel (1992). *The Satanizing of the Jews.* New York: Fromm International Publishing Corp.

Caron, Vicki (1999). *Uneasy Asylum: France and the Jewish Refugee Crisis, 1933–1942.* Stanford, CA: Stanford University Press.

Carotenuto, Aldo (1982). *A Secret Symmetry: Sabina Spielrein Between Jung and Freud.* Tr. Arno Pomerans et al. New York: Pantheon Books. New edition (1984). New York: Pantheon Books.

Carr, Steven Alan (2001). *Hollywood and Anti-semitism: A Cultural History, 1880–1941.* Cambridge: Cambridge University Press.

Carroll, James (2001). *Constantine's Sword: The Church and the Jews: A History.* Boston: Houghton Mifflin.

Carto, Willis Allison (Ed.). (1982). *Profiles in Populism.* Old Greenwich, CT: Flag Press.

Caruso, J.C., et al. (2001). Reliability of Scores from the Eysenck Personality Question-naire: A Reliability Generalization Study. *Educational and Psychological Measurement,* vol. 61, pp. 675–689.

Cazzullo, Aldo (2007) Ariel Toaff, dolore e minacce: "Usano mio padre contro di me." L'autore di "Pasque di sangue": non mi fanno parlare con lui "Non voglio perdere il suo affetto per aver violato un tabù." *Corriere della Sera,* February 8. [Italian].

Celan, Paul (1975). *Die Todesfuge.* In Celan, Paul, *Gedichte.* 2 vols. Frankfurt am Main; Suhrkamp. [German].

Céline [Destouches], Louis-Ferdinand (1937). *Bagatelles pour un massacre.* Paris: Denoël. New edition (1943). *Nouvelle édition avec 20 photographies.* Paris: Denoël. [French].

Cesarani, David (1995). *A History of the Holocaust.* Ed. Jonathan Freedland & Jon Mendelsohn. London: The Holocaust Educational Trust.

Cesarani, David (1996). *The Holocaust.* London: Macmillan Press.

Cesarani, David (2004). *Eichmann: His Life and Crimes.* London: William Heinemann.

Cesarani, David (2006). *Becoming Eichmann: Rethinking the Life, Crimes, and Trial of a "Desk Murderer."* New York: Da Capo Press.

Chaitin, Julia (2000). Facing the Holocaust in Generations of Families of Survivors: The Case of Partial Relevance and Interpersonal Values. *Contemporary Family Therapy,* vol. 22, no. 3, pp. 289–313.

Chalier, Corinne (1990). Plus de lumière. In Hazan, Barbara, et al. (1990). *Shoah, le film: des psychanalystes écrivent,* pp. 27–33. Paris: Jacques Grancher. [French].

Chamberlain, Houston Stewart (1899). *Die Grundlagen des neunzehnten Jahrhunderts.* 2 vols. Munich: F. Bruckmann. [German].

Chamberlain, Houston Stewart (1911). *The Foundations of the Nineteenth Century.* Tr. John Lees, Intro. by Lord Redesdale. 2 vols. London and New York: John Lane.

Chamberlain, Sigrid (1997). *Adolf Hitler, die deutsche Mutter und ihr erstes Kind: über zwei NS-Erziehungsbücher.* Mit einem Nachwort von Gregor Dill. Giessen: Psychosozial-Verlag. 2nd edition (1998). Giessen: Psychosozial-Verlag. 3rd edition (2000). Giessen: Psychosozial-Verlag. [German].

Chamberlain, Sigrid (2004). The Nurture and Care of the Future Master Race. *The Journal of Psychohistory,* vol. 31, pp. 367–394.

Chanes, Jerome A. (2004). *Antisemitism: A Reference Handbook.* Santa Barbara, CA: ABC-CLIO.

Chanes, Jerome A. (Ed.). (1995).*Antisemitism in America Today: Outspoken Experts Explode the Myths.* Secaucus, NJ: Carol Publishing Group.

Charlton, H.B. (1934). *Shakespeare's Jew.* Manchester: Manchester University Press. Reprinted (1973). Folcroft, PA: Folcroft Press.

Charny, Israel W. (1982). *How Can We Commit the Unthinkable? Genocide, the Human Cancer.* 2 vols. In collaboration with Chanan Rapaport. Foreword by Elie Wiesel. New York: Hearst Books. Boulder, CO: Westview Press.

Charny, Israel W. (1986). Genocide and Mass Destruction: Doing Harm to Others as a Missing Dimension of Psychopathology. *Psychiatry,* vol. 49, pp. 144–157.

Charny, Israel W. (2005). *Fascism and Democracy in the Human Mind.* Lincoln: University of Nebraska Press.

Charny, Israel W. (Ed.). (1984). *Toward the Understanding and Prevention of Genocide: Proceedings of the International Conference on the Holocaust and Genocide.* Boulder, CO: Westview Press.

Charny, Israel W. (Ed.). (1999). *Encyclopedia of Genocide.* Forewords by Desmond M. Tutu and Simon Wiesenthal. Santa Barbara, CA: ABC-CLIO.

Charny, Israel W. et al. (Eds.). (1988–1994). *Genocide: A Critical Bibliographic Review.* 4 vols. Vol. 1 (1988). *Genocide: A Critical Bibliographic Review.* Contributing Editors Alan L. Berger et al. New York: Facts on File Publications. London: Mansell Publications. Vol. 2 (1991). *Genocide: A Critical Bibliographic Review.* New York: Facts on File Publications. London: Mansell Publications. Vol. 3 (1994). *The Widening Circle of Genocide.* Foreword by Irving Louis Horowitz. New Brunswick, New Jersey: Transaction Publishers. Vol. 4 (1994). *Medical and Psychological Effects of Concentration Camps on Holocaust Victims.* Eds. Robert Krell and Marc I. Sherman. New Brunswick, NJ: Transaction Publishers.

Chase, A. (1979). *The Legacy of Malthus: The Social Costs of the New Scientific Racism.* New York: Alfred A. Knopf.

Chasseguet-Smirgel, Janine (1985). Perversion and the Universal Law. *Israel Journal of Psychiatry and Related Sciences,* vol. 20, no. 1–2, pp. 169–178. Reprinted (1984). In Chasseguet-Smirgel, Janine, *Creativity and Perversion.* New York: W. W. Norton. Reprinted (1985). London: Free Association Books.

Chasseguet-Smirgel, Janine (1986). *Sexuality and Mind: The Role of the Father and the Mother in the Psyche.* New York: New York University Press.

Chasseguet-Smirgel, Janine (1999). Briseur d'idoles, briseur d'illusions: le Juif. In Chasseguet-Smirgel, Janine, & Suied, Alain (Eds.), *Hommage à Béla Grunberger, un psychanalyste dans le siècle: du narcissisme au Judaïsme,* pp. 73–82. Paris: L'Harmattan. [French].

Chasseguet-Smirgel, Janine (2004). "Du vin vieux dans de jeunes outres?" *Pardès: Études et Culture Juives,* no. 37, *Psychanalyse de l'antisémitisme contemporain,* pp. 51–61. [French].

Chazan, Robert (1986). Medieval Anti-Semitism. In Berger, David (Ed.), *History and Hate: The Dimensions of Anti-Semitism.* Philadelphia: Jewish Publication Society of America. New edition (1997). Philadelphia: Jewish Publication Society.

Chazan, Robert (1997). *Medieval Stereotypes and Modern Antisemitism.* Berkeley: University of California Press.

Chazan, Robert (Ed.). (1980). *Church, State, and Jews in the Middle in the Middle East.* New York: Behrman House.

Chesler, Phyllis (2003). *The New Anti-Semitism: The Current Crisis and What We must Do about It.* San Francisco: Jossey-Bass.

Chesler, Phyllis (2004). The Psychoanalytic Roots of Islamic Terrorism. *Front Page Magazine,* May 3.

Chevalier, Yves (1988). *L'antisémitisme: le Juif comme bouc émissaire.* Préface de François Bourricaud. Paris: Les Éditions du Cerf. [French].

Cheyette, Brian (1989). Hilaire Belloc and the "Marconi Scandal" 1900–1914: A Reassessment of the Interactionist Model of Racial Hatred. *Immigrants and Minorities,* vol. 8, no. 1, March. Reprinted (1990) in Kushner, Tony, & Lunn, Kenneth (Eds.), *The Politics of Marginality,* pp. 128–139. London: Frank Cass.

Cheyette, Brian (2007). *Diasporas of the Mind: Literature and Race after the Holocaust.* London and New Haven, CT: Yale University Press.

Cheyette, Brian (Ed.). (1993). *Constructions of "The Jew" in English Literature and Society: Racial Representations, 1875–1945.* Cambridge and New York: Cambridge University Press.

Cheyette, Brian (Ed.). (1996). *Between "Race" and Culture: Representations of "The Jew" in English and American Literature.* Stanford, CA: Stanford University Press.

Christophersen, Thies (1973). *Die Auschwitz-Lüge: ein Erlebnisbericht.* Lausanne: Courrier du Continent. 5th edition (1975). Mohrkirch: Kritik-Verlag. [German].

Christophersen, Thies (1979). *Auschwitz: A Personal Account.* Intro. by Manfred Roeder. Schwarenborn: Deutsche Bürgerinitiative. Reedy, WV: Liberty Bell Publications.

Chrysostom, John (1979). *Discourse Against Juadizing Pagans.* Tr. T. W. Hawkins. Washington, DC: Catholic University Press.

Churchill, Ward (1997). *A Little Matter of Genocide: Holocaust and Denial in the Americas, 1492 to the Present.* San Francisco: City Lights Books.

Churchill, Ward (2003). Some People Push Back. In Churchill, Ward, *On the Justice of Roosting Chickens: Reflections on the Consequences of U.S. Imperial Arrogance and Criminality.* Intro. by Chellis Glendinning. Oakland, CA: AK Press.

Churchill, Winston Leonard Spencer (1920). Zionism Versus Bolshevism: a Struggle for the Soul of the Jewish People. *Illustrtaed Sunday Herald,* February 8, p. 5.

Clark, Gordon (1894). *Shylock as Banker, Bondholder, Corruptionist, Conspirator.* Washington, DC: Gordon Clark. Reprinted (1977). In Quinley, Harold E. (Ed.), *Anti-semitism in America, 1878–1939.* New York: Arno Press.

Clarke, Simon (2003). *Social Theory, Psychoanalysis, and Racism.* Houndmills, Basingstoke, England, and New York: Palgrave Macmillan.

Claussen, Detlev (1987a). *Grenzen der Aufklärung.* Frankfurt am Main: Fischer Verlag. [German].

Claussen, Detlev (1987b). Über Psychoanalyse und Antisemitismus. *Psyche: Zeitschrift für Psychoanalyse und ihre Anwendungen,* vol. 41, no. 1, pp. 1–21. [German].

Claussen, Detlev (1987c). *Vom Judenhass zum Antisemitismus: Materialien einer verleugneten Geschichte.* Darmstadt: Hermann Luchterhand. 2nd edition (1988). Munich: Deutsche Taschenbuch Verlag. [German].

Claussen, Detlev (1995). Die Banalisierung des Bösen: über Auschwitz, Alltagsreligion und Gesellschaftstheorie. In Werz, Michael (Ed.), *Antisemitismus und Gesellschaft,* pp. 13–28. Frankfurt am Main: Verlag Neue Kritik. [German].

Cocks, Geoffrey (1985). *Psychotherapy in the Third Reich: The Göring Institute.* Oxford and New York: Oxford University Press. 2nd edition (1997). Oxford and New York: Oxford University Press. New Brunswick, NJ: Transaction Publishers.

Cocks, Geoffrey (1996). The Politics of the Psychoanalytic Movement in Germany. *The Psychohistory Review,* vol. 24, no. 2, pp. 207–215.

Cocks, Geoffrey (2001). The Devil and the Details. *The Psychoanalytic Review,* vol. 88, pp. 225–244.

Cohen, Abraham (1933). *The Psychology of Antisemitism.* London: Woburn Press.

Cohen, Élie Aron (1953). *Human Behavior in the Concentration Camp.* Tr. M. H. Braaksma. New York: W. W. Norton.

Cohen, Hermann (1919). *Die Religion der Vernunft aus den Quellen des Judentums.* Leipzig: Fock. 2nd edition (1929). Frankfurt am Main: J. Kauffmann. New edition (1966). Ed. Bruno Strauss. With a Photograph of the Author by Max Liebermann. Darmstadt: J. Melzer. New edition (1988). Wiesbaden: Fourier. New edition (2000). Hildesheim: Olms. [German].

Cohen, Hermann (1924). Deutschtum und Judentum. In *Hermann Cohens jüdische Schriften.* Intro. by Franz Rosenzweig. Ed. Bruno Strauss. Berlin: C.A. Schwetschke.

Cohen, Hermann (1971). *Reason and Hope; Selections from the Jewish Writings of Hermann Cohen.* Tr. Eva Jospe. New York: Norton. New edition (1993). Cincinnati, OH: Hebrew Union College Press.

Cohen, Hermann (1972). *The Religion of Reason: Out of the Sources of Judaism.* Tr. Simon Kaplan. Intro. by Simon Kaplan & Leo Strauss. New York: F. Ungar Publishing Co. New edition (1995). Intro. by Steven S. Schwarzschild & Kenneth Seeskin. Atlanta, GA: Scholars Press.

Cohen, Jeremy (1982). *The Friars and the Jews: The Evolution of Medieval Anti-Judaism.* Ithaca, NY: Cornell University Press.

Cohen, Jeremy (Ed.). (1991). *Essential Papers on Judaism and Christianity.* New York: New York University Press.

Cohen, Mark R. (1994). *Under Crescent and Cross: The Jews in the Middle Ages.* Princeton, NJ: Princeton University Press.

Cohen, Norman J. (Ed.). (1990). *The Fundamentalist Phenomenon: A View from Within; a Response from Without.* Grand Rapids, MI: W.B. Eerdmans.

Cohen, Shaye J.D. (1986). Anti-Semitism in Antiquity: The Problem of Definition. In Berger, David (Ed.), *History and Hate: The Dimensions of Anti-Semitism.* Philadelphia: Jewish Publication Society of America. New edition (1997). Philadelphia: Jewish Publication Society.

Cohn, Norman Rufus Colin (1967). *Warrant for Genocide: The Myth of the Jewish World-Conspiracy and the Protocols of the Elders of Zion.* London: Eyre & Spottiswoode. New York: Harper & Row. New edition (1970). Harmondsworth: Penguin Books. New edition (1981). Chico, CA: Scholars Press. Revised edition (1996). London: Serif.

Cohn, Norman Rufus Colin (1970). *The Pursuit of the Millennium.* Oxford and New York: Oxford University Press.

Cohn, Norman Rufus Colin (1975). *Europe's Inner Demons: An Enquiry Inspired by the Great Witch Hunt.* London: Chatto, Heinemann Educational for Sussex University Press. New York: Meridian Books. Reprinted (1977). New York: New American Library. Revised edition (1993). Chicago: University of Chicago Press.

Colovic, Ivan (2000). The Renewal of the Past: Time and Space in Contemporary Political Mythology. Tr. Nenad Stefanov and John Abromeit. *Other Voices,* vol. 2, no. 1.

Comte, Bernard (1990). *Le Génocide nazi et les négationnistes.* Villeurbanne: Agir Ensemble Pour Les Droits de l'homme. [French].

Conan, Eric (1999). Les Secrets d'une manipulation antisémite. *L'express,* November 18. [French].

Cooper, Abraham (1986). *Portraits of Infamy: A Study of Soviet Antisemitic Caricatures and Their Roots in Nazi Ideology.* Los Angeles: Simon Wiesenthal Center.

Cooper, Judy (1994). *Speak of Me as I Am: the Life and Work of Masud Khan.* London: Karnac Books.

Cooper, Judy (1996). Anti-semitism in Therapists and Patients. *European Judaism,* vol. 29, No. 1, pp. 4–17.

Coudenhove-Kalergi, Heinrich Johann Maria von (1901). *Das Wesen des Antisemitismus.* Berlin: S. Calvary. New edition (1929). Intro. by Richard von Coudenhove-Kalergi. [German].

Coudenhove-Kalergi, Heinrich Johann Maria von (1935). *Anti-Semitism Throughout the Ages.* London: Hutchinson. New edition (1972). Ed. Richard von Coudenhove-Kalergi. Tr. Angelo S. Rappoport. Westport, CT: Greenwood Press.

Coughlin, Charles Edward (1939). "Am I an Anti-semite?" Nine Addresses on Various "Isms," Answering the Question…Broadcast over a National Network, Nov. 6, 1938–Jan. 1, 1939. Detroit, MI: Condon Printing Co. Reprinted (1977). In Harold E. Quinley (Ed.). *Anti-semitism in America, 1878–1939.* New York: Arno Press.

Cox, Earnest Sevier (1923). *White America: The American Racial Problem as Seen in a Worldwide Perspective.* Richmond, VA: White America Society. Reprinted (1937). Richmond, VA: White America Society.

Curtis, Michael (1988). Antisemitism: The Baffling Obsession. In Bauer, Yehuda (Ed.), *Present-Day Antisemitism.* Jerusalem: The Vidal Sassoon International Center for the Study of Antisemitism, The Hebrew University of Jerusalem.

Cutler, Allan Harris, & Cutler, Helen Elmquist (1986). *The Jew as Ally of the Muslim: Medieval Roots of Anti-Semitism.* Notre Dame, IN: University of Notre Dame Press.

Czermak, Gerhard (1981). *Der Alltägliche Fascismus: Frauen Im Dritten Reich.* Berlin: n.p. [German].

Czermak, Gerhard (1989). *Christen gegen Juden: Geschichte einer Verfolgung.* Nördlingen: Greno. [German].

Czyzewka, M. (1994). *The Concept of the Human Nature and the Readiness for Antisemitic Behavior.* Unpublished thesis, University of Wroclaw, Poland.

D'Alessio, S.J., & Stolzenberg, L. (1991). Antisemitism in America: the Dynamics of Prejudice. *Sociological Inquiry,* vol. 61, pp. 359–366.

Dahmer, Helmut (1979). "Holocaust" und die Amnesie (kritische Glosse). *Psyche: Zeitschrift für Psychoanalyse und ihre Anwendungen,* vol. 33, pp. 1039–1045.

Dahmer, Helmut (1984). Psychoanalyse unter Hitler: Rückblick auf eine Kontroverse. *Psyche: Zeitschrift für Psychoanalyse und ihre Anwendungen,* vol. 38, pp. 927–942.

Dahmer, Helmut (2001). Antisemitism and Xenophobia: How to Solve the Riddle of the Sphinx. *Australian Journal of Jewish Studies,* vol. 15, pp. 72–87.

Dana, Guy (2004). L'antisémitisme et les formes discursives de la modernité. *Pardès: Études et Culture Juives,* no. 37, *Psychanalyse de l'antisémitisme contemporain,* pp. 63–74. [French].

Daniel, Jerry L. (1979). Anti-Semitism in the Hellenistic-Roman Period. *Journal of Biblical Literature,* vol. 98, no. 1, pp. 45–65.

Darwin, Charles Robert (1859). *On the Origin of Species by Means of Natural Selection, or the Preservation of Favoured Races in the Struggle for Life.* London: John Murray. Reprinted (1860). New York: Appleton & Co.

Davidson, G.M. (1943). An Interpretation of Anti-Semitism. *Psychiatric Quarterly,* vol. 17, pp. 123–134.

Davies, Alan T. (Ed.). (1979). *Antisemitism and the Foundations of Christianity.* New York: Paulist Press.

Davies, Alan T. (Ed.). (1992) *Antisemitism in Canada: History and Interpretation.* Waterloo, Ontario: Wilfred Laurier University Press.

Dawidowicz, Lucy S. (1970). Can Anti-semitism Be Measured? *Commentary,* vol. 50, pp. 36–43.

Dawidowicz, Lucy S. (1975). *The War Against the Jews, 1933–1945.* New York: Holt, Rinehart and Winston. 10th anniversary edition (1986). New York: Bantam Books. Ardmore, PA: Seth Press.

Dawidowicz, Lucy S. (1978). *Hitler's War Against the Jews: A Young Reader's Version of the War Against the Jews, 1933–1945.* Ed. David A. Altshuler. New York: Behrman House.

Dawidowicz, Lucy S. (1981). *The Holocaust and the Historians.* Cambridge, MA: Harvard University Press.

De Boor, Wolfgang (1985). *Hitler: Mensch, Übermensch, Untermensch: eine kriminalpsychologische Studie.* Frankfurt: R.G. Fischer. [German].

De Wind, E. (1968). Begegnung mit dem Tod. *Psyche: Zeitschrift für Psychoanalyse und ihre Anwendungen,* 22, 423–441. n.p. [German].

Delisle, Esther (1993). *The Traitor and the Jew.* Toronto: Robert Davies Publishing.

DeMause, Lloyd (2005). The Childhood Origins of the Holocaust. *The Journal of Psychohistory,* vol. 33, no. 3, pp. 204–222.

Demos, John Putnam (1982). *Entertaining Satan: Witchcraft and the Culture of Early New England.* Oxford and New York: Oxford University Press. Updated edition (2004). Oxford and New York: Oxford University Press.

Des Pres, Terrence (1976). *The Survivor: An Anatomy of Life in the Death Camps.* Oxford and New York: Oxford University Press. New edition (1980). Oxford and New York: Oxford University Press.

Dessuant, Pierre (1999). *Béla Grunberger.* Paris: Presses Universitaires de France. [French].

Deutsch, Akiva W. (1974). *The Eichmann Trial in the Eyes of Israeli Youngsters: Opinions, Attitudes, and Impact.* Ramat-Gan, Israel: Bar-ilan University.

Deutsch, Emeric (2004). La haine des origines. *Pardès: Études et Culture Juives,* no. 37, *Psychanalyse de l'antisémitisme contemporain,* pp. 107–119. [French].

Dickens, Charles (1859). *A Tale of Two Cities.* In Three Books. London: Chapman and Hall. New edition (2006). Ed. Harold Bloom. New York: Chelsea House.

Dicks, Henry Victor (1972). *Licensed Mass Murder: A Socio-Psychological Study of Some SS Killers.* London: Chatto, Heinemmann Educational for Sussex University Press. Reprinted (1973). New York: Basic Books.

Didier, Eric (1990a). Compter jusqu'à un. In Hazan, Barbara, et al. (1990). *Shoah, le film: des psychanalystes écrivent,* pp. 197–198. Paris: Jacques Grancher. [French].

Didier, Eric (1990b). De l'impensable à l'irréparable. In Hazan, Barbara, et al. (1990). *Shoah, le film: des psychanalystes écrivent,* pp. 21–25. Paris: Jacques Grancher. [French].

Dietrich, Donald J. (1995). *God and Humanity in Auschwitz: Jewish-Christian Relations and Sanctioned Murder.* New Brunswick, NJ: Transaction Publishers.

Dietrich, Walter, et al. (Eds.). (1999). *Antijudaismus: christliche Erblast.* Stuttgart: W. Kohlhammer. [German].

Dinnerstein, Leonard (1968). *The Leo Frank Case.* New York: Columbia University Press. New edition (1987). Athens: University of Georgia Press.

Dinnerstein, Leonard (1982). *America and the Survivors of the Holocaust.* New York: Columbia University Press.

Dinnerstein, Leonard (1994). *Antisemitism in America.* New York: Oxford University Press.

Dinnerstein, Leonard (Ed.). (1971). *Antisemitism in the United States.* New York, Holt, Rinehart and Winston.

Dinter, Artur (1927). *Die Sünde wider das Blut: ein Zeitroman.* Leipzig: Verlag Ludolf Beust. [German].

Dion, K.L., & Earn, B.M. (1975). The Phenomenology of Being a Target of Prejudice. *Journal of Personality and Social Psychology,* vol. 32, pp. 944–950.

Disraeli, Benjamin (1847). *Tancred, Or, the New Crusade.* London: Henry Colburn. Philadelphia: Carey & Hart. New edition (1877). (1887). New York: G. Routledge. New edition (1970). Westport, CT: Greenwood Press.

Distel, Barbara, & Benz, Wolfgang (Eds.). (1994). *Das Konzentrationslager Dachau, 1933–1945: Geschichte und Bedeutung.* With Zdenek Zofka & Monika Mayr. Munich: Bayerische Landeszentrale für Politische Bildungsarbeit. [German].

Dobkowski, Michael N. (1979). *The Tarnished Dream: The Basis of American Anti-Semitism.* Westport, CT: Greenwood Press.

Dobkowski, Michael N., & Wallimann, Isidor (Eds.). (1983). *Towards the Holocaust: Antisemitism and Fascism in Weimar Germany.* Westport, CT: Greenwood Press. Alternative Title (1983). *Towards the Holocaust: The Social and Economic Collapse of the Weimar Republic.* Westport, CT: Greenwood Press.

Donaldson, Frances Lonsdale Annesley (1962). *The Marconi Scandal.* London: Rupert Hart-Davis. New York: Harcourt, Brace & World.

Douglas, M. (1966). *Purity and Danger: An Analysis of Concepts of Pollution and Taboo.* London: Routledge and Kegan Paul.

Downing, David (2006). *Origins of the Holocaust.* Milwaukee, WI: World Almanac Library.

Drumont, Edouard (1886). *La "France Juive" devant l'opinion.* Paris: C. Marpon et E. Flammarion. 43rd edition (1886). *La France Juive: essai d'histoire contemporaine.* Paris: C. Marpon et E. Flammarion. New edition (1888). *La France Juive: édition populaire.* Paris: V. Palmé. [French].

Duby, G. (Ed.). (1988). *A History of Private Life: Revelations of the Medieval World.* Cambridge, MA: Harvard University Press.

Duckitt, John (1992). Psychology and Prejudice: An Historical Analysis and Integrated Framework. *American Psychologist,* vol. 27, no. 10, pp. 1182–1193.

Dühring, Carl Eugen (1881). *Die Judenfrage als Rassen-, Sitten- und Kulturfrage, mit einer weltgeschichtlichen Antwort.* Karlsruhe: H. Reuther. 4th edition (1892). *Die Judenfrage als Frage der Rassenschädlichkeit für Existenz, Sitte und Kultur der Völker. mit einer weltgeschichtlichen, relgionsbezüglich, social und politisch freiheitlichen Antwort.* Karlsruhe: H. Reuther. New edition (1901). *Antichebraica.* Karlsruhe: H. Reuther. New edition

(1930). *Die Judenfrage als Frage des Rassencharakters und Seiner Schädlichkeiten für Existenz und Kultur der Völker.* Leipzig: O.R. Reisland. [German].

Dührssen, Annemarie (1994). *Ein Jahrhundert psychoanalytische Bewegung in Deutschland: die Psychotherapie unter dem Einfluss Freuds.* Göttingen: Vandenhoeck & Ruprecht. [German].

Dunbar, E. (1995). The Prejudiced Personality, Racism and Anti-semitism: The *Pr* Scale Forty Years Later. *Journal of Personality Assessment,* vol. 65, pp. 270–277.

Dunbar, E., & Simonova, L. (2003). Individual Difference and Social Status Predictors of Anti-Semitism and Racism Us and Czech Findings with the Prejudice/tolerance and Right Wing Authoritarianism Scales. *International Journal of Intercultural Relations,* vol. 27, pp. 507–523.

Dundes, Alan (1984). *Life Is Like a Chicken Coop Ladder: A Portrait of German Culture Through Folklore.* New York: Columbia University Press. New edition (1989). Detroit, MI: Wayne State University Press.

Dundes, Alan (1991). The Ritual Murder or Blood Libel Legend: A Study of Anti-Semitic Victimization through Projective Inversion. In Dundes, Alan (Ed.), *The Blood Libel Legend: A Casebook in Anti-Semitic Folklore.* Madison: University of Wisconsin Press.

Dundes, Alan (1997). *From Game to War and Other Psychoanalytic Essays on Folklore.* Lexington: University of Kentucky Press.

Dundes, Alan (2002). *The Shabbat Elevator and Other Sabbath Subterfuges: An Unorthodox Essay on Circumventing Custom and Jewish Character.* Lanham, MD: Rowman & Littlefield.

Dundes, Alan (Ed.). (1991). *The Blood Libel Legend: a Casebook in Anti-Semitic Folklore.* Madison: University of Wisconsin Press.

Dundes, Alan, & Hauschild, Thomas (1983). Auschwitz Jokes. *Western Folklore,* vol. 42, no. 4, pp. 249–260.

Durbin, Evan Frank Mottram, & Bowlby, John (1939). *Personal Aggressiveness and War.* London: Kegan Paul, Trench, Trubner & Co.

Dvořak, Josef (1987). Kein Antisemitismus... *Forum: kulturelle Freiheit, politische Gleichheit, solidarische Arbeit,* vol. 34, Nos. 406–408, pp. 3–4. [German].

Ebbinghaus, A. (Ed.). (1987). *Opfer und Täterinnen.* Nördlingen: Greno. [German].

Eckert, Willehad Paul, & Ehrlich, Ernst Ludwig (Eds.). (1964). *Judenhass: Schuld der Christen?! Versuch eines Gesprächs.* Essen: H. Driewer. [German].

Edelheit, Abraham J., & Edelheit, Hershel (1994). *History of the Holocaust: A Handbook and Dictionary.* Boulder, CO: Westview Press.

Edelheit, Hershel, & Edelheit, Abraham J. (2000). *History of Zionism: A Handbook and Dictionary.* Boulder, CO: Westview Press.

Editors of *Psyche* (Eds.). (1984). *Psychoanalyse unter Hitler: Dokumentation einer Kontroverse.* Frankfurt am Main: Masch. [German].

Edwards, Mark U. (1991). Against the Jews. In Cohen, Jeremy (Ed.), *Essential Papers on Judaism and Christianity.* New York: New York University Press.

Eickhoff, F.W. (1995). The Formation of the German Psychoanalytic Association (DPV).: Regaining the Psychoanalytical Orientation Lost in the Third Reich. *International Journal of Psychoanalysis,* vol. 76, no. 5 (October), 945–956.

Eidelson, R.J. & Eidelson, J.I. (2004). They Both Matter: Reality and Belief. *American Psychologist,* vol. 59, pp. 82–183.

Eisenstadt, Shmuel Noah (1967). *Israeli Society.* London: Weidenfeld & Nicolson. New York: Basic Books.

Eisenstadt, Shmuel Noah (1983). Some Comments on the "Ethnic" Problem in Israel. *Israel Social Science Research,* vol. 1, no. 2, pp. 20–29.

Eisenstadt, Shmuel Noah (1992). *Jewish Civilization: The Jewish Historical Experience in a Comparative Perspective.* Albany: State University of New York Press.

Eisner, Will (2005). *The Plot: The Secret Story of the Protocols of the Elders of Zion.* Intro. by Umberto Eco. New York: W.W. Norton

Eissler, Kurt R. (1963). Die Ermordung von wie vielen seiner Kinder muss ein Mensch Symtomfrei ertragen können, um eine normale Konstitution zu haben? *Psyche: Zeitschrift für Psychoanalyse und ihre Anwendungen,* vol. 17, pp. 241–291.

Elbogen, Ismar (1946). *A Century of Jewish Life.* Tr. Moses Hadas. Philadelphia: Jewish Publication Society of America.

Eley, Geoff (Ed.). (2000). *The Goldhagen Effect: History, Memory, Nazism—Facing the German Past.* Ann Arbor: University of Michigan Press.

Eliot, George [Mary Ann Evans Cross] (1876). *Daniel Deronda.* New York: Harper.

Elon, Amos (1975). *Herzl.* New York: Holt, Rinehart & Winston.

Elsässer, Jürgen, & Markovits, Andrei S. (Eds.). (1999). *Die Fratze der eigenen Geschichte: von der Goldhagen-Debatte zum Jugoslawien-Krieg.* Berlin: Antifa Edition. Berlin: Elefanten Press. [German].

Elshtain, Jean Bethke (2004). The Nazi Seduction: Why Do Hitler and the Nazis Continue to Fascinate? *Books & Culture,* vol. 10, no. 3 (May–June).

Emery, D.B. (1989). *Genocide and the Self.* Unpublished dissertation, Rutgers University.

Endelman, Todd M. (1986). Comparative Perspectives on Modern Anti-Semitism in the West. In Berger, David (Ed.), *History and Hate: The Dimensions of Anti-Semitism.* Philadelphia: Jewish Publication Society of America. New edition (1997). Philadelphia: Jewish Publication Society.

Endelman, Todd M. (2002). *The Jews of Britain, 1656 to 2000.* Berkeley: University of California Press.

Enders, J. (2005). Dramatic Rumors and Truthful Appearances: The Medieval Myth of Ritual Murder by Proxy. In Fine, G.A. et al. (Eds.). *Rumor Mills.* New Brunswick, NJ: Transaction Books.

Erb, Rainer (Ed.). (1993). *Die Legende vom Ritualmord: zur Geschichte der Blutbeschuldigung gegen Juden.* Berlin: Metropol. [German].

Erikson, Erik Homburger (1942). Hitler's Imagery and German Youth. *Psychiatry,* vol. 5, pp. 475–493.

Erikson, Erik Homburger (1958). *Young Man Luther: A Study in Psychoanalysis and History.* New York: W.W. Norton. New edition (1962). New York: W. W. Norton. New edition (1993). New York: W. W. Norton.

Erikson, Erik Homburger (1963). The Legend of Hitler's Childhood. In Erikson, Erik H., *Childhood and Society,* 2nd edition, pp. 326–358. New York: W.W. Norton.

Erlenmeyer, Arvid (2001). Nach der Katastrophe: Auschwitz in Jungs Texten. *Analytische Psychologie,* vol. 32, pp. 107–121. [German].

Ettinger Chodakowska, Elzbieta (1995). *Hannah Arendt/Martin Heidegger.* New Haven, CT: Yale University Press.

Ettinger, Shmuel (1976). The Origins of Modern Anti-Semitism. In Gutman, Yisrael, & Rothkirchen, Livia (Eds.), *The Catastrophe of European Jewry.* Jerusalem: Yad Vashem.

EUMC–the European Monitoring Centre on Racism and Xenophobia (2004). *Perceptions of Antisemitism in the European Union.* Vienna: European Monitoring Centre on Racism and Xenophobia.

Evans, R.I. (1952). Personal Values as Factors in Anti-Semitism. *Journal of Abnormal Psychology,* vol. 47, no. 4, pp. 749–756.

Evans, Richard J. (1997). *Rereading German History: From Unification to Reunification, 1800–1996.* London: Routledge.

Evans, Richard J. (2001). *Lying about Hitler: History, Holocaust, and the David Irving Trial.* New York: Basic Books.

Evard, Jean-Luc (1994). *La faute à Moise: essais sur la condition juive.* Paris: L'Harmattan. [French].

Eysenck, Hans Jürgen, & Eysenck, S.B.G. (1975). *The Eysenck Personality Questionnaire.* London: Hodder & Stoughton.

Ezriel, Henry (1950). A Psychoanalytic Approach to Group Treatment. *British Journal of Medical Psychology,* vol. 23, pp. 59–75.

Ezriel, Henry (1956). Experimentation Within the Psychoanalytic Session. *British Journal of the History of Science,* vol. 7, pp. 29–48.

Fackenheim, Emil L. (1982). *To Mend the World: Foundations of Future Jewish Thought.* New York: Schocken Books. New edition (1989). *To Mend the World: Foundations of Post-Holocaust Thought.* New York: Schocken Books. New edition (1994). *To Mend the World: Foundations of Post-Holocaust Jewish Thought.* Bloomington: Indiana University Press.

Factor, Alexander (1956). *A History of Anti-Semitism.* Ilfracombe: Arthur H. Stockwell.

Falk, Avner (1975–1976). Identity and Name Changes. *The Psychoanalytic Review,* vol. 62, no. 4, Pp. 647–657.

Falk, Avner (1978). Freud and Herzl. *Contemporary Psychoanalysis,* vol. 14, no. 3 (July), pp. 357–387.

Falk, Avner (1993). *Herzl, King of the Jews: A Psychoanalytic Biography of Theodor Herzl.* Lanham, MD: University Press of America.

Falk, Avner (1996). *A Psychoanalytic History of the Jews.* Madison, NJ: Fairleigh Dickinson University Press. Cranbury, NJ: Associated University Presses.

Falk, Avner (2004). *Fratricide in the Holy Land: A Psychoanalytic View of the Arab-Israeli Conflict.* Madison: University of Wisconsin Press.

Falk, Avner (2006). Collective Psychological Processes in Anti-Semitism. *Jewish Political Studies Review,* vol. 18, nos. 1–2, pp. 37–55.

Falwell, Jerry, et al. (Eds.). (1981). *The Fundamentalist Phenomenon: the Resurgence of Conservative Christianity.* Garden City, NY: Doubleday.

Faurisson, Robert (1980). *Mémoire en défense contre ceux qui m'accusent de falsifier l'histoire: la question des chambres à gaz.* Préface de Noam Chomsky. Paris: La Vieille Taupe. [French].

Faurisson, Robert (1982). *Réponse à Pierre Vidal-Naquet.* 2e Édition Augmentée. Paris: La Vieille Taupe. [French].

Faurisson, Robert (1994). *Réponse à Jean-Claude Pressac: sur le problème des chambres à gaz.* Vichy and Colombes: RHR. [French].

Faurisson, Robert et al. (2000). *Réponse à Valérie Igounet, auteur du livre "Histoire du négationnisme en France."* Honfleur: V. Reynouard. [French].

Feder, R. (1993). Antisemitism and the Collective Unconscious. *American Journal of Psychiatry,* vol. 150, No. 3 (March), pp. 527–528.

Federal Republic of Germany (1961). *Eichmann Trial Exploited for Defamation Campaign Against the Federal Republic by Eastern Propaganda and Agitation: Documentary Report, February 22, 1961.* Bonn: Federal Republic of Germany.

Fein, Helen (Ed.). (1987). Explanations of the Origin and Evolution of Antisemitism. In Fein, Helen (Ed.), *The Persisting Question: Sociological Perspectives and Social Context of Modern Antisemitism.* Berlin and New York: Walter de Gruyter.

Feldkamp, Michael F. (2003). *Goldhagens unwillige Kirche: alte und neue Fälschungen über Kirche und Papst während der NS-Herrschaft.* Munich: Olzog. [German].

Feldman, Linda E., & Orendi, Diana (Eds.). (2000). *Evolving Jewish Identities in German Culture: Borders and Crossings.* Westport, CT: Praeger.

Feldman, Louis H. (1958–1959). Philo-Semitism Among Ancient Intellectuals. Tradition, vol. 1, pp. 27–39. Reprinted (1993) in Feldman, Louis H., *Jew and Gentile in the Ancient World: Attitudes and Interactions from Alexander to Justinian.* Princeton, NJ: Princeton University Press.

Feldman, Louis H. (1968) Antisemitism in the Ancient World. In Berger, David (Ed.), *History and Hate: The Dimensions of Anti-Semitism.* Philadelphia: Jewish Publication Society of America. New edition (1997). Philadelphia: Jewish Publication Society.

Feldman, Louis H. (1993). *Jew and Gentile in the Ancient World: Attitudes and Interactions from Alexander to Justinian.* Princeton, NJ: Princeton University Press.

Felsenstein, Frank (1995). *Anti-Semitic Stereotypes.* Baltimore: Johns Hopkins University Press.

Fenichel, Otto (1940). Psychoanalysis of Anti-Semitism. *American Imago: A Psychoanalytic Journal for Culture, Science and the Arts,* vol. 1, pp. 24–39.

Fenichel, Otto (1946). Elements of a Psychoanalytic Theory of Antisemitism. In Simmel, Ernst (Ed.), *Anti-Semitism: A Social Disease,* pp. 11–32. New York: International Universities Press. New edition (1948). New York: International Universities Press.

Fenyvesi, Charles (2006). Antisemites Rally in Moscow: Police Stand By. *Bigotry Monitor: A Weekly Human Rights Newsletter on Antisemitism, Xenophobia, and Religious Persecution in the Former Communist World and Western Europe,* vol. 6, No. 9 (Friday, March 3). Washington, DC: Union of Councils for Jews in the Former Soviet Union.

Ferraroti, Franco (1994). *The Temptation to Forget: Racism, Anti-Semitism, Neo-nazism.* Westport, CT: Greenwood Press.

Finkelstein, Norman G. (2005). *Beyond Chutzpah: On the Misuse of Anti-Semitism and the Abuse of History.* Berkeley: University of California Press.

Finkielkraut, Alain (1980). *Le juif imaginaire.* Paris: Editions du Seuil. [French].

Finkielkraut, Alain (1982). *L'avenir d'une négation: réflexion sur la question du génocide.* Paris: Editions du Seuil. [French].

Finkielkraut, Alain (1997). *The Imaginary Jew.* Lincoln: University of Nebraska Press.

Finkielkraut, Alain (1998). *The Future of a Negation: Reflections on the Question of Genocide.* Tr. Mary Byrd Kelly. Intro. by Richard J. Golsan. Lincoln: University of Nebraska Press.

Finkielkraut, Alain (2003). *Au nom de l'autre: réflexions sur l'antisémitisme qui vient.* Paris: Gallimard. [French].

Finkielkraut, Alain, & Lévy, Benny (2003). *Le Livre et les livres: entretiens sur la laïcité.* Paris: Editions Verdier. [French].

Finlay, W.M.L. (2004). Pathologizing Dissent: Identity Politics, Zionism and the "Self-hating Jew." *British Journal of Social Psychology,* vol. 44, no. 2, pp. 201–222.

Fischer, Gerhard, & Lindner, Ulrich (1999).*Stürmer für Hitler: vom Zusammenspiel zwischen Fussball und Nationalsozialismus.* Mit Beiträgen von Werner Skrentny und Dietrich Schulze-marmeling. Göttingen: Die Werkstatt. [German].

Fischer, Jens Malte (1987). Literarischer Antisemitismus im zwanzigsten Jahrhundert: zu seinen Stereotypen und seiner Pathologie. In Fischer, Jens Malte, et al. (Eds.), *Erkundungen: Beiträge zu einem erweiterten Literaturbegriff. Festschrift für Helmut Kreuzer,* pp. 117–138. Göttingen: Vandenhoeck & Ruprecht. [German].

Fischer, Klaus P. (1998). *The History of an Obsession: German Judeophobia and the Holocaust.* New York: Continuum.

Fischer, Malvine (2004). *Nazi Laws and Jewish Lives: Letters from Vienna.* Ed. Edith Kurzweil. New Brunswick, NJ: Transaction Publishers.

Flannery, Edward H. (1965). *The Anguish of the Jews: Twenty-three Centuries of Anti-semitism.* Preface by John M. Oesterreicher. New York: Macmillan. New edition (1985). New York: Paulist Press. New edition (2004). Foreword by Philip A. Cunningham. New York: Paulist Press.

Flavin, Michael (2005). *Benjamin Disraeli: The Novel as Political Discourse.* Brighton and Portland: Sussex Academic Press.

Fleischner, Eva (Ed.) (1977). *Auschwitz: Beginning of a New Era? Reflections on the Holocaust.* New York: Ktav Publishing Co.

Fornari, Franco (1974). *The Psychoanalysis of War.* Tr. Alenka Pfeifer. Garden City, NY: Doubleday Anchor Press. Reprinted (1975). Bloomington: Indiana University Press.

Forster, Arnold (1950). *A Measure of Freedom: An Anti-defamation League Report.* Garden City, NY: Doubleday.

Forster, Arnold, & Epstein, Benjamin R. (1952). *The Trouble-Makers: an Anti-defamation League Report.* Garden City, NY: Doubleday. New edition (1970). Westport, CT: Negro Universities Press.

Forster, Arnold, & Epstein, Benjamin R. (1974). *The New Anti-Semitism.* New York: McGraw-Hill.

Forster, Arnold et al. (1948). *Anti-semitism in the United States in 1947.* New York: B'nai B'rith Anti-Defamation League.

Foulkes, Siegmund Heinz, & Anthony, Elwyn James (1957). *Group Psychotherapy: The Psychoanalytic Approach.* Harmondsworth, Middlesex: Penguin Books. 2nd edition (1965). Baltimore: Penguin Books.

Framer, William R. (Ed.). (1999). *Anti-Judaism and the Gospels.* Harrisburg, PA: Trinity Press International.

Frankel, Jonathan (1972). *The Anti-Zionist Press Campaigns in the USSR 1969–1971: Political Implications.* Jerusalem: Soviet and East European Research Centre, The Hebrew University of Jerusalem.

Frankel, Jonathan (1984). *The Soviet Regime and Anti-Zionism: An Analysis.* Jerusalem: Soviet and East European Research Centre, the Hebrew University of Jerusalem.

Frankel, Jonathan (1997). *The Damascus Affair: "Ritual Murder," Politics, and the Jews in 1840.* Cambridge and New York: Cambridge University Press.

Frankel, Jonathan (Ed.). (1997). *The Fate of the European Jews, 1939–1945: Continuity or Contingency?* New York: Oxford University Press.

Frankel, Jonathan (Ed.). (2000). *Jews and Gender: The Challenge to Hierarchy.* Oxford and New York: Oxford University Press.

Frankfurter, Naphtali, & Auerbach, Berthold (1838). *Gallerie der ausgezeichneten Israeliten aller Jahrhunderte: ihre Portraits und Biographien.* Paris: Imprimerie de A. Auffray. [German].

Frankl, Viktor Emil (1959). *From Death-camp to Existentialism: A Psychiatrist's Path to a New Therapy.* Tr. Ilse Lasch. Preface by Gordon W. Allport. Boston: Beacon Press.

Frankl, Viktor Emil (1997). *Man's Search for Ultimate Meaning.* Foreword by Swanee Hunt. New York: Insight Books.

Fraser, Steven (Ed.). (1995). *The Bell Curve Wars: Race, Intelligence, and the Future of America.* New York: Basic Books.

Fredrickson, George M. (2002). *Racism: A Short History.* Princeton, NJ: Princeton University Press.

Freedman, Mervin B. (1987). American Anti-Semitism Now: A Political Psychology Perspective. In Freedman, Mervin B. (Ed.), *Social Change and Personality.* New York: Springer.

Freedman, Robert O. (1989). *Soviet Jewry in the 1980s: The Politics of Anti-Semitism and Emigration and the Dynamics of Resettlement.* Durham, NC: Duke University Press.

Freiman, Grigori A. (1980). *It Seems I Am a Jew: A Samizdat Essay.* Tr. Melvyn B. Nathanson. London and Amsterdam: Feffer & Simons. Carbondale and Edwardsville, IL: Southern Illinois University Press.

Frenkel-Brunswick, Else, & Sanford, R. Nevitt (1945). Some Personality Factors in Anti-semitism. *Journal of Psychology,* vol. 20, pp. 271–291.

Frenkel-Brunswick, Else & Sanford, R. Nevitt (1946). The Anti-Semitic Personality: A Research Report. In Simmel, Ernst (Ed.), *Anti-Semitism: A Social Disease,* pp. 33–78. New York: International Universities Press. New edition (1948). New York: International Universities Press.

Fresco, Nadine (1990). Les "révisionnistes" négateurs de la Shoah. In "Révisionnisme," *Encyclopaedia Universalis.* [French].

Fresco, Nadine (1999). *Fabrication d'un antisémite.* Paris: Éditions du Seuil. [French].

Fresco, Nadine (2004). Négationnisme. *Encyclopaedia Universalis.* [French].

Freud, Sigmund (1910). Eine Kindheiterinnerung des Leonardo da Vinci. *Schriften zur angewandten Seelenkunde,* no. 7. Leipzig and Vienna: Deuticke. [German].

Freud, Sigmund (1921). *Massenpsychologie und Ich-analyse.* Leipzig, Vienna, and Zurich: Internationaler Psychoanalytischer Verlag. [German].

Freud, Sigmund (1930). *Das Unbehagen in der Kultur.* Vienna: Internationaler Psychoanalytischer Verlag. [German].

Freud, Sigmund (1939). *Der Mann Moses und die Monotheistische Religion: drei Anhandlungen.* Amsterdam: Verlag Albert De Lange. [German].

Freud, Sigmund (1955). Group Psychology and the Analysis of the Ego. In *The Standard Edition of the Complete Psychological Works of Sigmund Freud,* Vol. 18, pp. 65–143. Tr.

and Ed. James Strachey et al. London: The Hogarth Press and the Institute of Psycho-analysis.

Freud, Sigmund (1957). *Leonardo Da Vinci and a Memory of His Childhood.* In *The Standard Edition of the Complete Psychological Works of Sigmund Freud,* Vol. 11, pp. 57–137. Tr. And Ed. James Strachey et al. London: The Hogarth Press and the Institute of Psycho-Analysis.

Freud, Sigmund (1961). *Civilization and its Discontents.* In *The Standard Edition of the Complete Psychological Works of Sigmund Freud,* Vol. 21, pp. 57–145. Tr. and Ed. James Strachey et al. London: The Hogarth Press and the Institute of Psycho-Analysis.

Freud, Sigmund (1964). *Moses and Monotheism: Three Essays.* In *The Standard Edition of the Complete Psychological Works of Sigmund Freud,* Vol. 23, pp. 1–137. Tr. And Ed. James Strachey et Al. London: The Hogarth Press and the Institute of Psycho-Analysis.

Freud, Sigmund (1973). Zwangshandlungen und Religionsübungen. In Freud, Sigmund, *Studienausgabe,* Vol. 7, pp. 12–21. Frankfurt am Main: Fischer Verlag. [German].

Freud, Sigmund, & Abraham, Karl (1965). *Psychoanalytic Dialogue: The Letters of Sigmund Freud and Karl Abraham, 1907–1926.* Tr. B. Marsh & H.C. Abraham. Ed. H.C. Abraham & E.L. Freud. New York: Basic Books.

Freudmann, Lillian C. (1994). *Antisemitism in the New Testament.* Lanham, MD: University Press of America.

Freund, Ismar (1912). *Die Emanzipation der Juden in Preussen, unter besonderer Berücksichtigung des Gesetzes von 11. März 1812: ein Beitrag zur Rechtsgeschichte der Juden in Preussen.* Two Volumes. Berlin: M. Poppelauer. Reprinted (2004). Hildesheim, Zurich, and New York: Georg Olms. [German].

Friedländer, David (1799). *Sendschreiben an Seine Hochwürden Herrn Oberconsistorial-rath und Probst Teller zu Berlin, von Einigen Hausvätern Jüdischer Religion . . .* Berlin: David Friedländer. New edition (1975). Tr. Miriam Di-Nur. Intro. by Richard Cohen. Jerusalem: Zalman Shazar Center.

Friedländer, David (1812). *David Friedländers Schrift über die durch die neue Organisation der Judenschaften in den preußischen Staaten nothwendig gewordene Umbildung 1). Ihres Gottesdienstes in den Synagogen, 2). Ihrer Unterrichts-anstalten und deren Lehrgegenstände, Und 3). Ihres Erziehungwesens überhaupt: ein Wort zu seiner Zeit.* Berlin: W. Dieterich. New edition (1934). Berlin: Verlag Hausfreund. [German].

Friedländer, David, et al. (2004). *A Debate on Jewish Emancipation and Christian Theology in Old Berlin.* Tr. & Ed. Richard Crouter & Julie Klassen. Indianapolis: Hackett Publishing.

Friedlander, Henry (1995). *The Origins of the Nazi Genocide.* Chapel Hill: University of North Carolina Press.

Friedlander, Henry, & Milton, Sybil (Eds.) (1980). *The Holocaust: Ideology, Bureaucracy and Genocide.* New York: Kraus International Publications.

Friedländer, Saul (1971). *L'antisémitisme nazi.* Paris: Éditions du Seuil. [French].

Friedländer, Saul (1975). *Histoire et Psychanalyse: essai sur les possibilités et les limites de la psychohistoire.* Paris: Éditions du Seuil. [French].

Friedländer, Saul (1978). *History and Psychoanalysis: An Inquiry into the Possibilities and Limits of Psychohistory.* Tr. Susan Suleiman. New York and London: Holmes & Meier.

Friedländer, Saul (1993). *Memory, History, and the Extermination of the Jews of Europe.* Bloomington: Indiana University Press.

Friedländer, Saul (1997–2006). *Nazi Germany and the Jews.* 2 vols. New York: Harper-Collins.

Friedländer, Saul, & Hussein, Mahmoud [Bahgat Elnadi & Adel Rifaat] (1975). *Arabs and Israelis: A Dialogue. Moderated by Jean Lacouture.* Tr. Paul Auster and Lydia Davis. New York: Holmes & Meier.

Friedländer, Saul, et al. (1985). *Visions of Apocalypse: End or Rebirth?* New York: Holmes and Meier.

Friedman, Jerome (1987). Jewish Conversion, the Spanish Pure Blood Laws and Reformation: A Revisionist View of Racial and Religious Antisemitism. *The Sixteenth Century Journal,* vol. 18, no. 1, pp. 3–30.

Friedman, Lawrence J. (1999). *Identity's Architect: A Biography of Erik H. Erikson.* New York: Scribner.

Friedman, Saul S. (1984). *The Oberammergau Passion Play: A Lance Against Civilization.* Carbondale and Edwardsville, IL: Southern Illinois University Press.

Frindte, W., et al. (2005). Old and New Anti-semitic Attitudes in the Context of Authoritarianism and Social Dominance Orientation. *Peace and Conflict,* vol. 11, pp. 239–266.

Fromm, Erich (1932). Über Methode und Aufgabe einer analytischen Sozialpsychologie. *Zeitschrift Für Sozialforschung,* vol. 1, pp. 28–54. [German].

Fromm, Erich (1942). *The Fear of Freedom.* London: Kegan Paul, Trench, Trubner & Co. New edition (1975). London: Routledge and Kegan Paul.

Fromm, Erich (1973). *The Anatomy of Human Destructiveness.* New York: Holt, Rinehart and Winston. New edition (1992). New York: Henry Holt.

Frosh, Stephen (2003). Psychoanalysis, Nazism and "Jewish Science." *International Journal of Psychoanalysis,* vol. 84, pp. 1315–1332.

Frosh, Stephen (2004). Freud, Psychoanalysis and Anti-semitism. *The Psychoanalytic Review,* vol. 91, pp. 309–330.

Frosh, Stephen (2005). *Hate and the "Jewish Science": Antisemitism, Nazism, and Psychoanalysis.* New York and Houndmills: Palgrave Macmillan.

Fuchs, Eduard (1921). *Die Juden in der Karikatur: ein Beitrag zur Kulturgeschichte.* Munich: Albert Langen Verlag. [German].

Furlong, Patrick J. (1991) *Between Crown and Swastika: The Impact of the Radical Right on the Afrikaner Nationalist Movement in the Fascist Era.* Johannesburg: Witwatersrand University Press.

Gachnochi, Georges (2004). De l'antisémitisme traditionnel à l'islamo-gauchisme: facteurs inconscients du passage. *Pardès: Études et Culture Juives,* no. 37, *Psychanalyse de l'antisémitisme contemporain,* pp. 21–33.

Gager, John G. (1985). *The Origins of Anti-Semitism: Attitudes Toward Judaism in Pagan and Christian Antiquity.* New York: Oxford University Press.

Galinier, Pierre (2005). "Mahmoud Hussein," jumeaux de l'Islam. *Le Monde,* March 2, p. 16. [French].

Galton, Francis (1869). *Hereditary Genius: An Enquiry into its Laws and Consequences.* London: n.p. New edition (1914). London: Macmillan and Co.

Galton, Francis (1909). *Essays in Eugenics.* London: The Eugenics Education Society. Reprinted (1985). New York: Garland Publishing Co.

Garaudy, Roger (1995). *Les Mythes fondateurs de la politique israélienne.* Paris: Roger Garaudy and Samiszdat. [French].

Garaudy, Roger (1997). *The Mythical Foundations of Israeli Policy.* London: Studies Forum International. Reprinted (1997). As *The Founding Myths of the Israeli Policy.* Annandale, VA: United Association for Studies and Research. Reprinted (2000). As *The Founding Myths of Modern Israel.* Newport Beach, CA: Institute for Historical Review.

García Düttmann, Alexander (1991). *Das Gedächtnis des Denkens: Versuch über Heidegger und Adorno.* Frankfurt am Main: Suhrkamp. [German].

García Düttmann, Alexander (2002). *The Memory of Thought: An Essay on Heidegger and Adorno.* Tr. Nicholas Walker. London and New York: Continuum.

García Márquez, Gabriel (1982). *Chronicle of a Death Foretold.* Tr. Gregory Rabassa. London: Jonathan Cape. Reprinted (1983). New York: Alfred A. Knopf.

Gates, H.L. (1992). Why Target the Jews? *The New York Times,* July 20.

Geisel, E., & Broder, Henryk M. (Eds.). (1992). *Premiere und Pogrom: der jüdische Kulturbund 1933–1941.* Texte Und Bilder. Berlin: Siedler. [German].

Gellately, Robert, & Kiernan, Ben (Eds.). (2003). *The Specter of Genocide: Mass Murder in Historical Perspective.* Cambridge: Cambridge University Press.

Geller, Jay Howard (1999). The Godfather of Psychoanalysis: Circumcision, Antisemitism, Homosexuality, and Freud's "Fighting Jew." *Journal of the American Academy of Religion,* vol. 67, no. 2, pp. 355–386.

Geller, Jay Howard (2004). The Psychopathology of Everyday Vienna: Psychoanalysis and Freud's Familiars. *International Journal of Psychoanalysis,* vol. 85, no. 5, pp. 1209–1224.

Geller, Jay Howard (2005). *Jews in Post-Holocaust Germany, 1945–1953.* Cambridge and New York: Cambridge University Press.

General Jewish Council (1939). *Father Coughlin: His "Facts" and Arguments.* New York: General Jewish Council.

Gerber, David A. (1986) Cutting Out Shylock: Elite Anti-Semitism and The Quest for Moral Order in the Mid-Nineteenth Century American Marketplace. In Gerber, David A. (Ed.), *Anti-Semitism in American History.* Urbana: University of Illinois Press.

Gerber, Doris A. (Ed.). (1986). *Antisemitism in American History.* Urbana: University of Illinois Press.

Gerber, Jane (1986) Anti-Semitism and the Muslim World. In Berger, David (Ed.). *History and Hate: The Dimensions of Anti-Semitism.* Philadelphia: Jewish Publication Society of America. New edition (1997). Philadelphia: Jewish Publication Society.

Gerlach, Wolfgang (2000). *And the Witnesses Were Silent: The Confessing Church and the Persecution of the Jews.* Tr. Victoria J. Barnett. Lincoln: University of Nebraska Press.

Gerstenfeld, Manfred (2007). Ahmadinejad, Iran, and Holocaust Manipulation: Methods, Aims, and Reactions. Jerusalem Center for Public Affairs Web site, February 1.

Gerstenfeld, Manfred (Ed.). (2003). *Europe's Crumbling Myths.* Jerusalem: Jerusalem Center for Public Affairs.

Gerstenfeld, Manfred, & Trigano, Shmuel (Eds.). (2004). *Les Habits neufs de l'antisémitisme en Europe.* Ile de Noirmoutier: Café Noir. [French].

Gewen, Barry (2006). The Everyman of Genocide: Review of David Cesarani's *Becoming Eichmann.* In *The New York Times Sunday Book Review,* May 14.

Gibson, Jamers L., & Duch, Raymond M. (1992). Anti-Semitic Attitudes of the Mass Public: Estimates and Explanations Based on a Survey of the Moscow Oblast. *Public Opinion Quarterly,* vol. 56, pp. 1–28.

Gilbert, Martin (1985). *The Holocaust: A History of the Jews of Europe During the Second World War.* New York: Henry Holt & Co.

Gilbert, Martin (1996). *The Boys: The Untold Story of 732 Young Concentration Camp Survivors.* New York: Henry Holt & Co.

Gilligan, James (1996). *Violence: Our Deadly Epidemic and its Causes.* New York: Vintage Books.

Gilman, Sander L. (1986).*Jewish Self-Hatred: Anti-Semitism and the Hidden Language of the Jews.* Baltimore: Johns Hopkins University Press. New edition (1990). Baltimore: Johns Hopkins University Press.

Gilman, Sander L. (1990). Anti-Semitism and the Body in Psychoanalysis.*Social Research,* vol. 57, no. 4, pp. 993–1017.

Gilman, Sander L. (1991). *The Jew's Body.* New York and London: Routledge.

Gilman, Sander L. (1993a). *The Case of Sigmund Freud: Medicine and Identity at the Fin De Siècle.* Baltimore: Johns Hopkins University Press.

Gilman, Sander L. (1993b). *Freud, Race, and Gender.* Princeton, NJ: Princeton University Press.

Gilman, Sander L. (1994). Psychoanalysis and Anti-Semitism: Tainted Greatness in a Professional Context. In Harrowitz, Nancy A. (Ed.). *Tainted Greatness: Antisemitism and Cultural Heroes.* Philadelphia: Temple University Press.

Gilman, Sander L. (2003). *Jewish Frontiers: Essays on Bodies, Histories, and Identities.* New York: Palgrave Macmillan.

Gilman, Sander L., & Katz, Steven T. (Eds.). (1991).*Anti-semitism in Times of Crisis.* New York: New York University Press.

Gilman, Sander L., & Shain, Milton (Eds.). (1999). *Jewries at the Frontier: Accommodation, Identity, Conflict.* Urbana: University of Illinois Press.

Gilman, Sander L., & Zipes, Jack David (Eds.). (1997). *Yale Companion to Jewish Writing and Thought in German Culture, 1096–1996.* New Haven, CT: Yale University Press.

Gilmore, David D. (2001). *Misogyny: The Male Malady.* Philadelphia: University of Pennsylvania Press.

Ginsberg, Benjamin (1993). *The Fatal Embrace: Jews and the State.* Chicago: University of Chicago Press.

Girard, René (1972). *Violence and the Sacred.* Tr. Patrick Gregory. Baltimore: Johns Hopkins University Press.

Glagau, Otto (1876). *Der Börsen- und Gründungs-Schwindel in Berlin.* Leipzig: P. Frohberg. [German].

Glagau, Otto (1877). *Der Börsen- und Gründungs-Schwindel in Deutschland.* Leipzig: P. Frohberg. [German].

Glass, James M. (1997). *"Life Unworthy of Life": Racial Phobia and Mass Murder in Hitler's Germany.* New York: Basic Books.

Glass, James M. (2004). *Jewish Resistance During the Holocaust: Moral Uses of Violence and Will.* Houndmills, Basingstoke, Hampshire, England, and New York: Palgrave Macmillan.

Glassman, Bernard (1975). *Anti-Semitic Stereotypes Without Jews: Images of the Jews in England, 1290–1700.* Detroit, MI: Wayne State University Press.

Glassman, Bernard (2003). *Benjamin Disraeli: The Fabricated Jew in Myth and Memory.* Lanham, MD. University Press of America.

Glenn, Jules (1960). Circumcision and Anti-Semitism. *Psychoanalytic Quarterly,* vol. 29, pp. 395–399.

Glock, Charles Y., & Stark, Rodney (1966). *Christian Beliefs and Anti-Semitism.* New York: Harper & Row. New edition (1969). New York: Harper & Row. New edition (1979). Westport, CT: Greenwood Press.

Glock, Charles Y., et al. (1975). *Adolescent Prejudice.* New York: The Free Press.

Gobineau, Joseph-Arthur De (1915). *The Inequality of Human Races.* New York: G.P. Putnam's Sons. New edition (1967). Tr. Adrian Collins. Intro. by Oscar Levy. New York: Howard Fertig. New edition (1999). Preface by George L. Mosse. New York: Howard Fertig.

Gobineau, Joseph-Arthur De (1853–1855).*Essai sur l'inégalite des races humaines.* 4 vols. Paris: Firmin-didot. 2nd edition (1884). 2 Vols. Précédée D'un Avant-propos et D'une Biographie De L'auteur. Paris: Firmin-didot. New edition (1940). Paris: Firmin-didot. [French].

Godley, Wynne (2001). Saving Masud Khan. *London Review of Books,* vol. 23, no. 4 (February 22).

Goedsche, Hermann Ottomar Friedrich (1868). Auf dem Judenkirchhof in Prag. In Goedsche's *Biarritz: historisch-politischer Roman von Sir John Retcliffe.* . . . New edition (1924). Munich: Deutscher Volksverlag. Reprinted (1933). Berlin: P. Steegemann. [German].

Goetz, Aly, et al. (1994). *Cleansing the Fatherland: Nazi Medicine and Racial Hygiene.* Baltimore: Johns Hopkins University Press.

Goggin, James E., & Goggin, Eileen Brockman (2001). *Death of a "Jewish Science": Psychoanalysis in the Third Reich.* West Lafayette, IN: Purdue University Press.

Gold, Nora (1997). Canadian Jewish Women and Their Experiences of Antisemitism and Sexism. *Women in Judaism: A Multidisciplinary Journal,* vol. 1, no. 1.

Gold, Nora (2004). Sexism and Antisemitism as Experienced by Canadian Jewish Women: Results of a National Study. *Women's Studies International Forum,* vol. 27, pp. 55–74.

Goldberg, Carl (1996). *Speaking with the Devil: A Dialogue with Evil.* New York: Viking.

Goldberg, Carl (2000). *The Evil We Do: The Psychoanalysis of Destructive People.* Amherst, NJ: Prometheus Books.

Goldhagen, Daniel Jonah (1996a). *Hitlers Willige Vollstrecker: Ganz Gewöhnliche Deutsche und der Holocaust.* Tr. Klaus Kochmann. Berlin: Wolf Jobst Siedler Verlag. [German].

Goldhagen, Daniel Jonah (1996b). *Hitler's Willing Executioners: Ordinary Germans and the Holocaust.* New York: Alfred A. Knopf.

Goldhagen, Daniel Jonah et al. (1996). *The "Willing Executioners"/"Ordinary Men" Debate: Selections from the Symposium, April 8, 1996.* Intro. by Michael Berenbaum. Washington, DC: United States Holocaust Research Institute.

Goldstein, Jan E. (1985). The Wandering Jew and the Problem of Psychiatric Anti-Semitism in Fin-de-siècle France. *Journal of Contemporary History,* vol. 20, pp. 521–552.

Golomb, Abraham (1946). Jewish Self-Hatred. *Yivo Annual of Jewish Social Science,* vol. 1, pp. 250 H.

Gonen, Jay Y. (2000). *The Roots of Nazi Psychology: Hitler's Utopian Barbarism.* Lexington: University Press of Kentucky.

Goodman, David G. (1987). Japanese Anti-Semitism: It's Real, It's Obscene, and It's Potentially Dangerous. *The World & I,* vol. 2 (November), 401–409.

Goodman, David G., & Miyazawa, Masanori (1995). *Jews in the Japanese Mind: The History and Uses of a Cultural Stereotype.* New York: The Free Press.

Goodrick-Clarke, Nicholas (1998). *Hitler's Priestess: Savitri Devi, the Hindu-Aryan Myth and Neo-Nazism.* New York: New York University Press.

Gough, Harrison G. (1951). Studies in Social Intolerance: I. Some Psychological and Sociological Correlates of Anti-semitism. II. A Personality Scale for Anti-semitism [The Pr for Prejudice Scale]. III. Relationship of the Pr Scale to Other Variables. IV. Related Social Altitudes. *Journal of Social Psychology,* vol. 33, pp. 237–269.

Gould, Allan (Ed.) (1991). *What Did They Think of Jews?* New York: Jason Aronson

Graetz, Heinrich Z. (1853–1868). *Geschichte der Juden, von den Ältesten Zeiten bis auf die Gegenwart.* 12 vols. Leipzig: Oskar Leiner. [German].

Graetz, Heinrich Z. (1868). Voltaire und die Juden. *Monatsschrift,* pp. 161–174, 201, 223. [German].

Graml, Hermann (1992). *Antisemitism in the Third Reich.* Tr. Tim Kirk. Oxford: Blackwell

Grand, Sue (2000). *The Reproduction of Evil: A Clinical and Cultural Perspective.* Hillsdale, NJ: The Analytic Press.

Grant, Michael (1978). *History of Rome.* London: Weidenfeld & Nicolson.

Graus, P. (1987). *Pest, Geissler, Judenmorde: das 14. Jahrhundert als Krisenzeit.* Göttingen: Vandenhoek & Ruprecht. [German].

Graves, Philip (1921). The Truth about the Protocols: A Literary Forgery. *The Times,* August 16–18.

Grayzel, Solomon (1933). *The Church and the Jews in the XIIIth Century.* 2 vols. Philadelphia: The Dropsie College for Hebrew and Cognate Learning. New edition (1989). Ed. Kenneth R. Stow. New York: Jewish Theological Seminary of America. Detroit, MI: Wayne State University Press.

Grayzel, Solomon (1947). *A History of the Jews, from the Babylonian Exile to the End of World War II.* Philadelphia: Jewish Publication Society of America.

Grayzel, Solomon (1969). *A History of the Jews, from the Babylonian Exile to the Present.* 2nd edition. Philadelphia: Jewish Publication Society of America.

Greene, Melissa Fay (1996). *The Temple Bombing.* Reading, MA: Addison-Wesley.

Groener, Eberhard (1994). Christlicher AntiJudaismus und Psychologische Deutungsmuster: Versuch Einer Auseinandersetzung Mit Den Theorien D. W. Winnicotts. *Judaica,* vol. 50, no. 1, pp. 34–42. [German].

Grollman, Earl A. (1965). *Judaism in Sigmund Freud's World.* Foreword by Nathan W. Ackerman. New York: Bloch Pubishing Co.

Gröpler, Eva (1987). Sartres Überlegungen zur Judenfrage. *Babylon: Beiträge zur jüdischen Gegenwart,* no. 2 (July), pp. 108–115. [German].

Gross, Jan T. (2006). *Fear: Anti-Semitism in Poland after Auschwitz. An Essay in Historical Interpretation.* New York: Random House.

Gross, John (1992). *Shylock: Four Hundred Years in the Life of a Legend.* London: Chatto & Windus.

Gross, Raphael (2001). Die verspätete Holocaustforschung. *Buchzeichen,* Supplement to the *Tages-Anzeiger,* October 8. [German].

Grossarth-Maticek, R., et al. 1989). The Causes and Cures of Prejudice: An Empirical Study of the Frustration Aggression Hypothesis: *Personality and Individual Differences,* vol. 10, pp. 547–588.

Grosser, Paul E., & Halperin, Edwin G. (1978). *The Causes and Effects of Anti-Semitism: The Dimensions of Prejudice: An Analysis and Chronology of 1900 Years of Anti-Semitic Attitudes and Practices.* New York: Philosophical Library. New edition (1983). New York: Philosophical Library.

Grouès, Henri [Abbé Pierre], & Kouchner, Bernard (1993). *Dieu et les hommes: dialogues et propos recueillis par Michel-Antoine Burnier.* Avant-propos de Marek Halter. Paris: Robert Laffont. Reprinted (1993). Paris: Editions Corps. Paris: Le Grand Livre du Mois. Reprinted (1994). Paris: Editions Pocket. [French].

Gruber, Hansjörg (1995). *"Ohne Erinnerung": die Vergangenheitsbewältigung der Stadt W.: Eine Deutsche Chronik.* Tübingen: Silberburg. [German].

Grubrich-Simitis, I. (1979). Extremtraumatisierung Als Kumulatives Trauma. *Psyche: Zeitschrift für Psychoanalyse und ihre Anwendungen,* vol. 33, pp. 991–1023. [German].

Grunberger, Béla (1964). The Anti-Semite and the Oedipal Conflict. *International Journal of Psycho-analysis,* vol. 45, pp. 380–385.

Grunberger, Béla (1993). On Narcissism, Aggressivity and Anti-Semitism. *International Forum of Psychoanalysis,* vol. 2, no. 4, pp. 237–241.

Grunberger, Béla, & Chasseguet-Smirgel, Janine (1976). *Freud ou Reich? psychanalyse et illusion.* Paris: Tchou. [French].

Grunberger, Béla, & Dessuant, Pierre (1997). *Narcissisme, Christianisme, Antisémitisme: étude psychanalytique.* Arles: Actes Sud. [French].

Grynberg, Anne (1995). *La Shoah: l'impossible oubli.* Paris: Gallimard. [French].

Guntrip, Harry (1968). *Schizoid Phenomena, Object Relations and the Self.* New York: International Universities Press.

Gurock, Jeffrey S. (Ed.). (1998). *Anti-Semitism in America.* 2 vols. New York: Routledge.

Gutman, Israel [Yisrael] (1985). *Denying the Holocaust.* Jerusalem: Shazar Library, Institute of Contemporary Jewry, and Vidal Sassoon International Center for the Study of Antisemitism, The Hebrew University of Jerusalem.

Gutman, Israel [Yisrael] (1989). Polish Antisemitism Between the Wars: An Overview. In Gutman, Israel [Yisrael], et al. (Eds.), *The Jews of Poland between Two World Wars.* Hanover, NH: University Press of New England.

Guttman, Israel [Yisrael] (Ed.). (1990). *Encyclopedia of the Holocaust.* 4 vols. New York: Macmillan Publishing Co.

Gutman, Israel [Yisrael], & Berenbaum, Michael (Eds.) (1994). *Anatomy of the Auschwitz Death Camp.* Bloomington: Indiana University Press and Washington, DC: United States Holocaust Memorial Museum.

Haberman, Clyde (1987). Japanese Writers Critical of Jews. *The New York Times,* March 12, p. A13.

Hahn, Julius (1922). *Die Judenfrage.* Hamburg: Agentur des rauhen Hauses. [German].

Halkin, Hillel (2002). The Return of Anti-Semitism: To Be Against Israel Is to Be Against the Jews. *The Wall Street Journal's Opinion Journal,* February 5. Expanded Version in *Commentary,* vol. 113, No. 2.

Haller, M. (1963). *Eugenics: Hereditarian Attitudes in American Thought.* New Brunswick, NJ: Rutgers University Press.

Halliwell, Leslie (1989). *Halliwell's Film Guide.* 7th edition. New York: Harper & Row.

Hamburger Institut Für Sozialforschung (Ed.). (1987). *Die Auschwitz-Hefte: Texte der polnischen Zeitschrift "Przeglad Lekarski" über historische, psychische und medizinische Aspekte des Lebens und Sterbens in Auschwitz.* 2 vols. Tr. Jochen August et al. Weinheim: Beltz. [German].

Hanada, Kazuyoshi (1995). Editor's Note. *Marco Polo,* February. [Japanese].

Hanson, John (1984). Nazi Culture: The Social Uses of Fantasy as Repression. In Luel, Steven A., & Marcus, Paul (Eds.), *Psychoanalytic Reflections on the Holocaust: Selected Essays.* Denver, CO: Holocaust Awareness Institute, Center for Judaic Studies, University of Denver. New York: Ktav Publishing House.

Hardtmann, Gertrud (1995). Die "jüdische Mathematik": psychoanalytische Beobachtungen. In Benz, Wolfgang (Ed.), *Antisemitismus in Deutschland: zur Aktualität eines Vorurteils,* pp. 181–193. Munich: Deutscher Taschenbuch Verlag.

Hardtmann, Gertrud (2001). A Collective Psychosis? Interview with Mathilde Ter Heijne. *For a Better World,* vol. 10, no. 3 (October 13).

Hardtmann, Gertrud (Ed.). (1992). *Spuren der Verfolgung: seelische Auswirkungen des Holocaust auf die Opfer und ihre Kinder.* Gerlingen: Bleicher. [German].

Harel, Isser (1975). *The House on Garibaldi Street: The Capture of Adolf Eichmann.* London: Andre Deutsch. New York: Viking Press. New edition (1997). Ed. & Intro. by Shlomo J. Shpiro. London and Portland, OR: Frank Cass.

Harrowitz, Nancy A. (Ed.). (1994). *Tainted Greatness: Antisemitism and Cultural Heroes.* Philadelphia: Temple University Press.

Hart, Mitchell Bryan (2000). *Social Science and the Politics of Modern Jewish Identity.* Stanford, CA: Stanford University Press.

Hart, Mitchell Bryan (2005). Jews, Race, and Capitalism in the German-Jewish Context. *Jewish History,* vol. 19, no. 1, pp. 49–63.

Hart, Mitchell Bryan (2007). *The Healthy Jew: The Symbiosis of Judaism and Modern Medicine.* New York: Cambridge University Press.

Hartman, Geoffrey H. (2002). *The Longest Shadow: In the Aftermath of the Holocaust.* New York: Palgrave Macmillan.

Hartman, Geoffrey H. (Ed.). (1986). *Bitburg in Moral and Political Perspective.* Bloomington: Indiana University Press.

Hassan, Nasra (2001). Letter from Gaza: An Arsenal of Believers. Talking to the "Human Bombs." *The New Yorker,* November 19, pp. 36–41.

Hay, Malcolm (1950). *The Roots of Christian Antisemitism.* New York: B'nai B'rith Anti-Defamation League.

Hazan, Barbara (1990). Nettoyage. In Hazan, Barbara et al., *Shoah, le film: des psychanalystes écrivent* pp. 13–19. Paris: Jacques Grancher. [French].

Hazan, Barbara, et al. (1990). *Shoah, le film: des psychanalystes écrivent.* Paris: Jacques Grancher. [French].

Head, Thomas, & Landes, Richard Allen (Eds.). (1992). *The Peace of God: Social Violence and Religious Response in France Around the Year 1000.* Ithaca, NY: Cornell University Press.

Heggy, Tarek Ahmad (1991). *Egyptian Political Essays.* Cairo: Dar al-Shorouk.

Heine, Heinrich (1840). *Der Rabbi von Bacherach.* In Heine, Heinrich (1834–1840), *Der Salon,* Vol. 4. Lithographies by Max Liebermann. Hamburg: Hoffmann und Campe. New edition (1923). Berlin: Propyläen-Verlag. [German].

Heinsohn, Gunnar (1988). *Was ist Antisemitismus? der Ursprung von Monotheismus und Judenhass. warum Antizionismus?* Frankfurt am Main: Scarabäus Bei Eichborn. [German].

Heinsohn, Gunnar (1995). *Warum Auschwitz? Hitlers Plan und die Ratlosigkeit der Nachwelt.* Reinbek Bei Hamburg: Rowohlt. [German].

Heinsohn, Gunnar (1998). *Why Was the Holocaust Different from All Other Genocides?* Bremen: Uni-Druck.

Hellig, Jocelyn (2003). *The Holocaust and Anti-Semitism: A Short History.* Oxford: Oneworld Publications.

Henseler, Heinz, & Kuchenbuch, Albrecht (Eds.). (1982). *Die Wiederekehr von Krieg und Verfolgung in Psychoanalysen.* Ulm and Berlin: DPV. [German].

Herder, Johann Gottfried von (1784). *Ideen zur Philosophie der Geschichte der Menschheit.* Riga and Leipzig: J. F. Hartknoch. Reprinted in Herder, Johann Gottfried von (1877–1913), *Herder's Sämmtliche Werke.* Ed. Bernhard Suphan. 33 vols. Berlin: Weidmann. [German].

Herder, Johann Gottfried von (1968). *Reflections on the Philosophy of the History of Mankind.* Abridged & Intro. by Frank E. Manuel. Chicago: University of Chicago Press.

Hermann, Imre (1945). *Az Antiszemitizmus Lélektana.* Budapest: Bibliotheca. Reprinted (1990). Budapest: Cserépfalvi. [Hungarian].

Hermann, Imre (1972). *L'instinct filial.* Intro. by Nicolas Abraham. Tr. Georges Kassai. Paris: Denoël. [French].

Hermann, Imre (1986). *Psychologie de l'antisémitisme,* suivi de *La Préférence pour les marges en tant que processus primaire.* Tr. Georges Gachnochi, Georges Kassai, & Gyongyver Judith Gachnochi-Tattay. Paris: Editions De L'eclat. [French].

Herrnstein, Richard J., & Murray, Charles (1994). *The Bell Curve: Intelligence and Class Structure in American Life.* New York: The Free Press. Reprinted (1996). New York: Simon & Schuster.

Hertzberg, Arthur (1968). *The French Enlightenment and the Jews.* New York: Columbia University Press.

Hertzberg, Arthur (1989). *The Jews in America.* New York: Simon and Schuster.

Hertzberg, Arthur (1993). Is Antisemitism Dying Out? *New York Review of Books,* June 24.

Herzog, Herta (1994). The Jews as "Others": On Communicative Aspects of Antisemitism. *Analysis of Current Trends in Antisemitism,* no. 4. Jerusalem: The Vidal Sassoon International Center for the Study of Antisemitism, The Hebrew University of Jerusalem.

Hess, Moses (1862). *Rom und Jerusalem.* Leipzig: Eduard Wengler. New edition (1919). *Rom und Jerusalem: Die letzte Nationalitätsfrage.* Intro. by Hugo Bergmann. Vienna and Berlin: Verlag Richard Löwit. New edition (1935). Vienna and Jerusalem: Verlag Richard Löwit. Tel Aviv: Hozaah Ivrith. New edition (1939). Ed. Theodor Zlocisti. Tel Aviv: Hitachduth Olej Germania weOlej Austria. Reprinted (1969). In Heil, Helmut J. (Ed.), *Die neuen Propheten.* Fürth and Erlangen: Ner-Tamid-Verlag. [German].

Hess, Moses (1918). *Rome and Jerusalem: A Study in Jewish Nationalism.* Tr. Meyer Waxman. New York, Bloch Publishing Company. New edition (1958). *Rome and Jerusalem.* Tr. Maurice J. Bloom. New York: Philosophical Library. New edition (1995). *The Revival of Israel: Rome and Jerusalem, the Last Nationalist Question.* Tr. Meyer Waxman. Ed. Melvin I. Urofsky. Lincoln: University of Nebraska Press.

Hiden, John, & Farquharson, John (1983). *Explaining Hitler's Germany: Historians and the Third Reich.* Totowa, NJ: Barnes & Noble. 2nd edition (1989). London: Batsford Academic and Educational.

Higham, John (1975). *Send These to Me: Jews and Other Immigrants in Urban America.* New York: Atheneum.

Hilberg, Raoul (1961). *The Destruction of the European Jews.* Chicago: Quadrangle Books. New edition (1978). With a New Postscript by the Author. New York: Octagon Books. New edition (1985). 3 vols: New York: Holmes & Meier. 3rd edition (2003). 3 vols. New Haven, CT: Yale University Press.

Himmelfarb, S. (1966). Studies in the Perception of Ethnic Group Members. I. Accuracy, Response Bias, and Anti-Semitism. *Journal of Personality and Social Psychology,* vol. 4, no. 4, pp. 347–355.

Hirschfeld, Magnus (1938). *Racism.* Tr. & Ed. Eden and Cedar Paul. London: Victor Gollancz. Reprinted (1973). Port Washington, NY: Kennikat Press.

Hitchens, Christopher (2002). *Why Orwell Matters.* New York: Basic Books.

Hitler, Adolf (1925–1927). *Mein Kampf.* 2 vols. Munich: Franz Eher Nachfolger. [German].

Hitler, Adolf (1939). *Mein Kampf: The First Complete and Unexpurgated Edition Published in the English Language.* New York: Stackpole Sons. New edition (1969). Intro. by D.C. Watt, Tr. Ralph Mannheim. London: Hutchinson.

Hochheimer, Wolfgang (1962). Vorurteilsminderung in der Erziehung und die Prophylaxe des Antisemitismus. *Psyche: Zeitschrift für Psychoanalyse und ihre Anwendungen,* vol. 16, pp. 285–311. [German].

Hockenos, Paul (1993). Anti-Semitism Without Jews. In Hockenos, Paul, *Free to Hate: The Rise of the Right in Post-communist Europe.* New York: Routledge.

Hoffmann, Christhard, et al. (Eds.). (2002). *Exclusionary Violence: Antisemitic Riots in Modern German History.* Ann Arbor: University of Michigan Press.

Holden, Anthony (1999). *William Shakespeare: The Man Behind the Genius.* Boston, New York, and London: Little, Brown.

Holmes, Colin (1979). *Anti-Semitism in British Society, 1876–1939.* London: Edward Arnold. New York: Holmes & Meier.

Honneth, Alex (1987). Ohnmächtige Selbstbehauptung: Sartres Weg zu einer intersubjektivistischen Freiheitslehre. *Babylon: Beiträge zur jüdischen Gegenwart,* no. 2 (July), pp. 82–88. [German].

Hopkins, Linda B. (1998). D.W. Winnicott's Analysis of Masud Khan: A Preliminary Study of Failures of Object Usage. *Contemporary Psychoanalysis,* vol. 34, pp. 5–47.

Hopkins, Linda B. (2001a). Letter to the Editor on Godley's "Saving Masud Khan." *London Review of Books,* vol. 23, no. 6 (March 22).

Hopkins, Linda B. (2001b). Masud Khan's Descent into Alcoholism. In Petrucelli, Jean, & Stuart, Catherine (Eds.), *Hungers and Compulsions: The Psychodynamic Treatment of Eating Disorders and Addictions* pp. 319–346. Northvale, NJ: Jason Aronson.

Hopkins, Linda B. (2004). How Masud Khan Fell into Psychoanalysis. *American Imago,* vol. 61, no. 4, pp. 483–494.

Hopkins, Linda B. (2006). *False Self: The Life of Masud Khan.* New York: Other Press.

Hoppe, K.D. (1964). Verfolgung und Gewissen. *Psyche: Zeitschrift für Psychoanalyse und ihre Anwendungen,* vol. 18, pp. 305–313. [German].

Hoppe, K.D. (1965). Psychotherapie bei Konzentrationslageropfern. *Psyche: Zeitschrift für Psychoanalyse und ihre Anwendungen,* vol. 19, pp. 209–319.

Horkheimer, Max (1939). Die Juden und Europa. *Studies in Philosophy and Social Science,* vol. 8, pp. 115–137. [German].

Horkheimer, Max (1946). Sociological Background of the Psychoanalytic Approach. In Simmel, Ernst (Ed.). *Anti-Semitism. A Social Disease,* pp. 1–10. New York: International Universities Press.

Horkheimer, Max (1985a). Akademisches Studium. In Horheimer, Max (1985–1996), *Gesammelte Schriften,* 19 vols., vol. 8, pp. 381–390. Frankfurt am Main: S. Fischer Verlag. [German].

Horkheimer, Max (1985). Zur Psychologie des Antisemitismus. In Horheimer, Max (1985–1996), *Gesammelte Schriften,* 19 vols., vol. 12, Nachgelassene Schriften, pp. 173–183. Frankfurt am Main: S. Fischer. [German].

Horkheimer, Max (1989). The Jews and Europe. In Bronner, Stephen Eric, & Kellner, Douglas Mackay (Eds.). *Critical Theory and Society: A Reader,* pp. 77–94. London and New York: Routledge.

Horkheimer, Max, & Adorno, Theodor Wiesengrund (1944). Elemente des Antisemitismus: Grenzen der Aufklärung. In Horkheimer & Adorno's *Philosophische Fragmente.* New York: Social Studies Association. Reprinted (1947) in Horkheimer & Adorno's *Dialektik der Aufklärung: philosophische Fragmente.* Amsterdam: Querido-Verlag. Reprinted (1969) Frankfurt am Main: S. Fischer. Reprinted (1985) in Horheimer, Max (1985–1996), *Gesammelte Schriften,* 19 vols. Frankfurt am Main: S. Fischer. Reprinted (2006) in Horkheimer & Adorno's *Dialektik der Aufklärung: philosophische Fragmente,* 16th edition (2006). Frankfurt am Main: S. Fischer. [German].

Horkheimer, Max, & Adorno, Theodor Wiesengrund (1972). Elements of Anti-Semitism: Limits of Enlightenment. In Horkheimer & Adorno's *Dialectic of Enlightenment: Philosophical Fragments.* Tr. John Cumming. New York: Herder and Herder. Reprinted (1973). London: Allen Lane. Reprinted (1990). New York: Continuum.

Reprinted (1997). London: Blackwell Verso. New edition (2002). Ed. Gunzelin Schmid Noerr. Tr. Edmund Jephcott. Stanford, CA: Stanford University Press.

Horkheimer, Max, et al. (1936). *Studien über Autorität und Familie: Forschungsberichte aus dem Institut für Sozialforschung.* Paris: F. Alcan. [German].

Horwitz, Gordon J. (1990). *In the Shadow of Death: Living Outside the Gates of Mauthausen.* New York: The Free Press and Maxwell Macmillan International.

Houdebine-Gravaud, Anne-Marie (1990). L'écriture *Shoah.* In Hazan, Barbara et al. (1990). *Shoah, le film: des psychanalystes écrivent,* pp. 83–150. Paris: Jacques Grancher. [French].

Howe, Irving (1976). *The World of Our Fathers.* New York: Harcourt Brace Jovanovich.

Howe, Irving (1978). The East European Jews and American Culture. In Rosen, G. (Ed.). *Jewish Life in America.* New York: Institute of Human Relations Press of the American Jewish Committee.

Howe, Irving (1986). Writing and the Holocaust. *The New Republic,* October 27. Reprinted (1991). In Howe, Irving, *Selected Writings, 1950–1990* pp. 424–445. New York: Harcourt Brace Jovanovich.

Hsia, Ronnie Po-chia (1988). *The Myth of Ritual Murder, Jews and Magic in Reformation Germany.* New Haven, CT: Yale University Press.

Hsia, Ronnie Po-chia (1992). *Trent 1475: Stories of a Ritual Murder Trial.* New Haven, CT: Yale University Press in cooperation with Yeshiva University Library.

Hughes, Judith M. (1977). Toward a Psychological Drama of High Politics: The Case of Bismarck. *Central European History,* vol. 10, no. 4, pp. 271–285.

Hughes, Judith M. (1983). *Emotion and High Politics: Personal Relations at the Summit in Late Nineteenth-century Britain and Germany.* Berkeley: University of California Press.

Hughes, Richard Thomas (2003). *Myths America Lives By.* Foreword by Robert N. Bellah. Urbana: University of Illinois Press.

Hünichen, Liesel (1999). *Hitlers willige Vollstrecker?* Hamburg: Jahn & Ernst. [German].

Hussein, Mahmoud [Bahgat Elnadi & Adel Rifaat] (1969). *La Lutte de classes en Egypte de 1945 à 1968.* Paris: François Maspero. 2nd edition (1971). *La Lutte Des Classes En Egypte De 1945 À 1970.* Paris: François Maspero. New edition (1975). *L'Égypte: lutte de classes et libération nationale.* 2 vols. Paris: François Maspero. [French].

Hussein, Mahmoud [Bahgat Elnadi & Adel Rifaat] (1973). *Class Conflict in Egypt, 1945–1970.* Tr. Michel Chirman et al. New York: Monthly Review Press.

Hussein, Mahmoud [Bahgat Elnadi & Adel Rifaat] (2005). *Al-sîra: le prophète de l'Islam raconté par ses compagnons.* Paris: Grasset. [French].

Hussein, Mahmoud [Bahgat Elnadi & Adel Rifaat], Friedlälnder, Saul, & Lacouture, Jean (1974). *Arabes et Israéliens: un premier dialogue.* Paris: Editions du Seuil. [French].

Ichheiser, Gustav (1944). Fear of Violence and Fear of Fraud: With Some Remarks on the Social Psychology of Antisemitism. *Sociometry,* vol. 7, no. 4 (November), pp. 376–383.

Iganski, Paul, & Kosmin, Barry (2003). Globalized Judeophobia and Its Ramifications for British Society. In Iganski, Paul, & Kosmin, Barry (Eds.). *The New Antisemitism? Debating Judeophobia in 21st-Century Britain.* London: Institute for Jewish Policy Research.

Iganski, Paul, & Kosmin, Barry (Eds.). (2003). *The New Antisemitism? Debating Judeo-phobia in 21st-Century Britain.* London: Institute for Jewish Policy Research.

Igounet, Valérie (2000). *Histoire du négationnisme en France.* Paris: Editions du Seuil. [French].

Imbleau, Martin (2005). Der Stürmer. In Shelton, Dinah L. (Ed.), *Encyclopedia of Genocide and Crimes Against Humanity,* vol. 1, pp. 247–249. Detroit, MI: Macmillan Reference Books.

Irving, David John Cawdell (1977). *Hitler's War.* New York: Viking Press.

Isaac, Jules (1956). *Genèse de l'antisémitisme: essai historique.* Paris: Calmann-Lévy. New edition (1985). Paris: Calmann-Lévy. Reprinted (1998). Paris: Editions 10/18. [French].

Isaac, Jules (1964). *The Teaching of Contempt: Christian Roots of Anti-Semitism.* New York: Holt, Rinehart & Winston.

Isaac, Jules (1971). *Jesus and Israel.* New York: Holt, Rinehart & Winston.

ISIS-Meinungsprofile (1988). Antisemitismus in Österreich und Westdeutschland 1987. *Journal für Sozialforschung,* vol. 28, no. 1. [German].

Isser, Natalie (1991). *Antisemitism During the French Second Empire.* New York: Peter Lang.

Jacobs, Mike (1997). On Holocaust Denial and Japanese Judges. *The Jerusalem Post,* September 23, p. 6.

Jacoby, Russell, & Glauberman, Naomi (Eds.). (1995). *The Bell Curve Debate: History, Documents, Opinions.* New York: Times Books.

Jäger, Herbert (1967). *Verbrechen unter totalitärer Herrschaft.* Olten, Freiburg: Walter-Verlag. [German].

Jaher, Frederic Cople (1994). *A Scapegoat in the New Wilderness: The Origins and Rise of Anti-Semitism in America.* Cambridge, MA: Harvard University Press.

Jahoda, Marie Lazarsfeld (1947). An Approach to the Study of Prejudice. *Man,* vol. 47.

Janik, Allan (1987). Viennese Culture and the Jewish Self-Hatred Hypothesis: A Critique. In Oxaal, Ivar, et al. (Eds.), *Jews, Antisemitism, and Culture in Vienna.* London and New York: Routledge & Kegan Paul.

Janik, Allan (2001). *Wittgenstein's Vienna Revisited.* New Brunswick, NJ: Transaction Publishers.

Janik, Allan, & Toulmin, Stephen (1973) *Wittgenstein's Vienna.* New York: Simon and Schuster. London: Weidenfeld and Nicolson. Reprinted (1996) Chicago: Ivan R. Dee.

Jappe, Gemma (2002). Influence of External Reality on the Analytic Process. Panel: Psychoanalysis and Psychoanalysts in Germany after the Shoah. Introduction to the Panel. *European Psychoanalytic Federation Bulletin,* no. 56.

Jaspers, Karl (1946). *Die Schuldfrage, rin Beitrag zur deutschen Frage.* Zurich: Artemis-Verlag. New edition (1979). *Die Schuldfrage: für Völkermord gibt es keine Verjährung.* Munich: Piper Verlag. [German].

Jaspers, Karl (1947). *The Question of German Guilt.* Tr. E.B. Ashton. New York: Dial Press. New edition (1961). New York: Capricorn Books. New edition (1978). Westport, CT: Greenwood Press. New edition (2000). With a new introduction by Joseph W. Koterski. New York: Fordham University Press.

Jay, Martin (1974). Anti-Semitism and the Weimar Left. *Midstream,* vol. 20, no. 1. Reprinted (1985). In Jay, Martin, *Permanent Exiles: Essays on the Intellectual Migration from Germany to America,* pp. 79–89. New York: Columbia University Press.

Jay, Martin (1980). The Jews and the Frankfurt School: Critical Theory's Analysis of Anti-semitism. *New German Critique,* vol. 19. Reprinted (1985). In Jay, Martin, *Permanent Exiles: Essays on the Intellectual Migration from Germany to America,* pp. 90–100. New York: Columbia University Press. Reprinted (1986). In Rabinbach, Anson, & Zipes, Jack David (Eds.), *Germans and Jews Since the Holocaust: the Changing Situation in West Germany,* pp. 287–301. New York: Holmes and Meier.

Jesse, Eckehard, & Löw, Konrad (Eds.). (1997). *Vergangenheitsbewältigung.* Berlin: Duncker & Humblot. [German].

Jewish Theological Seminary of America (1995). *The Jew as Other: A Century of English Caricature, 1730–1830.* An Exhibition, April 6 to July 31, 1995. New York: The Library of the Jewish Theological Seminary of America.

Joffe, Josef (2004). The Demons of Europe. *Commentary,* vol. 117, no. 1.

Joffe, Josef (2005). Nations We Love to Hate: Israel, America and the New Antisemitism. In *Posen Papers in Contemporary Antisemitism,* no. 1. Jerusalem: The Vidal Sassoon International Center for the Study of Antisemitism (SICSA), the Hebrew University of Jerusalem.

Johnson, Douglas W. J. (1966). *France and the Dreyfus Affair.* London: Blandford. Reprinted (1967). New York: Walker.

Johnson, Paul (1987). *A History of the Jews.* London: Weidenfeld & Nicolson.

Johnson, Paul (2005). The Anti-Semitic Disease. *Commentary,* vol. 118, no. 6.

Joly, Maurice (1864). *Dialogue aux enfers entre Machiavel et Montesquieu, ou la Politique de Machiavel au xix. siècle, par un contemporain.* Brussels: Imprimerie de A. Mertens et Fils. [French].

Joly, Maurice (2002). *The Dialogue in Hell Between Machiavelli and Montesquieu.* Tr. & Ed. John S. Waggoner. Lanham, MD: Lexington Books.

Jones, Ernest (1951). The Psychology of the Jewish Question. In Jones, Ernest, *Essays in Applied Psycho-analysis,* vol. 1. London: The Hogarth Press.

Joos, Jean-Ernest (1993). La Haine antisémite: la loi de la haine, la haine de la loi. *Les Temps Modernes,* no. 559, pp. 45–58. [French].

Juergensmeyer, Mark (2000). *Terror in the Mind of God: The Global Rise of Religious Violence.* Berkeley: University of California Press.

Jülich, Dierk (1994). Abspaltung und Projektion: Zur Psychodynamik Antisemitischer Strukturen. In Schreier, Helmut, & Heyl, Matthias (Eds.), *Die Gegenwart der Schoah: zur Aktualität des Mordes an den Europäischen Juden,* pp. 175–194. Hamburg: Krämer. [German].

Julius, Anthony (1995). *T. S. Eliot: Anti-Semitism and Literary Form.* Cambridge and New York: Cambridge University Press. New edition (2003). With a Preface and a Response to the Critics. New York: Thames & Hudson.

Jung, Carl Gustav (1934). Zur gegenwärtigen Lage der Psychotherapie. *Zentralblatt für Psychotherapie und Ihre Grenzgebiete einschliesslich der medizinischen Psychologie und psychischen Hygiene,* vol. 7, pp. 1–16. Reprinted (1974). In Jung, Carl Gustav (1958–1994), *Gesammelte Werke,* Ed. Lilly Jung-Merker et al., vol. 10, *Zivilisation im Übergang.* Zürich and Stuttgrat: Rascher. Reprinted (1994). Solothurn and Düsseldorf: Walter-Verlag. [German].

Jung, Carl Gustav (1970). The State of Psychotherapy Today. In Jung, Carl Gustav (1953–1992), *The Collected Works of C. G. Jung.* 2nd edition. Vol. 10, *Civilization in Transition.* Tr. R. F. C. Hull. Eds. Herbert Read et al. New York: Pantheon Books. Princeton, NJ: Princeton University Press. Bollingen Press.

Kahane, David (1991). *Lvov Ghetto Diary.* Amherst: University of Massachusetts Press.

Kalecinska-Adamczyk, Ewa (1995). Religion and Anitsemitism: the Influences of the Social Approval of Prejudices on the Tendency to Manifest Them in Behavior. *Polish Psychological Bulletin,* vol. 26, pp. 157–160.

Kamenetsky, Christa (1984). *Children's Literature in Hitler's Germany: The Cultural Policy of National Socialism.* Athens: Ohio University Press.

Kaminer, Isidor Jehuda (1996). *Psychiatrie im Nationalsozialismus: das Philippshospital in Riedstadt (Hessen).* Frankfurt: Mabuse-Verlag. [German].

Kaminer, Isidor Jehuda (1997). Normalität und Nationalsozialismus. *Psyche: Zeitschrift für Psychoanalyse und ihre Anwendungen,* vol. 51, pp. 385–409. [German].

Kann, Jacobus Henricus (1910). *Erets Israël: Le Pays Juif.* Brussels: Librairie Falk Fils. [French].

Kaplan, Alice Yaeger (2000). *The Collaborator: The Trial & Execution of Robert Brasillach.* Chicago: University of Chicago Press.

Kaplan, Donald M. (1987). Review of Norbert Bromberg & Verna Volz Small's *Hitler's Psychopathology,* New York: International Universities Press, 1983. *Journal of the American Psychoanalytic Association,* vol. 35, pp. 759–761.

Kaplan, Leslie (1990). Shoah—une scène pour la parole. In Hazan, Barbara et al. (1990). *Shoah, le film: des psychanalystes écrivent,* pp. 151–154. Paris: Jacques Grancher. [French].

Karp, A. P. (1989). *Haven and Home: A History of the Jews in America.* New York: Schocken Books.

Katz, Daniel, & Braly, Kenneth W. (1933). Racial Stereotypes in One Hundred College Students. *Journal of Abnormal and Social Psychology,* vol. 28, pp. 280–290.

Katz, David (1994). *The Jews in the History of England, 1485–1850.* Oxford: The Clarendon Press. New York: Oxford University Press.

Katz, Jacob (1978). *Out of the Ghetto.* New York: Schocken Books.

Katz, Jacob (1980) *From Prejudice to Destruction: Anti-Semitism 1700 to 1933.* Cambridge, MA: Harvard University Press.

Katz, Jacob (1983). Misreadings of Anti-Semitism. *Commentary,* vol. 76, no. 1, pp. 39–44.

Katz, Jacob (1984). Lectures défectueuses de l'antisémitisme. *Sens,* vol. 36, no. 5–6, pp. 203–214. [French].

Katz, Jacob (1986). *The Darker Side of Genius: Richard Wagner's Anti-Semitism.* Hanover, NH: University Press of New England for Brandeis University Press.

Katz, Phyllis A. (Ed.). (1976). *Towards the Elimination of Racism.* New York: Pergamon Press.

Katz, Steven T. (1981). The "Unique" Intentionality of the Holocaust. *Modern Judaism,* vol. 1, no. 2, pp. 161–183. Reprinted (1996) in Rosenbaum, Alan S. (Ed.), *Is the Holocaust Unique? Perspectives on Comparative Genocide.* With a foreword by Israel W. Charny. Boulder, CO: Westview Press.

Katz, Steven T. (1992). *Historicism, the Holocaust, and Zionism: Critical Studies in Modern Jewish Thought and History.* New York: New York University Press.

Katz, Steven T. (1994). *The Holocaust in Historical Context.* Vol. 1: *The Holocaust and Mass Death before the Modern Age.* New York: Oxford University Press.

Katz, Steven T. (Ed.). (2005). *The Impact of the Holocaust on Jewish Theology.* New York: New York University Press.

Katz, Steven T. et al. (Ed.). (2006) *Wrestling with God: Jewish Responses During and After the Holocaust.* New York: Oxford University Press.

Kauders, Anthony (1996). *German Politics and the Jews: Düsseldorf and Nuremberg, 1910–1933.* Oxford: Oxford University Press.

Kautz, Fred (1998). *Goldhagen und die "hürnen Sewfriedte": die Holocaust-forschung in Sperrfeuer der Flakhelfer.* Berlin and Hamburg: Argument-Verlag. 2nd, expanded edition (2002). *Die Holocaust-Forschung im Sperrfeuer der Flakhelfer: vom befangenen Blick deutscher Historiker aus der Kriegsgeneration.* 2nd, expanded edition. Berlin and Hamburg: Argument-Verlag. [German].

Kautz, Fred (2003). *The German Historians:* Hitler's Willing Executioners *and Daniel Goldhagen.* Montreal: Black Rose Books.

Kautz, Fred (2004). *Im Glashaus der Zeitgeschichte: von der Suche der Deutschen nach einer passenderen Vergangenheit.* Berlin and Hamburg: Argument-Verlag. [German].

Kedward, Harry Roderick (1985). *Occupied France: Collaboration and Resistance, 1940–1944.* Oxford and New York: Basil Blackwell.

Keilson, Hans (1988). Linker Antisemitismus? *Psyche: Zeitschrift für Psychoanalyse und ihre Anwendungen,* vol. 42, no. 9, pp. 769–794. [German].

Keimowitz, Hazel Kahn, & Mieder, Wolfgang (Eds.). (1995). *The Jewish Experience of European Anti-Semitism: Harry H. Kahn Memorial Lectures (1990–1994).* Burlington, VT: Center for Holocaust Studies, University of Vermont.

Kellenbach, Katharina von (1994).*Anti-Judaism in Feminist Religious Writings.* Atlanta, GA: Scholars Press.

Kenny, Michael G. (2002). Toward a Racial Abyss: Eugenics, Wickliffe Draper, and the Origins of the Pioneer Fund. *Journal of History of the Behavioral Sciences,* vol. 38, no. 3, pp. 259–283.

Kershaw, Ian (1981). The Persecution of the Jews and German Popular Opinion in the Third Reich. *Leo Baeck Institute Year Book XXVI,* pp. 261–289. London: Leo Baeck Institute.

Kershaw, Ian (1987). *The "Hitler Myth": Image and Reality in the Third Reich.* Oxford: The Clarendon Press. New York: Oxford University Press.

Kershaw, Ian (1991). *Hitler.* London and New York: Longman. New edition (1999–2000). 2 vols. New York: W. W. Norton. Reprint of 1st edition (2000). Harlow: Longman. Reprint of 2nd edition (2001). New York: Longman.

Kershaw, Ian (2001). Trauma der Deutschen. *Spiegel Spezial,* no. 1, pp. 6–13. [German].

Kevles, D.J. (1985). *In the Name of Eugenics: Genetics and the Uses of Human Heredity.* New York: Knopf.

Khan, Mohammed Masud Raza (1983). The Evil Hand. In Khan's *Hidden Selves: Between Theory and Practice in Psychoanalysis.* London: The Hogarth Press.

Khan, Mohammed Masud Raza (1988). *When Spring Comes: Awakenings in Clinical Psychoanalysis.* London: Chatto & Windus. Reprinted (1989). As *The Long Wait and Other Psychoanalytic Narratives.* New York: Summit Books.

Kinastowski, W.T. (1996). *The Roles and Functions of National Myths: The Case of Poland.* Unpublished thesis, University of Waterloo.

Kingston, Paul J. (1983). *Anti-Semitism in France During the 1930s: Organisations, Personalities, and Propaganda.* Hull, England: University of Hull Press.

Kittel, Gerhard (1933). *Die Judenfrage.* Stuttgart: W. Kohlhammer. [German].

Kitzing, Wolfgang E. (1941). *Erziehung zur Gesundheit.* Berlin: ReichsgesundheitsVerlag. [German].

Klee, E., et al. (Eds.). (1988). *Judenmord aus der Sicht der Täter und Gaffer.* Frankfurt am Main: n.p. [German].

Klein, Charlotte (1978). *Anti-Judaism in Christian Theology.* Tr. Edward Quinn. Philadelphia: Fortress Press.

Klein, Dennis B. (1981). *Jewish Origins of the Psychoanalytic Movement.* New York: Praeger. New edition (1985). Chicago: University of Chicago Press.

Klein, Melanie (1948). *Contributions to Psycho-analysis, 1921–1945.* Intro. by Ernest Jones. London: The Hogarth Press.

Klein, Melanie (1957). *Envy and Gratitude: A Study of Unconscious Sources.* London: Tavistock Publications. New York: Basic Books.

Klein, Melanie (1971). *New Directions in Psycho-Analysis: The Significance of Infant Conflict in the Pattern of Adult Behaviour.* Eds. Melanie Klein, Paula Heimann & R.E. Money-Kyrle. Preface by Ernest Jones. London: Tavistock Publications.

Klemperer, Victor (1947). *LTI: Notizbuch eines Philologen.* Berlin: Aufbau-Verlag. New edition (1966). *Die unbewältigte Sprache: aus dem Notizbuch eines Philologen LTI.* Darmstadt: Melzer. New edition (1969). *LTI, Die Unbewältigte Sprache: aus dem Notizbuch eines Philologen.* Munich: Deutscher Taschenbuch-Verlag. 15th edition (1996). *LTI: Notizbuch eines Philologen.* Leipzig: Reclam. New edition (2004). Frankfurt am Main: Büchergilde Gutenberg. [German].

Klemperer, Victor (1995). *Ich will Zeugnis ablegen bis zum Letzten.* Ed. Walter Nowojski. With the Collaboration of Hadwig Klemperer. 2 vols. Berlin: Aufbau-Verlag. [German].

Klemperer, Victor (1997). *An Annotated Edition of Victor Klemperer's LTI: Notizbuch eines Philologen.* Ed. Roderick H. Watt. Lewiston, NY: Edwin Mellen Press. [German and English].

Klemperer, Victor (1998). *I Shall Bear Witness: The Diaries of Victor Klemperer, 1933–1941.* Abridged Version. Tr. Martin Chalmers. London: Weidenfeld & Nicolson. New edition (1998–2000). *I Will Bear Witness: A Diary of the Nazi Years.* 2 vols. Vol. 1. *1933–1941.* Vol. 2. *1942–1945.* New York: Random House. New edition (1999). *I Shall Bear Witness: The Diaries of Victor Klemperer, 1933–1941.* London: Phoenix. New edition (2000). *The Diaries of Victor Klemperer, 1933–1945: I Shall Bear Witness to the Bitter End.* London: Phoenix. New edition (1999–2001). *I Will Bear Witness: A Diary of the Nazi Years.* 2 vols. New York: Modern Library. New edition (2004). *The Diaries of Victor Klemperer, 1945–1959: The Lesser Evil.* London: Phoenix.

Klemperer, Victor (2000). *The Language of the Third Reich, LTI (Lingua Tertii Imperii): A Philologist's Notebook.* Tr. Martin Brady. London and New Brunswick, NJ: Athlone Press.

Knafo, Danielle (1999). Anti-Semitism in the Clinical Setting: Transference and Countertransference Dimensions. *Journal of the American Psychoanalytic Association,* vol. 47, no. 1, pp. 35–63.

Koch, Gertrud (1987). Sartres "J'accuse": ein Gespräch mit Claude Lanzmann. *Babylon: Beiträge zur jüdischen Gegenwart*, no. 2 (July), pp. 72–79. [German].

Kochan, Lionel (1990). *Jews, Idols and Messiahs: The Challenge of History.* Oxford: Basil Blackwell.

Koenigsberg, Richard A. (1975). *Hitler's Ideology: A Study in Psychoanalytic Sociology.* New York: Library of Social Science.

Kofta, Miroslaw, & Sedek, Grzegorz (2005). Conspiracy Stereotypes of Jews During Systemic Transformation in Poland. *International Journal of Sociology*, vol. 35, pp. 40–64.

Kogon, Eugen (2006). *The Theory and Practice of Hell: The German Concentration Camps and the System Behind Them.* Rev. edition. New York: Farrar, Straus and Giroux.

Kohn, M. (1995). *The Race Gallery: The Return of Racial Science.* London: Jonathan Cape.

Konig, Ruben, et al. (2000). Explaining the Relationship Between Christian Religion and Antisemitism in the Netherlands. *Review of Religious Research*, vol. 41, pp. 373–393.

Konig, Ruben et al. (2001). Research on Antisemitism: a Review of Previous Findings and the Case of the Netherlands in the 1990s. In Phalet, Karen, & Örkény, Antal (Eds.), *Ethnic Minorities and Inter-ethnic Relations in Context: A Dutch-Hungarian Comparison.* Aldershot, England, and Burlington, VT: Ashgate Publishing.

Koonz, Claudia (1987). *Mothers in the Fatherland: Women, the Family, and Nazi Politics.* New York: St. Martin's Press.

Korn, Bertram Wallace (1973). American Judeophobia: Confederate Version. In Dinnerstein, Leonard, & Paulson, Mary Dale, *Jews in the South.* Baton Rouge: Louisiana State University Press.

Kostyrchenko, Gennadi (1995). *Out of the Red Shadows: Anti-Semitism in Stalin's Russia.* Amherst, NY: Prometheus Books.

Kotek, Joël, & Kotek, Dan (2003). *Au nom de l'antisionisme: l'image des Juifs et d'Israël dans la Caricature depuis la Seconde Intifada.* Avant-propos De Plantu. Bruxelles: Éditions Complexe. [French].

Kött, Martin (1999). *Goldhagen in der Qualitätspresse: eine Debatte über "Kollektivschuld" und "Nationalcharakter" der Deutschen.* Konstanz: Uvk Medien. [German].

Kovács, András (1999). Antisemitic Prejudices in Contemporary Hungary. *Analysis of Current Trends in Antisemitism*, no. 16. Jerusalem: The Vidal Sassoon International Center for the Study of Antisemitism, The Hebrew University of Jerusalem.

Kovel, Joel (2007). *Overcoming Zionism: Creating a Single Democratic State in Israel/Palestine.* London: Pluto Press.

Kowalski, Sergiusz, & Tulli, Magdalena (2004). La Pologne. In Gerstenfeld, Manfred, & Trigano, Shmuel (Eds.). *Les Habits neufs de l'antisémitisme en Europe.* Ile De Noirmoutier: Café Noir. [French].

Kowitz, Stephanie (2004). *Jedwabne: kollektives Gedächtnis und tabuisierte Vergangenheit.* Berlin: Bebra Wissenschaftlicher Verlag. [German].

Kowner, Rotem (1997a). The Jewish Spot on the Rising Sun: Reconsidering Current Japanese Attitudes Towards Jews. *The Australia/Israel Review*, vol. 22, no. 15, pp. 19–21.

Kowner, Rotem (1997b). On Ignorance, Respect and Suspicion: Current Japanese Attitudes Towards Jews. *Analysis of Current Trends in Antisemitism,* no. 11. Jerusalem: The Vidal Sassoon International Center for the Study of Antisemitism, The Hebrew University of Jerusalem.

Kowner, Rotem (1999). Homogeneous Society with Exceptions: Prejudice and its Ideology in Japan. In Feldman, Ofer (Ed.), *Political Psychology in Japan,* pp. 233–255. New York: Nova Science Publications.

Kowner, Rotem (2001). Tokyo Recognizes Auschwitz: The Rise and Fall of Holocaust-denial in Japan, 1989–1999. *Journal of Genocide Research,* vol. 3, no. 2, pp. 257–272.

Kowner, Rotem (2006). On Symbolic Antisemitism: Motives for the Success of the *Protocols* in Japan and Its Consequences. *Posen Papers in Contemporary Antisemitism,* no. 3. Jerusalem: The Vidal Sassoon International Center for the Study of Antisemitism, The Hebrew University of Jerusalem.

Krajewski, Stanisław (2005). *Poland and the Jews: Reflections of a Polish Polish Jew.* Kraków: Klezmerhojs. Kraków: Wydawnia Austeria.

Krapf, E. Eduardo (1951). El Judío de Shakespeare: una contribución a la psychología del anti-semitismo. *Revista De Psicoanalisis,* vol. 8. no. 2, pp. 173–202. [Spanish].

Krapf, E. Eduardo (1955). Shylock and Antonio: A Psychoanalytic Study on Shakespeare and Antisemitism. *The Psychoanalytic Review,* vol. 42, no. 2, pp. 113–130.

Krauskopf, Joseph (1901). *A Rabbi's Impressions of the Oberammergau Passion Play, Being a Series of Six Lectures, with Three Supplemental Chapters Bearing on the Subject.* Philadelphia: E. Stern & Co.

Krekovicova, Eva (1997). Jewishness in the Eyes of Others: Reflection of the Jew in Slovak Folklore. *Human Affairs,* vol. 7, pp. 167–183.

Kremer, Lillian S. (1999). *Women's Holocaust Writing: Memory and Imagination.* Lincoln: University of Nebraska Press.

Kren, George (1979). "Psychohistory and the Holocaust." *The Journal of Psychohistory,* vol. 6, no. 3, pp. 409–418.

Kren, George, & Rappoport, Leon (1977). SS Atrocities: A Psychohistorical Perspective. *The Journal of Psychohistory,* vol. 3, no. 1, pp. 130–137.

Kren, George M., & Rappoport, Leon H. (1980). *The Holocaust and the Crisis of Human Behavior.* New York: Holmes & Meier.

Kreuzer-Haustein, U., & Schmidt, G. (1996). Kritische Bemerkungen über Annemarie Dührssens Buch "Ein Jahrhundert psychoanalytische Bewegung in Deutschland." *Psyche: Zeitschrift für Psychoanalyse und ihre Anwendungen,* vol. 50, no. 6, pp. 564–573. [German].

Krigier, Rivon (1985). Antisémitisme, Christianisme ou le complex d'Oedipe. *Ori: Mensuel israélien de pensée et d'actualité juives,* no. 1, pp. 19–20. [French].

Kristeller, Paul Oskar (1993). The Alleged Ritual Murder of Simon of Trent (1475) and Its Literary Repercussions: A Bibliographical Study. *Proceedings of the American Academy for Jewish Research,* vol. 59, pp. 103–135.

Kristeva, Julia (1993). *Nations Without Nationalism.* Tr. Leon S. Roudiez. New York: Columbia University Press.

Kristeva, Julia (2001). *Hannah Arendt.* Tr. Ross Guberman. New York: Columbia University Press. New edition (2001). *Hannah Arendt: Life Is a Narrative.* Tr. Frank Collins. Toronto: University of Toronto Press.

Krummel, Miriamne Ara (2002). *Fables, Facts, and Fictions: Jewishness in the English Middle Ages.* Unpublished dissertation, Lehigh University.

Krystal, Henry (Ed.) (1968). *Massive Psychic Trauma.* New York: International Universities Press.

Krystal, Henry, & Niederland, W.G. (1968). Clinical Observations on the Survivor Syndrome. In Krystal, Henry (Ed.). *Massive Psychic Trauma,* pp. 327–348. New York: International Universities Press.

Kühl, S. (1994). *Eugenics, American Racism, and German National Socialism.* New York: Oxford University Press.

Kulka, Otto Dov & Mendes-Flohr, Paul R. (1987). *Judaism and Christianity under the Impact of National Socialism.* Jerusalem: Historical Society of Israel and Zalman Shazar Center for Jewish History.

Küntzel, Matthias (2002). *Djihad und Judenhass: über den neuen antijüdischen Krieg.* Freiburg: Ça Ira Publications. [German].

Küntzel, Matthias (2005). National Socialism and Anti-Semitism in the Arab World. *Jewish Political Studies Review,* vol. 17, nos. 1–2, pp. 99–118.

Küntzel, Matthias (2005). The Booksellers of Tehran: Every Book Fair Exhibits Bestsellers. But Anti-Semitic Bestsellers? And in Germany, of All Places? *The Wall Street Journal Online,* October 28.

Küntzel, Matthias (2007). *Jihad and Jew-Hatred: Islamism, Nazism and the Roots of 9/11.* Tr. Colin Meade. New York: Telos Press.

Kurthen, Hermann, et al. (Eds.). (1997). *Antisemitism and Xenophobia in Germany after Unification.* New York: Oxford University Press.

Kurzweil, Edith (Ed.). (2001). Psychiatry, Psychotherapy, and Psychoanalysis in the Third Reich. *The Psychoanalytic Review,* vol. 88, no. 2 (April).

Kweller, Rion B. (1985). *Anti-Semitism in the Interpersonal Context.* Unpublished dissertation, Bowling Green State University.

Lacapra, Dominick (1998). *History and Memory after Auschwitz.* Ithaca, NY: Cornell University Press.

Landes, Richard Allen (2006). *Heaven on Earth: The Varieties of the Millennial Experience.* Cambridge and New York: Cambridge University Press.

Landes, Richard Allen, et al. (Eds.). (2003). *The Apocalyptic Year 1000: Religious Expectation and Social Change, 950–1050.* Oxford and New York: Oxford University Press.

Landres, J. Shawn, & Berenbaum, Michael (Eds.) (2004). *After The Passion Is Gone: American Religious Consequences.* Walnut Creek, CA: AltaMira Press.

Lang, Berel (1996). *Heidegger's Silence.* Ithaca, NY: Cornell University Press.

Langbein, Hermann (1972). *Menschen in Auschwitz.* Vienna: Europa-Verlag. [German].

Langer, Walter Charles (1972). *The Mind of Adolf Hitler: The Secret Wartime Report.* Foreword by William L. Langer. Afterword by Robert G.L. Waite. New York: Basic Books. Reprinted (1985). New York: New American Library.

Langmuir, Gavin I. (1990). *Antisemitism.* 2 vols. Volume 1. *Toward a Definition of Antisemitism.* Vol. 2. *History, Religion, and Antisemitism.* Berkeley: University of California Press. Reprinted (1993). Berkeley: University of California Press. Reprinted (1996). Berkeley: University of California Press.

Lanzmann, Claude (1985a). *Shoah.* Préface de Simone de Beauvoir. Paris: Fayard. New edition (1986). Paris: Librairie Générale Française. New edition (1997). Paris: Gallimard. New edition (2001). Paris: Gallimard. [French].

Lanzmann, Claude (1985b). *Shoah: An Oral History of the Holocaust. The Complete Text of the Film.* Preface by Simone de Beauvoir. Tr. A. Whitelaw and W. Byron. New York: Pantheon Books. New edition (1995). *Shoah: The Complete Text of the Acclaimed Holocaust Film.* New York: Da Capo Press.

Laqueur, Walter (1965). Footnotes to the Holocaust. Review of *And the Crooked Shall Be Made Straight: The Eichmann Trial, the Jewish Catastrophe and Hannah Arendt's Narrative* by Jacob Robinson. *New York Review of Books,* vol. 5, no. 7 (April 6).

Laqueur, Walter (1966). A Reply to Hannah Arendt. In Response to "The Formidable Dr. Robinson: a Reply" in the *New York Review of Books,* January 20. *New York Review of Books,* vol. 6, no. 1 (February 3).

Laqueur, Walter (1972). *A History of Zionism.* London: Weidenfeld & Nicolson. New York: Holt, Rinehart & Winston. Reprinted (1976). New York: Schocken Books.

Latour, Anny (1981). *The Jewish Resistance in France, 1940–1944.* Tr. Irene R. Ilton. New York: Holocaust Library.

Launer, John (1992). Jews, Christians and Family Therapy. *European Judaism,* vol. 25, no. 1, pp. 24–33.

Lazard, Iu (1884). Voltaire et les Juifs. *L'Univers israélite, journal des principes conservateurs du judaïsme,* vol. 41, no. 1, p. 126. [French].

Lazare, Bernard (1894). *L'antisémitisme: son histoire et ses causes.* Paris: L. Chailley. New edition (1934). Édition définitive. Étude d'André Fontainas, Orné d'un portrait de l'auteur. 2 vols. Paris: Editions Jean Crès. New edition (1969). Paris: H.-G. Coston. New edition (1982). Paris: Editions de la Différence. New edition (1985). Paris: La Vieille Taupe. New edition (1990). Préface De Jean-Denis Bredin. Paris: Les Éditions 1900.

Lazare, Bernard (1895). *Antisémitisme et révolution.* Paris: P.-V. Stock. New edition (1898). Paris: P.-V. Stock. New edition (1970). Paris: Cercle Bernard Lazare.

Lazare, Bernard (1896). *Contre l'antisémitisme: histoire d'une polémique.* Paris: P.-V. Stock.

Lazare, Bernard (1903). *Antisemitism: Its History and Causes.* New York: International Library Publishing Co. New edition (1967). London: Britons Publishing Co. New edition (1995). Lincoln: University of Nebraska Press,

Lazare, Lucien (1996). *Rescue as Resistance: How Jewish Organizations Fought the Holocaust in France.* Tr. Jeffrey M. Green. New York: Columbia University Press.

Le Bon, Gustave (1895). *Psychologie des foules.* Paris: F. Alcan. [French].

Le Bon, Gustave (1985). *Rôle des Juifs dans la civilisation.* Paris: Amis De Gustave Le Bon. [French].

Lee, Albert (1980). *Henry Ford and the Jews.* New York: Stein and Day.

Lelyveld, Toby (1961). *Shylock on the Stage.* London: Routledge.

Léon, Abraham [Abram Leon] (1946). *La Conception matérialiste de la question Juive.* Préface et postface de E. Germain. Paris: Édition Pionniers. New edition (1968). Nouvelle édition revue et préfacée par Maxime Rodinson. Préface originale de E. Germain. Textes complémentaires [traduits] de Isaac Deutscher et Léon Trotsky. Paris: Eìtudes et documentation internationales. [French].

Léon, Abraham [Abram Leon] (1970) *The Jewish Question: A Marxist Interpretation.* New York: Pathfinder Press.

Léon, Abraham [Abram Leon] (1971). *Judenfrage unde Kapitalismus: historisch-materialistische Analyse der Rolle der Juden in der Geschichte bis zur Gründung des Staates Israel.* Munich: Trikont-Verlag. [German].

Léon, Maurice (1946). *The Case of Dr. Carl Gustav Jung, Pseudo-Scientist Nazi Auxiliary: Report to U.S. Department of State and Nuremberg Tribunal.* Unpublished document. London: Foreign Office Archives.Baltimore: The Alan Mason Chesney Medical Archives at Johns Hopkins University.

Leuschen-Seppel, Rosemarie (1987). Refugees from Nazi Germany and the Scientific Study of Antisemitism. *Simon Wiesenthal Center Annual,* vol. 4, pp. 139–174.

Levi, Primo (1966). *If This Is a Man.* Tr. Stuart Woolf. London: Bodley Head. New edition (1986). *Survival in Auschwitz* and *The Reawakening: Two Memoirs.* New York: Summit Books. New edition (1993). *Survival in Auschwitz: The Nazi Assault on Humanity.* Including "A Conversation with Primo Levi by Philip Roth." New York: Collier Books. Toronto: Maxwell Macmillan Canada.

Levin, Kenneth (2005). *The Oslo Syndrome: Delusions of a People under Siege.* Hanover, NH: Smith and Kraus.

Levine, Hillel (1991). *Economic Origins of Antisemitism: Poland and Its Jews in the Early Modern Period.* New Haven, CT: Yale University Press.

Levine, Michael P., & Patak, Tamas (Eds.). (2004). *Racism in Mind.* Ithaca, NY: Cornell University Press.

Levine, Richard A. (1968). *Benjamin Disraeli.* New York: Twayne.

Levine, Robert M. (1991). Review of Robert S. Wistrich's *Between Redemption and Perdition: Modern Antisemitism and Jewish Identity,* London, Routledge, 1990. *History Teacher,* vol. 24, no. 3, pp. 364–366.

Levinger, Lee Joseph (1925). *The Causes of Anti-Semitism in the United States: A Study in Group and Sub-group.* Philadelphia: n.p. Reprinted (1925). As *Anti-Semitism in the United States.* New York: Bloch Publishing Co. New edition (1972).*Anti-Semitism in the United States: Its History and Causes.* Westport, CT: Greenwood Press.

Levinson, Daniel J. (1950). The Study of Anti-Semitic Ideology. In Adorno, Theodore Wiesengrund, Frenkel-Brunswick, Else, Levinson, Daniel J., & Sanford, R. Nevitt *The Authoritarian Personality,* pp. 57–101. New York: Harper. New edition (1969). New York: Norton. New edition (1982). New York: Norton.

Levkov, Ilya (Ed.) (1987). *Bitburg and Beyond: Encounters in American, German, and Jewish History.* New York: Shapolsky Publishers.

Lévy, Benny, and Sartre, Jean-Paul (1984). *Le nom de l'homme: dialogue avec Sartre.* Paris: Verdier. [French].

Levy, Richard S. (1975). *The Downfall of the Anti-Semitic Political Parties in Imperial Germany.* New Haven, CT: Yale University Press.

Levy, Richard S. (2002). Continuities and Discontinuities of Anti-Jewish Violence in Modern Germany, 1819–1938. In Hoffmann, Christhard, et al. (Eds). *Exclusionary Violence: Antisemitic Riots in Modern German History.* Ann Arbor: University of Michigan Press.

Levy, Richard S. (Ed.). (1990). *Antisemitism in the Modern World: An Anthology of Texts.* Lexington, MA: D.C. Heath.

Levy, Richard S. (Ed.). (2005). *Antisemitism: A Historical Encyclopedia of Prejudice and Persecution.* 2 vols. Santa Barbara, CA: ABC-CLIO.

Lewin, Kurt (1941). Self-Hatred among Jews. *Contemporary Jewish Record,* Vol. 4, pp. 219–232. Reprinted (1948). In Lewin, Kurt, *Resolving Social Conflicts: Selected Papers on Group Dynamics.* New York: Harper & Row.

Lewis, Bernard (1976). The Anti-Zionist Resolution. *Foreign Affairs,* October.

Lewis, Bernard (1984). *The Jews of Islam.* Princeton, NJ: Princeton University Press.

Lewis, Bernard (1986). *Semites and Anti-Semites: An Inquiry into Conflict and Prejudice.* New York: W.W. Norton. New edition (1999). With a new Afterword. New York and London: W.W. Norton.

Lewis, Bernard (1993). The Enemies of God. *The New York Review of Books,* vol. 40, no. 6.

Lewis, Bernard (2002) *What Went Wrong? The Clash Between Islam and Modernity in the Middle East.* London: Weidenfeld and Nicolson. U.S. version, *What Went Wrong? Western Impact and Middle Eastern Response.* New York: Oxford University Press.

Lewy, Gunther (1965). *The Catholic Church and Nazi Germany.* New York: McGraw-Hill.

Liefmann, E. (1951). Mittelalterliche Überlieferungen und Antisemitismus. *Psyche: Zeitschrift für Psychoanalyse und ihre Anwendungen,* vol. 5, pp. 481–496. [German].

Lifton, Robert Jay (1967). *Death in Life: Survivors of Hiroshima.* New York: Basic Books.

Lifton, Robert Jay (1979). *The Broken Connection: On Death and the Continuity of Life.* New York: Simon & Schuster. New edition (1980). New York: Simon & Schuster. New edition (1996). Washington, DC: American Psychiatric Press.

Lifton, Robert Jay (1986). *The Nazi Doctors: Medical Killing and the Psychology of Genocide.* New York: Basic Books. New edition (2000). With a new Preface by the author. New York: Basic Books.

Lifton, Robert Jay, & Markusen, Eric (1990). *The Genocidal Mentality: Nazi Holocaust and Nuclear Threat.* New York: Basic Books.

Lindemann, Albert S. (1991). *The Jew Accused: Three Anti-Semitic Affairs. (Dreyfus, Beilis, Frank, 1894–1915).* Cambridge: Cambridge University Press.

Lindemann, Albert S. (1997). *Esau's Tears: Modern Anti-Semitism and the Rise of the Jews.* Cambridge and New York: Cambridge University Press.

Lindemann, Albert S. (2000). *Anti-Semitism Before the Holocaust.* Boston: Addison-Wesley. Harlow and New York: Longman.

Linze, Dewey W. (1961). *The Trial of Adolf Eichmann.* Cover art by Bill Edwards. Illus. by Monte Rogers. Los Angeles: Holloway House Publishing Co.

Lipson, S.L. (2001). *Re-imagining Grimms' Fairy Tales.* Unpublished dissertation, Pacifica Graduate Institute.

Lipstadt, Deborah E. (1993). *Denying the Holocaust: The Growing Assault on Truth and Memory.* New York: The Free Press.

Lipstadt, Deborah E. (2005).*History on Trial: My Day in Court with Holocaust Denier David Irving.* New York: Ecco Press.

Livingston, Sigmund (1944). *Must Men Hate?* New York and London: Harper & Bros.

Lockot, Regine (1985). *Erinnern und Durcharbeiten: zur Geschichte der Psychoanalyse und Psychotherapie im Nationalsozialismus.* Frankfurt am Main: Fischer Taschenbuch Verlag. [German].

Lockot, Regine (1994). *Die Reinigung der Psychoanalyse: die deutsche psychoanalytische Gesellschaft im Spiegel von Dokumenten und Zeitzeugen (1933–1951).* Tübingen: Diskord Verlag. [German].

Loeblowitz-Lennard, Henry (1945). A Psychoanalytic Contribution to the Problem of Antisemitism. *The Psychoanalytic Review,* vol. 32 (July), pp. 359–361.

Loeblowitz-Lennard, Henry (1947). The Jew as Symbol. I. the Ritual Murder Myth. *The Psychoanalytic Quarterly,* vol. 16, pp. 33–38, 123–134. II. Anti-semitism and Transference. *Psychiatric Quarterly,* vol. 21, no. 2, pp. 253–260.

Loew-Beer, Martin (1987). Der seelische Haushalt eines Antisemiten: Überlegungen zu Sartres Erzählung "Die Kindheit eines Chefs. " *Babylon: Beiträge zur jüdischen Gegenwart,* no. 2 (July), pp. 99–107. [German].

Loewenberg, Peter (1971). The Unsuccessful Adolescence of Heinrich Himmler. *American Historical Review,* vol. 76, pp. 612–641. Reprinted (1983). In Loewenberg, Peter, *Decoding the Past: The Psychohistorical Approach,* pp. 209–239. New York: Alfred A. Knopf.

Loewenberg, Peter (1972). Die Psychodynamik des Antijudentums. In Grab, Walter (Ed.). *Jahrbuch des Instituts für deutsche Geschichte,* vol. 1, pp. 145–158. [German].

Loewenberg, Peter (1979). Antisemitismus und Jüdischer Selbsthass: eine sich wechselseitig verstärkende sozialpsychologische Doppelbeziehung. *Geschichte und Gesellschaft: Zeitschrift für historische Sozialwissenschaft,* vol. 5, no. 4, pp. 455–475. [German].

Loewenberg, Peter (1983). *Decoding the Past: The Psychohistorical Approach.* New York: Alfred A. Knopf.

Loewenberg, Peter (1985). Review of Norbert Bromberg & Verna Volz Small's *Hitler's Psychopathology,* New York: International Universities Press, 1983. *International Review of Psycho-analysis,* vol. 12, pp. 483–485.

Loewenberg, Peter (1987). The *Kristallnacht* as a Public Degradation in Ritual. *Leo Baeck Institute Year Book XXXII,* pp. 308–323. London: Leo Baeck Institute. Reprinted (1989). In Marrus, Michael Robert (Ed.), *The Nazi Holocaust,* vol. 2. *The Origins of the Holocaust,* pp. 582–596. Westport, CT: Meckler Press.

Loewenberg, Peter (1992). Die Psychodynamik des Antijudaismus in historischer Perspektive. *Psyche: Zeitschrift für Psychoanalyse und ihre Anwendungen,* vol. 46, no. 12 (December), pp. 1095–1121. [German].

Loewenberg, Peter (1995a). The Creation of a Scientific Community: The Burghölzli, 1902–1914. In Loewenberg, Peter, *Fantasy and Reality in History,* pp. 46–89. New York and Oxford: Oxford University Press.

Loewenberg, Peter (1995b). Racism in Comparative Historical Perspective. In Loewenberg, Peter, *Fantasy and Reality in History,* pp. 172–191. New York and Oxford: Oxford University Press.

Loewenstein, Rudolph Maurice (1947). The Historical and Cultural Roots of Anti-Semitism. *Psychoanalysis and the Social Sciences,* vol. 1, pp. 313–356.

Loewenstein, Rudolph Maurice (1951). *Christians and Jews: A Psychoanalytic Study.* Tr. Vera Damman. New York: International Universities Press.

Loewenstein, Rudolph Maurice (1952). *Psychanalyse de l'antisémitisme.* Paris: Presses Universitaires de France. New edition (2001). Préface De Nicolas Weill. Paris: Presses Universitaires de France. [French].

Loewenstein, Rudolph Maurice (1987). Anti-Semites in Psychoanalysis. In Bergmann, Werner (Ed.), *Error Without Trial: Psychological Research on Antisemitism.* Berlin and New York: Walter De Gruyter.

Lohmann, Hans-Martin (Ed.). (1984). *Psychoanalyse und Nationalsozialismus: Beiträge zur Bearbeitung eines unbewältigten Traumas.* Frankfurt: Fischer Taschenbuch Verlag.

Long, Emil J. (1953). *2,000 Years: A History of Anti-Semitism.* New York: Exposition Press.

Lord, Amnon (2002). Who Killed Muhammad Al-Dura? Blood Libel—Model 2000. *Jerusalem Letter/Viewpoints,* no. 482, July 15.

Lottman, Herbert R. (1986). *The Purge.* New York: William Morrow.

Lotto, David (2001). Freud's Struggle with Misogyny, Homosexuality, Guilt, in Irma's Dream. *Journal of the American Psychoanalytic Association,* vol. 49, pp. 1289–1314.

Louvish, Simon (2005). *The Question of Zion,* by Jacqueline Rose: How Words Went to War. *The Independent,* June 10.

Lowenstein, Steven M. (1994). *The Jewishness of David Friedländer and the Crisis of Berlin Jewry.* Ramat-Gan, Israel: Bar-Ilan University.

Lowenthal, Leo (1987). *False Prophets: Studies on Authoritarianism.* New Brunswick, NJ: Transaction Books.

Lowenthal, Leo, & Guterman, Norbert (1949). *Prophets of Deceit: A Study of the Techniques of the American Agitator.* New York: Harper and Brothers. New edition (1970). With a Foreword by Herbert Marcuse. Palo Alto, CA: Pacific Books. Reprinted (1987). In Lowenthal, Leo, *False Prophets: Studies on Authoritarianism.* New Brunswick, NJ: Transaction Books.

Lozowick, Yaacov (2000). *Hitlers Bürokraten: Eichmann, seine willigen Vollstrecker und die Banalität des Bösen.* Tr. Christoph Münz. Zurich: Pendo Verlag. [German].

Lozowick, Yaacov (2002). *Hitler's Bureaucrats: The Nazi Security Police and the Banality of Evil.* Tr. Haim Watzman. London and New York: Continuum.

Luel, Steven A., & Marcus, Paul (Eds.). (1984). *Psychoanalytic Reflections on the Holocaust: Selected Essays.* Denver, CO: Holocaust Awareness Institute, Center for Judaic Studies, University of Denver. New York: Ktav Publishing House.

Lukaszewski, Wieslaw (1995). The Attitude Towards Jews in Polish Psychological Studies. *Polish Psychological Bulletin,* vol. 26, pp. 97–112.

Lunn, Kenneth (1978). The Marconi Scandal and Related Aspects of British Anti-Semitism, 1911–1914. Unpublished PhD dissertation.

Luther, Martin (1523). Dass Jesus Christus ein geborener Jude sei. In Luther, Martin (1883–2002), *D. Martin Luthers Werke: Kritische Gesamtausgabe,* vol. 11 pp. 314–336. Weimar: Hermann Böhlau and Hermann Böhlaus Nachfolger. [German].

Luther, Martin (1543). Über die Juden und ihre Lügen. In Luther, Martin (1883–2002), *D. Martin Luthers Werke: Kritische Gesamtausgabe,* vol. 53 pp. 417–552. Weimar: Hermann Böhlau and Hermann Böhlaus Nachfolger. [German].

Luther, Martin (1955–1976). *Luther's Works.* 55 vols. Eds. Jaroslav Pelikan & Helmut T. Lehmann. St. Louis, MO: Concordia Publishing House. Philadelphia: Fortress Press.

Maccoby, Hyam (1983). The Greatness of Gershom Scholem. *Commentary,* vol. 76, no. 3 (September), pp. 37–46.

Maccoby, Hyam (1986). The Origins of Anti-Semitism. In Braham, Randolph L. (Ed.), *The Origins of the Holocaust: Christian Anti-Semitism.* Boulder: Social Science Monographs. New York: Institute for Holocaust Studies, City University of New York.

Maccoby, Hyam (1996). *A Pariah People: The Anthropology of Antisemitism.* London: Constable.

MacDonald, Kevin B. (1994). *A People That Shall Dwell Alone: Judaism as a Group Evolutionary Strategy.* Westport, CT: Praeger.

MacDonald, Kevin B. (1998). *Separation and Its Discontents: Toward an Evolutionary Theory of Anti-Semitism.* Westport, CT: Praeger.

Maciejewski, Franz (1994). Zur Psychoanalyse des geschichtlich Unheimlichen—das Beispiel der Sinti und Roma. *Psyche: Zeitschrift für Psychoanalyse und ihre Anwendungen,* vol. 48, pp. 30–49. [German].

Mack, John E. (1983). Nationalism and the Self. *The Psychohistory Review,* vol. 11, nos. 2–3, pp. 47–69.

Maidenbaum, Aryeh (Ed.) (2002). *Jung and the Shadow of Anti-Semitism: Collected Essays.* Berwick, ME: Nicolas-Hays.

Maidenbaum, Aryeh, & Martin, Stephen A. (Eds.) (1991). *Lingering Shadows: Jungians, Freudians, and Anti-Semitism.* Boston: Shambhala.

Mamet, David (2006). *The Wicked Son: Anti-Semitism, Self-Hatred, and the Jews.* New York: Schocken Books.

Mann, Michael (2005). *The Dark Side of Democracy: Explaining Ethnic Cleansing.* Cambridge: Cambridge University Press.

Mannes, Aaron ((2002–2003). A Reformer in Egypt: Aaron Mannes on *Egyptian Political Essay* by Tarek Heggy. *Policy Review,* December 2002–January 2003.

Manuel, Frank E. (1992). *The Broken Staff: Judaism through Christian Eyes.* Cambridge, MA: Harvard University Press.

Marais, Pierre (1994). *Les camions à gaz en question.* Préface par Robert Faurisson. Paris: Polémiques. [French].

Marcus, Jacob Rader (1951–1955). *Early American Jewry.* 2 vols. Reprinted (1970). Philadelphia: Jewish Publication Society of America. Detroit, MI: Wayne State University Press. Reprinted (1975). New York: Ktav Publishing House. New edition (1991–1995). Philadelphia: Jewish Publication Society. Detroit, MI: Wayne State University Press.

Marcus, Jacob Rader (1955–1956). *Memoirs of American Jews, 1775–1865.* 3 vols. Philadelphia: Jewish Publication Society of America.

Marcus, Jacob Rader (1970). *The Colonial American Jew, 1492–1776.* 3 vols. Philadelphia: Jewish Publication Society of America.

Marcus, Jacob Rader (1995). *The American Jew, 1585–1990: A History.* New York: Carlson.

Marcus, Paul (1997). Review of "Myth and Madness: The Psychodynamics of Antisemitism" by Mortimer Ostow. *Psychoanalytic Books,* vol. 8, pp. 236–245.

Marcus, Paul, & Rosenberg, Alan (1989). Another Look at Jewish Self-hatred. *Journal of Reform Judaism,* vol. 36, no. 3, pp. 37–59.

Marissen, Michael (1998). *Lutheranism, Anti-Judaism, and Bach's St. John Passion: With an Annotated Literal Translation of the Libretto.* New York: Oxford University Press.

Maritain, Jacques (1938). *Questions de conscience; essais et allocutions.* Paris: Desclée, De Brouwer et Cie. [French].

Maritain, Jacques (1939). *Antisemitism.* Ed. A.S. Oko, Emmanuel Chapman, & Harry McNeill. London: Geoffrey Bles, the Centenary Press.

Maritain, Jacques (1995). *L'impossible antisémitisme.* Précédé de *Jacques Maritain et les Juifs: réflexions sur un parcours,* par Pierre Vidal-Naquet. Malakoff: Desclée, De Brouwer. New edition (2003). Paris: Desclée, De Brouwer. [French].

Marks, Jonathan (1995). *Human Biodiversity: Genes, Race, and History.* Hawthorne, NY: Aldine De Gruyter.

Marr, Wilhelm (1879). *Der Sieg des Judenthums über das Germanenthum, vom nicht-confessionellen Standpunkt aus betrachtet.* Bern: Rudolph Costenoble. Reprinted (1998). Erlenbach: A. Vogt. [German].

Marr, Wilhelm (1880a). *Der Judenkrieg: seine Fehler und wie er zu organisieren Ist.* Chemnitz: E. Schmeitzner. [German].

Marr, Wilhelm (1880b). *Der Weg zum Siege des Germanentums über das Judentum.* Berlin: Otto Beusse's Verlag. [German].

Marrus, Michael Robert (1980). *The Politics of Assimilation: The French Jewish Community at the Time of the Dreyfus Affair.* Oxford: Clarendon Press.

Marrus, Michael Robert (1987). *The Holocaust in History.* Hanover, NH: University Press of New England. New edition (1989). New York: New American Library.

Marrus, Michael Robert (1988). Recent Trends in the History of the Holocaust. *Holocaust and Genocide Studies,* vol. 3, no. 3, pp. 257–265.

Marrus, Michael Robert (Ed.). (1989). *The Nazi Holocaust: Historical Articles on the Destruction of European Jews.* 15 vols. organized in nine. Vol. 1, *Perspectives on the Holocaust.* Vol. 2, *The Origins of the Holocaust.* Vol. 3, *The "Final Solution": The Implementation of Mass Murder* (2 vols.). Vol. 4, *The "Final Solution" Outside of Germany* (2 vols.). Vol. 5, *Public Opinion and Relations to the Jews in Nazi Europe* (2 vols.). Vol. 6, *The Victims of the Holocaust* (2 vols). Vol. 7, *Jewish Resistance to the Holocaust.* Vol. 8, *Bystanders to the Holocaust* (3 vols.). Vol. 9, *The End of the Holocaust.* Westport, CT: Meckler Press.

Marrus, Michael Robert, & Paxton, Robert O. (1981). *Vichy France and the Jews.* New York: Basic Books. Reprinted (1983). New York: Schocken Books. New edition (1995). Stanford, CA: Stanford University Press.

Martire, Gregory, & Clark, Ruth (1982). *Anti-Semitism in the United States: A Study of Prejudice in the 1980s.* New York: Praeger Scientific Publishing.

Marx, Karl (1844). Zur Judenfrage. *Deutsch-französische Jahrbücher,* First double issue, February. Ed. Arnold Ruge and Karl Marx. Paris: Im Bureau Der Jahrbücher. Reprinted (1973). Leipzig: Reclam. [German].

Marx, Karl (1959). *A World Without Jews.* Tr. & Intro. by Dagobert D. Runes. New York: Philosophical Library.

Massing, Paul W. (1949). *Rehearsal for Destruction: A Study of Political Anti-Semitism in Imperial Germany.* New York: Harper. New edition (1967). New York: Howard Fertig.

Mathis, Paul (1990). "Quel est le secret désir..." in Hazan, Barbara, et al. (1990). *Shoah, le film: des psychanalystes écrivent*, pp. 187–196. Paris: Jacques Grancher. [French].

Mayer, Arno J. (1988). *Why Did the Heavens Not Darken? The "Final Solution" in History.* New York: Pantheon Books.

Mazower, Mark (1999). *Dark Continent: Europe's Twentieth Century.* New York: Alfred A. Knopf.

McBoden, Allan (1878). *An Appeal to the Jews, to Stimulate Them to Obtain a Higher State of Civilization...* San Francisco: Francis & Valentine. Reprinted (1977). In Quinley, Harold E. (Ed.), *Anti-Semitism in America, 1878–1939.* New York: Arno Press.

McBoden, Allan (1879). *Coney Island and the Jews.* New York: G.W. Carleston & Co. Reprinted (1977). In Quinley, Harold E. (Ed.), *Anti-Semitism in America, 1878–1939.* New York: Arno Press.

McCalden, David (1982). *Exiles from History: A Psychohistorical Study of Jewish Self-Hate.* London: Londinium Press. Manhattan Beach, CA: David McCalden.

Meens, M. (1943). Comparisons of Racial Stereotypes of 1935 and 1942. *Journal of Social Psychology,* vol. 17, pp. 327–336.

Meghnagi, David (1990). The Dancer Balancing on the Tip of One Toe: Freud and the Man Moses. *Annali di storia dell'esegesi,* vol. 7, no. 1, pp. 311–321.

Meghnagi, David (Ed.). (1993). *Freud and Judaism.* London: Karnac Books.

Meghnagi, David, et al. (1989). *Ebraismo e antiebraismo: immagine e pregiudizio.* Presentazione Di Cesare Luporini. Florence: La Giuntina. [Italian].

Mehler, Barry (1983). The New Eugenics: Academic Racism in the U.S. Today. *Science for the People,* vol. 15, pp. 18–23.

Mehler, Barry (1988). *A History of the American Eugenics Society, 1921–1940.* Unpublished dissertation, University of Illinois at Urbana-Champaign.

Mehler, Barry (1989). Foundations for Fascism: The New Eugenics Movement in the United States. *Patterns of Prejudice,* vol. 23, pp. 17–25.

Mehler, Barry (1994). In Genes We Trust: When Science Bows to Racism. *Reform Judaism,* vol. 23, pp. 10–13, 77–79.

Mehler, Barry (1997). Beyondism: Raymond B. Cattell and the New Eugenics. *Genetica,* pp. 153–165.

Mehlman, Jeffrey (1983). *Legacies of Anti-Semitism in France.* Minneapolis: University of Minnesota Press.

Mendes-Flohr, Paul (1999). *German Jews: A Dual Identity.* New Haven, CT: Yale University Press.

Mendes-Flohr, Paul, & Reinharz, Jehuda (Eds.) (1980). *The Jew in the Modern World: A Documentary History.* New York: Oxford University Press. Second edition (1995). New York: Oxford University Press.

Menkis, Richard (1992). Antisemitism and Anti-Judaism in Pre-Confederation Canada. In Davies, Alan T. (Ed.), *Antisemitism in Canada: History and Interpretation.* Waterloo, Ontario: Wilfred Laurier University Press.

Merkl, Peter H. (1975). *Political Violence under the Swastika: 581 Early Nazis.* Princeton, NJ: Princeton University Press.

Meyer, Michael M. (1990). *Jewish Identity in the Modern World*. Seattle: University of Washington Press.

Meynell, Wilfrid (1903). *Benjamin Disraeli: An Unconventional Biography*. New York: D. Appleton and Company.

Michel, Henri (1950). *Histoire de la Résistance en France (1940–1944)*. Paris: Presses Universitaires de France. 5th edition (1969). Paris: Presses Universitaires de France. 6th edition (1972). Paris: Presses Universitaires de France. 7th edition (1975). Paris: Presses Universitaires de France. 8th edition (1980). Paris: Presses Universitaires de France. [French].

Middleton, R. (1973). Do Christian Beliefs Cause Antisemitism? *American Sociological Review*, vol. 10, pp. 511–515.

Miles, Robert (1989). *Racism*. London and New York: Routledge.

Miller, Arthur G. (Ed.) (1982). *In the Eye of the Beholder: Contemporary Issues in Stereotyping*. Westport, CT: Praeger.

Milner, Jean-Claude (2003). *Les penchants criminels de l'Europe démocratique*. Lagrasse: Verdier. [French].

Mintz, Alan L. (1984). *Hurban: Response to Catastrophe in Hebrew Literature*. New York: Columbia University Press.

Mintz, Frank P. (1985). *The Liberty Lobby and the American Right: Race, Conspiracy, and Culture*. Westport, CT: Greenwood Press.

Mitscherlich, Alexander, & Mitscherlich, Margarete (1967). *Die Unfähigkeit zu Trauern: Grundlagen kollektiven Verhaltens*. Munich: Piper Verlag. New edition (1982). Munich: Piper Verlag. [German].

Mitscherlich, Alexander, & Mitscherlich, Margarete (1975). *The Inability to Mourn: Principles of Collective Behavior*. Tr. Beverley R. Placzek. Preface by Robert Jay Lifton. New York Grove Press.

Mitscherlich, Margarete (1983). Antisemitismus—eine Männerkrankheit? *Psyche: Zeitschrift für Psychoanalyse und ihre Anwendungen*, vol. 37, No. 1, pp. 41–54. [German].

Mitscherlich, Margarete (1985). *Die friedfertige Frau: eine psychoanalytische Untersuchung zur Aggression der Geschlechter*. Frankfurt am Main: Fischer. [German].

Mitscherlich, Margarete (1987). *The Peaceable Sex: On Aggression in Women and Men*. Tr. Craig Tomlinson. New York: Fromm International Publishing.

Mitscherlich, Margarete (1997). Erinnern, Wiederholen und Durcharbeiten: anläßlich von Daniel Jonah Goldhagens Buch "Hitlers willige Vollstrecker." *Psyche: Zeitschrift für Psychoanalyse und ihre Anwendungen*, vol. 51, pp. 479–493. [German].

Mitten, Richard (1992). *The Politics of Antisemitic Prejudice: The Waldheim Phenomenon in Austria*. Boulder, CO: Westview Press.

Mittleman, Alan (2001). Continuity and Change in the Constitutional Experience of German Jewry. *Jewish Political Studies Review*, vol. 13.

Modder, Montagu Frank (1944). *The Jew in the Literature of England*. Philadelphia: Jewish Publication Society of America.

Mohler, Armin (1991). *Der Nasenring: Die Vergangenheitsbewältigung vor und nach dem Fall der Mauer*. München: Langen Müller. [German].

Molau, Andreas (1993). *Alfred Rosenberg, der Ideologe des Nationalsozialismus: eine politische Biografie*. Koblenz: S. Bublies. [German].

Mommsen, Christian Matthias Theodor (1880). *Auch ein Wort über unser Judenthum.* Berlin: Weidmannsche Buchhandlung. [German].

Moore, Robert I. (1987). *The Formation of a Persecuting Society.* Oxford and New York: Basil Blackwell.

Morais, Vamberto (1976). *A Short History of Anti-Semitism.* New York: W.W. Norton.

Morris, Leslie, & Zipes, Jack David (Eds.). (2002). *Unlikely History: The Changing German-Jewish Symbiosis, 1945–2000.* New York: Palgrave.

Morse, N.C., & Allport, F.H. (1952). The Causation of Antisemitism: An Investigation of Seven Hypotheses. *Journal of Psychology,* vol. 34, pp. 197–233.

Moscovici, Serge (1985). *The Age of the Crowd: A Historical Treatise on Mass Psychology.* Tr. J.C. Whitehouse. Cambridge and New York: Cambridge University Press. Paris: Editions de la Maison Des Sciences de L'homme.

Moscovitz, Jean-Jacques (1990). Savoir et non savoir en question. In Hazan, Barbara et al. (1990). *Shoah, le film: des psychanalystes écrivent,* pp. 35–63. Paris: Jacques Grancher. [French].

Moss, Donald (2001). Hating in the First Person Plural: Racism, Homophobia, Misogyny. *Journal of the American Psychoanalytic Association,* vol. 49, pp. 1315–1334.

Moss, Donald (Ed.). (2003). *Hating in the First Person Plural: Psychoanalytic Essays on Racism, Homophobia, Misogyny, and Terror.* New York: Other Press.

Mosse, George L. [Georg Lachmann] (1964). *The Crisis of German Ideology: The Intellectual Origins of the Third Reich.* New York: Grosset & Dunlap. New edition (1981). New York: Howard Fertig.

Mosse, George L. [Georg Lachmann] (1970). *Germans and Jews: The Right, the Left, and the Search for a "Third Force" in Pre-Nazi Germany.* New York: Howard Fertig. Reprinted (1987). Detroit, MI: Wayne State University Press. New edition (2004). Madison: University of Wisconsin Press.

Mosse, George L. [Georg Lachmann] (1978). *Toward the Final Solution: A History of European Racism.* New York: Howard Fertig. New edition (1985). Madison: University of Wisconsin Press.

Mosse, George L. [Georg Lachmann] (1985). *Nationalism and Sexuality: Respectablility and Abnormal Sexuality in Modern Europe.* New York: Howard Fertig. Reprinted (1988). Madison: University of Wisconsin Press.

Mosse, George L. [Georg Lachmann] (1987). *Masses and Man: Nationalist and Fascist Perceptions of Reality.* Detroit, MI: Wayne State University Press.

Mosse, George L. [Georg Lachmann] (2000). *Confronting History: A Memoir.* Foreword by Walter Laqueur. Madison: University of Wisconsin Press.

Mosse, George L. [Georg Lachmann] (Ed.). (1966). *Nazi Culture: Intellectual, Cultural, and Social Life in the Third Reich.* Tr. Salvatore Attanasio et al. New York: Grosset & Dunlap.

Mosse, George L. [Georg Lachmann], & Ledeen, Michael A. (1977). *Intervista sul nazismo.* Bari: Laterza-Feltrinelli. [Italian].

Mosse, George L. [Georg Lachmann], & Ledeen, Michael A. (1978). *Nazism: A Historical and Comparative Analysis of National Socialism.* New Brunswick, NJ: Transaction Books.

Mouttapa, Jean (2004). *Un Arabe face à Auschwitz.* Paris: Albin Michel. [French].

Müller, Filip (1979). *Sonderbehandlung: drei Jahre in den Krematorien und Gaskammern von Auschwitz.* Munich: n.p. [German].

Müller-Hill, Benno (1988). *Murderous Science: Elimination by Scientific Selection of Jews, Gypsies, and Others, Germany 1933–1945.* Tr. G.R. Fraser. Oxford: Oxford University Press.

Müller-Münch, Ingrid (1982). *Die Frauen von Majdanek: vom zerstörten Leben der Opfer und der Mörderinnen.* Reinbek Bein Hamburg: Rowohlt-Verlag. [German].

Muracciole, Jean-François (1993). *Histoire de la Résistance en France.* Paris: Presses Universitaires de France. 2nd edition (1996). Paris: Presses Universitaires de France. 3rd edition (2001). Paris: Presses Universitaires de France. 4th edition (2003). Paris: Presses Universitaires de France. [French].

Muracciole, Jean-François (1998). *Les Enfants de la défaite: la Résistance, l'éducation et la culture.* Paris: Presses De Sciences Po. [French].

Myers, D.G. (2002). Jean Améry: A Biographical Introduction. In Kremer, S. Lillian (Ed.), *Holocaust Literature: An Encyclopedia of Writers and Their Work.* New York: Routledge.

Nelson, B. (1949). *The Idea of Usury.* Princeton, NJ: Princeton University Press.

Nelson, B., & Starr, J. (1944). The Legend of the Divine Surety and the Jewish Moneylender. *Annuaire de l'institut de philologie et d'histoire orientales et slaves,* vol. 7. New York: Moretus Press.

Nettler, Ronald L. (1987). *Past Trials and Present Tribulations: A Muslim Fundamentalist's View of the Jews.* Oxford and New York: Published for the Vidal Sassoon International Center for the Study of Antisemitism, The Hebrew University of Jerusalem, by Pergamon Press.

Newby, I. (1969). *Challenge to the Court: Social Scientists and the Defense of Segregation, 1954–1996.* Baton Rouge: Louisiana State University Press.

Newhouse, Alana (2006). Finding Deeper Truths in Fiction. *The Jewish Daily Forward,* Friday, August 11.

Newman, Elias (1933). *The Jewish Peril and the Hidden Hand: The Bogey of Anti-Semitism's International Conspiracy.* Minneapolis: The Hebrew Christian Group of Minneapolis and St. Paul, Minnesota.

Newman, Leonard S., et al. (2002). *Understanding Genocide: The Social Psychology of the Holocaust.* Oxford and New York: Oxford University Press.

Nicholls, William (1993). *Christian Antisemitism: A History of Hate.* Northvale, NJ: Jason Aronson. Reprinted (1995). Northvale, NJ: Jason Aronson.

Nicolle, Olivier (2004). *"Times Are Changing..."*: notule sur des fantasmes collectifs de trahison. *Pardès: Études et Culture Juives,* no. 37, *Psychanalyse de l'antisémitisme contemporain,* pp. 43–50.

Niederland, William G. (1965). Psychische Spätschäden nach politischer Verfolgung. *Psyche: Zeitschrift für Psychoanalyse und ihre Anwendungen,* vol. 18, pp. 888–895.

Niederland, William G. (1968). Clinical Observations on the "Survivor Syndrome." *International Journal of Psycho-Analysis,* vol. 49, no. 2, pp. 313–315.

Niederland, William G. (1980). *Folgen der Verfolgung: das Überlebenden-Syndrom: Seelenmord.* Frankfurt am Main: Suhrkamp. [German].

Niewyk, Donald L. (1980). *The Jews in Weimar Germany.* Baton Rouge: Louisiana State University Press. New edition (2001). New Brunswick, NJ: Transaction Publishers.

Niewyk, Donald L. (Ed.). (1992). *The Holocaust: Problems and Perspectives of Interpretation.* Lexington, MA: D. C. Heath. 3rd edition (2003). Boston: Houghton Mifflin.

Niewyk, Donald L., & Nicosia, Francis R. (2000). *The Columbia Guide to the Holocaust.* New York: Columbia University Press.

Nilus, Sergei Aleksandrovich (1905). Протоколы СИонскИх Мудрецов [The Protocols of the Elders of Zion]. Ghostwritten by Matvei Vasilyevich Golovinski. Moscow: n.p. [Russian].

Nilus, Sergei Aleksandrovich (1920). *The Jewish Peril: Protocols of the Learned Elders of Zion.* Tr. & Ed. Boris Brazol in collaboration with Natalie De Bogory). London: Eyre & Spottiswoode. Boston: Maynard & Co. 4th edition (1921). London: The Britons.

Nirenstein, Fiamma (2002). *L'abbandono: come l'occidente ha tradito gli ebrei.* Milano: Rizzoli. [Italian].

Nirenstein, Fiamma (2005). *Terror: The New Anti-Semitism and the War Against the West.* Tr. Anne Milano Appel. Hanover, NH: Smith and Kraus.

Nishioka, Masanori (1995). The Greatest Taboo of Postwar World History: There Were No Nazi "Gas Chambers." *Marco Polo,* February. [Japanese].

Noguères Henri (1967–1981). *Histoire de la Résistance en France de 1940 à 1945.* En collaboration avec M. Degliame-Fouché et J.-L. Vigier. 5 vols. Paris: Robert Laffont. [French].

Noll, Richard (1994). *The Jung Cult: Origins of a Charismatic Movement.* Princeton, NJ: Princeton University Press. Reprinted (1997). New York: The Free Press.

Noll, Richard (1997). *The Aryan Christ: The Secret Life of Carl Jung.* New York: Random House.

Nolte, Ernst (1985). Between Myth and Revisionism. In Koch, H. W. (Ed.), *Aspects of the Third Reich.* New York: St. Martin's Press.

Nolte, Ernst (1991). *Lehrstück oder Tragödie? Beiträge zur Interpretation der Geschichte des 20. Jahrhunderts.* Cologne: Böhlau. [German].

Nolte, Ernst (1995). *Die Deutschen und ihre Vergangenheiten: Erinnerung und Vergessen von der Reichsgründung Bismarcks bis heute.* Berlin: Propyläen. [German].

Norenzayan, Ara, & Atran, Scott (2004). Cognitive and Emotional Processes in the Cultural Transmission of Natural and Nonnatural Beliefs. In Schaller, Mark, & Crandall, Christian S. (Eds.). *The Psychological Foundations of Culture,* pp. 149–170. Mahwah, NJ: Lawrence Erlbaum Associates.

Nova, Fritz (1986). *Alfred Rosenberg: Nazi Theorist of the Holocaust.* Foreword by Hans Jürgen Eysenck. Intro. by Robert M.W. Kempner. New York: Hippocrene Books.

Novick, Peter (1999). *The Holocaust in American Life.* Boston: Houghton Mifflin. Reprinted (1999). As *The Holocaust and Collective Memory: the American Experience.* London: Bloomsbury.

NSDAP [Nationalsozialistische Deutsche Arbeiter-partei] (1942). *Rassenpolitik.* Berlin: Der Reichsführer SS, SS Haumptamt. [German].

O'Dwyer De Macedo, Heitor (1990). Les trois savoirs de Claude Lanzmann. In Hazan, Barbara et al. (1990). *Shoah, le film: des psychanalystes écrivent,* pp. 177–186. Paris: Jacques Grancher. [French].

Oberman, Heiko Augustinus (1982). *Luther: Mensch zwischen Gott und Teufel.* Berlin: Severin und Siedler. [German].

Oberman, Heiko Augustinus (1984). *The Roots of Anti-Semitism in the Age of Renaissance and Reformation.* Philadelphia: Fortress Press.

Oberman, Heiko Augustinus (1989a). *Luther: Man Between God and the Devil.* Tr. Eileen Walliser-Schwarzbart. New Haven, CT: Yale University Press. New edition (2006). New Haven, CT: Yale University Press.

Oberman, Heiko Augustinus (1989b). The Stubborn Jews: Timing the Escalation of Antisemitism in Late Medieval Europe. *Leo Baeck Institute Year Book XXXIV.* London: Leo Baeck Institute. London: Secker & Warburg.

Oesterreicher, John [Johannes Maria] (1940). *Racisme-antisémitisme-antichristianisme: documents et critique.* Traduit de l'allemand. Avant propos de M. Robert d'Harcourt. Paris: Editions du Cerf. Reprinted (1943). New York: Editions de la Maison francaise. [French].

Oesterreicher, John [Johannes Maria] (1965). *Auschwitz, the Christian, and the Council.* Montreal: Palm Publishers.

Oesterreicher, John [Johannes Maria] (1993). *Rassenhass ist Christushass: Hitlers Jugendfeindlichkeit in zeitgeschichtlicher und in heilsgeschichtlicher Sicht. Dokumente und Kritik.* Tr. Eberhard Steinacker. Foreword by Franz König. Klagenfurt, Austria: Hermagoras/Mohorjeva.

Oisteanu, Andrei (2001). *The Image of the Jew in Romanian Culture.* Bucharest: Humanitas Publishing House.

Oisteanu, Andrei (2002). *Das Bild des Juden in der rumänischen Volkskultur: zum Problem scheinbar positiver Vorurteile.* Tr. Marie-Elisabeth Rehn. Ed. Erhard Roy Wiehn. Konstanz: Hartung-Gorre. [German].

Oliner, Samuel P. (2001). *Racial and Ethnic Attitudes in Rural America: Focus on Humboldt County, California.* Arcata, CA: Altruistic Personality and Prosocial Behavior Institute and the Center for Applied Social Analysis & Education at Humboldt State University.

Oliner, Samuel P., & Krause, J. D. (2001). Racial and Ethnic Attitudes in Rural America. *Humboldt Journal of Social Relations,* vol. 26, pp. 11–55.

Oliner, Samuel P., & Oliner, Pearl M. (1988). *The Altruistic Personality: Rescuers of Jews in Nazi Europe.* Foreword by Harold M. Schulweis. New York: The Free Press. London: Collier Macmillan.

Olson, Bernhard E. (1963). *Faith and Prejudice: Intergroup Problems in Protestant Curricula.* New Haven, CT: Yale University Press.

Olster, David M. (1994).*Roman Defeat, Christian Response and the Literary Construction of the Jew.* Philadelphia: University of Pennsylvania Press.

Ophir, Adi (1987). On Sanctifying the Holocaust: An Anti-Theological Treatise. *Tikkun,* vol. 2, no. 1, pp. 61–67.

Ophuls, Marcel (1969). *Le Chagrin et la pitié: chronique d'une ville française sous l'occupation.* Film in Two Parts. First Part: *L'Effondrement.* Second Part: *Le Choix.* Paris: Quetzal Films. [French].

Ophuls, Marcel (1972). *The Sorrow and the Pity.* Film. Intro. by Stanley Hoffmann. Tr. & Ed. Mireille Johnston. New York: Outerbridge & Lazard.

Oppenheim, Daniel (1990). Survivre, Transmettre. In Hazan, Barbara et al. (1990), *Shoah, le film: des psychanalystes écrivent,* pp. 159–170. Paris: Jacques Grancher. [French].

Oppenheimer, Paul (1996). *Evil and the Demonic: A New Theory of Monstrous Behavior.* New York: New York University Press.

Orr, Douglas (1946). Antisemitism and the Psychopathology of Daily Life. In Simmel, Ernst (Ed.), *Anti-Semitism: A Social Disease.* New York: International Universities Press. New edition (1948). New York: International Universities Press.

Orwell, George [Eric Blair] (1945). Antisemitism in Britain. *Contemporary Jewish Record,* April, pp. 332–341. Reprinted (1953). In Orwell, George, *England Your England and Other Essays.* London: Secker & Warburg. Reprinted (1953). In Orwell, George, *Such, Such Were the Joys.* London: Secker & Warburg. New York: Harcourt, Brace. Reprinted (1968). In Orwell, George, *The Collected Essays, Journalism and Letters of George Orwell.* Ed. Sonia Orwell & Ian Angus. London: Secker & Warburg.

Orwell, George [Eric Blair] (1949) *1984.* London: Secker & Warburg. New edition (2000). New York : Harcourt.

Ostow, Mortimer (1980). The Jewish Response to Crisis. *Conservative Judaism,* vol. 33, no. 4, pp. 3–25. Reprinted (1982). In Ostow, Mortimer, *Judaism and Psychoanalysis.* New York: Ktav Publishing.

Ostow, Mortimer (1993). Antisemitism and the Collective Unconscious. Letter to the Editor. *American Journal of Psychiatry,* vol. 150, no. 1, p. 173.

Ostow, Mortimer (1995). *Myth and Madness: The Psychodynamics of Antisemitism.* New Brunswick, NJ: Transaction Publishers.

Ostow, Mortimer (1996). Myth and Madness: Report of Psychoanalytic Study of Anti-semitism. *International Journal of Psycho-analysis,* vol. 77, pp. 15–32.

Ottolenghi, Emanuele (2006). Review of Jacqueline Rose's "The Question of Zion." *Israel Studies,* vol. 11, no. 1, pp. 194–203.

Ouzan, Françoise (2008). *Histoire des Américains juifs: de la marge à l'influence.* Brussels: André Versaille éditeur.

Oxall, Ivar, et al. (Eds.). (1987). *Jews, Antisemitism, and Culture in Vienna.* London and New York: Routledge & Kegan Paul.

Pagels, Elaine H. (1995). *The Origin of Satan.* New York: Vintage Books.

Pana, Georgetta (2004). Christian Anti-Judaism and the Holocaust. *Studia Hebraica,* vol. 4, pp. 69–74.

Papadatos, Petros A. (1964). *The Eichmann Trial.* London: Stevens & Sons.

Pappas, Theodore, et al. (Eds.) (2006). *Encyclopædia Britannica 2006 Ultimate Reference Suite DVD.* Chicago: Encyclopædia Britannica.

Pappé, Ilan (2005). *The Modern Middle East.* London and New York: Routledge.

Pappé, Ilan (Ed.) (1999). *The Israel/Palestine Question: A Reader.* London and New York: Routledge. New edition (2007). Milton Park and New York: Routledge.

Parin, Paul (1985). "The Mark of Oppression": ethnopsychoanalytische Studie über Juden und Homosexuelle in einer relativ permissiven Kultur. *Psyche: Zeitschrift für Psychoanalyse und ihre Anwendungen,* vol. 39, no. 3, pp. 193–219. [German].

Parkes, James William (1934). *The Conflict of the Church and the Synagogue: A Study in the Origins of Antisemitism.* London: The Soncino Press. New edition (1964). Cleveland, OH: World Publishing Co. Philadelphia: Jewish Publication Society of America. New edition (1974). New York: Hermon Press.

Parkes, James William (1936). *Jesus, Paul and the Jews.* With a Foreword by Herbert M.J. Loewe. London: Student Christian Movement Press.

Parkes, James William (1938a). *The Jew in the Medieval Community: A Study of His Political and Economic Situation.* London: The Soncino Press. New edition (1964).

Cleveland, OH: World Publishing Co. Philadelphia: Jewish Publication Society of America. New edition (1974). New York: Hermon Press.

Parkes, James William (1938b). *The Jew and His Neighbour: A Study of the Causes of Anti-Semitism.* London: Student Christian Movement Press.

Parkes, James William (1945). *An Enemy of the People: Antisemitism.* Harmondsworth: Penguin Books. Reprinted (1946). New York: Penguin Books. New edition (1964). *Antisemitism.* Chicago: Quadrangle Books. New edition (1969). *Antisemitism: A Concise World History.* Chicago: Quadrangle Books.

Parkes, James William (1954). *End of an Exile: Israel, the Jews, and the Gentile World.* London: Vallentine, Mitchell. New edition (1982). Marblehead, MA: Micah Publications. 3rd edition (2005). Eugene B. Korn & Roberta Kalechofsky (Eds.). Marblehead, MA: Micah Publications.

Parkes, James William (1963). *A History of the Jewish People.* Chicago: Quadrangle Books.

Patai, Raphael (1976). Ethnohistory and Inner History. *The Jewish Quarterly Review,* vol. 67, pp. 1–15. Reprinted (1977). In Patai, Raphael, *The Jewish Mind,* pp. 28–37. New York: Charles Scribner's Sons.

Patai, Raphael (1977). *The Jewish Mind.* New York: Charles Scribner's Sons.

Pauley, Bruce F. (1992). *From Prejudice to Persecution: A History of Austrian Anti-Semitism.* Chapel Hill: University of North Carolina Press.

Pawel, Ernst (1989). *The Labyrinth of Exile: A Life of Theodor Herzl.* New York: Farrar, Straus & Giroux.

Peabody, Dean (1961). Attitude Content and Agreement Set in Scales of Authoritarianism, Dogmatism, Anti-Semitism, and Economic Conservatism. *Journal of Abnormal and Social Psychology,* vol. 63, pp. 1–11.

Pellegrini, Ann (1997). *Performance Anxieties: Staging Psychoanalysis, Staging Race.* New York: Routledge.

Penslar, Derek Jonathan, et al. (Eds.). (2005). *Contemporary Antisemitism: Canada and the World.* Toronto: University of Toronto Press.

Perednik, Gustavo Daniel (2001). *La Judeofobia: cómo y cuándo nace, dónde y por qué pervive.* Barcelona: Flor del Viento Ediciones. [Spanish].

Perry, Marvin, & Schweitzer, Frederick M. (2002). *Antisemitism: Myth and Hate from Antiquity to the Present.* New York: Palgrave Macmillan.

Perry, Marvin, & Schweitzer, Frederick M. (Eds.). (1994). *Jewish-Christian Encounters over the Centuries: Symbiosis, Prejudice, Holocaust, Dialogue.* New York: Peter Lang.

Petit, Chris (2004). The Technocrat of Massacre. Review of David Cesarani's *Eichmann: His Life and Crimes.* In *The Guardian,* Saturday, August 28.

Phalet, Karen, & Örkény, Antal (Eds.). (2001). *Ethnic Minorities and Inter-ethnic Relations in Context: a Dutch-Hungarian Comparison.* Aldershot, England, and Burlington, VT: Ashgate Publishing.

Philostratus Flavius, the Athenian (2005). *The Life of Apollonius of Tyana.* Tr. And Ed. Christopher Jones. Cambridge, MA: Harvard University Press.

Pines, Malcolm (1994). Sigmund Freud and Siegfried Heinrich Fuchs/Foulkes: Psychoanalysis and Group Analysis and German-Jewish Relations. *European Judaism,* vol. 27, no. 2, pp. 46–57.

Pinsker, Leo [Lev Semyonovich] (1882) *Auto-Emancipation! Mahnruf an seine Stammesgenossen, von einem russischen Jude.* Berlin: Commissions-Verlag von W. Issleib.

Pinsker, Leo [Lev Semyonovich] (1916). *Auto-Emancipation: An Appeal to His People by a Russian Jew.* New York: Federation of American Zionists. Reprinted (1944). Washington, DC: Zionist organization of America. Reprinted (1969). In Hertzberg, Arthur (Ed.), *The Zionist Idea: A Historical Analysis and Reader,* pp. 178–198. New York: Atheneum. New edition (1984). New York: Atheneum.

Pinson, Koppel Shub (Ed.). (1942). *Essays on Antisemitism.* New York: Conference on Jewish Relations. 2nd edition (1946). New York: Conference on Jewish Relations.

Piven, Jerry S. (2004). *Death and Delusion: A Freudian Analysis of Mortal Terror.* Greenwich, CT: Information Age Publishing.

Piven, Jerry S. (Ed.). (2004). *The Psychology of Death in Fantasy and History.* Westport, CT: Praeger.

Piven, Jerry S., et al. (Eds.). (2001–2002). *Psychological Undercurrents of History.* 4 vols. Vol. 1, *Psychological Undercurrents of History.* Vol. 2, *Terror and Apocalypse.* Vol. 3, *Jihad and Sacred Vengeance.* Vol. 4, *Judaism and Genocide.* Lincoln, NE: iUniverse. San Jose, CA: Author's Choice Press, Writer's Showcase Press, Writer's Club Press.

Piven, Jerry S., et al. (Eds.). (2004). *Terrorism, Jihad and Sacred Vengeance.* Giessen: Psychosozial-Verlag.

Plessner, Helmuth (1935). *Das Schicksal des deutschen Geistes im Ausgang seiner bürgerlichen Epoche.* Zurich and Leipzig: Niehans. New edition (1959). *Die verspätete Nation: über die politische Verführbarkeit bürgerlichen Geistes.* Stuttgart: Kohlhammer. [German].

Poliakov, Léon (1954). *Harvest of Hate: the Nazi Program for the Destruction of the Jews of Europe.* Foreword by Reinhold Niebuhr. Syracuse, NY: Syracuse University Press. Reprinted (1971). Westport, CT: Greenwood Press. New edition (1979) New York: Holocaust Library.

Poliakov, Léon (1955–1977). *Histoire de l'antisémitisme.* 4 vols. Vol. 1. *Du Christ aux Juifs de cour.* Vol. 2. *De Mahomet aux Marranes, (suivi de) Les Juifs au Saint-Siège, les Morisques d'Espagne et Leur Expulsion.* Vol. 3. *De Voltaire à Wagner.* Vol. 4. *L'Europe Suicidaire, 1870–1933.* Paris: Calmann-Lévy. New edition (1991). 2 vols. Paris: Editions du Seuil. [French].

Poliakov, Léon (1964). *Auschwitz.* Paris: Julliard. [French].

Poliakov, Léon (1965–1985). *The History of Anti-Semitism.* 4 vols. Vol. 1. *From the Time of Christ to the Court Jews.* Vol. 2. *From Mohammed to the Marranos.* Vol. 3. *From Voltaire to Wagner.* Vol. 4. *Suicidal Europe, 1870–1933.* Tr. Richard Howard et al. London: Routledge & Kegan Paul. Oxford: Published for the Littman Library by Oxford University Press. New York: Vanguard Press. New York: Schocken Books. Reprinted (1966–1985). London: Elek Books. New edition (1974–1985). Tr. Miriam Kochan. London: Routledge and Kegan Paul. New York: Vanguard Press. Reprinted (2003). Philadelphia: University of Pennsylvania Press.

Poliakov, Léon (1969). *De l'antisionisme à l'antisémitisme.* Paris: Calmann-Lévy. [French].

Poliakov, Léon (1974). *The Aryan Myth: A History of Racist and Nationalist Ideas in Europe.* Tr. Edmund Howard. New York: Basic Books. London and Edinburgh: Chatto & Windus Heinemann for Sussex University Press.

Poliakov, Léon (Ed.). (1994). *Histoire de l'antisémitisme, 1945–1993.* Paris: Editions du Seuil. [French].

Poliakov, Léon, & Wulf, Josef (Eds.). (1955). *Das Dritte Reich und die Juden: Dokumente und Aufsätze.* Berlin: Arani. [German].

Polonsky, Antony (Ed.). (1990). *My Brother's Keeper? Recent Polish Debates on the Holocaust.* London: Routledge.

Porter, Brian (2000). *When Nationalism Began to Hate: Imagining Modern Politics in Nineteenth Century Poland.* New York: Oxford University Press.

Post, Jerrold M. (1996). The Loss of Enemies, Fragmenting Identities, and the Resurgence of Ethnic/Nationalist Hatred and Anti-Semitism in Eastern Europe. *Journal for the Psychoanalysis of Culture & Society,* vol. 1, no. 2, pp. 27–33.

Postone, Moishe (1993). *Time, Labor and Social Domination.* Cambridge: Cambridge University Press.

Potok, Chaim (1978). *Wanderings: Chaim Potok's History of the Jews.* New York: Alfred A. Knopf.

Prager, Dennis, & Telushkin, Joseph (1983). *Why the Jews? The Reason for Antisemitism.* New York: Simon and Schuster. Reprinted (1985). New York: Simon and Schuster. New edition (2003). New York: Simon and Schuster. Touchstone Books.

Proctor, R. (1988). *Racial Hygiene: Medicine under the Nazis.* Cambridge, MA: Harvard University Press.

Proctor, Robert N. (1999). *The Nazi War on Cancer.* Princeton, NJ: Princeton University Press.

Pulos, L., & Spilka, B. (1961). Perceptual Selectivity, Memory, and Anti-Semitism. *Journal of Abnormal and Social Psychology,* vol. 62, pp. 690–692.

Pulzer, Peter G.J. (1964). *The Rise of Political Anti-Semitism in Germany and Austria.* New York: John Wiley & Sons. New edition (1988). Cambridge, MA: Harvard University Press. London: Peter Halban.

Pulzer, Peter G.J. (2003). *Jews and the German State: The Political History of a Minority, 1848–1933.* Detroit, MI: Wayne State University Press.

Pulzer, Peter G.J. (2005). Third Thoughts on German and Austrian Antisemitism. *Journal of Modern Jewish Studies,* vol. 4, no. 2, pp. 137–178.

Quinley, Harold E. (Ed.). (1977). *Anti-Semitism in America, 1878–1939.* New York: Arno Press. London: Ayer Company Publishers.

Quinley, Harold E., & Glock, Charles Y. (1979). *Anti-Semitism in America.* New York: The Free Press. New edition (1983). New Introduction by Harold E. Quinley, New Foreword by Theodore Freedman. New Brunswick, NJ: Transaction Publishers.

Rabinbach, Anson (1997). *In the Shadow of Catastrophe: German Intellectuals Between Apocalypse and Enlightenment.* Berkeley: University of California Press.

Rabinbach, Anson (2004). Eichmann in New York: The New York Intellectuals and the Hannah Arendt Controversy. *October,* vol. 108, no. 1, pp. 97–111.

Rabinbach, Anson, & Zipes, Jack David (Eds.). (1986). *Germans and Jews since the Holocaust: The Changing Situation in West Germany.* New York: Holmes and Meier.

Rabinovitch, Gérard H. (1990). La Déchirure du rêve éveillé. In Hazan, Barbara et al. (1990). *Shoah, le film: des psychanalystes écrivent,* pp. 155–157. Paris: Jacques Grancher. [French].

Rabinowitz, Dan, & Abu-Baker, Khawla (2005). *Coffins on Our Shoulders: The Experience of the Palestinian Citizens of Israel.* Berkeley: University of California Press.

Radai, Itamar (2007). From Father to Son: Attitudes to Jews and Israel, in Asad's Syria. *Analysis of Current Trends in Antisemitism,* no. 29. Jerusalem: The Vidal Sassoon International Center for the Study of Antisemitism, The Hebrew University of Jerusalem.

Rancour-Laferriere, Daniel (1985). Solzhenitsyn and the Jews: A Psychoanalytical View. *Soviet Jewish Affairs,* vol. 15, no. 3, pp. 29–54.

Rancour-Laferriere, Daniel (2001). Anti-Semitism in Russia: Some Interactions of Paranoia and Masochism in the Ethnic Realm. *Journal for the Psychoanalysis of Culture and Society,* vol. 6, pp. 73–82.

Rappaport, Ernest A. (1975). *Anti-Judaism: A Psychohistory.* Chicago: Perspective Press.

Rappaport, Ernest A. (1976). Adolf Eichmann: The Travelling Salesman of Genocide. *International Review of Psycho-Analysis,* vol. 3, no. 1, pp. 111–119.

Rassial, Jean-Jacques (1984). Comme le nez au milieu de la figure. In Rassial, Adélie, & Rassial, Jean-Jacques (Eds.), *L'interdit de la représentation: colloque de Montpellier.* Éditions du Seuil. [French].

Rassinier, Paul (1955). *Le Mensonge D'Ulysse.* Mâcon: Paul Rassinier. 6th edition (1979). Paris: La Vieille Taupe. 8th edition (1998). Paris: France Libre. [French].

Rassinier, Paul (1964). *Le Drame des Juifs européens.* Paris: Les Sept Couleurs. [French].

Rather, Lelland Joseph (1986). Disraeli, Freud and Jewish Conspiracy Theories. *Journal of the History of Ideas,* vol. 47, no. 1, pp. 111–131.

Rauschenbach, Brigitte (Ed.). (1992). *Erinnern, Wiederholen, Durcharbeiten: zur Psychoanalyse deutscher Wenden.* Berlin: Aufbau Taschenbuch Verlag. [German].

Rauschning, Hermann (1940). *Hitler Speaks: A Series of Political Conversations.* London: Butterworth.

Rausky, Franklin (2004). La Conspiration secrète pour la domination du monde: explorations freudiennes. *Pardès: Études et Culture Juives,* no. 37, *Psychanalyse de l'antisémitisme contemporain,* pp. 121–127. [French].

Ray, John Jay (1972). Is Antisemitism a Cognitive Simplification? Some Observations on Australian Neo-Nazis. *Jewish Journal of Sociology,* vol. 15, pp. 207–213.

Ray, John Jay (1973). Antisemitic Types in Australia. *Patterns of Prejudice,* vol. 7, no. 1, pp. 6–16.

Ray, John Jay (1984). Half of All Racists Are Left-wing. *Political Psychology,* vol. 5, pp. 227–236.

Ray, John Jay (1985). Racism and Rationality: A Reply to Billig. *Ethnic and Racial Studies,* vol. 8, pp. 441–443.

Ray, John Jay (Ed.) (1974). *Conservatism as Heresy: An Australian Reader.* Sydney: Australia and New Zealand Book Co.

Ray, John Jay, & Furnham, Adrian (1984). Authoritarianism, Conservatism and Racism. *Ethnic & Racial Studies,* vol. 7, pp. 406–412.

Ray, John Jay, & Lovejoy, F. H. (1986). The Generality of Racial Prejudice. *Journal of Social Psychology,* vol. 126, pp. 563–564.

Redeker, Robert (1996). La toile d'arraignée du révisionnisme. *Les Temps Modernes,* no. 589, August–September. [French].

Redlich, Fritz (1999). *Hitler: Diagnosis of a Destructive Prophet.* New York: Oxford University Press.

Reed, Brian (1992). Monsters, Magic, and Murder: Ideological Anxiety in Chaucer's "The Prioress's Tale." *Mosaic,* vol. 13, pp. 1–9.

Reich, Wilhelm (1946). *The Mass Psychology of Fascism.* Tr. Theodore P. Wolfe. 3rd, rev., and enlarged ed. New York: Orgone Institute Press. New edition (1970). Tr. Vincent R. Carfagno. Ed. Mary Higgins & Chester R. Raphael. New York: Farrar, Straus & Giroux. New edition (1972). London: Souvenir Press. New edition (1975). Harmondsworth: Penguin Books. Reprinted (1991). London: Souvenir Press.

Reich, Wilhelm (1975). *The Murder of Christ: The Emotional Plague of Mankind.* London: Souvenir Press.

Reinach, Joseph (1901–1911). *Histoire de l'affaire Dreyfus.* 7 vols. Paris: Éditions de la Revue Blanche. [French].

Reinharz, Jehuda (1987). *Living with Antisemitism: Modern Jewish Responses.* Hanover, NH: University Press of New England.

Reinicke, Helmut (1988). Rede Auf Ulrich Sonnemann. In Schmied-Kowarzik, Wolfdietrich (Ed.), *Einsprüche Kritischer Philosophie. Kleine Festschrift für Ulrich Sonnemann,* pp. 221–227. Kassel: Gesamthochschule Kassel. [German].

Reitlinger, Gerald (1953). *The Final Solution: The Attempt to Exterminate the Jews of Europe, 1939–1945.* London: Vallentine, Mitchell. 2nd, revised, and augmented edition (1961). London: Vallentine, Mitchell. Reprinted (1968). London: Vallentine, Mitchell. South Brunswick, NJ: Thomas Yoseloff. New edition (1987). Northvale, NJ: Jason Aronson.

Reitter, Paul (2003). Karl Kraus and the Jewish Self-Hatred Question. *Jewish Social Studies* (new series), vol. 10, no. 1, pp. 78–116.

Renan, Ernest (1855) *Histoire générale et système comparé des langues sémitiques.* Paris: Imprimerie impériale. [French].

Rensmann, Lars P. (1996). Psychoanalytic Anti-semitism. *The Psychohistory Review,* vol. 24, no. 2, pp. 197–206.

Rex, John, & Mason, David (Eds.). (1986). *Theories of Race and Ethnic Relations.* Cambridge and New York: Cambridge University Press.

Reznik, Serge (1990). Au-delà du principe de souvenir? la chose, l'objet, le nom *Shoah.* In Hazan, Barbara et al. (1990), *Shoah, le film: des psychanalystes écrivent,* pp. 171–175. Paris: Jacques Grancher. [French].

Rezzori, Gregor von (1981). *Memoirs of an Anti-Semite.* New York: Viking Press. Reprinted (1982). Harmondsworth and New York: Penguin Books. New edition (1991). New York: Vintage Books.

Rice, Emanuel (1990). *Freud and Moses: The Long Journey Home.* Albany: State University of New York Press.

Richards, G. (1997). *"Race," Racism and Psychology: Towards a Reflexive History.* London: Routledge.

Rickels, Laurence A. (2002). *Nazi Psychoanalysis.* 3 vols. Foreword by Benjamin Bennett. Minneapolis: University of Minnesota Press.

Rickman, John (1957). *Selected Contributions to Psycho-Analysis.* Ed. W. Clifford M. Scott. Intro. by Sylvia M. Payne. London: The Hogarth Press. New York: Basic Books.

Rickman, John (2003). *No Ordinary Psychoanalyst: The Exceptional Contributions of John Rickman.* Ed. Pearl King. London: Karnac Books.

Rieff, Philip (1964). Jung's Confession: Psychology as a Language of Faith. *Encounter,* vol. 22, no. 5 (May), pp. 45–50.

Rintala, Marvin (1984). The Love of Power and the Power of Love: Churchill's Childhood. *Political Psychology,* vol. 5, pp. 375–390.

Rintala, Marvin (1995). *Lloyd George and Churchill: How Friendship Changed Politics.* Lanham, MD: Madison Books.

Ritsert, Jürgen (1997). Zur Dialektik der Subjektivität bei Adorno. *Zeitschrift für kritische Theorie,* vol. 4, no. 1, pp. 29–51. [German].

Robertson, Ritchie (1999). *The "Jewish Question" in German Literature, 1749–1939: Emancipation and Its Discontents.* Oxford and New York: Oxford University Press.

Robins, Robert S., & Post, Jerrold M. (1997). *Political Paranoia: The Psychopolitics of Hatred.* New Haven, CT: Yale University Press.

Robinson, D., & Rohde, S. (1945). A Public Opinion Study of Anti-Semitism in New York City. *American Sociological Review,* vol. 10, pp. 511–515.

Robinson, Jacob (1965). *And the Crooked Shall Be Made Straight: The Eichmann Trial, the Jewish Catastrophe, and Hannah Arendt's Narrative.* New York: Macmillan.

Rodman, F. Robert (2003). *Winnicott: Life and Work.* New York: Perseus Publishing.

Rogat, Yosal (1961). *The Eichmann Trial and the Rule of Law.* Santa Barbara, CA: Center for the Study of Democratic Institutions.

Rogow, Arnold A. (1986). Review of Norbert Bromberg & Verna Volz Small's *Hitler's Psychopathology,* New York: International Universities Press, 1983. *The Psychoanalytic Quarterly,* vol. 55, pp. 536–538.

Rogozinski, Jacob (1989). L'enfer sur la terre (Hannah Arendt devant Hitler). *Revue des sciences humaines,* vol. 213, no. 1, pp. 183–206. [French].

Rokeach, Milton (1960). *The Open and Closed Mind: Investigations into the Nature of Belief Systems and Personality Systems.* In collaboration with Richard Bonier [and others]. New York: Basic Books.

Rose, Jacqueline (2003). *On Not Being Able to Sleep: Psychoanalysis in the Modern World.* Princeton, NJ: Princeton University Press.

Rose, Jacqueline (2005). *The Question of Zion.* Princeton, NJ: Princeton University Press.

Rose, Paul Lawrence (1990). *German Question/Jewish Question: Revolutionary Antisemitism from Kant to Wagner.* Princeton, NJ: Princeton University Press.

Rosenbaum, Alan S. (1993). *Prosecuting Nazi War Criminals.* Boulder, CO: Westview Press.

Rosenbaum, Ron (1998). *Explaining Hitler: The Search for the Origins of His Evil.* New York: Random House.

Rosenberg, Alfred (1920). *Die Spur des Juden im Wandel der Zeiten.* Munich: Deutscher Volks-Verlag. 4th edition (1939). Munich: Zentralverlag Der Nsdap; F. Eher Nachfolger. New edition (1943). Munich: F. Eher Nachfolger. [German].

Rosenberg, Alfred (1921). *Das Verbrechen der Freimaurerei: Judentum, Jesuitismus, deutsches Christentum.* Munich: Hoheneichen-Verlag. 2nd edition (1922). Munich: J.F. Lehmanns Verlag. [German].

Rosenberg, Alfred (1941). *Die Judenfrage als Weltproblem.* Vortrag Am 28. März 1941 in Frankfurt am Main Anlässlich Der Eröffnung Des Institits Zur Erforschung Der Judenfrage. Munich: F. Eher Nachfolger. [German].

Rosenbloom, Maria Hirsch (1995). *What Can We Learn from the Holocaust?* Occasional Papers in Jewish History and Thought, no. 3. New York: Hunter College of the City University of New York.

Rosenfeld, Alvin H. (2006). *"Progressive Jewish Thought" and the New Anti-Semitism.* New York: American Jewish Committee.

Rosenkötter, Lutz (1981). Idealbildung in der Generationsfolge. *Psyche: Zeitschrift für Psychoanalyse und ihre Anwendungen,* vol. 35, pp. 593–599.

Rosenkötter, Lutz (1979). Vergangenheitsbewältigung in Psychoanalysen. *Psyche: Zeitschrift für Psychoanalyse und ihre Anwendungen,* vol. 33, pp. 593–599. [German].

Rosenkranz, H. (1978). *Verfolgung and Selbstbehauptung: Die Juden in Österreich, 1938–1945.* Vienna: n.p. [German].

Rosenman, Stanley (1977). Psychoanalytic Reflections on Anti-Semitism. *Journal of Psychology and Judaism,* vol. 1, no. 2, pp. 3–23.

Rosenman, Stanley (1998a). A Critique of Classical Psychoanalytic Theories of Anti-Semitism: a Commentary on M. Ostrow's [*sic*] *Myth and Madness: The Psychodynamics of Anti-semitism. American Journal of Psychoanalysis,* vol. 58, no. 4, pp. 417–433.

Rosenman, Stanley (1998b). Japanese Anti-Semitism: Conjuring up Conspiratorial Jews in a Land Without Jews. *The Journal of Psychohistory,* vol. 25, no. 1, pp. 2–32.

Rosenman, Stanley (2000). Zealous Antisemitism Without Jews: Fanaticism in Search of an Object. Review Essay. *Journal of Psychology and Judaism,* vol. 24, no. 4, pp. 275–285.

Rosenman, Stanley, & Handelsman, Irving (1992). When Victim Encounters Alien Victim in Grisly Circumstances: a Study in Hatred and Scorn. *The Journal of Psychohistory,* vol. 19, no. 4, pp. 421–462.

Rosenthal, Amy K. (2007) Historian Ignites Uproar in Italy. *New York Sun,* Arts and Letters, February 3.

Rosenthal, Denise (2001). The Mythical Jew: Antisemitism, Intellectuals and Democracy in Post-Communist Romania. *Nationalities Papers,* vol. 29, pp. 419–439.

Roskies, David G. (1984). *Against the Apocalypse: Responses to Catastrophe in Modern Jewish Culture.* Cambridge, MA: Harvard University Press. New edition (1999). Syracuse, NY: Syracuse University Press.

Roth, John K., & Berenbaum, Michael (Eds.). (1989). *Holocaust: Religious and Philosophical Implications.* New York: Paragon House.

Roth, Nathan (1985). Review of Norbert Bromberg & Verna Volz Small's *Hitler's Psychopathology,* New York: International Universities Press, 1983. *Journal of American Academy of Psychoanalysis,* vol. 13, pp. 547–548.

Roth, Philip (1986). *The Counterlife.* New York: Farrar, Straus, Giroux. Reprinted (1989). New York: Penguin Books. Reprinted (1996). New York: Vintage International.

Rothschild, Berthold (1991). Vom täglichen Umgang mit einem schlechten Gefühl: Rassismus aus der Sicht des Psychoanalytikers. In Rosenstein, Gaby (Ed.). *Fremdenfeindlichkeit, Rassismus, Antisemitismus: Symposium 1990 der israelitischen*

Cultusgemeinde Zürich und der Gesellschaft für Minderheiten, pp. 31–43. Konstanz: Hartung-Gorre. [German].

Roudinesco, Elisabeth (1995). Georges Mauco (1899–1988)—un psychanalyste au service de vichy: de l'antisémitisme à la psychopédagogie. *L'infini,* no. 51, pp. 69–84. [French].

Roudinesco, Elisabeth (1998). Carl Gustav Jung—de l'archetype au nazisme: dérives d'une psychologie de la différence. *L'Infini,* no. 63, pp. 73–94. [French].

Rousso, Henry (1987). *Le Syndrome De Vichy.* Paris: Editions du Seuil. New edition (1990). Paris: Editions du Seuil. [French].

Rousso, Henry (1991). *The Vichy Syndrome.* Cambridge, MA: Harvard University Press.

Rozzo, Ugo (1997). Il presunto omicidio rituale di Simonino da Trento e il primo santo "tipografico." *Atti dell'Accademia di Scienze e Lettere di Udine,* vol. 90, pp. 185–223. [Italian].

Rubenstein, Richard L. (1966). *After Auschwitz: Radical Theology and Contemporary Judaism.* Indianapolis: Bobbs-Merrill. 2nd edition (1992). Baltimore: Johns Hopkins University Press.

Rubenstein, Richard L. (1975). *The Cunning of History: Mass Death and the American Future.* New York: Harper & Row.

Rubenstein, Richard L., & Roth, John K. (1987). *Approaches to Auschwitz: The Holocaust and its Legacy.* Atlanta, GA: John Knox Press. 2nd edition (2003). Louisville, KY: Westminster John Knox Press.

Rubin, Daniel (Ed.). (1987). *Anti-Semitism and Zionism: Selected Marxist Writings.* New York: International Publishers.

Rubin, Miri (1999). *Gentile Tales: The Narrative Assault on Late Medieval Jews.* New Haven, CT: Yale University Press. New edition (2004). Philadelphia: University of Pennsylvania Press.

Rudski, Jeffrey (2003). What Does a Superstitious Person Believe? Impressions of Participants. *Journal of General Psychology,* vol. 130, no. 4, pp. 431–445.

Ruether, Rosemary Radford (1974). *Faith and Fratricide: The Theological Roots of Anti-Semitism.* New York: Seabury Press.

Ruether, Rosemary Radford (1987). The Theological Roots of Anti-Semitism. In Fein, Helen (Ed.), *The Persisting Question: Sociological Perspectives and Social Context of Modern Antisemitism.* Berlin and New York: Walter de Gruyter.

Ruether, Rosemary Radford (1991). The *Adversus Judaeos* Tradition in the Church Fathers: The Exegesis of Christian Anti-Judaism. In Cohen, Jeremy (Ed.), *Essential Papers on Judaism and Christianity.* New York: New York University Press.

Ruether, Rosemary Radford & Ellis, Marc H. (Eds.) (1990). *Beyond Occupation: American Jewish, Christian, and Palestinian Voices for Peace.* Boston: Beacon Press.

Ruether, Rosemary Radford, & Ruether, Herman J. (1989). *The Wrath of Jonah: The Crisis of Religious Nationalism in the Israeli-Palestinian Conflict.* New York: Harper & Row. 2nd edition (2002). Minneapolis: Fortress Press.

Rule, B.G. (1966). Anti-Semitism, Stress, and Judgments of Strangers. *Journal of Personality and Social Psychology,* vol. 3, no. 1, pp. 132–134.

Russell, Edward Frederick Langley [Lord Russell of Liverpool] (1962). *The Trial of Adolf Eichmann.* London: Heinemann. Reprinted (1963). London: Transworld Publishers.

Russell, Jeffrey Burton (1981). *Satan: The Early Chrisrian Tradition.* Ithaca, NY: Cornell University Press.

Russell, Jeffrey Burton (1984). *Lucifer: The Devil in the Middle Ages.* Ithaca, NY: Cornell University Press.

Rutschky, Katharina (1983). *Deutsche Kinder-Chronik.* Cologne: Kiepenheuer & Witsch. [German].

Safrai, Shmuel & Stern, Menahem (Eds.) (1974–1976). *Jewish People in the First Century: Historical Geography, Political History, Social, Cultural and Religious Life and Institutions.* 2 vols. In cooperation with David Flusser and Willem Cornelis van Unnik. Amsterdam: Assen, Van Gorcum.

Said, Edward (2000). My Encounter with Sartre. *London Review of Books,* vol. 22, no. 11 (June 1).

Salamon, Hagar (1999). *The Hyena People: Ethiopian Jews in Christian Ethiopia.* Berkeley: University of California Press.

Samuel, Maurice (1924). *You Gentiles.* New York: Harcourt, Brace & Co.

Samuel, Maurice (1940). *The Great Hatred.* New York: Alfred A. Knopf. Reprinted (1943). London: Victor Gollancz. New edition (1988). Lanham, MD: University Press of America.

Samuel, Maurice (1966). *Blood Accusation: The Strange History of the Beiliss Case.* New York: Alfred A. Knopf. Reprinted (1967). London: Weidenfeld & Nicolson.

Samuels, Andrew (1993). Jung, Anti-Semitism and the Nazis. In Samuels, Andrew, *The Political Psyche.* London and New York: Routledge.

Samuels, Andrew (1994). Jung and Antisemitism. *Jewish Quarterly,* vol. 40, no. 5, pp. 59–63.

Samuels, Andrew (1996). Jung's Return from Banishment. *The Psychoanalytic Review,* vol. 83, no. 4, pp. 469–489.

Sanford, R. Nevitt (1973). Authoritarian Personality in Contemporary Perspective. In Knutson, Jeanne N. (Ed.), *Handbook of Political Psychology,* pp. 139–170. San Francisco: Jossey-Bass.

Sanford, R. Nevitt, et al. (Eds.). (1971).*Sanctions for Evil: Sources of Social Destructiveness.* San Francisco: Jossey-Bass. Reprinted (1972). Boston: Beacon Press.

Sanua, Victor D. (1997). Review of "Myth and Madness: The Psychodynamics of Anti-Semitism." *Journal of Nervous & Mental Disease,* vol. 185, no. 8, pp. 527–528.

Sapriel, Guy (2004). La Permanence antisémite: une étude psychanalytique: la trace mnésique irréductible. *Pardès: Études et Culture Juives,* no. 37, *Psychanalyse de l'antisémitisme contemporain,* pp. 11–20. [French].

Sargant, William Walters (1957). *Battle for the Mind.* London: Heinemann. Garden City, NY: Doubleday. New edition (1961). Harmondsworth and Baltimore: Penguin Books. New edition (1975). *Battle for the Mind: a Physiology of Conversion and Brainwashing.* Westport, CT: Greenwood Press. New edition (1997). Preface by Charles Swencionis. Cambridge, MA: Malor Books.

Saroglou, Vassilis, & Galand, Philippe (2004). Identities, Values, and Religion: A Study among Muslim, Other Immigrant, and Native Belgian Young Adults after the 9/11 Attacks. *Identity,* vol. 4, no. 2, pp. 97–132.

Sartre, Jean-Paul (1939). *L'enfance d'un chef.* In Sartre, Jean-Paul,*Le Mur.* 2nd edition. Paris: Gallimard. New edition (1945). Paris: Gallimard. New edition (1958). Paris: Le Club du Meilleur Livre. [French].

Sartre, Jean-Paul (1946a). Portrait of an Antisemite. *Partisan Review,* vol. 13, pp. 163–178.

Sartre, Jean-Paul (1946b). *Réflexions sur la Question Juive.* Paris: P. Morihien. Reprinted (1954). Paris: Gallimard. New edition (1961). Paris: Gallimard. New edition (1985). Paris: Gallimard. New edition (1993). Paris: Gallimard. [French].

Sartre, Jean-Paul (1948). *Anti-Semite and Jew.* Tr. George J. Becker. New York: Schocken Books. Reprinted (1995). New York: Schocken Books.

Sartre, Jean-Paul (1987). What Is an Anti-Semite? In Fein, Helen (Ed.), *The Persisting Question: Sociological Perspectives and Social Context of Modern Antisemitism,* pp. 58–66. Berlin and New York: Walter De Gruyter.

Sartre, Jean-Paul, & Lévy, Benny (1980). Entretiens. *Le Nouvel Observateur.* Book edition (1991). *L'Espoir maintenant: les entretiens de 1980.* Paris: Verdier. [French].

Sartre, Jean-Paul, & Lévy, Benny (1996). *Hope Now: The 1980 Interviews.* Tr. Adrian Van Den Hoven. Intro. by Ronald Aronson. Chicago: University of Chicago Press.

Schäfer, Peter (1997). *Judeophobia: Attitudes Toward the Jews in the Ancient World.* Cambridge, MA: Harvard University Press.

Schaffner, Bertram (1948). *Fatherland: A Study of Authoritarianism in the German Family.* New York: Columbia University Press.

Schapira, Esther (2002). *Das rote Quadrat: drei Kugeln und ein totes Kind.* Ein Film von Esther Schapira geht der Frage nach: "Wer erschoss Mohammed Al-Dura?" Ard-TV, Monday, March 18, 9:45 PM. [German video].

Scharfstein, Sol (1996–1997). *Understanding Jewish History: From the Patriarchs to the 21st Century.* Design & Graphics by Dorcas Gelabert. Hoboken, NJ: Ktav Publishing House. New edition (1999). Hoboken, NJ: Ktav Publishing House.

Schatz, Jaff (1991). *The Generation: The Rise and Fall of the Jewish Communists of Poland.* Berkeley: University of California Press.

Scheidlinger, S. (1974). On the Concept of the Mother Group. *International Journal of Group Psychotherapy,* vol. 4, pp. 417–428.

Schermerhorn, Richard Alonzo (1970). *Comparative Ethnic Relations: A Framework for Theory and Research.* Ed. Peter I. Rose. New York: Random House. New edition (1978). With a new preface. Chicago: University of Chicago Press.

Schindler, Ronald Jeremiah (1996). *The Frankfurt School Critique of Capitalist Culture: A Critical Theory for Post-Democratic Society and its Re-Education.* Aldershot, England, and Brookfield, VT: Avebury. New edition (1998). Aldershot, England, and Brookfield, VT: Ashgate Publishing.

Schlant, Ernestine (1999).*The Language of Silence: West German Literature and the Holocaust.* New York: Routledge.

Schmidt, Alfred (1988). *Emanzipatorische Sinnlichkeit.* Munich: Piper Verlag. [German].

Schmidt. Marita, & Dietz, Gabi (Eds.). (1983). *Frauen unterm Hakenkreuz.* Berlin: Elefanten-presse. [German].

Schneider, Michael (1997). *Die "Goldhagen-Debatte": ein Historikerstreit in der Mediengesellschaft.* Ed. Dieter Dowe. Bonn: Forschungsinstitut Der Friedrich-Ebert-Stiftung, Historisches Forschungszentrum. [German].

Schneider, Wolfgang (2001). *Frauen unterm Hakenkreuz.* Hamburg: Hoffmann Und Campe, [German].

Schoenfeld, Charles George (1966). Psychoanalysis and Anti-Semitism. *The Psychoanalytic Review,* vol. 53, no. 1, pp. 24–37.

Schoenfeld, Gabriel (2004). *The Return of Anti-Semitism.* San Francisco: Encounter Books.

Scholem, Gershom (1973). *Sabbatai Sevi: The Mystical Messiah.* Princeton, NJ: Princeton University Press.

Schorsch, Ismar (1972). *Jewish Reactions to German Anti-Semitism, 1870–1914.* New York: Columbia University Press. Philadelphia: Jewish Publication Society of America.

Schott, Robin May (1992). The Domination of Women and Jews: A Critique of Horkheimer's and Adorno's Dialectic of Enlightenment. *Tel Aviver Jahrbuch für deutsche Geschichte,* vol. 21, pp. 259–269. Minerva-Institut für deutsche Geschichte, Tel Aviv University. Göttingen: Wallstein-Verlag.

Schreier, Helmut, & Heyl, Matthias (Eds.). (1994). *Die Gegenwart der Schoah: zur Aktualität des Mordes an den europäischen Juden.* Hamburg: Krämer. [German].

Schudrich, Michael J. (1987). Antisemitism in Japan. *IJA Research Reports,* no. 12 (December), pp. 8–11.

Schul, Yaacov (Ed.) (1995). *The "Other" as Threat: Demonization and Antisemitism.* Jerusalem: the Vidal Sassoon International Center for the Study of Antisemitism, The Hebrew University of Jerusalem.

Schürer, Emil (1886–1890). *Lehrbuch Der neutestamentlichen Zeitgeschichte.* Leipzig: J.C. Hinrichs. 2nd edition (1890). *Geschichte des jüdischen Volkes im Zeitalter Jesu Christi.* Leipzig: J.C. Hinrichs. [German].

Schürer, Emil (1961). *A History of the Jewish People in the Time of Jesus.* Edited and Introduced by Nahum N. Glatzer. New York: Schocken Books.

Schwaab, Edleff H. (1992). *Hitler's Mind: A Plunge into Madness.* Foreword by Peter H. Wolff. New York: Praeger.

Schwartz, Adi (2007). The Wayward Son. *Ha'aretz,* Thursday, March 1.

Schwarz, Daniel R. (1979). *Disraeli's Fiction.* London: Macmillan. New York: Barnes & Noble.

Schwarzschild, Steven S. (1979). Germanism and Judaism: Hermann Cohen's Normative Paradigm of the German-Jewish Symbiosis. In Bronsen, David (Ed.), *Jews and Germans from 1860 to 1933: The Problematic Symbiosis,* pp. 129–172. Heidelberg: Winter.

Segel, Benjamin Wolf (1934). *The Protocols of the Elders of Zion: the Greatest Lie in History.* Tr. Sascha Czaczkes-Charles, with 10 letters of endorsement from eminent German non-Jewish scholars. New York: Bloch Publishing Co. New edition (1995). *A Lie and a Libel: The History of the Protocols of the Elders of Zion.* Tr. & Ed. Richard S. Levy. Lincoln: University of Nebraska Press. Reprinted (1996). Lincoln: University of Nebraska Press.

Segev, Tom (1988). *Soldiers of Evil: The Commandants of the Nazi Concentration Camps.* Tr. Haim Watzman. New York: McGraw-Hill.

Seibel, Wolfgang (2002). The Strength of Perpetrators: The Holocaust in Western Europe, 1940–1944. *Governance,* vol. 15, no. 2.

Seltzer, Robert M. (1980). *Jewish People, Jewish Thought: The Jewish Experience in History.* New York: Macmillan Publishing Co.

Selznick, Gertrude Jaeger, & Steinberg, Stephen (1969). *The Tenacity of Prejudice: Anti-Semitism in Contemporary America.* New York: Harper & Row. New edition (1979). Westport, CT: Greenwood Press.

Semi, Antonio Alberto (1993). Psychopathology of Everyday Antisemitism. In Meghnagi, David (Ed.), *Freud and Judaism,* pp. 141–151. London: Karnac Books.

Senkman, Leonardo (2006). Democratization and Antisemitism in Argentina: an Assessment. *Analysis of Current Trends in Antisemitism,* no. 28. Jerusalem: The Vidal Sassoon International Center for the Study of Antisemitism, The Hebrew University of Jerusalem.

Šeparović, Zvonimir Paul (Ed.). *Victimology: International Action and Study of Victims: Papers Given at the Fifth International Symposium on Victimology, 1985, in Zagreb, Yugoslavia.* Zagreb, Croatia: University of Zagreb.

Sereny, Gitta (1974). *Into That Darkness: From Mercy Killing to Mass Murder.* London: Andre Deutsch. New York: McGraw-Hill. New edition (1983). *Into That Darkness: An Examination of Conscience.* New York: Vintage Books.

Sereny, Gitta (2000). *The German Trauma: Experiences and Reflections, 1938–1999.* London: Penguin Press. New edition (2001). *The Healing Wound: Experiences and Reflections on Germany, 1938–2001.* New York: W.W. Norton.

Serrano Fernández , Miguel Joaquín Diego del Carmen (1966). *C. G. Jung and Hermann Hesse: A Record of Two Friendships.* Tr. Frank Macshane. New York: Schocken Books.

Shachar, Isaiah (1974). *The Judensau: A Medieval Anti-Jewish Motif and Its History.* London: Warburg Institute.

Shain, Milton (1994). *The Roots of Antisemitism in South Africa.* Charlottesville: University Press of Virginia.

Shain, Milton (1998). *Antisemitism.* London: Bowerdean Publishing Co. in Association with the Kaplan Centre for Jewish Studies and Research at the University of Cape Town.

Shain, Milton, & Mendelsohn, Richards (Eds.). (2002). *Memories, Realities and Dreams: Aspects of the South African Jewish Experience.* Johannesburg: Jonathan Ball Publishers.

Shandley, Robert R. (Ed.). (1998). *Unwilling Germans? The Goldhagen Debate.* With Essays Translated by Jeremiah Riemer. Minneapolis: University of Minnesota Press.

Shapiro, James (1996). *Shakespeare and the Jews.* New York: Columbia University Press.

Sharpe, Barry (1999). *Modesty and Arrogance in Judgment: Hannah Arendt's "Eichmann in Jerusalem."* Westport, CT: Praeger.

Shatzmiller, Joseph (1990). *Shylock Reconsidered: Jews, Moneylending, and Medieval Society.* Berkeley: University of California Press.

Shavit, Jacob (1988). *Jabotinsky and the Revisionist Movement, 1925–1948.* London, and Totawa, NJ: Frank Cass.

Shaw, John, A. (1998). Narcissism, Identity Formation, and Genocide.*Adolescent Psychiatry.*

Shelton, Dinah L. (Ed.). (2005). *Encyclopedia of Genocide and Crimes Against Humanity.* 3 vols. Detroit, MI: Macmillan Reference Books.

Shermis, Michael, & Zannoni, Arthur E. (Eds.). *Introduction to Jewish-Christian Relations.* New York: Paulist Press.

Sherwin-White, A.N. (1967) Racial Prejudice in Imperial Rome. Cambridge: Cambridge University Press.

Shipman, P. (1994). *The Evolution of Racism: Human Differences and the Use and Abuse of Science.* New York: Simon & Schuster.

Shirer, William Lawrence (1960). *The Rise and Fall of the Third Reich: A History of Nazi Germany.* New York: Simon and Schuster. New edition (1990). With a new afterword by the author. New York: Simon & Schuster.

Shirer, William Lawrence (1961). *The Rise and Fall of Adolf Hitler.* New York: Random House.

Shoham, Shlomo Giora (1995). *Valhalla, Calvary, and Auschwitz.* Cincinnati: Bowman & Cody Academic Publishing. Tel Aviv: Ramot Publishing House at Tel Aviv University. Reprinted (1997). New York: Bloch Publishing Co.

Sibony, Daniel (1991). *Du vecu et de l'invivable: psychopathologie du quotidien.* Paris: Albin Michel. [French].

Sidahmed, Abdel Salam, & Ehteshami, Anoushiravan (Eds.). (1996). *Islamic Fundamentalism.* Boulder, CO: Westview Press.

Sigal, Gerald (2004). *Anti-Judaism in the New Testament.* New York: Gerald Sigal.

Siker, Jeffrey S. (1991). *Disinheriting the Jews: Abraham in Early Christian Controversy.* Louisville, KY: Westminster John Knox Press.

Silbermann, Alphons (1962). Zur Soziologie des Antisemitismus. *Psyche: Zeitschrift für Psychoanalyse und ihre Anwendungen,* vol. 16, pp. 246–254.

Silbermann, Alphons, & Schoeps, Julius Hans (Eds.). (1986). *Antisemitismus nach dem Holocaust: Bestandsaufnahme und Erscheinungsformen in Deutschsprachigen Ländern.* Cologne: Wissenschaft und Politik. [German].

Simmel, Ernst (1946). Antisemitism and Mass Psychopathology. In Simmel, Ernst (Ed.). *Anti-Semitism: A Social Disease.* New York: International Universities Press. New edition (1948). New York: International Universities Press.

Simmel, Ernst (1978). Antisemitismus und Massen-Psychopathologie (1946). (aus dem Archiv der Psychoanalyse). *Psyche: Zeitschrift für Psychoanalyse und ihre Anwendungen,* vol. 32, pp. 492–527. [German].

Simmel, Ernst (Ed.). (1946). *Anti-Semitism: A Social Disease.* New York: International Universities Press. New edition (1948). New York: International Universities Press.

Simmel, Ernst (Ed.). (1993). *Antisemitismus.* Ed. Elisabeth Dahmer-Kloss. Frankfurt am Main: Fischer Taschenbuch Verlag. New edition (2002). Frankfurt am Main: Fischer Taschenbuch Verlag. [German].

Simon, Hermann (2003). *Moses Mendelssohn: gesetzestreuer Jude und deutscher Aufklärer.* Teetz: Hentrich & Hentrich. [German].

Simon, Marcel (1996). *Verus Israel: A Study of the Relations between Christians and Jews in the Roman Empire, AD 135–425.* London: Littman Library of Jewish Civilization.

Sinsheimer, Hermann (1947). *Shylock: The History of a Character.* New York: Benjamin Blom.

Sklare, Marshall (Ed.). (1958). *The Jews: Social Patterns of an American Group.* Glencoe, IL: The Free Press.

Skolnik, Fred, & Berenbaum, Michael (Eds.). (2007). *Encyclopaedia Judaica,* 2nd edition. Detroit and Jerusalem: Macmillan Reference USA and Keter Publishing House.

Slochower, Harry (1981). Freud as Yahweh in Jung's Answer to Job. *American Imago,* vol. 38, no. 1, pp. 3–39.

Smiga, George M. (1992). *Pain and Polemic: Anti-Judaism in the Gospels.* New York: Paulist Press.

Smith, Bradley F. (1967). *Adolf Hitler: His Family, Childhood, and Youth.* Stanford, CA: Hoover Institution on War, Revolution, and Peace.

Smith, Bradley F. (1978). Two Alibis for the Inhumanities: Reviews of A. R. Butz, "The Hoax of the Twentieth Century" and David Irving, "Hitler's War." *German Studies Review,* vol. 1, no. 3, pp. 327–335.

Smith, David Norman (1996). The Social Construction of Enemies: Jews and the Representation of Evil. *Sociological Theory,* vol. 14, pp. 203–240.

Smith, David Norman (1997). Judeophobia: Myth and Critique. In Breslauer, S. Daniel (Ed.). *The Seductiveness of Jewish Myth: Challenge or Response?* Albany: State University of New York Press.

Smith Thomas W. (1993). The Polls—a Review: Actual Trends or Measurement Artifacts? A Review of Three Studies of Anti-Semitism. *Public Opinion Quarterly,* vol. 57, pp. 380–393.

Smith, Thomas W. (1999). The Religious Right and Anti-Semitism. *Review of Religious Research,* vol. 40, pp. 244–259.

Smith, Thomas W. (2005). *Jewish Distinctiveness in America: A Statistical Portrait.* New York: American Jewish Committee.

Solomon, Zahava (1995). From Denial to Recognition: Attitudes Toward Holocaust Survivors from World War II to the Present. *Journal of Traumatic Stress,* vol. 8, no. 2, pp. 215–228.

Sombart, Nicolaus (1991). *Die deutschen Männer und ihre Feinde: Carl Schmitt—ein deutsches Schicksal zwischen Männerbund und Matriarchatsmythos.* Munich: Carl Hanser Verlag. [German].

Sorkin, David Jan (1996). *Moses Mendelssohn and the Religious Enlightenment.* Berkeley: University of California Press.

Springer, Anne (1990). The Return of the Repressed in the Mask of the Victim. *The Journal of Psychohistory,* vol. 17, no. 3, pp. 237–256.

Stäglich, Wilhelm (1979). *Der Auschwitz-Mythos: Legende oder Wirklichkeit? eine kritische Bestandsaufnahme.* Tübingen: Grabert. [German].

Stäglich, Wilhelm (1986). *The Auschwitz Myth: A Judge Looks at the Evidence.* Torrance, CA: Institute for Historical Review.

State of Israel Ministry of Justice (1992). *The Trial of Adolf Eichmann: Record of Proceedings in the District Court of Jerusalem, Criminal Case 40/61.* 9 vols. Jerusalem: Trust for the Publication of the Proceedings of the Eichmann Trial, the Israel State Archives, and *Yad Vashem.* New edition (1998). Jerusalem: Rubin Mass.

Staub, Ervin (1989). *The Roots of Evil: The Origins of Genocide and Other Group Violence.* New York: Cambridge University Press.

Stav, Arieh (1999). *Peace: The Arabian Caricature. A Study of Anti-Semitic Imagery.* Jerusalem and New York: Gefen Publishing House. Reprinted (2000). Jerusalem and New York: Gefen Publishing House.

Stein, Howard F. (1975). American Judaism, Israel, and the New Ethnicity. *Cross Currents,* vol. 25, no. 1, pp. 51–66.

Stein, Howard F. (1977). The Binding of the Son: Psychoanalytic Reflections on the Symbiosis of Anti-Semitism and Anti-Gentilism. *The Psychoanalytic Quarterly,* vol. 46, pp. 650–683.

Stein, Howard F. (1978). Judaism and the Group Fantasy of Martyrdom: The Psychodynamic Paradox of Survival Through Persecution. *The Journal of Psychohistory,* vol. 6, no. 2, pp. 151–210.

Stein, Howard F. (1979). The Nazi Holocaust, History and Psychohistory. *The Journal of Psychohistory,* vol. 7, no. 2, pp. 215–227.

Stein, Howard F. (1984). The Holocaust, the Uncanny, and the Jewish Sense of History. *Political Psychology,* vol. 5, no. 1, pp. 5–35.

Stein, Howard F. (1987). *Developmental Time, Cultural Space: Studies in Psychogeography.* Norman: University of Oklahoma Press.

Stein, Howard F. (1993). The Holocaust, the Self, and the Question of Wholeness. *Ethos,* vol. 21, no. 4, pp. 485–512.

Stein, Howard F. (1994). "The Eternal Jew": Resurgent Anti-Semitism in the Post–Cold War World. *The Journal of Psychohistory,* vol. 22, no. 1, pp. 39–57. Updated version (2002) in Piven, Jerry S., & Boyd, Chris (Eds.), *Judaism and Genocide.* Lincoln, NE: iUniverse.

Stein, Ruth (2002). Evil as Love and Liberation: the Mind of a Suicidal Religious Terrorist. *Psychoanalytic Dialogues: A Journal of Relational Perspectives,* vol. 12, no. 3, pp. 393–420. Reprinted (2002) in Piven, Jerry S., et al. (Eds.), *Terror and Apocalypse,* Vol. 2 of *Psychological Undercurrents of History.* Lincoln, NE: iUniverse. San Jose, CA: Author's Choice Press, Writer's Showcase Press, Writer's Club Press. Reprinted (2003) in Moss, Donald (Ed.), *Hating in the First Person Plural: Psychoanalytic Essays on Racism, Homophobia, Misogyny, and Terror,* pp. 281–310. New York: Other Press. Reprinted (2004) in Piven, Jerry S., et al. (Eds.). *Terrorism, Jihad and Sacred Vengeance.* Giessen: Psychosozial-Verlag.

Steiner, George (1971). *In Bluebeard's Castle: Some Notes Towards the Redefinition of Culture.* New Haven, CT: Yale University Press.

Steinsaltz, Adin (1976). The Persecution and Banning of the Talmud. In Steinsalz, Adin, *The Essential Talmud,* part I, chapter 11. Tr. Chaya Galai. New York: Basic Books. Reprinted (1984). New York: Basic Books.

Stember, Charles Herbert et al. (1966). *Jews in the Mind of America.* Preface by John Slawson. Ed. George Salomon. New York: Basic Books.

Stern, Anne-Lise (1988). Eclats de la "Nuit de cristal. " *Les Temps Modernes,* no. 509, pp. 30–40. [French].

Stern, Anne-Lise (1989). "Penser" Auschwitz, par la psychanalyse? *Pardès: Études et Culture Juives,* no. 9–10, pp. 239–247. [French].

Stern, Anne-Lise (2004). *Le Savoir-déporté: camps, histoire, psychanalyse.* Précédé de *Une vie à l'œuvre* Par Nadine Fresco et Martine Leibovici. Paris: Editions du Seuil. [French].

Stern, Fritz Richard (1961). *The Politics of Cultural Despair: A Study in the Rise of the Germanic Ideology.* Berkeley: University of California Press. New edition (1974). Berkeley: University of California Press.

Stern, Kenneth Saul (1990). *Anti-Zionism: The Sophisticated Anti-Semitism.* New York: American Jewish Committee, Institute of Human Relations.

Stern, Kenneth Saul (1993). *Holocaust Denial.* New York: American Jewish Committee.

Stern, Kenneth Saul (2007). *Antisemitism Today: How It Is The Same, How It Is Different, and How To Fight It.* New York: American Jewish Committee.

Stern, Menachem (1976). The Jew in Greek and Latin Literature. In Safrai, Shmuel, & Stern, Menahem (Eds.) (1974–1976), *Jewish People in the First Century: Historical Geography, Political History, Social, Cultural and Religious Life and Institutions,* vol. 2. In cooperation with David Flusser and Willem Cornelis van Unnik. Amsterdam: Assen, Van Gorcum.

Stern, Menahem (Ed.). (1980). *Greek and Latin Authors on Jews and Judaism.* Jerusalem: Israel Academy of Sciences and Humanities.

Sternhell, Zeev (1988). *Antisemitism and the Right in France.* Jerusalem: Shazar Library, Institute of Contemporary Jewry, the Vidal Sassoon International Center for the Study of Antisemitism, The Hebrew University of Jerusalem.

Sternhell, Zeev (1998). *The Founding Myths of Israel: Nationalism, Socialism, and the Making of the Jewish State.* Tr. David Maisel. Princeton, New Jersey: Princeton University Press.

Stewart, Desmond (1974). *Theodor Herzl: Artist and Politician.* London: Hamish Hamilton. Garden City, NY: Doubleday.

Stiegnitz, Peter (1975). Angst und Antisemitismus: Sozialpsychologie der Judenfeindlichkeit in Deutschland und Österreich. *Tribüne,* vol. 14, pp. 6368–6374. [German].

Stierlin, Helm (1975). *Adolf Hitler: Familienperspektiven.* Frankfurt am Main: Suhrkamp. [German].

Stierlin, Helm (1976). *Adolf Hitler: A Family Perspective.* New York: The Psychohistory Press.

Stillman, Norman (1979). *The Jews of Arab Lands.* Philadelphia: Jewish Publication Society of America.

Stöcklein, Paul (1985). Zur Psychologie des Hasses: Joseph Roths Deutung des Judenhassen, mit einem Blick auf Freud. In Brochmeyer, Dieter, & Heimeran, Till (Eds.), *Weimar am Pazifik: literarische Wege zwischen den Kontinenten. Festschrift für Werner Vordtriede,* pp. 78–89. Tübingen: Max Niemeyer. [German].

Stone, William F., et al. (1993). *Strength and Weakness: The Authoritarian Personality Today.* New York: Springer-Verlag.

Strack, Hermann Leberecht (1909). *The Jew and Human Sacrifice: Human Blood and Jewish Ritual, an Historical and Sociological Inquiry.* Tr. Henry Blanchamp. New York: Block Publishing Co.

Stratton, Jon (2000). *Coming out Jewish: Constructing Ambivalent Identities.* London: Routledge.

Strauss, Herbert A. (Ed.). (1993). *Hostages of Modernization: Studies on Modern Antisemitism, 1870–1933/39.* 2 vols. Berlin and New York: Walter De Gruyter.

Strong, Donald S. (1941). *Organized Anti-Semitism in America: The Rise of Group Prejudice During the Decade 1930–40.* Washington, DC: American Council on Public Affairs. New edition (1979). Westport, CT: Greenwood Press.

Strozier, Charles B. (1994). *Apocalypse: On the Psychology of Fundamentalism in America.* Boston: Beacon Press.

Strozier, Charles B., & Flynn, Michael (Eds.). (1996). *Genocide, War, and Human Survival.* Lanham, MD: Rowman & Littlefield Publishers.

Suied, Alain (1996). *Paul Celan et le corps juif.* Bordeaux: William Blake & Co. [French].

Sutton, Nina (1996). *Bettelheim: A Life and a Legacy.* Tr. David Sharp, with the author. New York: Basic Books.

Sylvanus, Pal (1895). *Tit for Tat: Satirical Universal History.* Chicago: The Satirical Historical Association. Reprinted (1977). In Quinley, Harold E. (Ed.), *Anti-Semitism in America, 1878–1939.* New York: Arno Press.

Szafran, André Willy (1976). *Louis-Ferdinand Céline: essai psychanalytique.* Brussels: Éditions de l'Université de Bruxelles. [French].

Szafran, André Willy (1984). Psychological Aspects of Anti-Semitism in Fascist Writers. *Acta Psychiatrica Belgica,* vol. 84, no. 3, pp. 273–283.

Szarmach, Paul E. (Ed.). (1979). *Aspects of Jewish Culture in the Middle Ages.* Papers of the Eighth Annual Conference of the Center for Meieval and Early Renaissance Studies, State University of New York at Binghamton, May 3–5, 1974. Albany: State University of New York Press.

Szasz, Thomas (1978). Sigmund Freud: the Jewish Avenger. In Szasz, Thomas, *The Myth of Psychotherapy: Mental Healing as Religion, Rhetoric, and Repression,* pp. 138–157. Garden City, NY: Doubleday Anchor.

Szekely, Lajos (1988). Tradition and Infantile Fantasy in the Shape of Modern Antisemitism. *Scandinavian Psychoanalytic Review,* vol. 11, no. 2, pp. 160–177.

Szwec, Gerard (1990). *Shoah,* une nevrose traumatique. In Hazan, Barbara et al. (1990), *Shoah, le film: des psychanalystes écrivent,* pp. 78–81. Paris: Jacques Grancher. [French].

Taguieff, Pierre-André (1992). *Les Protocoles Des Sages De Sion.* 2 vols. Paris: Berg International. [French].

Taguieff, Pierre-André (2001). *The Force of Prejudice: On Racism and its Doubles.* Tr. & Ed. Hassan Melehy. Minneapolis: University of Minnesota Press.

Taguieff, Pierre-André (2002). *La nouvelle Judéophobie.* Paris: Mille et Une Nuits. [French].

Taguieff, Pierre-André (2004). *Rising from the Muck: The New Anti-Semitism in Europe.* Tr. Patrick Camiller. Foreword by Radu Ioanid. Chicago: Ivan R. Dee.

Taguieff, Pierre-André et al. (1999). *L'Antisémitisme de plume, 1940–1944: études et documents.* Par Pierre-André Taguieff, Grégoire Kauffmann, Michaël Lenoire; Sous La Direction De Pierre-André Taguieff; avec la participation de Robert Belot, Annick Duraffour, Marc Knobel...[et al.] Paris: Berg International. [French].

Tajfel, Henry (Ed.). (1982). *Social Identity and Intergroup Relations.* Cambridge: Cambridge University Press.

Takahama, Tatou (1995). Holocaust Denial in Japan: *Marco Polo* Demonstrates Insensitivity. *Japan Policy Research Institute Critique,* vol. 2, no. 3 (March).

Tal, Uriel (1975). *Christians and Jews in Germany: Religion, Politics, and Ideology in the Second Reich, 1870–1914.* Tr. Noah Jonathan Jacobs. Ithaca, NY: Cornell University Press.

Talmon, Jacob Leib (1973). European History—Seedbed of the Holocaust. *Midstream,* vol. 19, no. 5 (May).

Talmon, Jacob Leib (1981). *The Myth of the Nation and the Vision of Revolution: The Origins of Ideological Polarisation in the Twentieth Century.* London: Secker & Warburg. Berkeley: University of California Press.

Tarnero, Jacques (1995). *Le Racisme.* Toulouse: Milan. [French].

Tarnero, Jacques (1999). Le Négationnisme, ou le symptôme des temps pervers: une énigne récurrente: le signe antijuif. *Revue D'histoire De La Shoah,* vol. 3, no. 166. [French].

Taylor, Miriam S. (1995). *Anti-Judaism and Early Christian Identity: A Critique of the Scholarly Consensus.* Leiden and New York: E.J. Brill.

Teicher, Samy (1987). *Die Beurteilung jüdischer KZ-verfolgter und ihrer Kinder in Hinblick auf ihre spätere Integration.* Unpublished dissertation, University of Vienna. [German].

Tenenbaum, Joseph (1976). *Race and Reich: The Story of an Epoch.* Westport, CT: Greenwood Press.

Terman, David (1984). Anti-Semitism: A Study in Group Vulnerability and the Vicissitudes of Group Ideals. *The Psychohistory Review,* vol. 12, no. 4, pp. 18–24.

Tewarson, Heidi Thomann (1998). *Rahel Levin Varnhagen: The Life and Work of a German Jewish Intellectual.* Lincoln: University of Nebraska Press.

Tewes, Henning, & Wright, Jonathan (Eds.). (2001). *Liberalism, Anti-Semitism, and Democracy: Essays in Honour of Peter Pulzer.* Oxford and New York: Oxford University Press.

Thalmann, R. (Ed.). (1986). *Femmes et Fascisme.* Paris: n.p. [French].

Thion, Serge (1980). *Vérité historique ou vérité politique? le dossier de l'affaire Faurisson, la question des chambres à gaz.* Avec la collaboration de Jacob Assous, Denis Authier, Jean-Gabriel Cohn-Bendit, Maurice Di Scuillo, et al. Paris: La Vieille Taupe. [French].

Thoma, Clemens (1980). *A Christian Theology of Judaism.* Tr. Helga Croner. Foreword by David Flusser. New York: Paulist Press.

Tietze, Hans (1987). *Die Juden Wiens.* Vienna: E.P. Tal. [German].

Toaff, Ariel (2007) *Pasque di Sangue: ebrei d'Europa e omicidi rituali.* Bologna: Il Mulino. [Italian].

Tobacyk, Jerome, & Milford, Gary (1983). Belief in Paranormal Phenomena: Assessment Instrument Development and Implications for Personality Functioning.*Journal of Personality and Social Psychology,* vol. 44, pp. 648–655

Tobin, Gary A., & Sassler, Sharon L. (1988). *Jewish Perceptions of Antisemitism.* New York: Plenum Press.

Tokudome, Kinue (1999). *Courage to Remember: Interviews on the Holocaust.* St. Paul, MN: Paragon House.

Torner, Carles (2001). *Shoah, une pédagogie de la mémoire.* Paris: Editions de L'atelier. [French].

Totten, Samuel, Parsons, William S., & Charny, Israel W. (1997). *Century of Genocide: Eyewitness Accounts and Critical Views.* New York: Garland Publications. 2nd edition (2004). *Century of Genocide: Critical Essays and Eyewitness Accounts.* London and New York: Routledge.

Trachtenberg, Joshua (1943). *The Devil and the Jews: The Medieval Conception of the Jews and Its Relation to Modern Antisemitism.* New Haven, CT: Yale University Press. London: Henry Milford, Oxford University Press. New edition (1983). Foreword by Marc Saperstein. Philadelphia: Jewish Publication Society. Reprinted (1993). Philadelphia: Jewish Publication Society.

Trachtenberg, Moises (1989). Circumcision, Crucifixion and Anti-Semitism: the Anti-thetical Character of Ideologies and Their Symbols Which Contain Crossed Lines. *International Review of Psycho-Analysis,* vol. 16, no. 4, pp. 459–471.

Traub-Werner, D. (1979). A Note on Counter-transference and Anti-Semitism. *Canadian Journal of Psychiatry,* vol. 24, no. 6, pp. 547–548.

Traverso, Enzo (1995). *The Jews and Germany: From the "Judeo-German Symbiosis" to the Memory of Auschwitz.* Tr. Daniel Weissbort. Lincoln: University of Nebraska Press.

Traverso, Enzo (1999). *Understanding the Nazi Genocide: Marxism after Auschwitz.* Tr. Peter Drucker. London and Sterling, VA: Pluto Press.

Traverso, Enzo (2003). *The Origins of Nazi Violence.* Tr. Janet Lloyd. New York: The New Press.

Treitschke, Heinrich Gotthard von (1880). *Ein Wort über unser Judenthum.* Berlin: G. Reimer. Reprinted in Treitschke, Heinrich Gotthard von (1886–1897), *Historische und Politische Aufsätze.* 4 vols. Leipzig: S. Hirzel. [German].

Trigano, Shmuel (1979). *La nouvelle question Juive: l'avenir d'un espoir.* Paris: Gallimard. [French].

Trigano, Shmuel (1998). *France Faces Its Past: French Jews Face an Uncertain Future.* Jerusalem: Institute of the World Jewish Congress.

Trigano, Shmuel (2003a). *La Démission de la République: Juifs et Musulmans en France.* Paris: Presses Universitaires de France. [French].

Trigano, Shmuel (2003b). *L'é(xc)lu: Entre Juifs et Chrétiens.* Paris: Denoël. [French].

Trigano, Shmuel (Ed.). (1992–1993). *La Société juive à travers l'histoire.* 4 vols. Paris: Fayard. [French].

Trivouss-Widlöcher, Hélène (2004). L'antisémitique, une sémantique. *Pardès: Études et Culture Juives,* no. 37, *Psychanalyse de l'antisémitisme contemporain,* pp. 97–105. [French].

Trunk, Jechiel Jeszaja (1958). Anti-Semitism: A Contribution to its Freudian Interpretation. *Psychiatric Quarterly,* vol. 32, no. 3, pp. 574–588.

Tucker, W.H. (1994). *The Science and Politics of Racial Research.* Urbana: University of Illinois Press.

Tucker, William H. (2002). *The Funding of Scientific Racism: Wickliffe Draper and the Pioneer Fund.* Urbana: University of Illinois Press.

Tugend, Tom (1995). Japanese Publisher to Make Amends for Holocaust Denial. *The Jerusalem Post,* February 6, p. 4.

Tumin, Melvin M. (Ed.). (1961). *An Inventory and Appraisal of Research on American Anti-Semitism.* New York: Freedom Books.

Turner, John C., & Giles, Howard (Eds.). (1981). *Intergroup Behavior.* Oxford: Basil Blackwell.

Tyaglyy, M.I. (2004). The Role of Antisemitic Doctrine in German Propaganda in the Crimea, 1941–1944. *Holocaust and Genocide Studies,* vol. 18, pp. 421–459.

Union of Soviet Socialist Republics (1946). *Soviet Government Statements on Nazi Atrocities.* London and New York: Hutchinson.

United States Department of State (2005). *Report on Global Anti-Semitism.* July 1, 2003–December 15, 2004, submitted by the Department of State to the Committee on Foreign Relations and the Committee on International Relations in accordance with

Section 4 of PL 108-332, December 30, 2004. Released by the Bureau of Democracy, Human Rights, and Labor, January 5, 2005. Washington, DC: United States Department of State.

Utgaard, Peter (2003). *Remembering and Forgetting Nazism: Education, National Identity, and the Victim Myth in Postwar Austria.* New York: Oxford University Press.

Valabrega, Jean-Paul (1980). *Phantasme, mythe, corps et sens: une théorie psychanalytique de la connaissance.* Paris: Payot. 2nd revised edition (1992). 2e édition révisée, avec des notes nouvelles, une bibliographie complétée et une préface inédite. Paris Payot. New edition (2000). Paris: Payot. [French].

Valabrega, Jean-Paul (2001). *Les Mythes, conteurs de l'inconscient: questions d'origine et de fin.* Paris: Payot & Rivages. [French].

Valentin, Hugo Mauritz (1936). *Antisemitism Historically and Critically Examined.* Tr. A. G. Chater. London: Victor Gollancz. New York: The Viking Press. New edition (1971). Freeport, NY: Books for Libraries Press.

Van Buren, Paul M. (1980). Changes in Christian Theology. In Friedlander, Henry, & Milton, Sybil (Eds.), *The Holocaust: Ideology, Bureaucracy and Genocide.* New York: Kraus International Publications.

Victor, George (1998). *Hitler: The Pathology of Evil.* Washington, DC: Brassey's.

Victor, Pierre [Benny Lévy], Sartre, Jean-Paul, et al. (1974). *On a raison de se révolter.* Paris: Gallimard. [French].

Vidal-Naquet, Pierre (1987). *Les Assassins de la mémoire: "un Eichmann de papier" et autres essais sur le révisionnisme.* Paris: La Découverte. New edition (1995). Paris: Editions du Seuil. New edition (2005). Paris: La Découverte. [French].

Vidal-Naquet, Pierre (1992). *The Assassins of Memory: Essays on the Denial of the Holocaust.* Tr. Jeffrey Mehlman. New York: Columbia University Press.

Vidal-Naquet, Pierre (1995) *Jacques Maritain et les Juifs: réflexions sur un parcours.* In Maritain, Jacques, *L'impossible antisémitisme.* Malakoff: Desclée de Brouwer. New edition (2003). Paris: Desclée de Brouwer. [French].

Villano, P. (1999). Anti-semitic Prejudice in Adolescence: An Italian Study on Shared Beliefs. *Psychological Reports,* vol. 84, pp. 1372–1378.

Vital, David (1999). *A People Apart: the Jews in Europe, 1789–1939.* Oxford and New York: Oxford University Press.

Vogt, Rolf, & Vogt, Barbara (1997). Goldhagen und die Deutschen: psychoanalytische Reflexionen über die Resonanz auf ein Buch und seinen Autor in der deutschen Öffentlichkeit. *Psyche: Zeitschrift für Psychoanalyse und ihre Anwendungen,* vol. 51, pp. 494–569. [German].

Volkan, Vamık D. (1988). *The Need for Enemies and Allies: From Clinical Practice to International Relationships.* Northvale, NJ: Jason Aronson.

Volkan, Vamık D. (1997). *Bloodlines: From Ethnic Pride to Ethnic Terrorism.* New York: Farrar, Straus and Giroux.

Volkan, Vamık D. (2004). *Blind Trust: Large Groups and Their Leaders in Times of Crisis and Terror.* Charlottesville, VA: Pitchstone Publishing.

Volkov, Shulamit (1978). Antisemitism as a Cultural Code: Reflections on the History and Historiography of Antisemitism in Imperial Germany. *Leo Baeck Institute Year Book XXIII,* pp. 25–45. London: Leo Baeck Institute.

Volovici, Leon (1991). *Nationalist Ideology and Antisemitism.* Oxford: Pergamon Press.

Volovici, Leon (1994). Antisemitism in Post-Communist Eastern Europe: A Marginal or Central Issue? *Analysis of Current Trends in Antisemitism,* no. 5. Jerusalem: The Vidal Sassoon International Center for the Study of Antisemitism, The Hebrew University of Jerusalem.

Volovici, Leon (2001). Exorcizing Myths and Taboos in Romanian Society. *East European Jewish Affairs,* vol. 31, pp. 115–121.

Voltaire [François-Marie Arouet] (1764). Les Juifs. In Voltaire's *Dictionnaire Philosophique, Portatif.* London and Nancy: n.p. Reprinted (1968–1977). In *Oeuvres Complètes de Voltaire.* (The Complete Works of Voltaire). 81 vols. Ed. Theodore Besterman et al. Geneva: Institut et Musée Voltaire. Toronto and Buffalo: University of Toronto Press. Reprinted (1980–2006). In *Oeuvres Complètes de Voltaire* (The Complete Works of Voltaire). 85 vols. Ed. Nicholas Cronk et al. Oxford: Voltaire Foundation, University of Oxford. Reprinted (1994). In Voltaire's *Dictionnaire Philosophique.* Ed. Marie-Hélène Cotoni. Paris: Klincksieck. [French].

Von Dirke, Sabine (1996). "Where Were You 1933–1945?" The Legacy of the Nazi Past Beyond the Zero Hour. In Brockmann, Stephen, & Trommler, Frank (Eds.), *Revisiting Zero-Hour 1945: The Emergence of Postwar German Culture.* Washington, DC: American Institute for Contemporary German Culture, Johns Hopkins University.

Westernhagen, Dörte von (1987). *Die Kinder der Täter: Das Dritte Reich und die Generation danach.* Munich: Kösel. [German].

Waite, Robert George Leeson (1977). *The Psychopathic God: Adolf Hitler.* New York: Basic Books. Reprinted (1993). New York: Da Capo Press.

Walberer, Ulrich (Ed.). (1983). *10. Mai 1933: Bücherverbrennung in Deutschland und die Folgen.* Contributrors Wolfgang Benz et Al. Frankfurt am Main: Fischer Taschenbuch Verlag. [German].

Waller, James (2002). *Becoming Evil: How Ordinary People Commit Genocide and Mass Killing.* Oxford and New York: Oxford University Press.

Wangh, Martin (1962). Psychoanalytische Betrachtungen zur Dynamik und Genese des Vorurteils, des Antisemitismus und des Nazismus. *Psyche: Zeitschrift für Psychoanalyse und ihre Anwendungen,* vol. 16, pp. 273–284. Reprinted (1992). In *Psyche: Zeitschrift für Psychoanalyse und ihre Anwendungen,* vol. 46, pp. 1152–1176. [German].

Wangh, Martin (1964). National Socialism and the Genocide of the Jews: a Psychoanalytic Study of a History Event. *International Journal of Psycho-Analysis,* vol. 45, pp. 386–395.

Wangh, Martin (1996). Die Deutsche Psychoanalyse und die nationalsozialistische Vergangenheit. *Psyche: Zeitschrift für Psychoanalyse und ihre Anwendungen,* vol. 50, pp. 97–122.

Ward, C. W. (1973). Anti-semitism at College: Changes since Vatican II. *Journal of Scientific Study of Religion,* vol. 12, pp. 85–88.

Weatherley, Donald (1961). Anti-Semitism and the Expression of Fantasy Aggression. *Journal of Abnormal and Social Psychology,* vol. 62, pp. 454–457.

Weatherley, Donald (1963). Maternal Response to Childhood Aggression and Subsequent Anti-Semitism. *Journal of Abnormal and Social Psychology,* vol. 66, pp. 183–185.

Wegner, Gregory Paul (2002). *Anti-Semitism and Schooling under the Third Reich.* New York: Routledge Falmer.

Wehler, Hans-Ulrich (1996). Wie ein Stachel im Fleisch. *Die Zeit,* May 24, p. 40.

Weil, Fredericl D. (1985). The Variable Effects of Education on Liberal Attitudes: a Comparative Historical Analysis of Antisemitism Using Public Opinion Survey Data. *American Sociological Review,* vol. 50, pp. 458–474.

Weiland, Daniela (2004). *Otto Glagau und „Der Kulturkämpfer": zur Entstehung des modernen Antisemitismus im frühen Kaiserreich.* Berlin: Metropol. [German].

Weill, T.L. (1981). Anti-Semitism: Selected Psychodynamic Insights. *American Journal of Psychoanalysis,* vol. 41, no. 2, pp. 139–148.

Weinberg, Meyer (1986). *Because They Were Jews: A History of Anti-Semitism.* New York and London: Greenwood Press.

Weiner, Marc A. (1995). *Richard Wagner and the Anti-Semitic Imagination.* Lincoln: University of Nebraska Press.

Weinrach, Stephen G. (2002). The Counseling Profession's Relationship of Jews and the Issues That Concern Them: More Than a Case of Selective Awareness. *Journal of Counseling and Development,* vol. 80, pp. 300–314.

Weintraub, Ruth G. (1949). *How Secure These Rights? Anti-Semitism in the United States in 1948: An Anti-Defamation League Survey.* Garden City, NY: Doubleday.

Weintraub, Stanley (1993). *Disraeli: A Biography.* New York: Dutton's Truman Valley Books.

Weiss, John (1996). *Ideology of Death: Why the Holocaust Happened in Germany.* Chicago: Ivan R. Dee.

Weiss, John (2003). *The Politics of Hate: Anti-Semitism, History, and the Holocaust in Modern Europe.* Chicago: Ivan R. Dee.

Wells, Leon Weliczker (1966). *The Janowska Road.* London: Jonathan Cape. New edition (1978). *The Death Brigade = The Janowska Road.* New York: Holocaust Library. New edition (1999). *The Janowska Road.* Washington, DC: United States Holocaust Memorial Museum.

Wells, Leon Weliczker (1987). *Who Speaks for the Vanquished? American Jewish Leaders and the Holocaust.* Ed. Michael Ryan. New York: Peter Lang.

Wells, Leon Weliczker (1995). *Shattered Faith: A Holocaust Legacy.* Lexington: University Press of Kentucky.

Werz, Michael (1998). Personality, Authority, Society: Remarks on the Analysis of Authoritarianism and Prejudice in the Social Sciences. *Social Thought and Research,* vol. 21, no. 1 & 2.

Werz, Michael (Ed.). (1995). *Antisemitismus und Gesellschaft.* Frankfurt am Main: Verlag Neue Kritik. [German].

Wiener, Philip P. (Ed.). (1968). *Dictionary of the History of Ideas: Studies of Selected Pivotal Ideas.* 5 vols. New York: Charles Scribner's Sons. New edition (1973–1974). New York: Charles Scribner's Sons.

Wiesel, Elie (1960). *Night.* Foreword by François Mauriac. Tr. Stella Rodway. New York: Hill and Wang. Reprinted (1972). In Wiesel, Elie, *Night, Dawn, the Accident; Three Tales.* New York: Hill and Wang. Reprinted (1985). In Wiesel, Elie, *Night; Dawn; Day.* New York: Jason Aronson and B'nai B'rith. New edition (2001). *Elie Wiesel's*

Night. Ed. Harold Bloom. Philadelphia: Chelsea House Publishers. New edition (2005). Tr. Marion Wiesel. New York: Hill and Wang.

Wiesenthal, Simon (1967). *The Murderers Among Us.* Edited, with a profile of the author, by Joseph Wechsberg. London: Heinemann. New York: Mcgraw-Hill.

Wiggershaus, Renate (1984). *Frauen unterm Nationalsozialismus.* Wuppertal: P. Hammer. [German].

Wiggershaus, Rolf (1986). *Die Frankfurter Schule: Geschichte, Theoretische Entwicklung, Politische Bedeutung.* Munich: Carl Hanser Verlag. [German].

Wiggershaus, Rolf (1994). *The Frankfurt School: Its History, Theories, and Political Significance.* Tr. Michael Robertson. Cambridge, MA: MIT Press.

Wilentz, Gay (2001). Healing the "Sick Jewish Soul": Psychoanalytic Discourse in Jo Sinclair (Ruth Seid)'s "Wasteland." *Literature and Psychology,* vol. 47, nos. 1–2, pp. 68–93.

Williamson, Gordon (1995). *Loyalty Is My Honor.* Osceola, WI: Motorbooks International.

Willoughby, Roger (2005). *Masud Khan: The Myth and the Reality.* Foreword by Pearl King. London: Free Association Books.

Wilson, Andrew Norman (2005). When it Finally Occurred to Me That Disraeli Was a Racist. *The Daily Telegraph,* February 7.

Wilson, Stephen (1982). *Ideology and Experience: Antisemitism in France at the Time of the Dreyfus Affair.* Rutherford, NJ, and London: Fairleigh Dickinson University Press.

Winfield, Ann Gibson (2006). *Eugenics and Education in America: Institutionalized Racism and the Implications of History, Ideology, and Memory.* New York: Peter Lang.

Winnicott, Donald Woods (1971). *Playing and Reality.* London: Tavistock Publications. New York: Basic Books. Reprinted (1980). London and New York: Tavistock Publications.

Winston, Andrew S. (1996). "As His Name Indicates..." R.S. Woodworth's Letters of Reference and Employment for Jewish Psychologists in the 1930s. *Journal for the History of the Behavioral Sciences,* vol. 32, pp. 30–43.

Winston, Andrew S. (1996). The Context of Correctness: A Comment on Rushton. *Journal of Social Distress and the Homeless,* vol. 5, pp. 231–249.

Winston, Andrew S. (1998). "The Defects of His Race": E.G. Boring and Antisemitism in American Psychology, 1923–1953. *History of Psychology,* vol. 1, no. 1, pp. 27–51.

Winston, Andrew S. (1998). Science in the Service of the Far Right: Henry E. Garrett, the IAAEE and the Liberty Lobby. *Journal of Social Issues,* vol. 53, pp. 179–209.

Winston, Andrew S. (Ed.). (2004). *Defining Difference: Race and Racism in the History of Psychology.* Washington, DC: American Psychological Association,

Winter, Jay M. (1995). *Sites of Memory, Sites of Mourning: The Great War in European Cultural History.* Cambridge and New York: Cambridge University Press.

Winter, Jay M. (2006). *Remembering War: The Great War between Memory and History in the Twentieth Century.* New Haven, CT: Yale University Press.

Winter, Jay M., & Sivan, Emmanuel (Eds.). (1999). *War and Remembrance in the Twentieth Century.* Cambridge and New York: Cambridge University Press.

Winter, Jean-Pierre (2004). De l'antisémitisme comme perversion. *Pardès: Études et Culture Juives,* no. 37, *Psychanalyse de l'antisémitisme contemporain,* pp. 35–42. [French].

Wippermann, Wolfgang (1999). Goldhagen und die deutschen Historiker: strukturalistische Verkürzungen, böswillige Verdrehungen und antisemitische Untertöne. In

Elsässer, Jürgen, & Markovits, Andrei S. (Eds.), *Die Fratze der eigenen Geschichte: von der Goldhagen-Debatte zum Jugoslawien-Krieg.* Berlin: Antifa Edition. Berlin: Elefanten Press. [German].

Wistrich, Robert Solomon (1982). *Who's Who in Nazi Germany.* London: Weidenfeld and Nicolson. New York: Macmillan. New edition (1984). New York: Bonanza Books. New edition (1995). London and New York: Routledge. New edition (2002). London and New York: Routledge.

Wistrich, Robert Solomon (1990). *Between Redemption and Perdition: Modern Anti-Semitism and Jewish Identity.* London and New York: Routledge.

Wistrich, Robert Solomon (1991). *Antisemitism: The Longest Hatred.* London: Thames Mandarin. New York: Pantheon Books. New edition (1994). New York: Schoken Books.

Wistrich, Robert Solomon (1993). Anti-Semitism in Europe Since the Holocaust. In Singer, David (Ed.), *American Jewish Year Book,* vol. 93. Philadelphia: Jewish Publication Society.

Wistrich, Robert Solomon (1999). The Devil, the Jews and Hatred of the "Other." in Wistrich, Robert Solomon (Ed.), *Demonizing the Other: Antisemitism, Racism, and Xenophobia.* Amsterdam: Harwood Academic Publishers.

Wistrich, Robert Solomon (2005). *European Antisemitism Reinvents Itself.* New York: American Jewish Committee.

Wolin, Richard (2006). *The Frankfurt School Revisited, and Other Essays on Politics and Society.* New York: Routledge.

Wrong, Dennis H. (1966). The Psychology of Prejudice and the Future of Anti-Semitism in America. In Stember, Charles Herbert (Ed.), *Jews in the Mind of America.* New York: Basic Books.

Wuthnow, R. (1982). Anti-Semitism and Stereotyping. In Miller, Arthur G. (Ed.), *In the Eye of the Beholder.* Westport, CT: Praeger.

Yavetz, Zvi (1997). *Judenfeindschaft in der Antike: die münchener Vorträge.* Intro. by Christian Meier. München: C. H. Beck. [German].

Yelland, Linda M., & Stone, William F. (1996). Belief in the Holocaust: Effects of Personality and Propaganda. *Political Psychology,* vol. 17, no. 3, pp. 551–562.

Yerushalmi, Yosef Hayim (1981). *From Spanish Court to Italian Ghetto.* Seattle: University of Washington Press.

Yerushalmi, Yosef Hayim (1982a). *Assimilation and Racial Anti-Semitism: The Iberian and the German Models.* New York: Leo Baeck Institute.

Yerushalmi, Yosef Hayim (1982b). *Zakhor: Jewish History and Jewish Memory.* Seattle: University of Washington Press. New edition (1989). Foreword by Harold Bloom, with a new Preface and Postscript by the author. New York: Schocken Books. Reprinted (1996). Seattle: University of Washington Press.

Yerushalmi, Yosef Hayim (1990). *Freud's Moses: Judaism Terminable and Interminable.* New Haven, CT: Yale University Press. New edition (1991). New Haven, CT: Yale University Press.

Yerushalmi, Yosef Hayim (1997). Exile and Expulsion in Jewish History. In Gampel, Benjamin R. (Ed.), *Crisis and Creativity in the Sephardic World, 1391–1648,* pp. 3–22. New York: Columbia University Press. New edition (1998). New York: Columbia University Press.

Yerushalmi, Yosef Hayim (1998). *Sefardica: essais sur l'histoire des Juifs, des Marranes et des Nouveaux-Chrétiens d'origine hispano-portugaise.* Tr. Cyril Aslanoff, Éric Vigne, Paul Teyssier et Jean Letrouit. Paris: Chandeigne. [French].

Young, T. J. & French, L. A. (1996). Hitler's Psychopathology: Advantages and Limitations of Psychohistorical Assessments of Personality.*Psychological Reports,* vol. 78, no. 1, pp. 349–350.

Young-Bruehl, Elisabeth (1996). *The Anatomy of Prejudices.* Cambridge, MA: Harvard University Press.

Zafiropoulos, Markos, Condamin, Christine, & Nicolle, Olivier (Eds.). (2001). *L'Inconscient toxique.* Paris: Anthropos. [French].

Zamyslovsky, Gheorghi G. (1917). *Ubystvo Andriushi Yushchinskago* [The Murder of Andrei Yushchinsky]. Petrograd (St. Petersburg): n.p. [Russian].

Zanicky, R. M. (1997). *Anti-Judaism in Contemporary Christian Preaching.* Unpublished dissertation, Princeton Theological Seminary.

Zank, Michael (1998). Goldhagen in Germany: Historians' Nightmare and Popular Hero. An Essay on the Reception of *Hitler's Willing Executioners* in Germany. *Religious Studies Review,* vol. 24, no. 3, pp. 231–240.

Zeitoun, Sabine (1990).*L'œuvre de secours aux enfants (O.S.E.). sous l'occupation en France: du légalisme à la Résistance, 1940–1944.* Préface de Serge Klarsfeld. Paris: L'harmattan. [French].

Zertal, Idith (2005). *Israel's Holocaust and the Politics of Nationhood.* Tr. Chaya Galai. Cambridge and New York: Cambridge University Press.

Zick, A., & Kupper, B. (2005). Transformed Antisemitism: A Report on Anti-semitism in Germany. *Journal of Conflict and Violence Research,* vol. 7, pp. 50–92.

Zilmer, Eric A., et al. (1995). *The Quest for the Nazi Personality: A Psychological Investigation of Nazi War Criminals.* Hillsdale, NJ: Lawrence Erlbaum Associates.

Zimmerman, Joshua D. (2003). *Contested Memories: Poles and Jews During the Holocaust and its Aftermath.* New Brunswick, NJ: Rutgers University Press.

Zimmermann, Moshe (1986). *Wilhelm Marr: The Patriarch of Antisemitism.* Oxford and New York: Oxford University Press.

Zimmermann, Moshe (Ed.). (2006). *On Germans and Jews under the Nazi Regime: Essays by Three Generations of Historians.* A *Festschrift* in Honor of Otto Dov Kulka. Jerusalem: The Richard Koebner Minerva Center for German History, The Hebrew University of Jerusalem and the Magnes Press.

Zipes, Jack David (1991). *The Operated Jew: Two Tales of Anti-Semitism.* New York: Routledge.

Zuccotti, Susan (1993). *The Holocaust, the French, and the Jews.* New York: Basic Books. Reprinted (1999). Lincoln: University of Nebraska Press.

Zuckermann, Moshe (Ed.). (2005). Antisemitismus, Antizionismus, Israelkritik. *Tel Aviver Jahrbuch für deutsche Geschichte,* vol. 33, Minerva-Institut für Deutsche Geschichte, Tel Aviv University. Göttingen: Wallstein-Verlag. [German].

Index

ABOUT THE AUTHOR

AVNER FALK is an internationally known Israeli scholar in the fields of psychohistory and political psychology. He trained in Clinical Psychology at the Hebrew University of Jerusalem and Washington University in St. Louis, and practiced psychotherapy for 25 years before becoming a full-time independent scholar. He has authored six previous books and dozens of articles. His last book was a psychobiography of Napoleon.